SOMETHING ABOUT THE AUTHOR®

OUTSTANDING REFERENCE · SOURCE ·

ALA RUSA

Something about
the Author *was named
an "Outstanding
Reference Source,"
the highest honor given
by the American
Library Association
Reference and Adult
Services Division.*

ISSN 0276-816X

SOMETHING ABOUT THE AUTHOR®

Facts and Pictures about Authors
and Illustrators of Books for Young People

volume 208

GALE
CENGAGE Learning™

Detroit • New York • San Francisco • New Haven, Conn • Waterville, Maine • London

Something about the Author, Volume 208

Project Editor: Lisa Kumar

Editorial: Laura Avery, Pamela Bow, Jim Craddock, Amy Fuller, Andrea Henderson, Margaret Mazurkiewicz, Tracie Moy, Jeff Muhr, Kathy Nemeh, Mary Ruby, Mike Tyrkus

Permissions: Barb McNeil, Leitha Etheridge-Sims, Tracie Richardson

Imaging and Multimedia: Leitha Etheridge-Sims, John Watkins

Composition and Electronic Capture: Amy Darga

Manufacturing: Drew Kalasky

Product Manager: Janet Witalec

For product information and technology assistance, contact us at
Gale Customer Support, 1-800-877-4253.
For permission to use material from this text or product,
submit all requests online at **www.cengage.com/permissions.**
Further permissions questions can be emailed to
permissionrequest@cengage.com

Gale
27500 Drake Rd.
Farmington Hills, MI, 48331-3535

LIBRARY OF CONGRESS CATALOG CARD NUMBER 62-52046

ISBN-13: 978-1-4144-4221-1
ISBN-10: 1-4144-4221-1

ISSN 0276-816X

This title is also available as an e-book.
ISBN-13: 978-1-4144-6440-4
ISBN-10: 1-4144-6440-1
Contact your Gale sales representative for ordering information.

Printed in the United States of America
1 2 3 4 5 6 7 14 13 12 11 10

Contents

Authors in Forthcoming Volumes

Below are some of the authors and illustrators that will be featured in upcoming volumes of SATA. These include new entries on the swiftly rising stars of the field, as well as completely revised and updated entries (indicated with *) on some of the most notable and best-loved creators of books for children.

*Anne Laurel Carter ▌ Carter mines both contemporary life and Canadian history in her picture books, stories, and novels for young readers. Beginning her career writing award-winning short stories, she soon turned to picture books, producing *Tall in the Saddle*, *From Poppa*, and *Under a Prairie Sky*, while her novels for teen readers include the highly praised *Girl on Evangeline Beach* and *The Shepherd's Daughter*. Carter has also contributed to the popular "Our Canadian Girl" series, and has compiled the anthology *No Missing Parts, and Other Stories about Real Princesses*, a preteen's guide to inspiring and independent-minded young women from history.

Eleanor Davis ▌ An illustrator and cartoonist based in Athens, Georgia, Davis grew up reading comics. Unlike many children, her habit was encouraged by her parents and she began producing original comics at age fourteen. *Stinky*, her first children's book, was created when its author was still in college and focuses on a spiky-haired, pickle-loving monster. Published by Toon Books, an innovative graphic-novel imprint, Davis's debut was named a Theodor Seuss Geisel Award honor book.

Rachna Gilmore ▌ Born in India and a resident of Canada, Gilmore draws on her experiences as an immigrant and as a child of diverse cultures in writing her books for children. In addition to producing picture books such as *A Screaming Kind of Day*, *When-I-Was-a-Little-Girl*, and *Grandpa's Clock*, she is also the author of the young-adult novel *A Group of One*, the middle-grade fantasy *The Sower of Tales*, and a series of elementary-grade novels featuring an engaging young girl named Gita.

*Ron Koertge ▌ The bumpy ride from adolescence into adulthood is the focus of Koertge's novels for award-winning teen readers, and he has continued to win fans since beginning his publishing career in the mid-1980s. The protagonists in novels such as *The Arizona Kid*, *Tiger, Tiger, Burning Bright*, *The Brimstone Journals*, and *Margaux with an X* suffer universal teen anxieties, ponder their futures, toy with romance, and quarrel with eccentric or domineering parents. While Koertge often uses humor in his stories, he never downplays the seriousness of adolescent concerns, and his integrity as a writer extends to the many popular books he has written for middle-grade readers.

Bruce McCall ▌ McCall is a Canadian-born cartoonist, illustrator, and humorist whose work has appeared in the prestigious *New Yorker* magazine for over three decades. Known for his ironic, and sometimes cynical take on modern life, his detailed artwork, which he has characterized as both "faux nostalgia" and "retrofuturism," draws on the stylized images of the 1930s and 1940s

while satirizing the belief that the modern world will be improved by technology. In addition to *New Yorker* essays and covers, humor collections, and the memoir *Thin Ice: Coming of Age in Canada*, McCall has also produced the quirky and imaginative children's book *Marveltown*.

Susan Orlean ▌ A journalist, editor, and writer for the *New Yorker*, Orlean has translated several of her feature articles into award-winning books such as *The Orchid Thief: A True Story of Beauty and Obsession*, *The Bullfighter Checks Her Makeup: My Encounters with Extraordinary People*, and *My Kind of Place: Travel Stories from a Woman Who's Been Everywhere*. Like her books for adult readers, her picture book *Lazy Little Loafers*, had its roots in a magazine article and introduces young readers to a testy young narrator who bemoans the unfairness of the fact that cute infants can do no wrong.

*Meg Rosoff ▌ Rosoff began her work as a novelist shortly after the death of her younger sister, leaving her job in the New York advertising industry and relocating to England to write. The winner of several awards, her debut YA novel *How I Live Now* was acclaimed by critics and was followed by *What I Was*, *The Bride's Farewell*, and the Carnegie Medal-winning *Just in Case*. In addition, Rosoff entertains younger children with a series of amusing picture books about poorly behaved wild animals that feature engaging cartoon art by Sophie Blackall.

Bob Staake ▌ The abstract artwork of self-trained illustrator and cartoonist Staake has been featured in advertisements, editorial cartoons, animated cartoons, and books since the late 1980s. Characterized by flat, geometric shapes and a layered, Colorforms effect, his work has also inspired Staake to explore opportunities in children's books, with successful results. In addition to illustrating works by other writers, he has created board books, original picture books such as *The Red Lemon* and *The Donut Chef*, and a self-illustrated retelling of nineteenth-century writer Heinrich Hoffman's macabre children's book *Struwwelpeter and Other Disturbing Tales for Human Beings*.

Shadra Strickland ▌ An illustrator and graphic designer, Strickland earned the John Steptoe Award for New Talent for her artwork in *Bird*, a picture book with a text by New York City poet and playwright Zetta Elliott. Living and working in both her native Atlanta and New York City, Strickland has continued to develop her illustration career by creating art for books such as Renee Watson's *A Place Where Hurricanes Happen* while also traveling and teaching at schools and through community organizations.

Susan Marie Swanson ▌ Swanson lives and works in St. Paul, Minnesota, where she has dedicated a large part of her career to children's poetry and literature. In addition to editing the children's book supplement of the *Hungry Mind Review* for many years, Swanson is a published poet and author of award-winning picture books such as *To Be like the Sun* and the Caldecott Medal-winning *The House in the Night*, a story featuring artwork by Beth Krommes.

Introduction

Something about the Author (*SATA*) is an ongoing reference series that examines the lives and works of authors and illustrators of books for children. *SATA* includes not only well-known writers and artists but also less prominent individuals whose works are just coming to be recognized. This series is often the only readily available information source on emerging authors and illustrators. You'll find *SATA* informative and entertaining, whether you are a student, a librarian, an English teacher, a parent, or simply an adult who enjoys children's literature.

What's Inside *SATA*

SATA provides detailed information about authors and illustrators who span the full time range of children's literature, from early figures like John Newbery and L. Frank Baum to contemporary figures like Judy Blume and Richard Peck. Authors in the series represent primarily English-speaking countries, particularly the United States, Canada, and the United Kingdom. Also included, however, are authors from around the world whose works are available in English translation. The writings represented in *SATA* include those created intentionally for children and young adults as well as those written for a general audience and known to interest younger readers. These writings cover the entire spectrum of children's literature, including picture books, humor, folk and fairy tales, animal stories, mystery and adventure, science fiction and fantasy, historical fiction, poetry and nonsense verse, drama, biography, and nonfiction. Obituaries are also included in many volumes of *SATA* and are intended not only as death notices but also as concise overviews of people's lives and work. Additionally, each edition features newly revised and updated entries for a selection of *SATA* listees who remain of interest to today's readers and who have been active enough to require extensive revisions of their earlier biographies.

Autobiography Feature

Beginning with Volume 103, many volumes of *SATA* feature one or more specially commissioned autobiographical essays. These unique essays, averaging about ten thousand words in length and illustrated with an abundance of personal photos, present an entertaining and informative first-person perspective on the lives and careers of prominent authors and illustrators profiled in *SATA*.

Two Convenient Indexes

In response to suggestions from librarians, *SATA* indexes no longer appear in every volume but are included in alternate (odd-numbered) volumes of the series, beginning with Volume 57.

SATA continues to include two indexes that cumulate with each alternate volume: the Illustrations Index, arranged by the name of the illustrator, gives the number of the volume and page where the illustrator's work appears in the current volume as well as all preceding volumes in the series; the Author Index gives the number of the volume in which a person's biographical sketch, autobiographical essay, or obituary appears in the current volume as well as all preceding volumes in the series.

These indexes also include references to authors and illustrators who appear in *Gale's Yesterday's Authors of Books for Children*, *Children's Literature Review*, and *Something about the Author Autobiography Series*.

Easy-to-Use Entry Format

Whether you're already familiar with the *SATA* series or just getting acquainted, you will want to be aware of the kind of information that an entry provides. In every *SATA* entry the editors attempt to give as complete a picture of the person's life and work as possible. A typical entry in *SATA* includes the following clearly labeled information sections:

PERSONAL: date and place of birth and death, parents' names and occupations, name of spouse, date of marriage, names of children, educational institutions attended, degrees received, religious and political affiliations, hobbies and other interests.

ADDRESSES: complete home, office, electronic mail, and agent addresses, whenever available.

CAREER: name of employer, position, and dates for each career post; art exhibitions; military service; memberships and offices held in professional and civic organizations.

MEMBER: professional, civic, and other association memberships and any official posts held.

AWARDS, HONORS: literary and professional awards received.

WRITINGS: title-by-title chronological bibliography of books written and/or illustrated, listed by genre when known; lists of other notable publications, such as plays, screenplays, and periodical contributions.

ADAPTATIONS: a list of films, television programs, plays, CD-ROMs, recordings, and other media presentations that have been adapted from the author's work.

WORK IN PROGRESS: description of projects in progress.

SIDELIGHTS: a biographical portrait of the author or illustrator's development, either directly from the biographee— and often written specifically for the *SATA* entry—or gathered from diaries, letters, interviews, or other published sources.

BIOGRAPHICAL AND CRITICAL SOURCES: cites sources quoted in "Sidelights" along with references for further reading.

EXTENSIVE ILLUSTRATIONS: photographs, movie stills, book illustrations, and other interesting visual materials supplement the text.

How a *SATA* Entry Is Compiled

SATA editors examine a wide variety of published sources to gather information for an entry. Biographical and bibliographic sources are consulted, as are book reviews, feature articles, published interviews, and material sometimes obtained from the biographee's family, publishers, agent, or other associates. Whenever possible, the author or illustrator is sent a copy of the entry to check for accuracy and completeness.

Entries that have not been verified by the biographees or their representatives are marked with an asterisk (*).

Contact the Editor

We encourage our readers to examine the entire *SATA* series. Please write and tell us if we can make *SATA* even more helpful to you. Give your comments and suggestions to the editor:

Editor
Something about the Author
Gale, Cengage Learning
27500 Drake Rd.
Farmington Hills MI 48331-3535

Toll-free: 800-877-GALE
Fax: 248-699-8070

Something about the Author Product Advisory Board

The editors of *Something about the Author* are dedicated to maintaining a high standard of excellence by publishing comprehensive, accurate, and highly readable entries on a wide array of writers for children and young adults. In addition to the quality of the content, the editors take pride in the graphic design of the series, which is intended to be orderly yet inviting, allowing readers to utilize the pages of *SATA* easily and with efficiency. Despite the longevity of the *SATA* print series, and the success of its format, we are mindful that the vitality of a literary reference product is dependent on its ability to serve its users over time. As literature, and attitudes about literature, constantly evolve, so do the reference needs of students, teachers, scholars, journalists, researchers, and book club members. To be certain that we continue to keep pace with the expectations of our customers, the editors of *SATA* listen carefully to their comments regarding the value, utility, and quality of the series. Librarians, who have firsthand knowledge of the needs of library users, are a valuable resource for us. The *Something about the Author* Product Advisory Board, made up of school, public, and academic librarians, is a forum to promote focused feedback about *SATA* on a regular basis. The nine-member advisory board includes the following individuals, whom the editors wish to thank for sharing their expertise:

Eva M. Davis
Director,
Canton Public Library,
Canton, Michigan

Joan B. Eisenberg
Lower School Librarian,
Milton Academy,
Milton, Massachusetts

Francisca Goldsmith
Teen Services Librarian,
Berkeley Public Library,
Berkeley, California

Susan Dove Lempke
Children's Services Supervisor,
Niles Public Library District,
Niles, Illinois

Robyn Lupa
Head of Children's Services,
Jefferson County Public Library,
Lakewood, Colorado

Victor L. Schill
Assistant Branch Librarian/Children's Librarian,
Harris County Public Library/Fairbanks Branch,
Houston, Texas

Caryn Sipos
Community Librarian,
Three Creeks Community Library,
Vancouver, Washington

Steven Weiner
Director,
Maynard Public Library,
Maynard, Massachusetts

SOMETHING ABOUT THE AUTHOR

ANCONA, George 1929-

Personal

Born Jorge Efraín Ancona, December 4, 1929, in New York, NY; son of Efraín José (an accountant and amateur photographer) and Emma (a seamstress) Ancona; married Patricia Apatow, March 4, 1951 (divorced, 1966); married Helga Von Sydow (a journalist), June 20, 1968; children: (first marriage) Lisa, Gina, Tomas; (second marriage) Isabel, Marina, Pablo. *Ethnicity:* "Mexican-American." *Education:* Attended Academia San Carlos, 1949-50, Art Students League, 1950-51, and Cooper Union, 1951-52. *Politics:* Democrat.

Addresses

Home—Santa Fe, NM. *E-mail*—geoancona@cybermesa. com.

Career

Photographer, filmmaker, and author. *New York Times,* New York, NY, member of promotions department, 1950-51; *Esquire* magazine, New York, NY, art director, 1951-53; *Seventeen* magazine, New York, NY, head of promotion department, 1953-54; Grey Advertising, New York, NY, art director, 1954-57; Daniel & Charles, New York, NY, art director, 1957-61; George Ancona, Inc., New York, NY, photographer and filmmaker, 1961—. Instructor at Rockland Community College, School of Visual Arts, and Parsons School of Design; lecturer on film, design photography, and books.

George Ancona (Photograph by Helga Ancona. Reproduced by permission.)

Member

Authors Guild.

Awards, Honors

Art Director's Show award, 1959, 1960, 1967; Cine Golden Eagle Award, Council on Non-Theatrical Events, 1967, for film *Reflections,* and 1972, for film *Cities of the Web*; award from American Institute of Graphic Arts, 1967, 1968, 1974; Cindy Award, Industry Film Producers Association, 1967; Science Book Awards Nonfiction Younger Honor, New York Academy of Sciences, 1975, for *Handtalk,* and 1988, for *Turtle Watch*; Golden Kite Award, Society of Children's Book Writers and Illustrators, 1980, for *Finding Your First Job*; American Library Association Notable Book designation, and Notable Children's Trade Book in the Field of Social Studies designation, National Council for the Social Studies (NCSS)/Children's Book Council (CBC), 1986, both for *Sheep Dog*; Best Illustrated Children's Books of the Year citation, *New York Times,* 1987, for *Handtalk Birthday*; Carter G. Woodson Book Award for Outstanding Merit, NCSS, 1987, for *Living in Two Worlds*; Notable Children's Trade Book in the Field of Social Studies designation, NCSS/CBC, c. 1989, for *Spanish Pioneers of the Southwest*; Texas Blue Bonnet Award, c. 1989, for *The American Family Farm*; Notable Children's Trade Book in the Field of Social Studies designation, NCSS/CBC, c. 1990, for *Riverkeeper* and *Mom Can't See Me*; Pick of the Lists citation, American Booksellers Association, 1991, for *The Aquarium Book*; Children's Book of the Year citation, Bank Street College Children's Book Committee, 1993, for *Pablo Remembers*; Best 100 Children's Books citation, New York Public Library, 1993, for *Powwow*; John Burroughs Nature Books for Young Readers listee, 1993, for *Earth Keepers,* by Joan Anderson; Parents' Choice Award, 1994, for *The Piñata Maker/El piñatero*; Children's Book of the Year citation, Bank Street College Children's Book Committee, 1994, for *Twins on Toes*; Golden Duck Award for excellence in children's science fiction, 1994, for *Richie's Rocket*; Outstanding Science Trade Book for Children citation, National Science Teachers Association/CBC, 1995, for *The Golden Lion Tamarin Comes Home*; Americas Award for Children's and Young-Adult Literature, Consortium of Latin-American Studies Programs, 1998, and Pura Belpré Honor Book designation, Association for Library Service to Children/National Association to Promote Library and Information Services to Latinos and the Spanish Speaking, 2000, both for *Barrio*; *Washington Post*/Children's Book Guild Nonfiction Award, 2002, for body of work; Bank Street College Children's Book Committee Children's Book of the Year designation, Americas Award Commended designation, and Cooperative Children's Book Center Choice designation, all 2007, all for *Capoeira*; New Mexico Book Association Special Recognition award, 2008.

Writings

AND PHOTOGRAPHER

Monsters on Wheels, Dutton (New York, NY), 1974.
And What Do You Do?, Dutton (New York, NY), 1976.
I Feel: A Picture Book of Emotions, Dutton (New York, NY), 1977.
Growing Older, Dutton (New York, NY), 1978.
It's a Baby!, Dutton (New York, NY), 1979.
Dancing Is . . ., Dutton (New York, NY), 1981.
Bananas: From Manolo to Margie, Clarion (New York, NY), 1982.
Teamwork: A Picture Essay about Crews and Teams at Work, Crowell (New York, NY), 1983.
Monster Movers, Dutton (New York, NY), 1983.
Freighters, Crowell (New York, NY), 1985.
Sheep Dog, Lothrop (New York, NY), 1985.
Helping Out, Clarion (New York, NY), 1985.
Turtle Watch, Macmillan (New York, NY), 1987.
Riverkeeper, Macmillan (New York, NY), 1990.
The Aquarium Book, Clarion (New York, NY), 1991.
Man and Mustang, Macmillan (New York, NY), 1992.
My Camera, Crown (New York, NY), 1992.
Pablo Remembers: The Fiesta of the Day of the Dead, Lothrop (New York, NY), 1993.
Powwow, Harcourt (San Diego, CA), 1993.
Ser util, Scholastic (New York, NY), 1993.
The Golden Lion Tamarin Comes Home, Macmillan (New York, NY), 1994.
The Piñata Maker/El piñatero, Harcourt (San Diego, CA), 1994.
Ricardo's Day/El día de Ricardo, Scholastic (New York, NY), 1995.
Fiesta U.S.A., Dutton (New York, NY), 1995.
Stone Cutters, Carvers, and the Cathedral, Lothrop (New York, NY), 1995.
Earth Daughter: Alicia of Acoma Pueblo, Simon & Schuster (New York, NY), 1995.
In City Gardens, Celebrations Press (Glenview, IL), 1996.
Mayeros: A Yucatec Maya Family, Lothrop (New York, NY), 1997.
Let's Dance!, Morrow/Avon (New York, NY), 1998.
Fiesta Fireworks, Lothrop (New York, NY), 1998.
Barrio: José's Neighborhood, Harcourt (San Diego, CA), 1998.
Carnaval, Harcourt (San Diego, CA), 1999.
Charro: The Mexican Cowboy, Harcourt (San Diego, CA), 1999.
Cuban Kids, Marshall Cavendish (Tarrytown, MD), 2000.
Harvest, Marshall Cavendish (Tarrytown, MD), 2001.
Come and Eat, HarperCollins (New York, NY), 2001.
Murals: Walls That Sing, Marshall Cavendish (Tarrytown, MD), 2003.
Capoeira: Game! Dance! Martial Art!, Lee & Low (New York, NY), 2007.
Self Portrait, Robert C. Owen (New York, NY), 2007.
Ole! Flamenco, 2010.

Authors works have been translated into Spanish.

"HANDTALK" SERIES; AND PHOTOGRAPHER

(With Remy Charlip and Mary Beth Miller) *Handtalk: An ABC of Finger Spelling and Sign Language,* Parents' Magazine Press (New York, NY), 1974.

(With Remy Charlip and Mary Beth Miller) *Handtalk Birthday: A Number and Story Book in Sign Language,* Four Winds Press (New York, NY), 1987.

(With Mary Beth Miller) *Handtalk Zoo,* Four Winds Press (New York, NY), 1989.

(With Mary Beth Miller) *Handtalk School,* Four Winds Press (New York, NY), 1991.

"VIVA MEXICO!" SERIES; AND PHOTOGRAPHER

The Fiestas, Marshall Cavendish (Tarrytown, MD), 2002.

The Folk Arts, Marshall Cavendish (Tarrytown, MD), 2002.

The Past, Marshall Cavendish (Tarrytown, MD), 2002.

The People, Marshall Cavendish (Tarrytown, MD), 2002.

The Foods, Marshall Cavendish (Tarrytown, MD), 2002.

"SOMOS LATINOS" SERIES; AND PHOTOGRAPHER

Mi barrio/My Neighborhood, Children's Press (Danbury, CT), 2004.

Mi casa/My House, Children's Press (Danbury, CT), 2004.

Mi escuela/My School, Children's Press (Danbury, CT), 2004.

Mi familia/My Family, Children's Press (Danbury, CT), 2004.

Mis amigos/My Friends, Children's Press (Danbury, CT), 2004.

Mi musica/My Music, Children's Press (Danbury, CT), 2005.

Mis abuelos/My Grandparents, Children's Press (Danbury, CT), 2005.

Mis comidas/My Foods, Children's Press (Danbury, CT), 2005.

Mis fiestas/My Celebrations, Children's Press (Danbury, CT), 2005.

Mis juegos/My Games, Children's Press (Danbury, CT), 2005.

Mis quehaceres/My Chores, Children's Press (Danbury, CT), 2005.

PHOTOGRAPHER

Barbara Brenner, *A Snake-lover's Diary,* Scott Young Books, 1970.

Barbara Brenner, *Faces,* Dutton (New York, NY), 1970.

Barbara Brenner, *Bodies,* Dutton (New York, NY), 1973.

Louise Jackson, *Grandpa Had a Windmill, Grandma Had a Churn,* Parents' Magazine Press (New York, NY), 1977.

Jean Holzenthaler, *My Feet Do,* Dutton (New York, NY), 1979.

Louise Jackson, *Over on the River,* Lothrop (New York, NY), 1980.

Sue Alexander, *Finding Your First Job,* Dutton (New York, NY), 1980.

Howard Smith, *Balance It,* Four Winds Press (New York, NY), 1982.

Maxine B. Rosenberg, *My Friend Leslie: The Story of a Handicapped Child,* Lothrop (New York, NY), 1983.

Joan Anderson, *First Thanksgiving Feast,* Clarion (New York, NY), 1984.

Maxine B. Rosenberg, *Being Adopted,* Lothrop (New York, NY), 1984.

Joan Anderson, *Christmas on the Prairie,* Clarion (New York, NY), 1985.

Maxine B. Rosenberg, *Being a Twin, Having a Twin,* Lothrop (New York, NY), 1985.

Joan Anderson, *The Glorious Fourth at Prairietown,* Morrow (New York, NY), 1986.

Maxine B. Rosenberg, *Making a New Home in America,* Lothrop (New York, NY), 1986.

Maxine B. Rosenberg, *Living in Two Worlds,* Lothrop (New York, NY), 1986.

Joan Anderson, *Pioneer Children of Appalachia,* Clarion (New York, NY), 1986.

Floreva G. Cohen, *My Special Friend,* Board of Jewish Education (New York, NY), 1986.

Sam and Beryl Epstein, *Jackpot of the Beagle Brigade,* Macmillan (New York, NY), 1987.

Joan Anderson, *Joshua's Westward Journal,* Morrow (New York, NY), 1987.

Maxine B. Rosenberg, *Artists of Handcrafted Furniture at Work,* Lothrop (New York, NY), 1988.

Maxine B. Rosenberg, *Finding a Way: Living with Exceptional Brothers and Sisters,* afterword by Stephen Greenspan, Lothrop (New York, NY), 1988.

Joan Anderson, *From Map to Museum: Uncovering Mysteries of the Past,* introduction by David Hurst Thomas, Morrow Junior Books (New York, NY), 1988.

Joan Anderson, *A Williamsburg Household,* Clarion (New York, NY), 1988.

Joan Anderson, *The American Family Farm: A Photo Essay,* Harcourt (San Diego, CA), 1989.

Marcia Seligson, *Dolphins at Grassy Key,* Macmillan (New York, NY), 1989.

Joan Anderson, *Spanish Pioneers of the Southwest,* Dutton (New York, NY), 1989.

Shirley Climo, *City! New York,* Macmillan (New York, NY), 1990.

Shirley Climo, *City! San Francisco,* Macmillan (New York, NY), 1990.

Joan Anderson, *Harry's Helicopter,* Morrow (New York, NY), 1990.

Sally Hobart Alexander, *Mom Can't See Me,* Macmillan (New York, NY), 1990.

Joan Anderson, *Pioneer Settlers of New France,* Dutton (New York, NY), 1990.

Maxine B. Rosenberg, *Brothers and Sisters,* Clarion (New York, NY), 1991.

Joan Anderson, *Christopher Columbus: From Vision to Voyage,* Dial (New York, NY), 1991.

Shirley Climo, *City! Washington, DC,* Macmillan (New York, NY), 1991.

Christine Loomis, *My New Baby-sitter,* Morrow (New York, NY), 1991.

Bonnie Larkin Nims, *Just beyond Reach and Other Riddle Poems,* Scholastic (New York, NY), 1992.

Sally Hobart Alexander, *Mom's Best Friend,* Macmillan (New York, NY), 1992.

Joan Anderson, *Earth Keepers,* Gulliver Green/Harcourt (San Diego, CA), 1993.

Mildred Leinweber Dawson, *Over Here It's Different: Carolina's Story,* Macmillan (New York, NY), 1993.

Joan Anderson, *Richie's Rocket,* Morrow (New York, NY), 1993.

Joan Anderson, *Twins on Toes: A Ballet Debut,* Lodestar (New York, NY), 1993.

Joan Anderson, *Sally's Submarine,* Morrow (New York, NY), 1995.

Joan Anderson, *Cowboys: Roundup on an American Ranch,* Scholastic (New York, NY), 1996.

Barbara Beasley Murphy, *Miguel Lost and Found in the Palace,* Museum of New Mexico Press (Santa Fe, NM), 2002.

Pat Mora, *Join Hands: The Ways We Celebrate Life,* Charlesbridge (New York, NY), 2008.

OTHER

Also author of film scripts, including *Doctor and Dentist,* two short films for *Sesame Street; Faces* and *The River,* for children; *Getting It Together,* a documentary film about the Children's Television Workshop and Neighborhood Youth Corps; *Cities of the Web,* produced by Macmillan; *Looking for Pictures, Looking for Color,* and *Seeing Rhythm,* a series; *Reflections,* produced by American Crafts Council; *The Link,* produced by Orba Corporation; and *Expansion,* produced by Diamond International Corporation.

Sidelights

George Ancona is renowned for creating vivid photo essays that allow children to immerse themselves in new ideas and cultures, to appreciate the labor that so often goes unnoticed behind the scenes of daily life, and to accept themselves as well as others. Many of his images, as well as his writings, also celebrate his own Mexican heritage and the Spanish language. His books for children include *The Golden Lion Tamarin Comes Home, Mayeros: A Yucatec Maya Family,* and *Cuban Kids.*

Ancona began his career as a freelance photographer by taking photographs for *Vogue Children.* In addition, he made films for *Sesame Street* and filmed the children's series *Big Blue Marble.* As he worked, he traveled to Brazil, Pakistan, Hong Kong, Japan, Iceland, Tunisia, and Switzerland. It was during this time that Ancona and his first wife divorced. Ancona's three children, Lisa, Gina, and Tomas, stayed with him, and he later married Helga Von Sydow. With Von Sydow, Ancona had three more children: Isabel, Marina, and Pablo. By 2008 he could also boast four grandchildren and three great grandchildren.

Ancona began creating photographs for children's books in 1970, when Barbara Brenner, a friend and an established writer, asked him if he would be interested in illustrating her work. Ancona collaborated with Brennan on *Faces, Bodies,* and *A Snake-lover's Diary.* Later, when Brenner's editor suggested that Ancona write as well as illustrate a book, Ancona decided to use his interest in construction, and the result was *Monsters on Wheels.* This detailed book describes machines that "push, lift, crush, and haul," from cranes to the Lunar Roving Vehicle that explored the moon. John S. Radosta, writing in the *New York Times Book Review,* considered *Monsters on Wheels* "excellent."

Similar in focus, *Monster Movers* features sixteen machines, from a walking dragline to a clamshell bucket loader, that move mountains of coal, grain, and cargo over land and on and off ships. One of these machines, a crawler-transporter, is pictured moving the U.S. space shuttle. "Once again Ancona has mixed striking photographs, a lucid text and a fascinating subject with winning results," Connie Tyrrell Burns commented in *School Library Journal.* Like *Monsters on Wheels* and *Monster Movers, Freighters* presents various machines that help people work. In *Freighters* Ancona focuses on the people who control the machines as well as on the machines themselves; with his camera, he follows the qualifications, training, and daily routine of a freighter crew. Many of his books are entirely devoted to workers and the jobs they perform. Even *Sheep Dog,* which features a very intelligent breed of dogs, is about an important kind of work: guarding and herding sheep.

According to *School Library Journal* reviewer Andy Ward, Ancona's *And What Do You Do?* presents twenty-one jobs, including carpenter, costume designer, dental assistant, barber, and nurse by pairing "outstanding photographs" and a "lucid writing style." Denise M. Wilms noted in *Booklist* that Ancona's photographs feature "men and women of varying racial and ethnic backgrounds" and that there is a "conscious attempt to avoid stereotyping." *Teamwork: A Picture Essay about Crews and Teams at Work* follows the efforts of mountain climbers, a nursing crew, a sailing crew, a film crew, and other team-based workers. As in *And What Do You Do?,* the women and men in *Teamwork* are not cast in stereotypical roles.

Ancona has also made photo essays focusing on specific jobs. *Man and Mustang* shows how feral horses are captured, transported, and tamed by prison inmates for the Bureau of Land Management, while *Stone Cutters, Carvers, and the Cathedral* illuminates an esoteric and fascinating profession. With black-and-white photographs and text, *Riverkeeper* follows John Cronin, the riverkeeper of the Hudson River in New York, as he works to protect the water, plants, and wildlife. Ancona demonstrates that Cronin cannot fight pollution from the seat of his powerboat, named *Riverkeeper;* as a representative of the Hudson River Fishermen's Association, the man must deal with corporate polluters and a host of government agencies to ensure the water's cleanliness. According to Mary M. Burns in *Horn Book*, Ancona provides a "balanced, rational presentation" that "speaks directly to our times in a manner as informative as it is appealing." Betsy Hearne, writing in the *Bulletin of the Center for Children's Books*, concluded that *Riverkeeper* "will energize kids" to view its subject "in the light of ecological responsibility."

Many children are interested in learning about careers and the world of work, and Ancona dealts with a variation on this theme in *Helping Out*. According to a *Publishers Weekly* critic, *Helping Out* is based on a "stimulating" idea—children can help out (washing cars, planting seeds, doing chores) to the satisfaction of all. The children featured in Ancona's black-and-white pictures smile and, as the reviewer noted, "show clearly that they like what they're doing."

Children are fascinated with babies, and the photographer received several requests for a book discussing babies and how they grow. Ancona met this need by staying home to photograph the first twelve months in the life of his son Pablo. As he noted in a *Junior Literary Guild* article, the text of *It's a Baby!* "grew out of the questions children would ask" about Pablo when they saw him. This book shows the boy nursing, playing, climbing, and taking his first steps. In *Horn Book*, Kate M. Flanagan described Ancona's black-and-white photographs as "exquisite."

Ancona's photographs have also helped children learn to accept themselves and others by bringing life to books featuring physically challenged children and adults. *Mom Can't See Me* and *Mom's Best Friend*, both by Sally Hobart Alexander, show how a blind woman lives a fulfilling life. *Finding a Way: Living with Exceptional Brothers and Sisters*, by Maxine B. Rosenberg, demonstrates how children can help physically challenged siblings in a caring, positive manner. In *Handtalk Zoo*, a book in the popular "Handtalk" series with a text by Mary Beth Miller, children visit the zoo and communicate in sign language. Ancona's color photographs for *Handtalk Zoo* clearly show the signs the children make, as well as capturing hands in rapid movement. As Hanna B. Zeiger observed in *Horn Book*, some "photos of signs capture very clearly the essence of the animal" the children are viewing. In the words of *School Library Journal* contributor Susan Nemeth McCarthy, *Handtalk Zoo* introduces children to sign-language vocabulary in a "creative and exuberant manner."

Ancona's travels to countries around the world have provided him with alternate settings in which to explore his favorite topics: machines, working and occupations, and nature. He was inspired to write *Bananas: From Manolo to Margie* while visiting a Honduran village. This book demonstrates how bananas are cultivated on a Honduran plantation, picked by plantation workers, and sent on a two-week trip to a grocery store in the United States, where Margie and her mother buy some. The mostly black-and-white photos focus on the equipment used in picking and transporting bananas as well as on the people who operate it. They also feature the families of the plantation workers. The photos in *Bananas* are "fair: workers live poorly and work hard," Terry Lawhead noted in *School Library Journal*. As Zena Sutherland observed in the *Bulletin of the Center for Children's Books*, information about the plantation workers is offered, although the text does not really discuss the "personal lives" of Margie and the transportation and marketing workers.

Turtle Watch follows the efforts of oceanographers attempting to replenish the sea turtle population in northeastern Brazil. During nesting season, both oceanographers and the people of Praia do Forte have important responsibilities. The local people, especially fishermen, must encourage one another to leave the eggs and turtles they find instead of selling them. Oceanographers must observe female turtles laying eggs, recover the eggs for safe hatching, and then, after the baby turtles emerge from their eggs, help them make their way to the ocean. According to Karey Wehner, writing for *School Library Journal*, in *Turtle Watch* "Ancona conveys some of the excitement and wonder scientists must feel when observing animals firsthand, in the field." Ancona noted in *Junior Literary Guild* that photographing the turtles was difficult. "We would arrive either too early or too late to see them emerge from the sea." Although it took a long time for Ancona to finally get his photos, he did not mind because "Brazil is a wonderful place to be stranded in." Ancona returned to Brazil to research and take photos for his 1994 book *The Golden Lion Tamarin Monkey Comes Home*.

Pablo Remembers: The Fiesta of the Day of the Dead features a Mexican family as its members prepare for and enjoy the festival of the Day of the Dead. During the festival's three days (All Hallow's Eve, All Saints' Day, and All Souls' Day), which honor the dead in a combination of Aztec and Catholic traditions, altars are decorated, children eat candy skulls, and Pablo takes time to remember his deceased grandmother. According to *Bulletin of the Center for Children's Books* contributor Roger Sutton, the book's "photography has the intimacy of high-quality family snapshots." Margaret A. Bush concluded of *Pablo Remembers* in *Horn Book* that the "beautiful book" serves as a fitting "tribute to Mexican home life."

The Piñata Maker/El piñatero also focuses on life in Mexico, offering text written in both Spanish and English. Ancona follows Don Ricardo Nuñez Gijon—better known as Tío Rico in the village—as he carefully crafts fantastic, delightful piñatas. Ancona's photos demonstrate how Tío Rico makes a paste out of old newspapers and paper bags, and then shapes the paste into the form of a carrot, swan, star, or other figure. The next series of photos demonstrates how Daniela, a young girl, chooses a piñata for her birthday party, and how her guests crack it open and spill the candy. "Ancona has created an authentic, detailed account of one aspect of Mexican culture which has particularly wide appeal to children," wrote Maeve Visser Knoth in *Horn Book.* According to Ann Welton in *School Library Journal,* the "balance between text and illustration is masterful."

Ancona did not have to travel far to meet the people he photographed for *Powwow.* With color photographs and a thoughtful introduction, he provides what *School Library Journal* reviewer Lisa Mitten described as an "exquisite kaleidoscope of Native-American music, customs, and crafts." The Crow Fair in Montana provides an opportunity for people from various tribes, including the Crow, Lakota, Cheyenne, Cree, and Ojibwa, to dance traditional, fancy, grass, and jingle-dress dances competitively. Ancona follows the celebration as it progresses from parade to dance; he focuses his camera on the people watching the dances as well as on the dancers themselves. As Bush noted in *Horn Book,* in *Powwow* Ancona's camera records "the ironies of traditional cultural practice in the modern setting" and "conveys the universal appeal of spectacle and celebration."

Ancona returns to Mexican-American themes with *Fiesta U.S.A.,* a book dealing with four of the holidays most celebrated by Latinos in North America. Featured holidays include El Día de los Muertos, or Day of the Dead; Los Matachines, celebrated on New Year's Day; La Fiesta de los Reyes Magos, or Three Kings' Day; and Los Posadas, a reenactment of Mary and Joseph's hunt for accommodations in Bethlehem. Ancona takes readers to a New Mexican pueblo in *Earth Daughter: Alicia of Acoma Pueblo,* an "attractive photo-essay," according to *Booklist* critic Stephanie Zvirin. Here young Alicia, who is learning to throw pottery, introduces readers to the simple life of her small town, which dates to the Spanish conquest.

Traveling farther south to the Yucatán Peninsula and his own heritage, Ancona features Mayan culture in *Mayeros,* including color photographs of not only people of the region, but also of their ancient artwork and temples. "Ancona ably interweaves the history of . . . the ancient Mayeros with the daily life of their descendants," claimed Karen Morgan in *Booklist.* Frances E. Millhouser, writing in *School Library Journal,* praised Ancona's "involving text" as well as the manner in which he "seamlessly interspersed" more factual information into the narrative of the present-day family. Millhouser concluded that in *Mayeros* "Ancona provides a unique perspective on the vibrant survival of an enduring way of life."

More Hispanic themes are served up in *Fiesta Fireworks,* in which Ancona follows Caren and her family of fireworks makers in Tultepec, a town near Mexico City, as they create the fireworks display for the annual festival of San Juan de Dios. Phelan found that the book "captures the excitement of a fiesta," while *School*

Library Journal critic Selene S. Vasquez called *Fiesta Fireworks* "an informative tribute to an enduring Mexican tradition."

Ancona deals with a year in the life of a Mexican American youth in San Francisco's Mission District in *Barrio: José's Neighborhood.* José strolls through this barrio and enjoys sights such as a soccer game, a colorful mural, and the traditional celebrations that mark the year. Annie Ayres, writing in *Booklist,* called the book "a fond and fascinating photo-essay focusing on the richness of the Latino experience." Similarly, Dina Sherman observed in *School Library Journal* that the "title successfully captures images of a particular place as seen through the eyes of a child."

Charro: The Mexican Cowboy is set in Guadalajara, Mexico, on the day of a local rodeo, or *charreada.* Ancona focuses on the riding and roping skills of the cowboys who take part in the event, and his color photographs also highlight the scene, complete with mariachi bands and the fancy dress of both men and women. Helen Rosenberg, writing in *Booklist,* called Ancona's book "beautiful and informative" and predicted that it "will satisfy any reader interested in the ways of today's cowboys." A reviewer for *Publishers Weekly* praised Ancona's "energetic" photographs in *Charro.* Ruth Semrau, writing in *School Library Journal,* maintained that "Ancona's pictures just keep getting better and better." Reviewing the book for the *Bulletin of the Center for Children's Books,* Deborah Stevenson concluded that "young buckaroos who enjoy a rodeo will be intrigued by this southern alternative."

Ancona deals with themes ranging from festivals to Caribbean children to Mexican field workers in *Carnaval, Cuban Kids,* and *Harvest.* In *Carnaval,* he documents celebrations in the Brazilian town of Olinda in an "appealing picture-book format" with an "accessible, lively text," according to Sherman. Similarly, a contributor for *Hungry Mind Review* noted that "full-page photographs bring all the wonder and energy of carnival to life." Paul Kelsey, writing in *School Library Journal,* concluded that *Carnaval* is "an excellent introduction in an inviting and visually pleasing format." Ancona illustrates life in Cuba through his photos of students in *Cuban Kids,* "a very fine portrait of modern Cuba," according to *Booklist* critic Denia Hester, who also praised the "well-written text." Marilyn Long Graham, writing in *School Library Journal,* deemed *Cuban Kids* "upbeat and positive." With *Harvest,* "Ancona puts a face on Mexican migrant workers," explained Ilene Cooper in a *Booklist* review. With photos and text, he shows the hard work these people do, picking produce on various West Coast farms. At the same time, the author/illustrator also introduces young readers to a wide variety of crops and to the work of labor organizer Cesar Chavez.

Ancona travels from the farm to the world of art in *Murals: Walls That Sing,* which focuses on prehistoric wall paintings in France, Mexican church Murals: and modern graffiti in Harlem. He not only deals with the use of materials in the execution of these very public works of art, but through a combination of close-up and wide-angle shots, he lets readers see the works in relation to the architecture they adorn. Once again, Ancona's work elicited praise from reviewers. Susannah Price, writing in *School Library Journal,* called *Murals* an "eye-catching book [that] just might whet the appetite of budding artists." In *Booklist* Gillian Engberg also felt that "the beautiful, sharp color photos and the unusual subject will attract plenty of browsers," while a *Kirkus Reviews* critic deemed *Murals* "a unique chronicle of our country's diversity and an engaging look at the connection between the arts and activism."

Ancona celebrates Mexico in the five-volume set "Viva Mexico!," whose titles include *The Fiestas, The Folk Arts, The Foods, The Past,* and *The People.* Blending clear color photos with an incisive text, Ancona illuminates these various aspects of contemporary Mexican life in works that provide a "visual feast," as *Booklist* critic Annie Ayres commented of the series. Reviewing *The Past, The Foods,* and *The People* in *School Library Journal,* Coop Renner called the books "breezy and upbeat," while Mary Elam, writing in the same journal, found *The Fiestas* and *The Folk Arts* to be "beautifully illustrated volumes," that "contain a wealth of information."

Ancona turns to Latinos living in the United States in the eleven-volume "Somos Latinos" series. Each volume is told from a child's point of view and covers an aspect of daily life, including school, family, and friends. Ancona's photographs illustrate the text, sometimes supplemented with children's drawings. Ann Welton noted in *School Library Journal* that "from city to country life, schools to dances, Latino life is presented in its great variety" in Ancona's work.

Capoeira: Game! Dance! Martial Art! examines a martial art developed in Brazil that has become increasingly popular in the United States as well. A mixture of fighting, dance, and game, capoeira involves a series of movements set to music. Several schools of capoeira have evolved over the centuries, and in *Capoeira* Ancona explains the differences between them. His photographs show how capoeira students learn the basic moves of the sport. Alana Abbott, writing in *School Library Journal,* concluded that Ancona's "action-packed pictures . . . make this an eye-catching title," and a critic in *Kirkus Reviews* recommended the book "for martial-arts fans, armchair travelers and anyone who wants to view a new way of having fun."

In *Self Portrait,* Ancona gives a brief overview of his life, taking readers behind the scenes of his work as a writer and illustrator of children's books. "Kids will learn about the entire process," according to a reviewer for *Children's Bookwatch.* Ancona also offers insight into his work through the pages of *My Camera,* which demonstrates how to use a 35mm camera similar to the one Ancona uses. He describes how to compose pictures, how to use the flash, and how to put together albums, photo essays, and storyboards. Ancona also includes a diagrammatic and textual explanation of how a camera works. "Evidence of Ancona's photographic talent and teaching ability radiates from every page," remarked Nancy E. Curran in her *School Library Journal* review of *My Camera.*

On his home page, Ancona noted: "It is very gratifying to be invited to speak at schools and conferences around the country and abroad. It warms my heart to see my well-worn books in classrooms and libraries. When teachers praise my books and kids run up to me to tell me my books are 'cool,' I figure I must be doing something right."

Biographical and Critical Sources

BOOKS

Ancona, George, *Self Portrait,* Robert C. Owen (New York, NY), 2007.
St. James Guide to Children's Writers, 5th edition, St. James Press (Detroit, MI), 1999.

PERIODICALS

Booklist, July 1, 1976, Denise M. Wilms, review of *And What Do You Do?,* p. 1525; October 1, 1995, Annie Ayres, review of *Fiesta U.S.A.,* pp. 305-306; October 15, 1995, Stephanie Zvirin, review of *Earth Daughter: Alicia of Acoma Pueblo,* p. 397; April 15, 1997, Karen Morgan, review of *Mayeros: A Yucatec Maya Family,* p. 1420; April, 1998, Carolyn Phelan, review of *Fiesta Fireworks,* p. 1323; September 1, 1998, Ellen Mandel, review of *Let's Dance!,* p. 121; December 1, 1998, Annie Ayres, review of *Barrio: José's Neighborhood,* p. 662; May 15, 1999, Helen Rosenberg, review of *Charro: The Mexican Cowboy,* p. 1689; November 15, 1999, Chris Sherman, review of *Carnaval,* p. 617; December 15, 2000, Denia Hester, review of *Cuban Kids,* p. 811; January 1, 2002, Ilene Cooper, review of *Harvest,* pp. 846-847; March 1, 2002, review of "Viva Mexico!" series, pp. 1121-1132; April 15, 2003, Gillian Engberg, review of *Murals: Walls That Sing,* p. 1467; April 15, 2007, Gillian Engberg, review of *Capoeira: Game! Dance! Martial Art!,* p. 45.
Black Issues Book Review, May-June, 2007, review of *Capoeira,* p. 30.
Bulletin of the Center for Children's Books, January, 1983, Zena Sutherland, review of *Bananas,* p. 81; July-August, 1990, Betsy Hearne, review of *Riverkeeper,* p. 259; May, 1993, Roger Sutton, review of *Powwow,* p. 276; December, 1993, Roger Sutton, review of *Pablo Remembers: The Fiesta of the Day of the Dead,* p. 114; May, 1999, Deborah Stevenson, review of *Charro,* pp. 306-307.

Childhood Education, fall, 2003, Gina Hoagland, review of *Murals,* p. 38.

Children's Bookwatch, June, 2007, review of *Self Portrait.*

Horn Book, February, 1980, Kate M. Flanagan, review of *It's a Baby!,* p. 7; November-December, 1989, Hanna B. Zeiger, review of *Handtalk Zoo,* p. 775; May-June, 1990, Mary M. Burns, review of *Riverkeeper,* p. 345; May-June, 1993, Margaret A. Bush, review of *Powwow,* p. 343; March-April, 1994, Margaret A. Bush, review of *Pablo Remembers,* pp. 213-214; July-August, 1994, Maeve Visser Knoth, review of *The Piñata Maker/El piñatero,* p. 469; November-December, 1995, Elizabeth S. Watson, review of *Fiesta U.S.A.,* pp. 728-729; May-June, 1998, Margaret A. Bush, review of *Fiesta Fireworks,* pp. 353-354.

Hungry Mind Review, fall, 1999, review of *Carnaval,* p. 34.

Junior Literary Guild, September, 1979, interview with Ancona; October, 1987-March, 1988, review of *Turtle Watch,* p. 25.

Kirkus Reviews, March 15, 2003, review of *Murals,* p. 458; May 1, 2007, review of *Capoeira;* June 15, 2008, review of *Join Hands!: The Ways We Celebrate Life.*

Language Arts, October, 1997, Rosalinda B. Barrera, "Profile—George Ancona: Photographer and Writer," pp. 477-481.

New York Times Book Review, January 19, 1975, John S. Radosta, review of *Monsters on Wheels,* p. 8.

Publishers Weekly, July 19, 1985, review of *Helping Out,* p. 53; June 7, 1999, review of *Charro,* p. 85; December 20, 1999, review of *Carnaval,* p. 82.

School Library Journal, September, 1976, Andy Ward, review of *And What Do You Do?,* p. 109; January, 1983, Terry Lawhead, review of *Bananas,* pp. 69-70; February, 1984, Connie Tyrrell Burns, review of *Monster Movers,* p. 65; October, 1987, Karey Wehner, review of *Turtle Watch,* p. 131; October, 1989, Susan Nemeth McCarthy, review of *Handtalk Zoo,* pp. 99-100; February, 1993, Nancy E. Curran, review of *My Camera,* p. 95; April, 1993, Lisa Mitten, review of *Powwow,* pp. 125-126; April, 1994, Ann Welton, review of *The Piñata Maker/El piñatero,* p. 116; November, 1995, Rose Zertuche Trevino, review of *Fiesta U.S.A.,* p. 136; December, 1995, Darcy Schild, review of *Earth Daughter,* p. 94; June, 1997, Frances E. Millhouser, review of *Mayeros,* p. 105; March, 1998, Selene S. Vasquez, review of *Fiesta Fireworks,* p. 191; November, 1998, Kit Vaughan, review of *Let's Dance!,* p. 101; December, 1998, Dina Sherman, review of *Barrio,* p. 99; June, 1999, Ruth Semrau, review of *Charro,* p. 110; February, 2000, Paul Kelsey, review of *Carnaval,* p. 107; January, 2001, Marilyn Long Graham, review of *Cuban Kids,* p. 112; February, 2002, Mary Elam, reviews of *The Folk Arts* and *The Fiestas,* pp. 138-139; March, 2002, Coop Renner, reviews of *The Foods, The Past,* and *The People,* pp. 240-241; April, 2002, Louise L. Sherman, review of *Harvest,* p. 162; July, 2002, Francisca Goldsmith, review of *Miguel Lost and Found in the Palace,* p. 123; May, 2003, Susannah Price, review of *Murals,* p. 161; May, 2005, Ann Welton, reviews of *Mi barrio/My Neighborhood, Mi casa/My House, Mi escuela/My School, Mi familia/My Family,* and *Mis amigos/My Friends,* p. 118; February, 2006, Maria Otero-Boisvert, reviews of *Mi musica/My Music, Mis abuelos/My Grandparents, Mis comidas/My Foods, Mis fiestas/My Celebrations, Mis juegos/My Games,* and *Mis quehaceres/My Chores,* p. 126; June, 2007, Alana Abbott, review of *Capoeira,* p. 129; November, 2008, Susan Lissim, review of *Join Hands!,* p. 111.

Skipping Stones, September-October, 2008, review of *Capoeira,* p. 31.

ONLINE

George Ancona Home Page, http://www.georgeancona.com (March 9, 2009).

Scholastic Author Studies Web site, http://www2.scholastic.com/ (March 9, 2009).

Autobiography Feature

George Ancona

George Ancona contributed the following auto-biographcial essay to *SATA:*

It was snowing on the streets of New York the night my father helped my mother into a taxi to take her to the hospital. She was in labor but also very worried because the taxi was so expensive. She would have preferred to take a trolley to the hospital. The following morning at about five o'clock I was born. They gave me the name of Jorge Efraín, Efraín being my father's name. Since we lived in the United States I was called George except by my family who called me by the diminutive, Jorgito (horhito).

Both my parents were born in small villages in the Yucatán, a region in the south of Mexico which is one of the centers of Mayan civilization. My mother's father died as a young man of thirty-three when he was injured during a bullfight in his village. A bull had gotten loose among the spectators and my grandfather had tried to distract it away from them. The bull hurt him in the chest and some time later he died from the injury. He left ten children. My grandmother went to work as a schoolteacher, leaving Emma, my mother who was the eldest girl, to keep house and raise the other children. Eventually the family left the village to live in the capital of the state, Mérida, where relatives could help them find work.

My father's family also left their village for the capital, where my grandfather opened a general store. Of all my aunts and uncles only two lived in the United States so I didn't get to know my other relatives until I had graduated high school and then visited them in Mexico. My father had come to the United States to study accounting. He liked it here so much that he decided to

George Ancona, photographing young Matachin dancers in New Mexico, 1993 (Reproduced by permission.)

"Georgie," first portrait 1930 (Reproduced by permission.)

stay beyond his student visa. This made him an illegal alien but nobody seemed to care in those days.

Since my mother had devoted so much of her time to raising the family, her brothers, who were now all working, decided to chip in to send her to New York to visit her other brothers, Mario and Carlos, who lived there. The trip was made by ship and I still have the fading photographs of the family on the dock of Progreso, the seaport closest to Mérida. The year was 1927, and little did my mother know that that was the last time she would see her family for many, many years.

My father was living in the same rooming house as my two uncles. When my mother arrived she promptly volunteered to wash her brothers' clothes. Finding more clothes than she expected, she discovered that my father had been adding his to her brothers' laundry. That's how my mother and father met. The following year they were married and the next year I arrived. That was 1929, the year of the big financial crash and the beginning of the Great Depression.

Our young family moved to Brooklyn because my father wanted to experience the melting pot of cultures that was America. Our neighbors were immigrants from Italy, Germany, Ireland, Poland, and other European countries. At home we spoke only Spanish while all around us we heard the heavily accented English which became the community's common language.

My uncle Carlos's wife, tía Isolina, had the most annoying habit of christening everyone with nicknames. She called my mother Am. Finally, after many years, I asked her why. She chuckled and responded, "Before your mother learned English she would go shopping and stand in front of the butcher or grocer's counter trying to think of the word for what she wanted. She would say 'Am, Am, Am,' groping for the right word." So my aunt and uncle ended up calling her Am.

She would call me Poochis, with a high squeak on the last syllable. Something that irritated me all my life. Recently I summoned up the courage to ask her why

that nickname. She told me that when I was a little boy we lived next door to a Polish family called Puchinsky. Unable to pronounce the name it would come out of my mouth as Poochis, hence to my chagrin, my nickname. Now it seems amusing but then it was infuriating.

We were living in Brooklyn when my sister, Neri Alicia, was born three years after me. She was born a blue baby, a heart condition that kept her weak and gave her lips a purple cast because her blood could not get enough oxygen. She was unable to attend school so she received home instruction.

Our apartment was over an Italian bakery and I remember waking up to the warm smells of fresh bread baking. Our playpen was the fire escape that was suspended over the backyard. Neri was trussed up in a harness and we spent hours together, sitting and playing on the blankets that my mother placed on the fire escape. Climbing over the windowsill was like entering a rocket ship to visit a new world. The top railing came up to my chin and I would grip the hard, paint-encrusted iron with all my might and peer down between the bars. Of course there were always the clotheslines suspended over the backyard with their family banners waving in the wind. One could tell the families by the makeup of the clothes suspended for the world to see: overalls, work shirts, dresses, corsets, shorts, and bloomers of varying sizes and styles.

Often I would sit at the kitchen table drawing and watching my mother do the washing, her arms rhythmically disappearing in and out of the sudsy water. As she washed she would sing to herself the Spanish songs which take me back to those warm sudsy days when I hear them today. The clothesline was attached to the rear window of the apartment. The sound of the squealing pulley would signal the end of my mother's washing for the day. My job was to unroll the squeezed coils of warm, wet clothes and hand them to her along with the weathered clothespins as she leaned out the window precariously to hang them on the line. The squeaking pulley would accompany my mother's humming that emerged through the wooden clothespins that she held between her teeth.

The depression years were difficult for my parents. My father studied and worked as an accountant, but it was sporadic. At one point he tried to sell apple dumplings on the streets. My mother would make them and he would go out to try to sell them. Business was not too good so we often ate them for dinner. He also enrolled with the Works Progress Administration, a government program that created jobs. He was assigned to work on a construction project. Since he didn't have any work clothes he went in his business suit. I have a photograph of him along with the rest of the work crew. There he is standing in his fedora hat, overcoat, suit, and tie behind a wheelbarrow with a shovel in his hand.

He also worked for a time as a men's suit salesman. He had several thick books of fabric swatches about six inches square. When the job ended he kept all these swatches, and my mother took and sewed them together to make me a quilted blanket. She sewed on a cotton backing to protect me from the scratchy tweed and wool fabric swatches. This somber-colored quilt kept me warm during the winters of my childhood. When I was sick and had to stay in bed, it became the canvas for my imagination. The squares became acres of farmland for my animals or the fields of battle for my collection of tin soldiers. With a stick propping it up in the middle, it became a Bedouin tent.

Somewhere in the attic of my memory is a cousin who had become part of the American mainstream. His father had a silk screen sign factory where many of our newly arrived relatives found employment, including my mother and father. My cousin's name was also George. He was older than I and his outgrown clothes were destined for me. One treasure was a leather aviator's helmet, complete with goggles. The other was a pair of knee-length boots that laced up and had a small pocket for a knife. I was in my glory with these treasures. The hat inspired many adventures. My favorite was flying around the world. The airplane was my mother's ironing board with a chair perched precariously on it and the toilet plunger held between my feet as the control stick. Many dog fights were battled out in our living room (while my mother was out), to the roar of the engine and rat-tat-tat of the machine gun produced through clenched teeth. All this to the delight of my sister who I was left to look after.

Another inherited treasure was my cousin's old Boy Scout uniform which I proudly wore to my first scout meeting. While all the other tenderfoots had spanking new uniforms, mine was older and more experienced.

*

By the time I was ready for school we had moved to Coney Island. Our first apartment was a cold-water flat in a two-story house that was reached through an alley. A wood-burning stove in the kitchen supplied the heat for the rest of the rooms. I slept in an enclosed porch which got very cold in the winter. I remember going to sleep wearing a wool hat to stay warm. Icicles formed on the windows during the night and my getting up to go to school involved a mad dash into the kitchen where I would change by the warmth of the stove, wash up, and have my breakfast. Toothpaste was a luxury, so my mother burned bread and crushed it into a charcoal powder for us to brush our teeth with. My mother was the first to rise and search the neighborhood for wood for the stove.

My first day at PS 80 was memorable. The sight of the imposing brick building with iron gates surrounding it and heavy wire mesh over the windows was not a welcoming one. Since we spoke only Spanish at home my English may not have been the same as my classmates. There were many strange faces in the class. At some point during the day I wet my pants, which only increased my sense of alienation.

Although we moved several times during the years it was only a few blocks from the previous apartments so I remained in PS 80. By now my mother's English was quite proficient and both she and my father enjoyed the PTA meetings at the school. It was with a mixture of pride and embarrassment that I listened and watched them at school meetings. For an international day the class experienced the foods from the various homes of the class. There were pasta fagiolo, egg rolls, knishes, noodle pudding, chicken soup, latkes, pizza, and my mother's tamales and tacos. Of course this made me very popular with my chums. Whenever we arrived at my house after school my mother made sure to sit us all down for tacos and Mexican hot chocolate which she beat in a carved wooden bowl.

By the time I was in sixth grade I was on the Safety Squad, which meant I wore a white Sam Browne belt and directed the corner crossings of the kids going to

The author cycling around the block, Coney Island, 1935 (Reproduced by permission.)

school. Most of my friends went to the parochial school which was on the same block. They couldn't care less about the public school rules which I was supposed to enforce for both schools. Of course this was a cause of confrontation between my schoolmates and my friends from the neighborhood. After the usual shoving match and threats of "I'll get you after school," we would end up brawling outside the school grounds. My mother was furious when I returned with torn shirts. I had to face her ire after dealing with my antagonists. Then I would run out and play stickball with the guys 1 had just had a fight with.

My mother helped with the family income by doing piecework—sewing that she could do at home. She would go out to a nearby sweatshop and pick up her work. During her absences I would take care of my sister. As the older child I maintained a sober aspect which only hid my imaginative flights of fancy. Another source of work for my mother was a very fashionable lingerie store in Manhattan. She would take the subway to pick up the unfinished lingerie and bring it home to sew on fancy lace and monograms. Eventually I was entrusted to trim the lace on the garments.

Sometimes my father would also bring piecework home. After dinner we would all sit around the table bending little wires which were used in displays while we chatted or listened to the radio. My favorite radio programs were "The Lone Ranger," the "Shadow," the "Green Hornet," and "Let's Pretend." I would sit with my head leaning against the speaker cloth of our radio and visualize the adventures I was listening to.

Coney Island was a wonderful place to grow up in. During the summer the amusement parks were crowded with people from all over the world. Most of the time I was in a bathing suit and barefoot. With my friends I would run to the beach and spend the days there swimming, fooling around, and sifting the sand for coins. During the winter months the ocean winds would drive the snow into drifts against the silent amusement rides. Clowns and garish signs would emerge from the crisp white snow. The boardwalk would have only a few intrepid strollers and cyclists. Occasionally the stocky members of the Polar Bear Club would be out doing calisthenics in bathing suits and then plunging into the frigid waves.

One of the biggest treats for us was to go to a restaurant that showed silent movies. We could sit at a table and have a waiter bring us hot dogs and sodas and spend the afternoon watching Charlie Chaplin, Buster Keaton, and the other greats of the silent film era.

It was during these years that my father would take me on outings to the various parts of the city. Perhaps what prepared me for my wanderlust years were these hours spent exploring the docks of the East River. There we would stand at the bow of a docked freighter and watch the unloading of cargo. Craning my neck to see the looming prow of a ship, I was filled with wonder and awe—feelings I have sought to experience all my life. The names of distant cities were stenciled on the sides of the crates and the smell of coffee from the sacks that were unloaded from Santos, Brazil, permeated the air. Years later, as a filmmaker, I would go to Brazil to shoot a documentary on the coffee industry and would visit Santos, the port that played a role in my childhood imaginings.

My father was an amateur photographer and these outings were always documented with his camera. He had set up a darkroom in the bathroom and I would watch him make prints. Watching just exhausted my patience and I knew that I would never be a photographer. But I would look through his photography books and try to copy the pictures, thoroughly enjoying the shading that I could achieve by using the side of a pencil.

Although my father spoke English well, it was my mother who became a U.S. citizen first. She had entered legally, but my father had simply stayed after his student visa expired. When World War II broke out, illegal aliens were investigated and my father feared he would be deported. My two uncles were drafted into the army and when it came time to be interviewed by the immigration service my father proudly told them I was a Boy Scout. He was permitted to stay because of his family and shortly after did become a citizen.

By then I was about twelve and had started to earn my own movie money. Every day after school I went to our neighbor Tony's garage to clean up. It was very exciting. I loved the smell of grease and gasoline. My job was to sweep up and to clean his tools. Tony was a quiet man and I admired his craftsmanship and independence. He did not have to go to a job but worked in his own garage next door to his house. Each morning when he arrived to work he would ceremoniously unwrap the cellophane from a knobby, twisted stick of tobacco, break it in half, pop one half into his mouth and clamp the other half between his teeth. Then, with a wooden match, he would proceed to light the stub until his face disappeared in a cloud of white smoke. The rest of the day would be spent keeping the stub lit and interrupting his puffing just long enough to hold the stub of the cigar between two grease-blackened fingers and spit a comet of tobacco juice across the garage. As the sweeper of the garage I became quite familiar with the brown tobacco spots and the black grease spots that covered the floor.

We never had a car so it was a thrill to slide behind the wheel of one of the cars waiting to be serviced. I could barely see over the steering wheel. The hard leather seats would squeak as I reached out with my feet to touch the pedals and take off on an imaginary trip. One day I made the mistake of turning on the ignition key while the car was in gear. The sudden lurch was enough to keep me away from the controls of a car for a long time.

This was my job after school, on Saturdays, and on school holidays. My reward came on Saturday when Tony would hand me a shiny fifty-cent coin for the week's work. It wasn't two quarters but a whole half-dollar, and I had earned it. I felt so grown-up as I held it in my pocket and went to the Saturday movie matinee to see the cartoons and the serial adventures of Flash Gordon, Tarzan, Zorro, or the Lone Ranger. The white uniformed matron would walk up and down the aisles during the showing, keeping the rowdy kids quiet. She carried her flashlight like a scepter and woe to the poor loudmouth who was revealed in her beam of light. Out they would go, never to know the conclusion of that week's chapter. Of course these adventures were reenacted in the empty lots which were our playgrounds. At the end of a cool fall day my friends and I would build a fire among the rubble and bring together sweet potatoes to throw into the ashes. When they were charred on the outside, we would pull them out of the fire, toss them into the air to cool off, and then break them open to savor the hot, moist sweetness.

There was a trolley line in Coney Island that ran from the last subway station to the western tip of the island. The older kids would hitch rides on the back of the car and the mischievous ones would disconnect the cable from the power line and run while the motorman would run out cursing at them. My first attempt to hitch was also my last. Under the guidance of the older kids I took my place alongside them and the car took off on its trip. As I hung onto the cable housing, the car came to a stop at a corner. My friends disappeared and, while I wondered why they had, a strong hand suddenly clasped me by the scruff of the neck. The motorman had snuck up on me by going around the outside of the car to take me by surprise. I hadn't pulled the cable off, but I was certainly in a position to do so.

He hauled me into the car and sat me down behind him as he resumed the trip. It was so humiliating to see the stern faces of the commuters frowning at me. The motorman was taking me to the end of the line and he threatened to turn me over to the police. By the time we arrived at the last stop I was terrified. Not so much of the police but of what my father would do to me when he heard of this. When the motorman pulled me out of the trolley, I burst into tears. He sent me off with a kick in the pants and I never did hitch again. It was a long walk home, but boy was I relieved.

My friend Artie and I had a lucrative business. Artie was an orphan who lived with his elderly uncle in a dilapidated house by the creek. Together we became junkies. Not that we dealt in drugs but in junk. Once a week at about five in the morning we would take a two-wheeled pushcart and make the rounds of the neighborhoods. We chose the day when the garbage would be collected and we got to the trash on the streets before the garbage collectors did. We picked up newspapers, rags, and metals (especially copper) and sold them to the junkyard down the street. This would net us about five dollars a week which we would split. The funny part was when we had a full cart and had to push down on the handle to level it off its stand. Both of us would hoist ourselves up on the handle and, with legs waving, bring the cart level so we could push it back home.

The Coney Island Creek was a foul-smelling, polluted body of water that separated the island from the Brooklyn mainland. It was also a source of endless adventures for my friends and me. During the war, a Coast Guard cutter was tied up there and we enjoyed talking to the sailors. We sometimes made rafts to pole about with. When our craft would tip and spill us into the foul waters I would return home and my mother would make me strip outside the house before getting into the bathtub. In later years the area near the creek became the place for me to paint. I spent many days behind an easel painting the barges, boat wrecks, tugs, and oil tanks along its shores.

These were my junior-high-school years. Mark Twain Junior High School was about a ten-block walk from where I lived. The classes I particularly enjoyed were my shop classes. Metal work, electrical wiring, and woodworking taught me new skills. Since this was during World War II, we made model airplanes for the government in the woodworking shop. They were painted black and used to train gunners to identify enemy aircraft.

The sign-painting class with Mr. Blutinger was the one that influenced my life's work. It was in his class that I

Painting by George Ancona, Mexico, 1950 (Reproduced by permission.)

discovered the feel of a chisel-edged brush and learned the joys of painting the letter S, with its curves and combination of heavy and thin strokes. I made extra money by painting signs for some of the Coney Island rides. I was even commissioned by my friend and classmate Bernie to paint the flavors and prices on his ice cream cart. Bernie managed to keep this business going through high school and college.

The sign-painting class was asked by the English teacher to make the backdrop scenery for the school play called *Intolerance*. This was my first introduction to mural painting. It was a huge, fire-spitting dragon that formed the fiery word HATE. Most of the painting was done by my friend Herbie and myself under Mr. Blutinger's guidance.

*

Entering Lincoln High School was the beginning of my career as a designer. The chairman of the art department was Mr. Leon Friend, who had come from Germany and was acquainted with the work of the graphic artists there. He had formed an "Art Squad," an after-school group of students interested in art. We designed the yearbook and did posters for competitions and school events. In retrospect, I think we all held Mr. Friend in such high esteem because he expected us to do our best and to be our own critics. We would work late into the night to render our ideas and the next morning we would pin our work on the board. He would walk about looking and then ask, "Is this your best, Mr. Ancona?" He always addressed us by Miss or Mr., which seemed to give us a sense of professionalism we would try to live up to. Of course this was a challenge to try again and see if it was the best that we could do. Somehow it always got better.

Mr. Friend made sure that the alumni of the Art Squad stayed in touch with the students. There were alumni meetings in New York City. Mr. Friend and the alumni would invite many of the top designers, artists, photographers, architects, and art directors to speak and show their work. As students we were in awe of what we heard and saw, and were exposed to a very professional group of people. Many of us got our first jobs through the alumni group. They once organized a benefit concert by the New York Philharmonic to raise money for scholarships for Art Squad students. I was fortunate enough to win one of these scholarships, which permitted me to attend the Art Students' League after graduation. My classmates have gone in many different directions but when we do meet we still remember and pay tribute to our mentor, Mr. Leon Friend.

It was in high school that the world of making books was introduced to me. The year-book, *Cargoes,* was designed by the students and I had my first experience in making illustrations. Sometimes they were paintings or drawings or linoleum cuts that were printed directly into the book. Poring through books in the library I dis-

"Painting in the kitchen," **1949** (Reproduced by permission.)

covered the work of Fritz Eichenberg, who did rich black-and-white woodcuts. Even today I am thrilled to hold a book that is beautifully printed in black and white.

It was during the time I was in high school that my sister died. It was very painful for all of us. My parents were devastated although her life had been full of illness and uncertainties. She had chosen to have an open-heart operation and took the risk because she looked forward to an improved life. She died during the operation. It was on that day that I grew up very quickly.

While in high school I attended classes at the Brooklyn Museum where I showed my work to the Mexican painter Rufino Tamayo. He invited me to visit him in Mexico which I did when I graduated high school. This was my first trip to Mexico. I had saved $500 from my earnings and took a bus to Mexico City. Señor Tamayo graciously arranged for me to attend the Academia de San Carlos, the leading art school in Mexico, and take any course I was interested in. I spent several months studying there.

At night I studied lithography in La Escuela de Arte del Libra (School for the Art of the Book). One night as I sat at my desk working on a lithograph, I felt someone behind me. When I turned I realized that it was Orozco, the great Mexican muralist, looking over my shoulder. He smiled at my astonishment and continued down the line of benches.

One of the courses I took was mural painting. Each student was assigned a panel which was prepared with fresh plaster each morning. The only problem was that we were never allowed to finish a painting. Each day our work was torn down and the panel prepared for the next day's work. I finally gave up and did an easel painting in oils of the subject I was trying to paint. What impressed upon me the most were subjects of poverty, of which I did several paintings—the old woman with the up-stretched hand, the blind man with the pockmarked face being led by his grandson, his hand outstretched. These images seared themselves into my conscience and memory. I traveled with a sketchbook and made quick drawings of these people and later worked the sketches up into paintings.

Through the school, students were able to attend performances at the Palacio de Bellas Artes, the museum and concert hall. I saw José Limon perform *The Moor's Pavane* and he gave me permission to photograph his rehearsal. I had borrowed my father's camera and this was the first time I attempted to work seriously with it.

When I look back on these times—I was nineteen and alone in a strange city—I realize that I learned a great deal. Meeting the masters was quite easy. Igor Stravinsky was conducting and I was introduced to him. Since my Spanish was learned in the kitchen with my parents, I was not too familiar with the formal way of addressing people so I used the familiar term of "tu" instead of "usted" with the maestro, much to the shock of my companions.

When I was introduced to Diego Rivera and his wife, I was too shy to take him up on his invitation to his home to taste "mole"—traditional turkey with chile and chocolate sauce. I'm sure he was quite genuine in his invitation, as were most of the Mexicans that I met in my travels. I was always impressed with the kindness and openness of the people I met.

As my money dwindled I decided to move on to the Yucatán to visit the family I had come to Mexico to meet. Traveling by bus, train, and finally plane, I arrived in Mérida. There were relatives from both sides of the family. All greeted me as if they had known me all my life. "Qué pasó, Jorgito!" was the greeting I heard whenever I entered a home, in the Yucatecan Spanish that has a Mayan accent.

It was a very moving experience to meet my mother's mother whom I called "Chichi." Chichi is the Mayan word for grandmother. She was a wonderful lady who had written to me since my birth. I still cherish her letters that are now faded and brown with age. She would write in the most elegant and flowery handwriting and would address me as "My most unforgettable and beloved grandson, Jorgito."

Chichi would take me on her rounds of visits to the family. Every morning a coachman with his tiny coach drawn by a tiny frail horse would call upon her. The coachman and my aunts would help Chichi get into the carriage. As she stepped into the carriage the entire coach would tip precariously to one side. Once settled, I would sit facing her and we would set off to visit my cousins, aunts, and uncles. Since getting in and out of the carriage was such a production, Chichi would stay in the carriage and everyone we visited would come out on the street to kiss her and bring her up-to-date on family events and gossip.

On my father's side only my grandfather, Don Silverio, was alive at that time. He was quite old by then and had white hair and a grand white mustache. He was a cause of much concern to my aunts, perhaps because he spent his life as a storekeeper—whenever he would receive a present he would take his hat and cane and go off and try to sell it to someone.

My days in the Yucatán were taken up with visiting the various limbs of the family tree. Breakfast at one aunt's home, lunch at an uncle's, dinner with a cousin, and in-between snacks and cups of hot chocolate. When I traveled into the Yucatán interior I always took a hammock along. In this way I was able to spend the night on the caretaker's porch at the ruins of Chichén Itzá. My first view of the ruins was at night by moonlight while I was wandering around alone. I recently took my son Pablo and my granddaughter Corina to see the ruins. It was hard for me to equate the crowds, the restaurants, the museum, and the tour buses with the magical night I spent there many years ago.

One of my uncles worked on a cattle ranch which he took me to visit. At night we sat in the kitchen with the cowboys, with the carcass of a deer hanging from the rafters. The Mayan women in their white dresses would cut off strips of meat and cook them in the traditional Mayan way. Huge wooden bowls filled with meat, vegetables, and tortillas were placed on the table and we all ate simply, using tortillas as our utensils.

I learned to eat this way on my trip to Taxco during a market day. Arriving in the town by bus I went to the market to eat. The wooden tubs filled with hot barbecued meat were carried in through the crowds. I bought a stack of tortillas from a woman who sold them to me from a basket. Then I asked for half a kilo of meat which was chopped up and weighed on a greasy scale. At another stand I bought a dollop of guacamole and onions and sat down on the curb with the other people who had come into town to trade. Pulling the bottom tortilla out I tore pieces off and used them to pick up the meat to eat. This went on until the meat was gone. With the remnant of the last tortilla I wiped my lips and ate it. Nothing to throw away or recycle.

*

Six months had gone by and my money was gone. There was just enough to take the ship to New Orleans and a bus back to New York City. On my return I entered the Art Students' League to study with the scholarship I had received from the Art Squad. At night I attended Cooper Union. My scholarship at the League ran for nine months, after which I went to work. My first jobs were as an apprentice in art studios where I spent as much time as I could looking over the artists' shoulders at what they were doing. My job was to change the water in their jars and make stencils for the retouchers. Finally I was allowed to sit at a drawing board to do layouts. My education came with going from job to job, always staying on a little longer in the new one than in the previous one. At last my portfolio was professional enough to get me a job in the promotion department of the *New York Times*. I was working so hard during the day that my evening schoolwork suffered, so I decided to continue with my work and left school. The other major decision I made was to get married. I was twenty-one at the time. I married Patricia Apatow, a girl from Lincoln High School who loved to dance.

My next job was as a staff designer at *Esquire* magazine. I was surrounded in the "bullpen," which is what the art department was called, by many talented young artists and designers. Among them were people like Henry Wolf, Ed Sorel, Seymour Chwast, Eddie Benguiat, and others who went on to make important contributions to the world of art and design. A few months into the job there was a major upheaval in the department. The head art director was fired and one by one we were called into the publisher's office and either fired or given new responsibilities. I was lucky. I stayed on and became art director for *Apparel Arts*, a men's fashion trade magazine.

After two years I decided it was time for a change and swapped jobs with a friend who was art director of the promotion department for *Seventeen* magazine. This gave me my first taste of advertising. I enjoyed the challenge of blending images with words to create a forceful message. From the world of magazines I was next drawn to the world of advertising. I joined an advertising agency as an art director for the NBC Television and Radio Networks. It was a heady and exciting experience. I was fortunate to work with very creative illustrators and photographers. From television advertising I moved on to the world of fashion, which opened up new experiences in photography for me. I would stand alongside a photographer and work toward creating an image that would convey an idea and concept. It was not esthetics that dominated our work but rather concepts. During these eight years I learned a great deal

about photography and film production. During my time at home I would photograph my three children and collaborate with a friend to make my first film.

The title of the film was *The Gift*. It was written by Herb Danska, who illustrated children's books. We borrowed a camera and asked friends to participate in the production. We learned by doing it. Working on weekends, our locations were Greenwich Village and an island in the East River occupied by many old, abandoned hospital buildings. The film told the story of the brief encounter between an older successful artist and a young couple on the island.

We received some good reviews for the film and this led us into another project. We were contracted to make a documentary of the South Bronx that gave an overall picture of the people and conditions in the neighborhood. The film was used as an introduction to new staff members of Lincoln Hospital who would be working in the community. Of course all this was done while we earned our living with other jobs.

The film experiences and my early attempts at photography seemed to be leading me into a different career direction. Having started out as someone who loved to draw and paint, I was spending more and more time with film and still cameras. Of course I still enjoyed drawing in my sketchbooks and attending a weekly sketch group of friends who drew from a model. Drawing was such a part of my discipline that I couldn't let it go. To me it is still one of the best ways of developing an "eye." Once you draw something it becomes part of your visual knowledge.

During family vacations I would travel with a camera and take on assignments for magazines. One of the earliest stories I did was for a Catholic layman's magazine called *Jubilee*. In Spain I photographed and wrote an article about the work the young priests did among the poor and rural people in the area around Málaga. In the towns, the French order of the Sisters of Charity nuns had established health centers which I photographed.

In one school I spent a morning photographing children in their classrooms. In one class, much to my delight, a teacher asked two students to perform a flamenco dance to the accompaniment of their classmates' clapping. After taking pictures of several classes I ended my visit. As I walked across the courtyard to leave, the recess bell rang. Children burst from their classrooms and, upon seeing me in the courtyard below, lined up around the balconies and began to sing to me. It was a very moving experience and it impressed me with the humanity of the situation. I was very grateful.

As a boy I remember the scrapbooks that my father kept of the progress of the Spanish Civil War. He was an ardent anti-fascist and I remember the images of war that he vehemently condemned. When I saw Picasso's *Guernica* mural, I understood the outrage and pain he expressed at his fellow man's violence and cruelty.

With wife Helga (right) and friend Margarida, New Mexico, 1993 (Reproduced by permission.)

During this time I was very interested in flamenco music and I studied the guitar for a while. In the office next to mine was a like-minded art director, Dave Charney, who was also a flamenco aficionado. During lunch he would practice his guitar while I did "palmas," the rhythmic clapping. All this to the consternation of our boss, the agency president, who would walk away shaking his head and mumbling something about "these creative types."

On another trip I did a story about a community farm in England that functioned on the Benedictine mode. It had been established by an architect who declared himself a conscientious objector during the Second World War. He had converted to Catholicism and adopted the rituals of the nearby Benedictine monastery. The entire community worked together, but individuals were able to pursue their own specialties such as pottery and weaving. This way of life interested me and years later I moved into a cooperative community in the Hudson Valley of New York. I suppose that, since I had grown up in the only Mexican family in the neighborhood, throughout my adult years I would search out a way of being part of a closer community.

By now a choice had to be made. Either I continued as an art director with a steady job and paycheck or moved into the uncertain world of freelancing. I was thirty years old and felt that it was now or never, so I took the plunge. I quit my job and started taking a portfolio of my family and travel photographs to magazines and advertising agencies. My first break came when I took children's fashion photographs for a magazine called *Vogue Children.* It all seemed so natural for me to be photographing children. In order to save money we rented out our house in the city and moved about twenty miles up the Hudson River. We had been invited to rent a house in a cooperative community in Stony Point, New York. Most of our neighbors were artists, musicians, and craftspeople.

The result of my first documentary in the South Bronx enabled me to produce films for *Sesame Street* and later to film a children's series called *Big Blue Marble.* This took me to Iceland, Tunisia, and Switzerland and later to other locations around the world. During these years I also worked on documentaries and industrial films in Brazil, Pakistan, Hong Kong, and Japan.

It was quite comfortable for me to work in both films and stills. One offered a solitary way of photographing while the other provided a collaborative experience by working and traveling as part of a film crew.

After fifteen years of marriage my wife and I were divorced. Our children, Lisa, Gina, and Tomas, stayed with me. I learned to balance both housework and career. About a year later the wife of a Brazilian friend came to visit with two friends. One of her companions was Helga Von Sydow. I escorted them around New York; her two friends left and Helga stayed. I introduced her to the kids and the following year we were married. Soon our first child was born and we named her Isabel. Two years after Isabel came Marina and six years later came Pablo.

*

My introduction to children's books was totally unexpected. It was at a dinner at our friends Barbara and Fred Brenner's home when "Bobbie" asked if I'd be interested in working with her on a children's book. She is an established children's author and had the idea of using photographs to illustrate a book idea she had written. Since I had never done a children's book I said yes. *Faces* was my first experience in the world of children's literature. It was published in 1970 and it is still in print. Two more books with Bobbie followed, *Bodies* and *A Snake-Lover's Diary.*

Our editor, Ann Troy, suggested I try writing the text for a book of my photographs. Well, it sounded pretty daunting. I had never studied writing or gone to college, but I gulped hard and said I would try. Ann said that if I were to write the text I would receive the other fifty percent of the royalties. That convinced me to try. I did and it worked. The first book I ever wrote was called *Monsters on Wheels.* It was based on the interest I've always had of watching construction sites and huge machinery. I spent several months photographing and describing these huge machines at work.

People ask me where I get my ideas for books. It seems that one book often leads me into another subject. Having done a book about machines, I made a book about the people who run them. Basically, I consider myself a people photographer. The book *And What Do You Do?* shows people at work who didn't go to college or study at a two-year school. This led to a book called *Teamwork,* which shows how people work in teams to get a job done. It was influenced by some of my experiences as a member of a film crew.

This was about the time when Helga and I were expecting Pablo. I decided to photograph Pablo's birth and his first year of life and growth. The book was called *It's a Baby!* When he was small, Pablo would tell people that he was born in a book. Now as a teenager he tends to be embarrassed about our showing the book.

Ever since I've been a teenager I've loved Latin music and would spend hours learning the steps and movements to the various rhythms. It wasn't important for me to do them correctly; it was just to have fun. At parties I would be surprised when some of my friends

would say they can't dance. This was hard to believe so I did a book called *Dancing Is . . .* It took a year of going to parties and festivals to photograph people dancing to the wide diversity of music that can be heard in New York.

There are times when I meet people or talk to friends that I come up with ideas for books. A friend, Remy Charlip, once asked me to suggest a way to photograph a book about signing for the deaf. This led to our working with Mary Beth and producing the "Handtalk" series.

Joan Anderson, one of the mothers at our children's school, had an idea for a Thanksgiving book. This led to the publication of *The First Thanksgiving Feast* and the many books that followed. By collaborating with other authors I learn about the subjects we are documenting and it broadens my outlook not only to my craft but to the world around me. It helps me to see things through someone else's perspective. It's teamwork.

In time I've discovered that the world of children's books suits me just fine. Not only can I go out and take pictures but I can also write the words and design the book. Half the time I will do my own books and the other half I will collaborate with other writers and do only the photography and sometimes the design.

In a way it is a fulfillment of my childhood fantasies to travel and explore other places. My approach is not that of the tourist but of a visitor trying to see things through the eyes of my hosts. In Honduras, I knew I had met the right family for my next book when I saw little Manolo greet his father upon his return from work in the banana plantation. When they saw each other their faces lit up in the sunniest of smiles. The result was *Bananas,* a book about all the people who bring bananas from the plantation to our stores.

"Editing slides in my studio," New Mexico, 1993 (Reproduced by permission.)

People seem to want to help me when they hear that I am trying to make a children's book. In Brazil, it was little Rosa and Flavia who took me through the experience of seeing the birth of turtles and the work being done to keep the sea turtle from extinction. *Turtle Watch* was the result. As I left in a taxi down the dusty street of the fishing village I heard, "Señor Jorge, Señor Jorge." Rosa was running down the street to give me a good-bye "abraço," or big hug. For me it was a sad departure. I did have the opportunity to return to Brazil with my family to visit Rosa and Flavia. We all ended up dancing on the beach one evening.

Recently I have been going back to my roots for subjects to photograph and write about. *Pablo Remembers* is an idea I'd had for at least five years. It took thirteen rejections from publishers before Lothrop, Lee & Shepard offered me the contract to do it. On one of my trips to Mexico I saw the way people there remembered their dead relatives and friends. It is a time for family reunions, meals, and an evening spent in the cemetery among flowers and candles on the decorated tombs of departed relatives. Children run and play among the graves while families and neighbors sit, eat, drink, and visit with the dead. In the streets people parade in costume and recite satiric poems in front of their neighbors' houses. When a Spanish edition of *Pablo Remembers* was printed, it gave me an opportunity to translate the text and use my Spanish name, Jorge Ancona Diaz.

A second Mexico book has just been published. This one is about Don Ricardo, the village piñata maker in a small town in Oaxaca, Mexico. The result is a bilingual book called, of course, *The Piñata Maker/El piñatador.*

The only problem I have with meeting and spending time with people is when I say good-bye. Time and time again when I enter the lives of strangers I leave as a friend. The departure is very sad for me because these people have become part of my life and I don't know if I will ever see them again.

The year after I did *Pablo Remembers* I was able to return to the same area to do *The Piñata Maker.* Naturally I went to the town to visit my friends from *Pablo Remembers.* When the children saw me walking down the street they all came running into my arms shouting "Don Jorge, Don Jorge." Samuel, the father, came out of the house beaming while Refugio, his wife, while wiping her hands on her apron the way my mother did, invited me to sit and drink, eat, and just be with them. I sat with them, relishing their warm welcome and affection. They have become an extension of my family. Someday I would like to take as much time as it would to visit all the people I have gotten to know through my travels and books.

At the moment I am finishing a book about the Golden Lion Tamarin monkey in Brazil. Since there were no hotels in the small town near the rain forest, I was invited to stay at the home of the coordinator of the

The author with his granddaughter, Maya (Reproduced by permission.)

project. She was an eldest daughter with ten brothers and sisters. I shared a room with the teenage brother while the other children slept on couches and mats on the floor. Running in and out of the house were dogs, puppies, cats, and kittens. In the yard were chickens, roosters, ducks, geese, pigs, guinea hens, and goats. In the evening the young bull was also brought into the yard to sleep. Added to the din of the animals and shouts of the kids was the radio with samba music and the television with the soap operas.

This was my home for ten days. After grueling days photographing the monkeys in the rain forest, I would return to the house to eat and relax but found that quiet was impossible. My place to rest was the town plaza. The mother would send three of the boys on bikes to keep me from getting lost and I would sit on a bench greeting newfound friends and reading. Before returning I would buy ice-cream pops for the boys and myself. By the time I left I felt not only part of the family but also of the town.

Processes fascinate me, whether I am doing it myself or watching others at their work. Much of my work is simply waiting and watching. This is time well spent because I learn and I try to sense what goes on beneath the surface. Sometimes it can be photographed, sometimes it can't, but it usually leads to an understanding of what I see. This helps me in the writing.

Working with words has been a delightful new experience for me. Before, I depended on photographs to convey the meanings. Now with words alongside my pictures I can enhance the image with a description of the sounds that I heard or the feelings I experienced. To me words seem like the colors that I would use to paint pictures. The struggle to find the right word can be frustrating and exciting at the same time. That's why I enjoy the rewriting process. I like to see how much I can tighten up a phrase and intensify its meaning.

I consider myself a primitive writer and I depend on my editors to tell me where my thoughts are muddy. My family are usually my first critics. Then I will take the manuscript and rewrite it again . . . and again . . . and again.

When I do a book I try to bring to it the same feeling I had when my father would show me the big ships. It's like seeing something awe-inspiring and you just have to say, "WOW."

And so I continue to wander the world and meet wonderful people who share their lives with me and in turn I hope to share these wonderful experiences with the readers of my books.

*

Ancona, working in his office (Reproduced by permission.)

George Ancona contributed the following update to *SATA* in 2009:

It's been sixteen years since my original essay for *Something about the Author.* So much has happened in those years. More books published, more children born in the family, and more wrinkles and white hair.

As a fledgling photographer I had the good fortune to be assigned by *Esquire* magazine to photograph Leonard Bernstein rehearsing the New York Philharmonic orchestra in New York City's Carnegie Hall. It was a piece by Manuel de Falla. As he conducted, he danced about the podium to the rhythm of the music. When he finished he came down to where I was standing, and I said, "You look like you are having a ball." His response was profound and influenced my approach to my work. He said, "If it isn't fun, it isn't worth doing."

I took this to heart. I found that children's books offered me the opportunity to explore and discover people and places I never would have known. I've followed paths I never would have considered. Been to places and met people who shared their lives with me. All because I said, "I'm doing a children's book."

My other guiding gem of wisdom came from Pablo Picasso, who said, "I do not search, I find." This taught me to be flexible. Photography being my medium requires a reliance on intuition. I've learned to be open to possibilities. With every direction I take there is a chance of failing, but there are probably other solutions that can be even better. It's worth a try.

I recently saw a sign over the entrance to a play school. It was another quote by Picasso. It said, "Every child is an artist. The problem is how to remain an artist once we grow up." I've been thinking about it, and it may evolve into another book.

With my more recent projects I've begun to look back at my roots. The stories my parents told me about our family have inspired me to return to Mexico and the Yucatán, where my parents came from. Looking at the books I've done I can now see a pattern of reaching back to my early experiences and stories, and exploring and producing books about these memories and roots.

By now I've produced over 113 books, sixty percent of which I have written and photographed. The others have been collaborations with other authors.

When I graduated high school I was asked to say something about my ambitions for the school paper. In a joking manner I said I wanted to have six children and be a great artist. Well, I did have the six children: Lisa, Gina, and Tom, from my first marriage, and Isabel, Marina, and Pablo from my marriage to Helga. The "great artist" I don't worry about. I'm too busy having a wonderful time being alive and doing what I like to do.

I've watched my children grow and blossom into creative and loving people. To date there are four grand-

Ancona with students on a school visit. (Reproduced by permission.)

children: Gina's daughter, Corina; Tom's two daughters Olivia and Natalie; and Isabel's new baby, Felix Thelonius. The oldest granddaughter Corina is six months older than our youngest son, Pablo. Corina was a third grade teacher. She is now the mother of three children, Maya, Alexander, and Leila, making me a great grandfather.

Unfortunately they are all living in different cities around the country. Pablo returned to finish his studies here in New Mexico and is now contemplating his future directions. The result is that I try to find projects that I can do in cities where my loved ones live. And I do.

One of the gratifying results of my books has been to visit schools to talk to children about reading and writing—particularly when their school has a large population of Spanish speaking children. I can identify with them as someone who grew up in a home where Spanish was spoken. It was my first language, and it was only when I was able to play outside that I began to learn English.

Our family was the only one in the neighborhood that spoke Spanish. Our neighborhood in Coney Island was made up of immigrants from a variety of European countries. Our immediate neighbors were predominantly Italian. When I was confirmed I asked my scoutmaster to be my godfather. He agreed. Our troop called him Patsy. I was under the impression that his name was Patrick.

When we stood in front of the bishop and I was anointed, I received the slap on the cheek to remind me of the hardships I would face in my new status of a man. It was then that I heard for the first time that I had accepted the name Pascual, not Patrick. So I became George Efraín Pascual Ancona Diaz.

Many years passed and I was driving around New Mexico with Helga, exploring the lands to where we would eventually move. In a small village we stopped to visit the home of a wood carver who carved wood figures of the saints. There on a shelf stood the carving of a saint holding a disc in each hand. When I asked the carver who the saint was and what the disks were he replied, "Those are tortillas he is holding. He is San Pascual, the patron saint of the kitchen." I bought the statue, and it stands behind me on a shelf in my studio.

My more recent books seem to be reaching back to events in my roots, drawing on stories about Mexico I heard when my uncles and my parents' friends came to visit. These long forgotten subjects seem to be coming to my consciousness. The result is that I've been returning to Mexico to produce several books about the region's people, places, and happenings.

I've also done a series of bilingual books about Spanish-speaking families in the United States. The children featured in the books seem to share some of the feelings I have had growing up speaking Spanish in this country. I've returned to the Yucatán where my parents came from and where I still have some aunts and cousins.

The more I wrote and photographed the Latino experience here, the more I've been intrigued with the history of the Spanish conquest of the New World and how it has resulted in the America of today.

About five years ago my son Tom was contracted to move to London to work on some projects. He went with his wife Laura and his two daughters, Olivia and Natalie. One day Natalie brought one of my books to the American School to show her teacher. The result was that the school invited me to London to visit and talk to the students. After the presentations I decided to go to Sevilla, Spain, to do some research for a book on flamenco. Tom suggested I take Natalie since she could afford to miss some school time. Olivia was in a higher class and was unable to take time away from school.

We went to Sevilla, Natalie and I, and began to explore flamenco, an interest I've had for many years. So here are Grandpa and ten-year-old little Natalie exploring the labyrinths of the old city and attending flamenco performances, where Natalie would often fall asleep on my shoulder. This trip was the beginning of a children's book that I have just completed called, *Ole! Flamenco.* On my most recent visit to Sevilla, I was accompanied by my youngest son, Pablo, who just graduated from college and is interested in documentary photography and music. He was a big help.

Sevilla is part of the Ancona history in that the first Ancona departed from that city and landed in the Yucatán in 1654. One of my cousins in the Yucatán has been researching the genealogy of the family name. Ancona is a city on the coast of the Adriatic just south of Venice.

During the years when Spain governed the southern part of Italy a Spanish duke was assigned to govern the area. In his court in Naples was a fifteen-year-old page called Ancona. When the duke was recalled to Sevilla, he brought the boy with him. The duke educated him, and Ancona became a distinguished doctor. He married and had four sons, the eldest of whom was sent by the king to be the vice-governor of the Yucatán.

I was able to do more research in the Archives of the Indies and found the family name on a list of passengers who embarked on a ship from Sevilla to Yucatán in 1654. This is quite exciting since an Ancona was the archbishop who built the cathedral in Merida, and a later Ancona wrote a five-volume history of the Yucatán published in 1874. The leather-bound volumes were left to me by my father.

I just returned from a tour of twenty schools in south east Washington State. It took three weeks. It was arduous but extremely exciting. I showed the kids parts of *Ole! Flamenco,* the book I have just finished. I explain how flamenco artists keep the rhythm of the dance by clapping. Then I showed each audience of about two hundred students how to do it. Imagine, all those clapping kids. And I end the clapping by shouting "Ole!" At one presentation one student shouted, "Dance!" I tried to avoid this request by saying, "I can't. I don't have a partner." One teacher obligingly hopped over the rows of kids and joined me in an impromptu Sevillanas to the clapping and shouts of "Ole!" of the kids. It was a blast.

A few days after I returned to Santa Fe I received a carton of letters and books written by the students I had just left. Many of the comments are hilarious, such as, "Love the 'stash!" and "Your books are cool and you are old but you are cool." Many of the letters were written in Spanish. There were so many Spanish-speaking students that I gave two presentations in Spanish. Looking at the faces of the kids sitting cross-legged on the floor of the gyms took me back to my early experiences in school. It was a profound experience to see them wave and shout "Ole!" as they left the gym. One little girl broke ranks and ran into my arms. I picked her up and spun her around. I felt very much at home.

More than ever I want to continue in the direction I seem to be going: that of celebrating the multicultural roots of the United States. I've become aware of the diversity in each culture that I have encountered. We are a nation of diversity, which is celebrated in the writings, music, dance, and languages of our native people and immigrants. These exchanges gave us flamenco, jazz, tango, samba, hip-hop, fusion, and salsa. These are living arts that will keep absorbing and renewing themselves. It is all very exciting.

Ancona, photographing a dancer (Reproduced by permission.)

ANDERSON, Carolyn Dunn
See DUNN, Carolyn

*   *   *

ARNOLD, Tedd 1949-

Personal

Born January 20, 1949, in Elmira, NY; son of Theodore (a machinist) and Gabriela Arnold; married Carol Clark (a teacher), August 15, 1970; children: Walter, William. *Education:* University of Florida, B.F.A.

Addresses

Office—Elmira, NY. *E-mail*—tarnold@stny.rr.com.

Career

Author and illustrator. Textbook illustrator, Tallahassee, FL, 1973-78; creative director and owner of a graphic design studio, 1978-81; Cycles USA, Tallahassee, advertising art director, 1981-84; Workman Publishing, New York, NY, book designer, 1984-86; freelance author and illustrator, beginning 1986. Presenter at schools. *Military service:* U.S. Army Reserve, medic, 1969-75.

Awards, Honors

Children's Choice Award, International Reading Association (IRA)/Children's Book Council (CBC), 1988, Georgia Children's Picture Storybook Award, 1990, North Dakota Children's Choice Picture-Book Award, 1991, and Volunteer State Book Award, 1992, all for *No Jumping on the Bed!;* North Dakota Flicker Tale Award, 1993, for *The Signmaker's Assistant;* Parent's Choice designation, 1993, and Children's Choice Award, IRA/ CBC, 1994, both for *Green Wilma;* Children's Choice Award, IRA/CBC, 1995, for *My Working Mom,* and 1996, for *No More Water in the Tub!;* National Association of Parenting Publications Award, 1996, for *Bialosky's Bedtime;* Tellable Stories for Ages 4-7 Award, *Storytelling World,* and Books Mean Business selection, American Booksellers Association/CBC, both 1998, and Colorado Children's Book Award, 1999, all for *Parts;* Notable Books for Children citation, *Smithsonian* magazine, 1999, for *Axle Annie;* Theodor Seuss Geisel Award Honor Book designation, 2006, for *Hi, Fly Guy!;* Edgar Allan Poe Award for Best Young-Adult Novel, Mystery Writers of America, 2008, for *Rat Life.*

Writings

FOR CHILDREN; SELF-ILLUSTRATED EXCEPT AS NOTED

Sounds, Little Simon (New York, NY), 1985.
Opposites, Little Simon (New York, NY), 1985.
Actions, Little Simon (New York, NY), 1985.

Tedd Arnold (Photograph by Carol Arnold. Reproduced by permission.)

Colors, Little Simon (New York, NY), 1985.
My First Drawing Book, Workman Publishing (New York, NY), 1986.
No Jumping on the Bed!, Dial (New York, NY), 1987.
My First Play House, Workman Publishing (New York, NY), 1987.
My First Play Town, Workman Publishing (New York, NY), 1987.
Ollie Forgot, Dial (New York, NY), 1988.
(Compiler) *Mother Goose's Words of Wit and Wisdom: A Book of Months,* Dial (New York, NY), 1990.
(And designer of samplers) *Cross-Stitch Patterns for Mother Goose's Words of Wit and Wisdom: Samplers to Stitch,* New American Library/Dutton (New York, NY), 1990.
The Signmaker's Assistant, Dial (New York, NY), 1992.
The Simple People, illustrated by Andrew Shachat, Dial (New York, NY), 1992.
Green Wilma, Dial (New York, NY), 1993.
No More Water in the Tub!, Dial (New York, NY), 1995.
Five Ugly Monsters, Scholastic (New York, NY), 1995.
Bialosky's Bedtime: An Opposites Book, Workman Publishing (New York, NY), 1996.
Bialosky's Big Mess: An Alphabet Book, Workman Publishing (New York, NY), 1996.
Bialosky's Bumblebees: A Counting Book, Workman Publishing (New York, NY), 1996.
Bialosky's House: A Color Book, Workman Publishing (New York, NY), 1996.

Parts, Dial (New York, NY), 1997.

Huggly Gets Dressed, Scholastic (New York, NY), 1997.

Huggly Takes a Bath, Scholastic (New York, NY), 1998.

Huggly and the Toy Monster, Scholastic (New York, NY), 1998.

Huggly's Pizza, Scholastic (New York, NY), 2000.

Huggly Goes to School, Scholastic (New York, NY), 2000.

More Parts, Dial (New York, NY), 2001.

Huggly's Christmas, Scholastic (New York, NY), 2001.

Huggly's Big Mess, Scholastic (New York, NY), 2001.

Huggly's Trip to the Beach, Scholastic (New York, NY), 2002.

Huggly's Snow Day, Scholastic (New York, NY), 2002.

Huggly's Halloween, Scholastic (New York, NY), 2002.

Huggly's Thanksgiving Parade, Scholastic (New York, NY), 2002.

Huggly's Valentines, Scholastic (New York, NY), 2003.

Huggly Goes Camping, Scholastic (New York, NY), 2003.

Even More Parts: Idioms from Head to Toe, Dial (New York, NY), 2004.

Catalina Magdalena Hoopensteiner Wallendiner Hogan Logan Bogan Was Her Name, Scholastic (New York, NY), 2004.

Hi, Fly Guy!, Scholastic (New York, NY), 2005.

Super Fly Guy!, Scholastic (New York, NY), 2006.

The Twin Princes, Dial (New York, NY), 2006.

Shoo, Fly Guy!, Scholastic (New York, NY), 2006.

Rat Life, Sleuth Dial (New York, NY), 2007.

There Was an Old Lady Who Swallowed Fly Guy, Scholastic (New York, NY), 2007.

Fly High, Fly Guy!, Cartwheel Books/Scholastic (New York, NY), 2008.

Hooray for Fly Guy!, Scholastic (New York, NY), 2008.

Green Wilma, Frog in Space, Dial Books for Young Readers (New York, NY), 2009.

I Spy Fly Guy, Scholastic (New York, NY), 2009.

Fly Guy Meets Fly Girl, Scholastic (New York, NY), 2010.

No Jumping on the Bed! was translated into Spanish.

ILLUSTRATOR

Helen Witty, *Mrs. Witty's Monster Cookies,* Workman Publishing (New York, NY), 1983.

Ron Atlas, *Looking for Zebra: Hotel Zoo: Happy Hunting from A to Z,* Little Simon (New York, NY), 1986.

Ron Atlas, *A Room for Benny,* Little Simon (New York, NY), 1987.

Rena Coyle, *My First Baking Book,* Workman Publishing (New York, NY), 1988.

Anne Kostick, *My First Camera Book,* Workman Publishing (New York, NY), 1989.

Laurie Abel, *Bisnipian Blast-off: An Action Counting Book,* Discovery Toys, 1991.

David Schiller and David Rosenbloom, *My First Computer Book,* Workman Publishing (New York, NY), 1991.

Peter Glassman, *My Working Mom,* Morrow (New York, NY), 1994.

Jim Sargena, *The Roly-Poly Spider,* Scholastic (New York, NY), 1994.

Alyssa Satin Capucilli, *Inside a Barn in the Country: A Rebus Read-along Story,* Scholastic (New York, NY), 1995.

David Galef, *Tracks,* Morrow (New York, NY), 1996.

Suzanne Williams, *My Dog Never Says Please,* Dial (New York, NY), 1997.

Alyssa Satin Capucilli, *Inside a House That Is Haunted: A Rebus Read-along Story,* Scholastic (New York, NY), 1998.

Robin Pulver, *Axle Annie,* Dial (New York, NY), 1999.

Alyssa Satin Capucilli, *Inside a Zoo in the City: A Rebus Read-along Story,* Scholastic (New York, NY), 2000.

Brod Bagert, *Giant Children,* Dial (New York, NY), 2002.

Barbara Larmon Failing, *Lasso Lou and Cowboy McCoy,* Dial (New York, NY), 2003.

Robin Pulver, *Axle Annie and the Speed Grump,* Dial (New York, NY), 2005.

Sidelights

Whimsy is a stock in trade of award-winning author and artist Tedd Arnold. A successful creator of children's picture books, Arnold fills the tales he writes—and those he illustrates for other authors—with lovable but quirky characters with a sense of fun. His breakthrough book, *No Jumping on the Bed!,* won numerous awards; its follow up, *No More Water in the Tub!,* prompted *School Library Journal* contributor Anne Connor to write that "Arnold's soft pencil and watercolor illustrations are full of amusing details" that "will keep young readers coming back again and again." While Arnold continues to entertain young children in books such as *Green Wilma, Parts,* and his "Huggly" and "Fly Guy" series, he also treats older readers to a complex tale in his award-winning young-adult novel *Rat Life.*

In **Huggly Takes a Bath** *Arnold introduces readers to another cute monster character.* (Copyright © 1998 by Tedd Arnold. Reprinted by permission of Scholastic, Inc.)

Born in 1949, Arnold attended the University of Florida where he earned a bachelor of fine arts degree. Although he originally specialized in textbook illustration and graphic design for advertising, Arnold became interested in picture-book illustration thanks to the books his wife, Carol, was collecting for her kindergarten classroom. He approached several publishers with samples of his work, eventually receiving as his first illustration project Helen Witty's *Mrs. Witty's Monster Cookies,* published in 1983. Since then, Arnold has authored dozens of books and contributed his humorous drawings to stories by Robin Pulver, Alyssa Satin Capucilli, and Peter Glassman, among others. Of Capucilli's *Inside a Barn in the Country: A Rebus Read-along Story, Booklist* contributor Stephanie Zvirin wrote that Arnold's "lively pictures, filled with exaggerated, bug-eyed, cartoon-like characters and melodrama, should make this a childhood favorite." His illustrations for *Axle Annie,* by Robin Pulver, prompted *Booklist* contributor Ilene Cooper to write that Arnold's "pictures shiver with energy and fun."

No Jumping on the Bed! was inspired by Arnold's oldest son, Walter, who at four years old was a notorious bed-jumper. Arnold was then living with his parents in an old apartment building in Yonkers, New York, and he became intrigued by the possibility of Walter's bed falling through the floor into the neighbor's apartment below. The success of that book with children and parents confirmed Arnold's decision to specialize in illustrating children's books. *Ollie Forgot* and *The Signmaker's Assistant* soon followed.

Having penned a book for his older son, Arnold soon needed a book for his younger son, William, and *No More Water in the Tub!* was published in 1995. It is a warmhearted take on bath time, featuring young William who looks forward to snorkeling in the tub. Arnold's rhyming prose and illustrations found favor with Ann A. Flowers, who wrote in her *Horn Book* review: "Young readers will love the ridiculous incidents and cumulative rhymes, and the illustrations . . . are hilarious.'

Arnold has continued to gain fans among young children due to the many volumes of children's books he has written and illustrated since beginning his career. In *Catalina Magdalena Hoopensteiner Wallendiner Hogan Logan Bogan Was Her Name* Arnold "once again embraces the absurd," according to *School Library Journal* critic Piper L. Nyman. The story tells of a strange-looking girl with big feet, only two hairs on her head, and ape-like arms. But she is happy with herself, and indeed has some abilities that make her stand out from the crowd. Based on a traditional campfire song, the story is told in verse and takes liberties with a tale that was already silly. A critic for *Kirkus Reviews* noted that the book is "impossible to read without bursting into song."

In the series that includes *Huggly Gets Dressed, Huggly Takes a Bath,* and *Huggly's Pizza,* Arnold introduces a

Arnold combines an amusing story with his characteristically goofy art in his series installment **Hi, Fly Guy!** (Copyright © 2005 by Tedd Arnold. Reproduced by permission.)

likable monster from under the bed whose forays into the world of humans uncover many curiosities. In *Huggly's Pizza* the monster, together with his non-human friends Booter and Grubble, leaves his home under the bed to search for some delicious human food. In *Huggly Takes a Bath* the green-skinned monster sets forth to explore and discovers a small room full of porcelain objects that swish or spray water, a slippery cube that makes suds, bottles of sudsy, pretty-smelling lotions just perfect for mixing together to make a monster slime pit, and a row of tiny long-handled brushes for which he finds a funny use. Calling Arnold's illustrations "cartoon-like" and "colorfully appealing," *Booklist* contributor Shelley Townsend-Hudson praised *Huggly Takes a Bath* as a "simple, efficient text [that] is sure to elicit many laughs."

Arnold's "Fly Guy" easy-reader saga, which begins with *Hi, Fly Guy!,* also includes the Theodor Seuss Geisel Award Honor book *Hooray for Fly Guy!* as well as *Super Fly Guy, Fly High, Fly Guy!,* and *Shoo, Fly Guy.* Featuring what a *Kirkus Reviews* critic described as "a spare but never-stilted text and child-appealing" cartoon illustrations, the self-illustrated series follows the adventures of Buzz and his pet fly, named Fly Guy. In *Fly High, Fly Guy!* Fly Guy joins Buzz and his family on a vacation that includes surfing at the beach and visiting an art museum, while the fly finds catching a large football to be a bit more than he can handle when he joins Buzz's team in *Hooray for Fly Guy!* Lunchtime finds the tenacious Fly Guy determined to find just the right gooey, brown snack among the many lunches being consumed in the lunchroom at Buzz's school, while tragedy strikes in *There Was an Old Lady Who Swallowed Fly Guy.* The author/illustrator "masterfully infuses funny, expressive . . . illustrations with actions that further the plot," maintained Laura Scott in her *School Library Journal* review of *Fly High, Fly Guy!*, and in the same periodical Linda Staskus dubbed *Hooray for Fly Guy!* an "easy reader [that] is chock-full of humor." *Shoo, Fly Guy!* "has tons of kid appeal" assured *School Library Journal* contributor Martha Simpson, the critic hailing Arnold's "Fly Guy" books as a "rollicking series" featuring "clear, bright pictures."

Equally fanciful, *Green Wilma* and *Green Wilma, Frog in Space* recount a frog's dream that she has turned into a human girl with a talent for catching flies with her tongue. A voyage into outer space is in store for the fly-crazy frog in *Green Wilma, Frog in Space,* when Wilma is mistaken for a little blue space alien and beamed aboard a space ship bound for the outer galaxies. "Fast, funny, and froggy, *Green Wilma* is guaranteed to be a hit with the story hour silly set," enthused Annie Ayres in a *Booklist* review of the book. Arnold's style of illustration in the "Green Wilma" books is particularly appropriate: rounded lines and exaggerated, saucer-like, "goggle" eyes give his characters a frog-like appeal. Characterizing *Green Wilma* as a "wacky action romp," a *Publishers Weekly* contributor praised Arnold for his use of both color and humor in making stories come alive for youngsters, and *School Library Journal* critic Susan Weitz wrote of *Green Wilma, Frog in Space* that "to say that the pictures complement the text is like declaring that the Sun complements the Earth. Children will adore Wilma."

In his books *Parts, More Parts,* and *Even More Parts: Idioms from Head to Toe,* Arnold examines common figures of speech and how they baffle and strike fear into a young boy. Expressions like "hold your tongue," "give me a hand," and "I want all eyes on me" are shown literally in drawings that capture the boy's vivid imagination. Alice Case Smith, reviewing *More Parts* for *School Library Journal,* admitted that "kids will love faces cracking, lungs being coughed up, and bodies flying apart." In her review of the same title, Natalie Soto concluded in the *Rocky Mountain News* that "readers will delight in this book." Speaking of *Even More Parts,* a critic for *Kirkus Reviews* found that "Arnold's squiggly, bright watercolor-and-pencil illustrations are again delightfully bizarre."

In addition to his original, self-illustrated books, Arnold has also contributed art to books by other writers, such as Robin Pulver, Brod Bagert, and Alyssa Satin Capucilli. In addition, he earned critical recognition for his Edgar Allan Poe Award Honor book *Rat Life,* which a *Publishers Weekly* critic hailed as "dark and consis-

Arnold's characteristic saucer-eyed characters sometimes encounter challenges, as is evidenced in his picture book **Parts.** (Copyright © 1998 by Tedd Arnold. Reprinted by permission of Scholastic, Inc.)

tently gripping." Narrated by fourteen-year-old Todd Anthony and taking place in New York State in the early 1970s, the novel focuses on the violence and trauma endured by an older boy Todd meets, a boy named Rat. Working alongside Rat at a local drive-in theatre, Todd slowly learns Rat's history and he weaves these details—growing up with a violent father, being fraudulently enlisted in the U.S. army by a mother wishing to unburdened herself of her fourteen-year-old son, and enduring battlefield violence during the Vietnam war—into the creative writing he does for school and his own understanding of the world. In *School Library Journal* Miranda Doyle praised *Rat Life* "a solid story . . . with a likable main character," the critic adding that the novel will reward "patient readers" with its philosophical focus and "details of small-town life."

Arnold once told *SATA:* "It still comes as a great surprise to me that I'm now an author. I've always drawn pictures, taken art classes, and thought of myself as an artist. In school, my cartoons graced many a desktop, chalkboard, and math paper. (The teachers and the girls always noticed.) In the army, extra duty could be avoided by letting the sergeants know how nice the barracks would look with 'inspirational' murals painted on the walls. After college, I quickly learned that art-related jobs were more comfortable than construction-related jobs. And even today I find that drawing pictures for books is a great way to avoid doing real work.

"Back in college, I began writing titles across the bottoms of my drawings. The titles became lengthy, growing into sentences and paragraphs. The drawings and writings were like fragments of stories, pages torn from books. My interest in the words developed into a re-newed interest in an old love—comics. It was in the form of comics that I first explored storytelling.

"However, the writing was always for the pictures. The pictures were the real thing, the reason for being, the fun. Which is why the label of 'author' still feels like brand-new dress shoes, while 'artist' feels like well-worn, street-running, tree-climbing, can-kicking, ball-park sneakers. But don't we all just love a new pair of shoes!"

Biographical and Critical Sources

PERIODICALS

Booklist, March 1, 1993, Annie Ayres, review of *Green Wilma,* p. 1234; January 15, 1995, Stephanie Zvirin, review of *Inside a Barn in the Country: A Rebus Read-along Story,* p. 935; February 1, 1999, Shelley Townsend-Hudson, review of *Huggly Takes a Bath,* p. 978; February 15, 2000, Ilene Cooper, review of *Axle Annie,* p. 1120; November 1, 2005, Julie Cummins, review of *Axle Annie and the Speed Grump,* p. 54; March 1, 2007, Jennifer Mattson, review of *The Twin Princes,* p. 84; November 15, 2007, Carolyn Phelan, review of *There Was an Old Lady Who Swallowed Fly Guy,* p. 52; September 1, 2008, Carolyn Phelan, review of *Hooray for Fly Guy!,* p. 115.

Horn Book, January-February, 1996, Ann A. Flowers, review of *No More Water in the Tub!,* p. 59; July-August, 2006, Betty Carter, review of *Super Fly Guy,* p. 433.

Kirkus Reviews, June 15, 2004, review of *Catalina Magdalena Hoopensteiner Wallendiner Hogan Logan Bogan Was Her Name,* p. 575; August 1, 2004, review of *Even More Parts: Idioms from Head to Toe,* p. 737; July 15, 2005, review of *Hi, Fly Guy!,* p. 785; August 1, 2006, review of *Shoo, Fly Guy!,* p. 779; April 15, 2008, review of *Fly High, Fly Guy!*; April 1, 2009, review of *Green Wilma, Frog in Space.*

Kliatt, March, 2007, Claire Rosser, review of *Rat Life,* p. 8.

Publishers Weekly, January 29, 1996, review of *Tracks,* p. 99; October 16, 2000, review of *Parts,* p. 78; July 18, 2005, review of *Hi, Fly Guy!,* p. 205; April 30, 2007, review of *The Twin Princes,* p. 160; May 7, 2007, review of *Rat Life,* p. 61.

Rocky Mountain News, September 28, 2001, Natalie Soto, review of *More Parts,* p. D29.

School Library Journal, October, 1995, Anne Connor, review of *No More Water in the Tub!,* p. 96; September, 2001, review of *More Parts,* p. 182; August, 2004, Piper L. Nyman, review of *Catalina Magdalena Hoopensteiner Wallendiner Hogan Logan Bogan Was Her Name,* p. 105; January, 2005, Marge Loch-Wouters, review of *Even More Parts,* p. 85; December, 2005, Susan Weitz, review of *Axel Annie and the Speed Grump,* p. 120; March, 2006, Bobbee Pennington, review of *Super Fly Guy,* p. 174; September, 2006, Martha Simpson, review of *Shoo, Fly Guy!,* p. 158; May, 2007, Miranda Doyle, review of *Rat Life,* p. 128; December, 2007, Linda M. Kenton, review of *There Was an Old Lady Who Swallowed Fly Guy,* p. 86; June, 2008, Laura Scott, review of *Fly High, Fly Guy!,* p. 94; November, 2008, Linda Staskus, review of *Hooray for Fly Guy!,* p. 84; June, 2009, Susan Weitz, review of *Green Wilma, Frog in Space,* p. 78.

ONLINE

Tedd Arnold Home Page, http://www.teddarnoldbooks.com (November 15, 2009).

B

BECHTOLD, Lisze

Personal
Married; children: three. *Education:* M.F.A.

Addresses
Home—South Pasadena, CA.

Career
Author, illustrator, animator, and educator. Animator for films, including: *Star Trek: The Motion Picture,* 1979; *Spirit Lodge,* 1986; *Back to Neverland,* 1990; *The Prince and the Pauper,* 1990; and *FernGully: The Last Rainforest,* 1992. University of California, Los Angeles, Extension, instructor in writers' program.

Awards, Honors
Oppenheim Toy Portfolio Gold Award, 2000, for *Buster, the Very Shy Dog;* Oppenheim Gold Award, and Maryland Blue Crab Honor Book designation, both 2005, both for *Buster and Phoebe: The Great Bone Game.*

Writings

SELF-ILLUSTRATED

Buster, the Very Shy Dog, Houghton Mifflin (Boston, MA), 1999.
Edna's Tale, Houghton Mifflin (Boston, MA), 2001.
Buster and Phoebe: The Great Bone Game, Houghton Mifflin (Boston, MA), 2003.
Sally and the Purple Socks, Philomel (New York, NY), 2008.

ILLUSTRATOR

Karla Kuskin, *Toots the Cat,* Henry Holt (New York, NY), 2005.

Sidelights
Lisze Bechtold worked as an animator for feature films for seventeen years before making the shift to picture books. While she has contributed artwork to Karla Kuskin's *Toots the Cat,* most of Bechtold's illustrations pair with original stories that have been inspired by her own life. Her "Buster" stories, which appear in a pair of early readers, are based on dogs Bechtold has known, while *Edna's Tale* was inspired by her memories of a pet cat with a fluffy white tail that always managed to be covered with leaves. Reviewing *Edna's Tale* for *Booklist,* Ilene Cooper maintained that Bechtold's "terrific artwork . . . elevates this above many picture books," while Genevieve Ceraldi concluded in *School Library Journal* that the story of the fluffy-tailed kitty "will appeal to cat lovers everywhere."

In her award-winning beginning chapter books *Buster, the Very Shy Dog* and *Buster and Phoebe: The Great Bone Game* Bechtold shares her warm memories of two beloved family pets. Buster is a shy dog, while older dog-sister Phoebe likes to be the center of attention. Together, the two dogs manage to tangle with trouble in the form of raccoons and skunks, come to the rescue of their human caretakers through their loyalty and doggy talents, and also create some humorous situations, as Bechtold's short stories reveal.

Reviewing *Buster, the Very Shy Dog,* Cooper praised the author's ability to pair an "agreeable, relatable story and above-average cartoon-style artwork," while in *Horn Book* a critic asserted that "the lively ink-and-watercolor illustrations have a well-drawn goofiness." The author/illustrator "exhibits her winning humor" again in *Buster and Phoebe: The Great Bone Game,* which contains three more illustrated stories "guaranteed to entertain," according to *School Library Journal* contributor Gay Lynn Van Vleck. Comparing Bechtold's ink drawings to the work of noted cartoonist James Thurber, a *Publishers Weekly* reviewer added that in *Buster, the Very Shy Dog* the canine characters are "very childlike . . . and youngsters will find much with which to identify."

Lisze Bechtold captures the essence of an independent young spirit in her self-illustrated Sally and the Purple Socks. (Copyright © 2008 by Lisze Bechtold. All rights reserved. Reproduced by permission of Philomel Books, a division of Penguin Putnam Books for Young Readers.)

Bechtold turns to whimsy in *Sally and the Purple Socks,* which pairs her "quirky, playful . . . illustrations" with a tale containing "just the right amount of suspense," according to *Booklist* critic Randall Enos. In the story, a duck named Sally loves her new purple knit socks. Although they are a bit too small at first, as she wears them, the socks stretch ever larger. Once they are too large for Sally's feet, the duck uses them as a warm cap and scarf. The socks keep stretching, however, and soon they are large enough to be used as blankets, then as a carpet. Finally, the socks are too large to remain in the house, and so the resourceful duck crafts them into a tent the perfect size to shelter all her friends at a party. Reviewing *Sally and the Purple Socks* in *Kirkus Reviews,* a critic praised the book's "pared-down text and artfully minimalist illustrations," adding that Bechtold's story captures a child's "uncanny ability to find wonder" in simple things.

"A child is far more demanding of clarity and brevity in books than an adult, and yet a child is delightfully more tolerant of silliness," Bechtold noted on the University of California, Los Angeles Extension Web site. "I love the challenge of expressing deep feelings with silliness and brevity."

Biographical and Critical Sources

PERIODICALS

Booklist, May 15, 1999, Ilene Cooper, review of *Buster, the Very Shy Dog,* p. 1704; May 1, 2001, Ilene Cooper, review of *Edna's Tale,* p. 1688; September 1, 2005, Hazel Rochman, review of *Toots the Cat,* p. 138; June 1, 2008, Randall Enos, review of *Sally and the Purple Socks,* p. 92.

Horn Book, July, 1999, review of *Buster, the Very Shy Dog,* p. 462; September-October, 2003, Roger Sutton, review of *Buster and Phoebe: The Great Bone Game,* p. 606; November-December, 2005, Susan Dove Lempke, review of *Toots the Cat,* p. 731.

Kirkus Reviews, August 1, 2005, Karla Kuskin, review of *Toots the Cat,* p. 852; April 15, 2008, review of *Sally and the Purple Socks.*

Publishers Weekly, January 18, 1999, review of *Buster, the Very Shy Dog,* p. 95; September 1, 2003, review of *Buster and Phoebe: The Great Bone Game,* p. 91; July 25, 2005, review of *Toots the Cat,* p. 74.

School Library Journal, June, 2001, Genevieve Ceraldi, review of *Edna's Tale,* p. 102; July, 2003, Gay Lynn Van Vleck, review of *Buster and Phoebe,* p. 87; January, 2006, Shawn Brommer, review of *Toots the Cat,* p. 120; June, 2008, Ieva Bates, review of *Sally and the Purple Socks,* p. 95.

ONLINE

California Readers Online, http://www.californiareaders. org/ (November 20, 2009), Bonnie O'Brian, interview with Bechtold.

University of California, Los Angeles, Extension Web site, http://www2.uclaextension.edu/writers/ (November 20, 2009), "Lisze Bechtold."*

*   *   *

BERGUM, Constance R. 1952-

Personal

Born June 23, 1952, in Helena, MT; daughter of Andrew J. (a draftsman) and Mary Eva (a secretary) Rummel; married Ron Bergum (a pharmacist), June 19, 1976; children: William, Elizabeth, Sophia. *Education:* Attended University of Montana, 1970-75; Marywood University, M.F.A. (illustration), 2000. *Politics:* "Liberal." *Religion:* Roman Catholic.

Addresses

Home—Helena, MT.

Career

Freelance illustrator, beginning 1981; artist at schools, beginning 1985. President and member of board of directors, Holter Museum of Art, 1993-99.

Member

Society of Children's Book Writers and Illustrators.

Awards, Honors

Ezra Jack Keats fellowship, 1993; Magazine Merit Award, Society of Children's Book Writers and Illustrators, 1996, for "Where Do the Ducks Go"; Washington

Constance R. Bergum (Reproduced by permission.)

State Writer's Award, 1998, for *Seya's Song;* Notable Social Studies Trade Book for Young People designation, National Council for Social Studies, 2007, for *Dancing with Katya* by Dori Chaconas.

Illustrator

Gayle Shirley, *M Is for Montana,* Falcon Press, 1988.

Gayle Shirley, *C Is for Colorado,* Falcon Press, 1989.

Gayle Shirley, *A Is for Animals,* Falcon Press, 1991.

Ron Hirschi, *Seya's Song,* Sasquatch Books, 1992.

Carol C. Stilz, *Grandma Buffalo, May, and Me,* Sasquatch Books, 1995.

Lester Laminack, *The Sunsets of Miss Olivia Wiggins,* Peachtree Press (Atlanta, GA), 1998.

Rick Watson, *Up a Tree,* Scholastic (New York, NY), 2002.

Lee Ann Landstrom, *Nature's Yucky: Gross Stuff That Helps Nature Work,* Mountain Press Pub. (Missoula, MT), 2003.

Wendy McCormick, *Daniel and His Walking Stick,* Peachtree Press (Atlanta, GA), 2005.

Dori Chaconas, *Dancing with Katya,* Peachtree Press (Atlanta, GA), 2006.

Melissa Stewart, *When Rain Falls,* Peachtree Press (Atlanta, GA), 2008.

Melissa Stewart, *Under the Snow,* Peachtree Press (Atlanta, GA), 2009.

Sidelights

Constance R. Bergum is an illustrator whose books often draw on the culture and history of her home state of Montana and the wider Pacific Northwest. Her illustrations for Ron Hirschi's *Seya's Song* accompany a text that was characterized by Janice Del Negro in *Booklist* as "simple, poetic, and concrete." Hirschi's story focuses on a young girl and celebrates the way of life of a small tribe of Native Americans from northwestern Washington state by depicting these people's relation-

ship to the salmon in the rivers, the seasons, and the cycle of life; it also includes thirty words from the nearly forgotten S'Klallam Indian language. Bergum's watercolor images for the book "interlace elements of the girl's modern life with aspects of the natural world and with references to traditional stories and dance," noted Carolyn Polese in *School Library Journal*. "Because of the high quality of text and art, [*Seya's Song*] . . . may speak eloquently to readers with a special affinity for . . . Native American tribes," concluded a reviewer for *Publishers Weekly*.

Bergum contributes her detailed pencil art to Ron Hirschi's picture book **Seya's Song.** (Sasquatch Books, 1992. Illustration copyright © 1992 by Constance R. Bergum. Reproduced by permission.)

Bergum's nature-themed illustration projects include two books by Melissa Stewart that focus on how animals adapt to changes in the weather in different biomes, from forest to wetland to desert to prairie. In *Under the Snow* she captures the region's winter beauty and shows how many creatures survive the bitter cold and heavy snows of the mountainous region. Stewart's focus on creatures like the red-spotted newt and the wood frog are reflected in Bergum's detailed paintings. A companion volume, *When Rain Falls,* focuses on how nature's creatures react to a heavy rain, showing ants nesting underground, squirrels using their fluffy long tails as umbrellas, and caterpillars sheltering themselves under leaves. Reviewing *When Rain Falls* for *School Library Journal,* Kathy Piehl noted that the artist's "well-rendered watercolors" will engage story-hour audiences and a *Kirkus Reviews* writer cited the artwork for its "naturalistic feel."

In her warm-toned illustrations for Carol C. Stilz's picture book *Grandma Buffalo, May, and Me* Bergum celebrates Montana's beauty, bringing to life the story of young Poppy, who is on a trip with her family to her grandmother's home in that state. Along the way, Poppy studies an album of family photographs and asks questions about her ancestors; among the sights seen is a buffalo ranch where live the descendants of a buffalo Poppy's Grandma May once fed. "Bergum's illustrations are colorful and warm," averred Jennifer Fleming in *School Library Journal,* and *Booklist* critic Leone McDermott dubbed *Grandma Buffalo, May, and Me* "a useful introduction to the concept of the family tree."

Daniel and His Walking Stick, Wendy McCormick's story about a little girl who learns about nature from a

Bergum's skill at capturing the joys of childhood are evident in her art for Carol Curtis Stilz's **Grandma Buffalo, May, and Me.** (Sasquatch Books, 1995. Illustration © 1995 by Constance R. Bergum. Reproduced by permission.)

surrogate grandfather, is brought to life by Bergum in "transparent watercolor paintings [that] are soft and colorful," according to *School Library Journal* critic Jessi Platt. In another multigenerational tale, *The Sunsets of Miss Olivia Wiggins,* author Lester L. Laminack tells a poignant story of an elderly woman with Alzheimer's disease who is visited by her daughter, Angel, and great-grandson, Troy. Throughout the visit, Miss Wiggins appears not to recognize or even notice her visitors, but the things they say and do trigger strong memories of earlier, joyful times. "Realistic watercolors flow gently between present and past in this tender depiction of a life well lived," remarked Susan Dove Lempke in *Booklist.* Although a reviewer for *Publishers Weekly* contended that Bergum's watercolor illustrations heighten the book's sentimental approach to aging, "children perplexed or upset by their own visits to deteriorating elders may find this book helpful and even consoling," the reviewer concluded.

Two sisters whose love of dancing sustains them during a family tragedy are the focus of *Dancing with Katya,* a story by Dori Chaconas that features Bergum's soft-toned art. In the tale, Anna and little sister Katya often pretend to be ballerinas, but then Katya contracts polio and her legs only work with the help of heavy metal braces. Fortunately, a pair of white gloves decorated with flowing pink ribbon—a gift from Anna to Katya—gives the younger girl hope by allowing her the means to dance in a new way. Calling *Dancing with Katya* an "inspiring" story, a *Kirkus Reviews* writer added that Bergum's "lovely realistic watercolors" for the book effectively capture both the rural setting and "the mood and spirit" of both girls. In *Booklist* Carolyn Phelan praised Chaconas's text as "complex" and "emotionally resonant" and the accompanying artwork as "full of light."

Bergum once told *SATA:* "As a child growing up in Helena, Montana, I had two sources of art and history to draw upon. The first was our only museum, the Montana Historical Society. Being the oldest girl among seven children, any of the younger ones who could walk were handed over to me on Sunday afternoons for a trip to the museum. For my mother, this was her only opportunity for an hour or two of comparative quiet; for me it was a mixed experience. I loved the museum. With the wonderful dioramas showing Montana history, the bison family gazing at me with those quiet brown eyes and a whole room of Charlie Russell paintings and sculpture. I wasn't crazy about the cowboy and Indian subject matter, but even I could tell that this guy could draw. But my quiet enjoyment was constantly interrupted by fussy little kids. And none of them were ever happy until we were at our last stop: the stuffed albino bison.

"My second visual resource was the Saint Helena Cathedral stained-glass windows. I still gaze at them in admiration. They were designed and executed by the F.X. Zettler Company of Munich, Germany, around

Bergum's light-filled art captures the spontaneity of nature in Melissa Stewart's picture book **When Rain Falls.** (Peachtree Publishers, 2008. Illustration © by Constance R. Bergum. Reproduced by permission.)

1912. The stained-glass pieces are painted to form the figures. Some unnamed master or masters drew Pre-Raphaelite figures with the most exquisite modeling of hands and feet and faces. Mass is still for me a weekly drawing lesson.

"To succeed in life, all of us need adults who make us feel special as children. I had an abundance of such people in my life: aunts and great aunts, and a wonderful art teacher throughout junior high and high school named Larry Hayes. At the University of Montana I retreated to the only corner of the art school that felt safe: watercolor painting, where the head teacher painted realistically. In the 1970s this was radical. After college, I found an entry-level job with the University of Montana as a graphic artist. Those four years were the time of my real design training, when I clearly formed my desire to be an illustrator. After a year on the West Coast working as an exhibit designer for a zoo, I returned to my home town with my husband, began raising children (three), and worked toward getting published as a children's-book illustrator.

"While pregnant with my third child, I formed a partnership with a local writer and we published our own book, *M Is for Montana,* the first of three alphabet books. It was a blockbuster of sorts and is now in its eighth printing. In 1991 I had the opportunity to illustrate *Seya's Song,* a S'Klallam Indian story. In the process of researching the story, I had the pleasure of working with members of the tribe, using some as models. The book served to reintroduce the S'Klallam language to the tribe's children and to remind them of their own stories and heritage. It was very satisfying to be illustrating a book that made such a contribution.

"Illustrating for children has introduced me to wonderful people whom I would never have had the pleasure of meeting otherwise. It has allowed me to celebrate childhood and old age, and my own culture and others."

Biographical and Critical Sources

PERIODICALS

Booklist, January 1, 1993, Janice Del Negro, review of *Seya's Song,* p. 806; October 1, 1995, Leone McDermott, review of *Grandma Buffalo, May, and Me,* p. 327; May 1, 1998, Susan Dove Lempke, review of *The Sunsets of Miss Olivia Wiggins,* p. 1521; September 1, 2006, Carolyn Phelan, review of *Dancing with Katya,* p. 134.

Kirkus Reviews, August 1, 2006, Dori Chaconas, review of *Dancing with Katya,* p. 783; February 15, 2008, review of *When Rain Falls.*

Publishers Weekly, November 9, 1992, review of *Seya's Song,* p. 82; March 30, 1998, review of *The Sunsets of Miss Olivia Wiggins,* p. 82.

School Library Journal, May, 1993, Carolyn Polese, review of *Seya's Song,* p. 99; December, 1995, Jennifer Fleming, review of *Grandma Buffalo, May, and Me,* p. 92; July, 1998, Martha Topol, review of *The Sunsets of Miss Olivia Wiggins,* p. 78; November, 2003, Patricia Manning, review of *Nature's Yucky!: Gross Stuff That Helps Nature Work,* p. 127; May, 2005, Jessi Platt, review of *Daniel and His Walking Stick,* p. 90; September, 2006, Debbie Stewart Hoskins, review of *Dancing with Katya,* p. 161; April, 2008, Kathy Piehl, review of *When Rain Falls,* p. 123.

ONLINE

Peachtree Publishers Web site, http://peachtree-online. com/ (November 15, 2009), "Constance R. Bergum."*

* * *

BERK, Ari

Personal

Born in CA; married; children: one son. *Education:* Humboldt State University, B.A. (ancient history), 1991; Oxford University, postgraduate study, 1993; University of Arizona, M.A. (American Indian studies), 1994, Ph.D. (comparative literature and culture), 1998.

Addresses

Home—MI. *Office*—Anspach Hall 301-G, Central Michigan University, Mount Pleasant, MI 48859. *E-mail*—berk1ad@cmich.edu.

Career

Author, folklorist, and educator. Assistant to author N. Scott Momaday, c. 1994; Central Michigan University, Mount Pleasant, MI, professor of English, 1999—; *Realms of Fantasy* magazine, editor of "Folkroots" section, 2008—. Mythic Imagination Institute, member of board of directors, 2005—.

Awards, Honors

Parent's Choice Recommended designation, 2008, and Notable Books selection, National Council of Teachers of English, 2009, both for *The Secret History of Giants; or, Codex Giganticum.*

Writings

The Runes of Elfland, illustrated by Brian Froud, Abrams (New York, NY), 2003.

Goblins!: A Survival Guide and Fiasco in Four Parts, illustrated by Wendy and Brian Froud, Abrams (New York, NY), 2004.

Lady Cottington's Pressed Fairy Letters, illustrated by Brian Froud, Abrams (New York, NY), 2005.

(With Carolyn Dunn) *Coyote Speaks: Wonders of the Native American World,* Abrams (New York, NY), 2008.

The Secret History of Giants; or, Codex Giganticum, illustrated by Wayne Anderson, Larry MacDougall, Gary Chalk, and Douglas Carrel, Candlewick Press (Somerville, MA), 2008.

How to Be a Viking, illustrated by Milivoj Ceran and others, Templar (Dorking, England), 2008.

The Secret History of Mermaids and Creatures of the Deep, illustrated by Matt Dangler, Virginia Lee, Gary Chalk, and Wayne Anderson, Candlewick Press (Somerville, MA), 2009.

Ari Berk (Photograph by Alan Lee. Reproduced by permission.)

Contributor of scholarly articles and poems to books and periodicals, including *Realms of Fantasy, The Quest for the Green Man,* and *Language Arts Journal of Michigan.* Author, with Elizabeth Jane Baldry, of screenplay *Lanval.*

Author's work has been translated into other languages, including Spanish, German, French, Italian, Finnish, Romanian, Bosnian-Herzegovinian, Slovenian, and Japanese.

Adaptations

The Secret History of Giants; or, Codex Giganticum was optioned as a film by Sony Pictures, 2009. *Goblins!: A Survival Guide and Fiasco in Four Parts* was optioned as a film by Disney Motion Pictures, 2009.

Sidelights

An award-winning writer and scholar of literature, iconography, and comparative myth, Ari Berk is also a folklorist, poet, and visual artist. A former student of Pulitzer Prize-winning writer N. Scott Momaday, Berk studied at Oxford University and traveled widely, making friends in many parts of the world. Now, in addition to teaching English at Central Michigan University, where he focuses on courses in mythology, folklore, Native American studies, and medieval literature, Berk spends his evenings "locked away within a high tower," as he told *SATA,* "working tirelessly on numerous writing projects surrounded by thousands of books and curious artifacts of ages past."

Berk's publications include several books about magical creatures that feature the fantasy art of Brian Froud. *The Runes of Elfland,* which was published in 2003, provides readers with a brief explanation of each rune, as well as the symbol's history and other related facts of interest. "Life lessons, folk wisdom, and psychotherapy all play a role" in the work, wrote *School Library Journal* critic Patricia D. Lothrop in her review of *The Runes of Elfland,* the critic dubbing the detailed artwork "classic Froud."

In addition to collaborating with Froud, Berk has worked with Native-American poet and writer Carolyn Dunn on *Coyote Speaks: Wonders of the Native American World* Illustrated with photographs of tribal artwork and artifacts, *Coyote Speaks* shares myths and legends from more than forty different peoples of the Americas, pairing a creative retelling of the story and a detailed explanation. For many reviewers, the book's blend of artwork, verse, story, and commentary resulted in a visually appealing collection. Writing in *Kirkus Reviews,* a critic described the collaborative story as "arresting in its presentation," while *School Library Journal* contributor Riva Pollard ranked the volume as "outstanding for its art and artifact pictures." A reviewer in *Children's Bookwatch* highlighted *Coyote Speaks* for its "ease of text," adding that the volume "encourages better understanding of Native American cultures . . . through word and image." In *Booklist* Hazel Rochman also found *Coyote Speaks* to be a "comprehensive" resource about a diverse group of people, calling the book "a rich collection of exciting art and story that keeps the past alive." In *Children's Literature,* Uma Krishnaswami called *Coyote Speaks* an "exquisitely presented mix of original poetry, retold traditional stories and linking commentary" that, "with a delicate and caring touch, invit[es] . . . both young readers and adults to explore its pages again and again."

Biographical and Critical Sources

PERIODICALS

Booklist, July 22, 2008, Hazel Rochman, review of *Coyote Speaks: Wonders of the Native American World.*
Children's Bookwatch, November, 2008, review of *Coyote Speaks.*
Kirkus reviews, July 15, 2008, review of *Coyote Speaks.*
School Library Journal, May, 2004, Patricia D. Lothrop, review of *The Runes of Elfland,* p. 162; October, 2008, Riva Pollard, review of *Coyote Speaks,* p. 164.
Voice of Youth Advocates, February, 2004, Kim Carter and Shane Bell, review of *The Runes of Elfland,* p. 502; October, 2008, Jenny Ingram and Daniel Antell, review of *Coyote Speaks,* p. 358.

ONLINE

Ari Berk Home Page, http://www.ariberk.com (November 14, 2009).

Ari Berk Web Log, http://ariberk.livejournal.com/ (November 14, 2009).

Children's Literature Newsletter, http://www.childrenslit.com (January 1, 2009), Uma Krishnaswami, review of *Coyote Speaks.*

* * *

BOSWELL, Addie
(Addie Kay Boswell)

Personal
Married. *Education:* American University, B.A., 2000.

Addresses
Home—Portland, OR. *E-mail*—artist@addieboswell.com.

Career
Author, artist, and art teacher. Blazers Boys and Girls Club, Portland, OR, art coordinator, 2002-04; Augustana Academy, Portland, co-director and art teacher, 2004-06; Lot Whitcomb Elementary, Milwaukie, OR, art specialist, 2006-08; Multnomah County Libraries, arts presenter, 2008-10. Right Brain Initiative, visiting artist, 2009-10. *Exhibitions:* Works included in exhibitions; murals have been installed throughout Portland, OR.

Member
Future Problem Solving International, Children's Cancer Association, Society of Children's Book Writers and Illustrators, Willamette Writers, School and Community Reuse Action Project, First Book-Portland.

Writings

The Rain Stomper, illustrated by Eric Velasquez, Marshall Cavendish (New York, NY), 2008.

Sidelights
A resident of Portland, Oregon, artist Addie Boswell also writes picture books, directs community mural projects, and visits hundreds of children each year through author/artist residencies in schools, libraries, and community programs. Illustrated by Eric Velasquez, Boswell's picture-book debut, *The Rain Stomper,* introduces Jazmin, a young African-American girl who leads parades with her trusty baton.

On the first day of spring, goes Boswell's tale, Jazmin wakes up to a storm in which the rain pours down in buckets and the thunder booms. Before the storm can cancel her parade and ruin her day, Jazmin points her baton at the sky and fights back. Soon the other children in the neighborhood join in to dance and stomp in the rain, helping Jazmin create something magical out of a stormy day.

Writing in *School Library Journal,* Mary N. Oluonye praised *The Rain Stomper* as "a delightful read-aloud that deals with making the best of a disappointing situation," while a *Kirkus Reviews* critic similarly thought that the author "shows how the spirit can overcome a rained-on parade." In *Booklist* Hazel Rochman cited Boswell's use of onomatopoeia in her debut effort, claiming that "the wordplay is part of the joyful uproar" and predicting that young readers will enjoy "shouting along" to the story.

Biographical and Critical Sources

PERIODICALS

Booklist, September 1, 2008, Hazel Rochman, review of *The Rain Stomper,* p. 107.

Kirkus Reviews, August 15, 2008, review of *The Rain Stomper.*

School Library Journal, September, 2008, Mary N. Oluonye, review of *The Rain Stomper,* p. 138.

Addie Boswell (Reproduced by permission.)

Boswell's energetic picture book The Rain Stomper *features quirky paintings by Eric Velasquez.* (Marshall Cavendish Children, 2008. Illustration copyright © 2008 by Eric Velasquez. Reproduced by permission.)

ONLINE

Addie Boswell Home Page, http://www.addieboswell.com (December 20, 2009).

* * *

BOSWELL, Addie Kay
See BOSWELL, Addie

* * *

BROADWAY, Hannah

Personal

Born in Oxfordshire, England; married Felix Hayes (an actor and writer). *Education:* Attended art school.

Addresses

Home—Bristol, England. *E-mail*—hannahkbroadway@ googlemail.com.

Career

Theatrical designer and illustrator. Network of Stuff Theatre, founder, 1998. Member of Number 40 (artists' collective), Bristol, England. *Exhibitions:* Work exhibited in galleries in Bristol, England.

Awards, Honors

Best Children's Book of the Year designation, Bank Street College of Education, 2009, for *Dog Day* by Sarah Hayes.

Illustrator

Sarah Hayes, *Dog Day,* Farrar, Straus & Giroux (New York, NY), 2008.

Biographical and Critical Sources

PERIODICALS

Bulletin of the Center for Children's Books, September, 2008, Deborah Stevenson, review of *Dog Day,* p. 20.
Kirkus Reviews, July 1, 2008, review of *Dog Day.*
Publishers Weekly, July 28, 2008, review of *Dog Day,* p. 73.
School Library Journal, July, 2008, Carolyn Janssen, review of *Dog Day,* p. 74.

Hannah Broadway (Photograph by Felix Hayes. Reproduced by permission.)

ONLINE

Hannah Broadway Web log, http://www.hannah-broadway-pictures.blogspot.com (January 10, 2010).
Macmillan Books Web site, http://us.macmillan.com/ (November 15, 2009).*

*   *   *

BUSH, Jenna 1981-
(Jenna Bush Hager)

Personal

Born November 25, 1981, in Dallas, TX; daughter of George W. (43rd U.S president and politician) and Laura (a teacher and librarian) Bush; married Henry Chase Hager (in politics), May 10, 2008. *Education:* University of Texas at Austin, earned degree (education), 2004.

Addresses

Home—Baltimore, MD.

Career

Journalist, educator, and author. Elsie Whitlow Stokes Community Freedom Public School, teacher, 2005-06; UNICEF, intern in Latin America, Young Leadership Ambassador, and chair of Next Generation Initiative; school reading coordinator, then sixth-grade teacher in Baltimore, MD. Educational correspondent for *Today* television program, c. 2009.

Writings

Ana's Story: A Journey of Hope, HarperCollins (New York, NY), 2007.
(With mother, Laura Bush) *Read All about It!,* illustrated by Denise Brunkus, HarperCollins (New York, NY), 2008.

Author's work has been translated into Spanish.

Sidelights

Jenna Bush, the daughter of former U.S. President George W. Bush, has followed in the path of her mother, former First Lady and teacher Laura Bush. Sharing her mother's passion for education and literacy, Jenna Bush trained as a teacher and even traveled to South America to study the role culture plays in a child's development. Committed to advancing the opportunities for all children, Bush has worked to inspire others in her generation to share her passion for urban education and children's issues through her role as the Young Leadership Ambassador and chair of UNICEF's Next Generation Initiative.

Born in 1981, Jenna and her sister, Barbara Bush, became the first twin children of a sitting president when their father took the oath of office in January of 2001. Although she was not enthusiastic about having her family put in the political spotlight, when her father ran for a second term of office Jenna joined her sister in promoting his candidacy, exhibiting some youthful hijinks while also showing composure and maturity when speaking before the Republican Convention in the summer of 2004. Jenna showed such impressive composure before the media, in fact, that she was asked to serve as an education correspondent for television's *Today* show and began working in that capacity in August of 2009.

While working as an intern for UNICEF in Latin America, Bush spent nine months getting to know a seventeen-year-old Panamanian woman who had been born with HIV/AIDS. In Latin America, as elsewhere, Ana's disease inspired fear, prejudice, and discrimination, and the girl was forced to hide her condition in order to be socially accepted. After both parents died, she spent the rest of her childhood shuttle between relatives who did not want her, even enduring sexual abuse. Eventually, Ana found a supportive home at an AIDS center; when she ultimately became a mother herself her child was born HIV-free.

In *Ana's Story: A Journey of Hope* Bush shares Ana's experiences with others, capturing the young woman's "pain and ability to transcend it," according to a *Pub-*

lishers Weekly critic. The author's "compassion for her subject comes through clearly," the reviewer added, and *Ana's Story* inspires readers "to feel strong empathy" for Ana and others like her. Citing Bush's "brisk" pace and "accessible language," *Booklist* critic Gillian Engberg concluded that the author "effectively sends an urgent message" about the many children and young people at risk due to ignorance regarding HIV/AIDS. Bush "has the good sense to let the story speak for itself," asserted *Horn Book* critic Roger Sutton, and Erin Montgomery wrote in the *Weekly Standard* that the author's "straightforward, unadorned language" effectively captures Ana's "grim" story and "enduring hopes for a better life." Noting the book's "unnerving dichotomy"—"a young woman born into a life of privilege and opportunity telling the story of another young woman born into a life that couldn't be more different"—Montgomery deemed *Ana's Story* an "incredibly powerful and humbling" read.

In 2008 Bush took time away from her teaching duties to collaborate with her mother on the picture book *Read All about It!* Geared for children in grades one through three, the book focuses on a boy named Tyrone as he

Cover of Jenna Bush's Ana's Journey, *a profile of one woman's challenges and triumphs.* (Cover photograph copyright © 2007 by Mia Baxter. Used by permission of HarperCollins Children's Books, a division of HarperCollins Publishers.)

discovers the magic of books. More interested in math, science, and being the class clown, Tyrone finds story hour boring. However, with no one to talk to, the boy decides that he might as well listen to the story after all, and he quickly becomes as caught up in reading as his classmates. Noting that the Bushs' well-intentioned story "gets a real kick" from Denise Brunkus's engaging watercolor illustrations, *Booklist* reviewer Ilene Cooper predicted that *Read All about It!* may inspire other "nonreaders . . . to give books a try," and a *Kirkus Reviews* writer dubbed the picture book a "well-meaning salute to the pleasures of reading."

Biographical and Critical Sources

PERIODICALS

Booklist, August, 2007, Gillian Engberg, review of *Ana's Story: A Journey of Hope,* p. 39; May 1, 2008, Ilene Cooper, review of *Read All about It!,* p. 94.
Foreign Affairs, January-February, 2008, Richard Feinberg, review of *Ana's Story,* p. 188.
Good Housekeeping, May, 2008, Rosemary Ellis, interview with Laura and Jenna Bush, p. 71.
Horn Book, November-December, 2007, Roger Sutton, review of *Ana's Story,* p. 693.
Kirkus Reviews, May 1, 2008, review of *Read All about It!*
Kliatt, September, 2008, Nola Theiss, review of *Ana's Story,* p. 36.
Newsweek, May 12, 2008, interview with Laura and Jenna Bush.
Publishers Weekly, September 17, 2007, review of *Ana's Story,* p. 56; May 26, 2008, Lucy Calkins, review of *Read All about It!,* p. 66.
School Library Journal, June, 2008, Grace Oliff, review of *Read All about It!,* p. 96.
Time, October 22, 2007, interview with Bush, p. 6.
Weekly Standard, November 12, 2007, Erin Montgomery, "Jenna's Story: The President's Daughter Appeals to Young Adults."

ONLINE

UNICEF Next Generation Web site, http://www.unicefusa.org/about/unicefs-next-generation/ (November 15, 2009).*

* * *

BUSH, Laura 1946-

Personal

Born November 4, 1946, in Midland, TX; daughter of Harold (a home builder and real-estate developer) and Jenna Louise (a bookkeeper) Welch; married George W. Bush (43rd U.S. president and politician), 1977; chil-

Laura Bush (Reproduced by permission. Photograph © Brooks Kraft/Corbis.)

dren: Jenna, Barbara (twins). *Education:* Southern Methodist University, B.S. (education), 1968; University of Texas at Austin, M.L.S., 1973. *Politics:* Republican.

Addresses

Home—Crawford, TX.

Career

Educator, author, and former First Lady. Teacher and librarian in public schools in Houston, Dallas, and Austin, TX, 1968-77; First Lady of Texas, 1995-2000; First Lady of the United States, 2001-09. Reading and literacy advocate; Texas Book Festival, founder; "Ready to Read, Ready to Learn" early-education initiative, founder, c. 2000; National Book Festival, founder, 2001; organizer of White House summits on education; Laura Bush Foundation for America's Libraries, founder, 2001.

Member

Kappa Alpha Theta.

Awards, Honors

Elie Wiesel Foundation for Humanity honor, 2000; American Library Association award, 2005, for support to America's libraries and librarians; Kuwait-American Foundation award, 2006; Nichols-Chancellor's Medal, Vanderbilt University, 2006; Christian Freedom International Freedom Award, 2008.

Writings

(With daughter, Jenna Bush) *Read All about It!,* illustrated by Denise Brunkus, HarperCollins (New York, NY), 2008.

Sidelights

One of the most beloved of First Ladies, Laura Bush was also the first librarian to ever hold that high honor. Through her influence as the wife of George W. Bush during his rise from governor of Texas to his service as the forty-third president of the United States, the causes of reading and literacy were brought to the political forefront, both through the speeches and personal appearances she made throughout the nation and also through her work establishing the "Ready to Read, Ready to Learn" early-education initiative, the National Book Festival, and the Laura Bush Foundation for America's Libraries.

Bush has loved books and reading since childhood, and she counts among her favorite books the "Little House" novels by Laura Ingalls Wilder. "When I was a young girl, [my mother] . . . often took me to our local library in the Midland County Courthouse," Bush recalled to *American Libraries* interviewer Leonard Kniffel. "These trips to the library were a defining part of my childhood. Even at 3 and 4 years of age I remember thinking how special the library must be—here were so many books with people of all ages enjoying them, located in the most important building in our town."

Anticipating a career as a teacher, Bush earned a degree in education at Southern Methodist University in 1968, and then taught second grade for several years. In 1973 she earned a master's degree in library science from another Texas school, the University of Texas at Austin. While working as a librarian, she was introduced to her future husband, and after a brief courtship the two were married in 1977. The Bushes have twin daughters Jenna and Barbara, who were born in 1981.

As she did as First Lady of Texas and First Lady of the United States, Bush continues to use her influence to advance education and literacy. Working with her daughter, Jenna Bush Hager, she has written *Read All about It!,* a picture book for early elementary graders that follows an imaginative young boy's excitement as he learns about the power of reading. Tyrone loves math and science, likes being the class clown, and thinks that books are boring. During story time he attempts to attract the attention of his classmates, but to no avail; the storytelling teacher has their rapt attention.

With nothing else to do, Tyrone listens to the story himself, and soon the tale works its inevitable magic on the high-spirited boy. In *School Library Journal,* Grace Oliff cited Denise Brunkus's "bright and cheerful watercolor art" for capturing the energy of Tyrone and his "multiethnic class," and a *Kirkus Reviews* writer dubbed *Read All about It!* a "well-meaning salute to the pleasures of reading." Noting that the Bushs' well-intentioned story "gets a real kick" from Brunkus's illustrations, Ilene Cooper concluded in her *Booklist* review that *Read All about It!* may inspire other "nonreaders . . . to give books a try."

Biographical and Critical Sources

PERIODICALS

American Libraries, February, 2001, Leonard Kniffel, "First Lady, First Librarian," p. 50.

Booklist, May 1, 2008, Ilene Cooper, review of *Read All about It!,* p. 94.

Good Housekeeping, May, 2008, Rosemary Ellis, interview with Laura and Jenna Bush, p. 71.

Kirkus Reviews, May 1, 2008, review of *Read All about It!*

Newsweek, May 12, 2008, interview with Laura and Jenna Bush.

Publishers Weekly, May 26, 2008, Lucy Calkins, review of *Read All about It!,* p. 66.

School Library Journal, June, 2008, Grace Oliff, review of *Read All about It!,* p. 96.

Texas Monthly, November, 1996, Skip Hollandsworth, "Reading Laura Bush," p. 120.

ONLINE

Laura Bush Foundation for America's Libraries Web site, http://www.laurabushfoundation.org (November 20, 2009).*

C

CHACONAS, D.J.
See CHACONAS, Dori

* * *

CHACONAS, Dori 1938-
(D.J. Chaconas, Doris J. Chaconas)

Personal
Born March 11, 1938, in Milwaukee, WI; daughter of Paul (a factory worker) and Kathryn (a homemaker) Kozak; married Nick Chaconas (in sales), October 12, 1957; children: Stacy DeKeyser, Stephanie Mielke, Michaela Ristaino, Nicki. *Ethnicity:* "Slovenian." *Religion:* Roman Catholic. *Hobbies and other interests:* Needlework, photography.

Addresses
Home—Germantown, WI. *E-mail*—dori@dorichaconas. com.

Career
Children's book author. Formerly worked as a needlework designer.

Member
Society of Children's Book Writers and Illustrators, Council for Wisconsin Writers.

Awards, Honors
Archer/Eckblad Children's Picture Book Award, Council for Wisconsin Writers (CWW), 2000, for *On a Wintry Morning;* Betty Ren Wright Picture Book Award CWW, 2002, for *One Little Mouse;* Chicago Public Library Best of the Best designation, 2005, for *Cork and*

Dori Chaconas (Reproduced by permission.)

Fuzz; American Library Association Notable Book designation, and Texas 2x2 Reading List inclusion, both 2007, both for *Cork and Fuzz: Short and Tall;* Notable Social Studies Trade Book for Young People designation, National Council for Social Studies, 2007, for *Dancing with Katya;* Cooperative Children's Book Center (CCBC) Choices designation, 2007, for *Cork and Fuzz: Short and Tall,* 2008, for *Cork and Fuzz: Good*

Sports, 2009, for *Cork and Fuzz: The Collectors;* Best Children's Book of the Year designation, 2009, for *Cork and Fuzz: The Collectors.*

Writings

FOR CHILDREN

(Under name D.J. Chaconas) *A Hat for Lily,* illustrated by Betsy Warren, Steck-Vaughn (Austin, TX), 1967.

(Under name D.J. Chaconas) *In a Window on Greenwater Street,* illustrated by Carroll Dolezal, Steck-Vaughn (Austin, TX), 1970.

(Under name Doris J. Chaconas) *The Way the Tiger Walked,* illustrated by Frank Bozzo, Simon & Schuster (New York, NY), 1970.

Danger in the Swamp (originally published in *Jack and Jill* magazine), illustrated by Haris Petie, Lantern Press (Mount Vernon, NY), 1971.

On a Wintry Morning, illustrated by Stephen T. Johnson, Viking (New York, NY), 2000.

One Little Mouse, illustrated by LeUyen Pham, Viking (New York, NY), 2002.

Goodnight, Dewberry Bear, illustrated by Florence S. Davis, Abingdon Press (Nashville, TN), 2003.

Momma, Will You?, illustrated by Steve Johnson and Lou Fancher, Viking (New York, NY), 2004.

That Blessed Christmas Night, illustrated by Deborah Perez-Stable, Abingdon Press (Nashville, TN), 2004.

When Cows Come Home for Christmas, illustrated by Lynne Chapman, Albert Whitman (Morton Grove, IL), 2005.

Christmas Mouseling, illustrated by Susan Kathleen Hartung, Viking (New York, NY), 2005.

Dancing with Katya, illustrated by Constance R. Bergum, Peachtree (Atlanta, GA), 2006.

Coriander the Contrary Hen, illustrated by Marsha Gray Carrington, Carolrhoda Books (Minneapolis, MN), 2006.

Pennies in a Jar, illustrated by Ted Lewin, Peachtree (Atlanta, GA), 2007.

Virginnie's Hat, illustrated by Holly Meade, Candlewick Press (Cambridge, MA), 2007.

Looking for Easter, illustrated by Margie Moore, Albert Whitman (Morton Grove, IL), 2008.

Mousie Love, illustrated by Josée Masse, Bloomsbury U.S.A. Children's Books (New York, NY), 2009.

Don't Slam the Door!, illustrated by Will Hillenbrand, Candlewick Press (Cambridge, MA), 2010.

Contributor of short stories to periodicals, including *Jack and Jill* and *Highlights for Children.*

"CORK AND FUZZ" EASY-READER SERIES

Cork and Fuzz, illustrated by Lisa McCue, Viking (New York, NY), 2005.

Cork and Fuzz: Short and Tall, illustrated by Lisa McCue, Viking (New York, NY), 2006.

Cork and Fuzz: Good Sports, illustrated by Lisa McCue, Viking (New York, NY), 2007.

Cork and Fuzz: The Collectors, illustrated by Lisa McCue, Viking (New York, NY), 2008.

Cork and Fuzz: Finders Keepers, illustrated by Lisa McCue, Viking (New York, NY), 2009.

Cork and Fuzz: The Babysitters, illustrated by Lisa McCue, Viking (New York, NY), 2010.

Sidelights

In the 1960s, Dori Chaconas published several children's books as well as numerous short stories for children that appeared in magazines, all under the pen name D.J. Chaconas. Then, drawing on her talent for needlework design, she left writing for thirty years to explore another career and raise her family. Chaconas rediscovered her desire to write in the late 1990s, inspired by questions from one of her adult daughters, who had become interested in writing for children. Joining a writers' support group on the Internet, she revived her former career and in the years since has produced such children's books as *When Cows Come Home for Christmas, One Little Mouse, Dancing with Katya,* and *Virginnie's Hat,* as well as books in the popular "Cork and Fuzz" easy-reader series.

Written years earlier and put aside, *One Little Mouse* is the story that rekindled Chaconas's writing career following her foray into needlework design. After retrieving the story manuscript from storage, she revised it and managed to sell it to a publisher within a month. An upbeat tale, *One Little Mouse* is both a counting book and a story told in rhyme that follows a little mouse as it goes out in search of a roomier place to

Cover of Chaconas's winter-themed picture book On a Wintry Morning, *featuring illustrations by Stephen T. Johnson.* (Illustration copyright © 2000 by Stephen T. Johnson. Reproduced by permission.)

Lynn Chapman's cartoon illustrations capture the humor in Chaconas's holiday-themed story in **When Cows Come Home for Christmas.** (Albert Whitman, 2005. Illustration copyright © 2005 by Lynne Chapman. Reproduced by permission.)

live. In the meadow, the creature encounters two moles, then three frogs, and so on, up to a crowd of ten critters. Ultimately, Mouse realizes that it is not comfortable in the homes of these other creatures, and on its way home it passes the abodes of its new animal friends, counting down from ten to one on its way. *One Little Mouse* was praised as "a charming counting book that will appeal especially to the read-aloud set" by Cathie E. Bashaw in a review for *School Library Journal.* Chaconas returns to mouse-centered fiction in *Mousie Love,* a "short, sweet, and old-fashioned" story about a love-struck mouse, according to *Booklist* critic Abby Nolan.

The first original story Chaconas penned after her return to picture-book writing, *On a Wintry Morning,* is characteristic of much of the author's work: it is a simple story told in a rhyming text. *On a Wintry Morning* describes a young girl and her father as the duo spend a brisk winter morning together. Father and daughter bundle up, then go out into the snow where they sled, hunt for animal tracks, go for a sleigh ride, and buy a puppy at a nearby market. Later the pair returns home to dry off and warm up, the tired girl soon falling asleep to the sound of her father's soothing voice. Chaconas's story, described as "by turns exuberant and soothing" by *School Library Journal* critic Jane Marino, serves as a "celebrat[ion of] . . . the small moments that a father and toddler share," according to the critic. Likewise, a contributor to *Publishers Weekly* noted the quiet, nostalgic tone of the tale, which by-

passes a dramatic plot in favor of "a cornucopia of child-pleasing images." The *Publishers Weekly* reviewer concluded by calling *On a Wintry Morning* a book "as nourishing as hearty winter soup."

In *Dancing with Katya* country-dwelling sisters Anna and Katya love to pretend that they are prima ballerinas, and often dance around the house together. However, when polio cripples five-year-old Katya and condemns her to walking only with heavy metal leg braces, older sister Anna finds a way that the two can continue to dance together: she creates a pair of ballerina gloves. These white gloves, which are beautifully embellished with long, loosely flowing pink ribbons, allow the disabled girl to dance with her hands rather than her feet. Noting that Chaconas's picture book was inspired by a family member who contracted the once-debilitating and all-too-common childhood disease years ago, *School Library Journal* critic Debbie Stewart Hopkins dubbed *Dancing with Katya* "a sincere, nostalgic effort," and a *Kirkus Reviews* writer described it as "a warm and inspiring tribute to one sister's love and the other's courage." In *Booklist,* Carolyn Phelan praised the picture book as a "complex, emotionally resonant story."

Other books by Chaconas include *Pennies in a Jar,* a World War II story that features Ted Lewin's "stunning, realistic" paintings, according to a *Publishers Weekly* critic. In the story, a boy overcomes his fear of horses in order to attain the perfect birthday gift for his father, who is fighting overseas. A "quiet story," according to *School Library Journal* critic Rachel Kamin, *Pennies in a Jar* introduces children to a bygone era in a story "that will resonate with contemporary children" whose parents are in the U.S. military.

Virginnie's Hat also pairs Chaconas's story with dramatic art, this time the mixed-media art by Holly Meade. In *Virginnie's Hat* a young girl walking near a swamp loses her hat to a gust of wind. When she tracks the hat to the branches of a nearby tree and uses her boots to dislodge it, the girl attracts the attention of a succession of toe-nibblers, from a crayfish to an alligator. Noting that "the conceit" in *Virginnie's Hat* "is quite clever," a *Kirkus Reviews* critic also cited the author's "faux-folksy verse text." Appraising the same book in *Booklist,* Kristen McKulski praised Meade's "spry watercolor and cut-paper" art as well as a "lively" story that treats read-aloud audiences to an energetic mix of "onomatopoeia, alliteration, and regional vocabulary."

Popular with beginning readers and featuring detailed illustrations by Lisa McCue, Chaconas's "Cork and Fuzz" books introduce Cork the muskrat and Fuzz the possum, who are best friends despite the fact that they look very different. Those differences are the focus of *Cork and Fuzz: Short and Tall,* as stubborn and single-minded Fuzz attempts to make Cork more possum-like. Citing the friends' "comical attempts to make Fuzz shorter, then Cork, taller," a *Kirkus Reviews* writer added that *Cork and Fuzz: Short and Tall* contains a kid-pleasing combination of "earnest endeavor and endearingly silly misapprehension." "Preschoolers will especially relate to the small critter who wants to take charge," predicted Hazel Rochman in her *Booklist* review of *Cork and Fuzz: Short and Tall*, while in *School Library Journal* Laura Scott wrote that the book's young readers "will find comfort and delight in . . . dialogue that reflect[s] their own relationships."

Other "Cork and Fuzz" books include *Cork and Fuzz: Good Sports, Cork and Fuzz: The Collectors, Cork and Fuzz: Finders Keepers,* and *Cork and Fuzz: The Babysitters,* all illustrated by McCue. Cork the muskrat and Fuzz the possum decide to play a range of games in *Good Sports,* but when Cork winds up losing more than his share his feelings get hurt. In *The Collectors* rock collector Fuzz discovers what he thinks are pretty, smooth stones while he and Cork are playing near the pond. When the stones turn out to be duck eggs, however, Mother Duck zeroes in on an unsuspecting Fuzz. In *Finders Keepers* Cork loses a very special green stone from his collection and then Fuzz finds it, resulting in a disagreement between the two friends. In *The Babysitters* Cork tries to enlist the aid of Fuzz in taking care of a baby porcupine. McCue's "lively illustrations" pair with a sprightly plot "filled with repeated vocabulary and simple sentences" in *Cork and Fuzz: Good Sports,* according to *School Library Journal* critic June Wolfe, and Mary Hazelton maintained in the same periodical that Chaconas's "text flows smoothly and re-

mains entertaining throughout" *Cork and Fuzz: The Collectors.* In *Kirkus Reviews* a critic cited the "adorably drawn" illustrations in *Cork and Fuzz: Finders Keepers,* adding that, in addition to being "timeless", Chaconas's "simple, sweet tale offers a lesson, wisely pronounced." Praising the series as a whole, Betty Carter cited Chaconas's use of short sentences and "easily decodable" vocabulary, concluding that the "Cork and Fuzz" books "will fit beginning readers well as they try out their newfound skills."

Chaconas's talent for spinning a rhyming tale continues to make her books popular with storytellers and young listeners alike. As she explained to Julia Durango in an online interview for *By the Book,* "I think I was born with a small clock ticking in my brain. I've always liked rhythms of any kind . . . music . . . poetry . . . sleet clicking on the window, or whatever. I think I remember every nursery rhyme and song I ever learned as a child, because I loved them so much. I'm lucky to have an ear for rhythms."

Biographical and Critical Sources

PERIODICALS

Booklist, September 15, 2000, Shelley Townsend-Hudson, review of *On a Wintry Morning,* p. 247; September 1, 2002, Kathy Broderick, review of *One Little Mouse,* p. 136; January 1, 2006, Hazel Rochman, review of *Cork and Fuzz: Short and Tall,* p. 109; September 1, 2006, Carolyn Phelan, review of *Dancing with Katya,* p. 134; June 1, 2007, Kristen McKulksi, review of *Virginnie's Hat,* p. 86; October 1, 2007, Abby Nolan, review of *Pennies in a Jar,* p. 66; February 1, 2009, Hazel Rochman, review of *Cork and Fuzz: Finders Keepers,* p. 44; May 1, 2009, Abby Nolan, review of *Mousie Love,* p. 88.

Bulletin of the Center for Children's Books, April, 2005, Timnah Card, review of *Cork and Fuzz,* p. 331.

Horn Book, May-June, 2006, Betty Carter, review of *Cork and Fuzz: Short and Tall,* p. 311.

Kirkus Reviews, February 15, 2006, review of *Cork and Fuzz: Short and Tall,* p. 179; August 1, 2006, review of *Dancing with Katya,* p. 783; March 15, 2007, review of *Coriander the Contrary Hen;* April 15, 2007, review of *Virginnie's Hat;* February 15, 2008, review of *Cork and Fuzz: Finders Keepers;* December 1, 2008, review of *Cork and Fuzz: Finders Keepers.*

Publishers Weekly, October 23, 2000, review of *On a Wintry Morning,* p. 74; September 17, 2007, review of *Pennies in a Jar,* p. 54; June 1, 2009, review of *Mousie Love,* p. 46.

School Library Journal, November, 2000, Jane Marino, review of *On a Wintry Morning,* p. 112; August, 2002, Cathie E. Bashaw, review of *One Little Mouse,* p. 148; April, 2006, Laura Scott, review of *Cork and Fuzz: Short and Tall,* p. 98; September, 2006, Debbie Stewart Hoskins, review of *Dancing with Katya,* p.

161; April, 2007, June Wolfe, review of *Cork and Fuzz: Good Sports,* p. 96; May, 2007, Martha Simpson, review of *Virginnie's Hat,* p. 86; June, 2007, Blair Christolon, review of *Coriander the Contrary Hen,* p. 94; October, 2007, Rachel Kamin, review of *Pennies in a Jar,* p. 110; March, 2008, Mary Hazelton, review of *Cork and Fuzz: The Collectors,* p. 156; January, 2009, Lisa Egly Lehmuller, review of *Cork and Fuzz: Finders Keepers,* p. 73.

ONLINE

By the Book Web site, http://www.geocities.com/julia durango/ (February 13, 2001), Julia Durango, "Dori Chaconas Warms up Winter."

Cynsations Web site, http://www.cynthialeitichsmith.com/ (June 12, 2003), Cynthia Leitich Smith, interview with Chaconas.

Dori Chaconas Home Page, http://www.dorichaconas.com (November 15, 2009).

Kezi Matthews Late Bloomers Page, http://kezimatthews. com/ (June 12, 2003), "Dori Chaconas."

* * *

CHACONAS, Doris J.
See CHACONAS, Dori

* * *

CLAFLIN, Willy 1944-

Personal

Born 1944, in Wolfeboro, NH; married Jacqueline Darrigrand; children: Brian. *Education:* Harvard University, degree, 1966; postgraduate study in Edinburgh, Scotland.

Addresses

Home—San Francisco, CA. *E-mail*—claflin@willy claflin.com.

Career

Storyteller, educator, and author. Taught school, c. 1960s-70s; performing and recording artist, beginning 1980. Performer at National Storytelling Festival, Jonesborough, TN, 2001, 2002, 2004, 2006, 2007, 2009, at International Storytelling Festival, Cape Clear, Ireland, and at festivals in United States and Europe. Artist-in-residence, International School, Jakarta, Indonesia, 2001.

Awards, Honors

Recommended Release designation, *Billboard* magazine, 1987, for *Bones of Love;* Notable Children's Recording designation, American Library Association

(ALA), and Parents' Choice Classic award, both 1992, both for *Maynard Moose;* Notable Children's Recording designation, ALA, and Parents' Choice Gold award, both for *The Wolf under the Bed;* Parents' Choice Gold award, *Storytelling World* Award, and National Parenting Publications Gold Award, all for recording *The Uglified Ducky;* Texas Bluebonnet Award Master List inclusion, 2010, for book *The Uglified Ducky; Storytelling World* Award, 2003, for *Where Were You in '72?: Live at the National Storytelling Festival.*

Writings

The Uglified Ducky: A Maynard Moose Tale (includes audio CD; also see below), illustrated by James Stimson, August House/LittleFolk (Atlanta, GA), 2008.

SOUND RECORDINGS

Stones along the Shore, Old Coyote Music, 1984.

Maynard Moose: Sleeping Beastly and Other Tales, August House (Atlanta, GA), 1992.

The Wolf under the Bed, August House (Atlanta, GA), 1996.

The Uglified Duckling, August House (Atlanta, GA), 2002.

Maynard Moose Tales, August House (Atlanta, GA), 2002.

Other recordings include *Willy Claflin and Friends,* 1986; *Bones of Love,* 1987; *Where Were You in '72?: Live at the National Storytelling Festival,* 2003; *The*

Willy Claflin's humorous picture book The Uglified Ducky *features James Stimson's entertaining digitized art.* (August House LittleFolk, 2008. Illustration copyright © 2008 by James Stimson. Reproduced by permission.)

George Washington Method for Blues Ukulele, 2006; *The Goat Whisperer: Live at Jonesborough,* 2009; (with Brian Claflin) *In Yonder's Wood;* and *Maynard Moose Live at the National Festival.*

Sidelights

Willy Claflin, an award-winning storyteller and musician, is the author of *The Uglified Ducky: A Maynard Moose Tale,* a humorous retelling of the Hans Christian Andersen fairytale "The Ugly Duckling." Born and raised in New Hampshire, Claflin acquired a love of storytelling from his father, who entertained his son with bedtime tales. Claflin, an accomplished guitarist, also developed an appreciation for folk music in his youth, and while attending Harvard University he performed in local clubs. After postgraduate work in Europe, he returned to the United States and began teaching, earning recognition for his clever lessons featuring a variety of puppets, including Maynard Moose, Boring Beaver, Socklops, Dr. Al, and Gorf. In the 1980s Claflin left the classroom to join the storytelling circuit; in the years since, he has been a featured performer at the National Storytelling Festival in Jonesborough, Tennessee, and at regional festivals throughout the United States.

According to *Sing Out!* contributor Dan Keding, Claflin's "rewrites of well-known fairy tales are wonderful, funny and border on genius." In *The Uglified Ducky,* a recorded story that became his debut picture book for young readers, Claflin relates the story of a wayward young moose that stumbles into a nest of duck's eggs and is raised with the other waterfowl, despite the animal's disastrous attempts to waddle, quack, swim, and fly. *The Uglified Ducky* is highlighted "by glossary-defined moose words and malapropisms, making it a tale just begging to be read aloud," observed a critic in *Kirkus Reviews.* Clafin's "fresh, lively story is laugh-out-loud funny," Lee Bock concluded in *School Library Journal.*

Biographical and Critical Sources

PERIODICALS

Kirkus Reviews, August 15, 2008, review of *The Uglified Ducky: A Maynard Moose Tale.*

School Library Journal, April, 1997, review of *The Wolf under the Bed,* p. 42; September, 2008, Lee Bock, review of *The Uglified Duckling,* p. 142.

Sing Out!, spring, 2003, Dan Keding, review of *The Wolf under the Bed,* p. 150.

ONLINE

Willy Claflin Home Page, http://www.willyclaflin.com (November 1, 2009).

CORACE, Jen

Personal

Born in NJ. *Education:* Rhode Island School of Design, B.F.A.

Addresses

Home—Providence, RI. *Agent*—Steven Malk, Writers House, 21 W. 26th St., New York, NY 10010. *E-mail*—jcn@jencorace.com.

Career

Artist, illustrator, and designer. *Exhibitions:* Work exhibited at galleries in Tokyo, Japan, Los Angeles, CA, New York, NY, Seattle, WA, Philadelphia, PA, and Portland, OR.

Illustrator

Amy Krouse Rosenthal, *Little Pea,* Chronicle Books (San Francisco, CA), 2005.

Amy Krouse Rosenthal, *Little Hoot,* Chronicle Books (San Francisco, CA), 2008.

Cynthia Rylant, reteller, *Hansel and Gretel,* Hyperion (New York, NY), 2008.

Dene Low, *The Entomological Tales of Augustus T. Percival: Petronella Saves Nearly Everyone,* Houghton Mifflin (Boston, MA), 2009.

Amy Krouse Rosenthal, *Little Oink,* Chronicle Books (San Francisco, CA), 2009.

Amy Krouse Rosenthal, *This + That,* HarperCollins (New York, NY), 2010.

Randall de Sève, *Mathilda, the Orange Balloon,* Balzer & Bray (New York, NY), 2010.

Contributor to periodicals, including *Portland Mercury, Sound Collector Audio Review,* and *Cricket.*

Sidelights

Jen Corace, a Providence, Rhode Island-based artist and illustrator, has provided the artwork for such critically acclaimed children's books as *Little Pea,* a work by Amy Krouse Rosenthal, and *Hansel and Gretel,* a retelling of the classic Brothers Grimm tale by Cynthia Rylant. Corace is recognized for her spare but charming watercolor-and-ink images that incorporate a muted color palette. "The minimal aspect of my work on one hand speaks to the bare necessities of the atmosphere or emotion of the piece but also address my more basic concerns with composition and drawing," she related to *Colouring Outside the Lines* online interviewer Melanie Maddison. "I also love negative space," Corace added. "I like playing with shapes. I like the spaces in between arms and bodies, between leaves, antlers, all sorts of objects."

Born and raised in New Jersey, Corace developed an interest in the arts at an early age. "I grew up always drawing, always painting," she related to Maddison. "I spent a lot of time in my room, by myself, door closed with pads and pads of paper. It's hard to say if a kindergartner or an elementary aged child 'excels' at art. It was just something I always loved to do." Corace also recalled that her mother was a strong proponent of her work: "The encouragement that I received from my mom in my early development definitively put me on the road to where I am now. She always enrolled me in after-school and summer art programs and when the time came, researched art schools with me. So she created this momentum that supported the idea that art was where I belonged." Corace eventually earned a bachelor's degree from the Rhode Island School of Design, began working on a diverse array of projects, such as illustrating record covers and designing Web sites, and refined her artistic style. "I wanted my work to reflect who I was, to be personal," she told Maddison.

Corace made her publishing debut in 2005, with the release of *Little Pea,* a humorous picture book. Rosenthal's title character, a happy, outgoing legume who enjoys spending time with family and friends, has just one problem: he cannot stomach candy, which is, unfortunately, a mainstay at the dinner table. "The ink-and-watercolor illustrations are as spare as the text," Wendy Woodfill observed in *School Library Journal,* and a *Publishers Weekly* critic noted that the "warm-hearted . . . paintings plays up the most of ample white space, which plays up the vibrant greenness of the Pea family."

Corace and Rosenthal team up again on *Little Hoot,* another story that offers a unique twist on a familiar childhood experience. The protagonist, a tiny owl, finds himself at odds with his parents each night at bedtime;

Little Hoot wants to go to sleep at a reasonable hour, like his friends, but his parents insist that he stay up late. "Text and art convey parental love, filial annoyance, and everything in between," remarked Catherine Callegari in *School Library Journal.* Daniel Handler, writing in the *New York Times Book Review,* felt that Corace's work here is bolder than that in *Little Pea,* stating that the "illustrations are more daring, throwing a wider color spectrum into the mix and showing a slight anime influence." In *Little Oink,* a young pig asserts his right to tidy up around the house. *New York Times Book Review* critic Bruce Handy praised Rosenthal's "Bizarro World trilogy for kids," adding that "all three [are] elevated further by . . . Corace's droll, fine-tuned illustrations."

Rylant's *Hansel and Gretel* focuses on the courage and resourceful of the two children. Corace's "settings resemble dark, dramatically lit stage sets, while her characters convey emotion adroitly," Joanna Rudge Long maintained in *Horn Book,* and Carolyn Phelan, writing in *Booklist,* observed that the "distinctive illustrations feature strong composition, confident line work, and a fine sense of color."

Biographical and Critical Sources

PERIODICALS

Booklist, August 1, 2008, Carolyn Phelan, review of *Hansel and Gretel,* p. 78.

Horn Book, November-December, 2008, Joanna Rudge Long, review of *Hansel and Gretel,* p. 720.

Kirkus Reviews, May 1, 2005, review of *Little Pea,* p. 545; August 1, 2008, review of *Hansel and Gretel.*

New York Times Book Review, May 11, 2008, Daniel Handler, review of *Little Hoot,* p. 18; May 10, 2009, Bruce Handy, review of *Little Oink,* p. 20.

Publishers Weekly, May 9, 2005, review of *Little Pea,* p. 69; January 21, 2008, review of *Little Hoot,* p. 169.

School Library Journal, May, 2005, Wendy Woodfill, review of *Little Pea,* p. 95; April, 2008, Catherine Callegari, review of *Little Hoot,* p. 121; September, 2008, Marilyn Taniguchi, review of *Hansel and Gretel,* p. 158.

ONLINE

Colouring Outside the Lines Web log, http://cotlzine. blogspot.com/ (July 19, 2008), Melanie Maddison, interview with Corace.

IndieFixx.com, http://indiefixx.com/ (June 18, 2008), interview with Corace.

Jen Corace's brightly colored art brings to life Amy Krouse Rosenthal's story in **Little Hoot.** (Illustration © 2008 by Jen Corace. Used with permission of Chronicle Books, LLC, San Francisco. Visit ChronicleBooks.com.)

Jen Corace Home Page, http://www.jencorace.com (November 1, 2009).

* * *

CROW, Kristyn

Personal

Born in CA; married Steve Crow (a police officer; children: seven. *Education:* Brigham Young University, degree.

Addresses

Home—UT. *Agent*—Kendra Marcus, BookStop Literary Agency, 67 Meadow View Rd., Orinda, CA 94563. *E-mail*—email@kristyncrow.com.

Career

Writer.

Member

Society of Children's Book Writers and Illustrators.

Awards, Honors

Bulletin of the Center for Children's Books Blue Ribbon selection, 2008, for *Cool Daddy Rat;* Washington Children's Choice Picture Book nomination, and Ladybug Picture Book Award nomination, both 2009, both for *Bedtime at the Swamp;* Utah Book Award nomination, 2009, for *Cool Daddy Rat.*

Writings

Cool Daddy Rat, illustrated by Mike Lester, Putnam (New York, NY), 2007.

Bedtime at the Swamp, illustrated by Macky Pamintuan, HarperCollins (New York, NY), 2008.

The Middle-Child Blues, illustrated by David Catrow, G.P. Putnam's Sons (New York, NY), 2009.

Skeleton Cat, Scholastic (New York, NY), 2011.

Sidelights

According to Utah author Kristyn Crow, reading a book should be fun, and in her picture books *Cool Daddy Rat, Bedtime at the Swamp,* and *The Middle-Child Blues* she serves up a rollicking mix of repetition, rhyme, and rhythm. With its toe-tapping text, *Cool Daddy Rat* tells the story of Ace, a rat whose musician father plays bass for jazz bands throughout New York City. When Ace hides in his dad's instrument case, he discovers how exciting a musician's life can be. Daddy Rat discovers

Kristyn Crow (Reproduced by permission.)

that his offspring is a scat-singing jazz star in the making, and as a *Kirkus Reviews* writer noted, Crow's story "pulses with liberally laced scat . . . and syncopated sound words." Reviewing *Cool Daddy Rat* for *Publishers Weekly* a contributor predicted that "Crow's hip ode to jazz . . . will sweep up its audience in its catch beat," while Teri Markson maintained in *School Library Journal* that "the text . . . jumps and jives and begs to be read aloud." The *Publishers Weekly* critic also praised Mike Lester's "kinetic cartoon art" for the book, noting that it adds "verve and wit," while Markson wrote that the cartoonist's "artwork pops with the same humor and zing as the text."

Crow imbues her picture books *Bedtime at the Swamp* and *Is there a Monster on the Loose* with the same high energy that fuels *Cool Daddy Rat.* An imaginative little boy is pursued through the dark of night by something large and strange and swampy in *Bedtime at the Swamp,* a book in which Crowe's "repetitive chorus, [and] a simple rhyming story . . . will draw readers in," according to *School Library Journal* critic Marian Creamer. Featuring "bright, . . . expressive art" by Macky Pamintuan, *Bedtime at the Swamp* also entertains readers with its "rhythmic chant and rhymed text," according to a *Kirkus Reviews* writer.

Another young child is the focus of Crowe's picture book *The Middle-Child Blues.* With an older brother who is the first to do, say, and think everything, as well as a cuter-than-cute little sister, Lee feels stuck. Too young to keep up with his brother, the boy is also too old to play games with his sister. Fortunately, Lee has a special gift that makes him stand out on his own, and he discovers it by strumming on his guitar. Praising the book's energetic cartoon art by David Catrow, Ieva Bates dubbed *The Middle-Child Blues* "a winner" in her *School Library Journal* appraisal.

***Crow's story of two jazzy rodents is brought to life in Mike Lester's scratchy art for* Cool Daddy Rat.** (G.P. Putnam's Sons, 2008. Illustration copyright © 2008 by Mike Lester. Reproduced by permission.)

On her home page, Crow offered encouragement to budding writers. "You have to decide: how serious am I about this quest? If you're dead serious, then you've got to treat it like a career, instead of a hobby. You've got to study, attend writer's conferences, schedule time to write, get into a critique group, and act like you're wearing an 'author' hat. Find out where other writers are meeting and what they're doing. Get in with the 'in crowd' of writing. There is a whole underworld you need to discover. Hone your craft, by writing and revising a lot. Understand the product you're trying to create, by reading lots of picture books regularly.

"I once read an interview from an editor who said that 80 percent of the manuscripts they received were written by people who had clearly not even looked at a recent picture book. You need to know your intended product very well. I think the biggest obstacle hopeful picture book authors face is their own misconception that writing for children is easy."

Biographical and Critical Sources

PERIODICALS

Kirkus Reviews, March 1, 2008, review of *Cool Daddy Rat;* July 1, 2008, review of *Bedtime at the Swamp.*
Publishers Weekly, March 17, 2008, review of *Cool Daddy Rat,* p. 68.
School Library Journal, August, 2008, Marian Creamer, review of *Bedtime at the Swamp,* p. 86; April, 2008, Teri Markson, review of *Cool Daddy Rat,* p. 104; November, 2009, Ieva Bates, review of *The Middle-Child Blues.*

ONLINE

Kristyn Crow Home Page, http://www.kristyncrow.com (November 15, 2009).
Kristyn Crow Web log, http://kristyncrow.blogspot.com/ (November 15, 2009).

D

DAVIS, Katie 1959(?)-

Personal

Born c. 1959, in New York, NY; married Jerry Davis (an animated-film producer); children: Benny, Ruby. *Education:* Attended American College of Paris; Boston University, B.S. *Hobbies and other interests:* Knitting, gardening, eating Hot Tamales candy.

Addresses

Home—Bedford Hills, NY. *E-mail*—katiedavis@katie davis.com.

Career

Author and illustrator. Formerly worked in public relations and advertising. Founder, Dirty Dishes (ceramics and design company), 1986—. Creator of "Scared Guy" (licensed character).

Member

Society of Children's Book Writers and Illustrators, PEN.

Awards, Honors

Oppenheim Toy Portfolio Platinum Award, and National Parenting Publications Award (NAPPA) Honors designation, both 1998, both for *Who Hops?;* Children's Book Council/International Reading Association Choice Award, and NAPPA Award, both 1999, both for *I Hate to Go to Bed!;* Oppenheim Toy Portfolio Gold Award, 2000, for *Who Hoots?,* and 2003, for *Mabel the Tooth Fairy and How She Got Her Job;* Best Children's Book designation, Bank Street College of Education, 2008, for *The Curse of Addy McMahon.*

Writings

SELF-ILLUSTRATED

Who Hops?, Harcourt Brace (San Diego, CA), 1998.

I Hate to Go to Bed!, Harcourt Brace (San Diego, CA), 1999.
Who Hoots?, HarcourtSanDiego (San Diego, CA), 2000.
Scared Stiff, HarcourtSanDiego (San Diego, CA), 2001.
Party Animals, HarcourtSanDiego (San Diego, CA), 2002.
Mabel the Tooth Fairy and How She Got Her Job, HarcourtSanDiego (San Diego, CA), 2003.
Kindergarten Rocks!, Harcourt (Orlandom FL), 2005.
The Curse of Addy McMahon, Greenwillow Books (New York, NY), 2008.

Davis's books have been translated into Spanish and Korean.

ILLUSTRATOR

Jerry Davis, *Little Chicken's Big Day,* Margaret K. McElderry Books (New York, NY), 2011.

Sidelights

As children's book author and illustrator Katie Davis stated on her home page, she is inspired to create her quirky picture books by "my life, my kids, and the world around me." After graduating from Boston University, Davis worked in public relations and advertising, but moved on to start her own business in 1986. Using the name Dirty Dishes, Davis sold hand-painted ceramics and also created a character she dubbed "Scared Guy" that she licensed for use on various products. In 1996, after being urged by her film-producer husband, Davis attended a conference for the Society of Children's Book Writers and Illustrators. It was then that she discovered a perfect career that fit in with her energetic, creative personality: creating picture books. Among Davis's highly praised books are titles such as *Who Hoots?, Kindergarten Rocks!,* and *Mabel the Tooth Fairy and How She Got Her Job.*

Davis's first published book, *Who Hops?,* focuses on identifying which animals do what by showcasing a glaring error that young listeners will immediately latch

***Katie Davis banishes all first-day-of-school fears in her self-illustrated* Kindergarten Rocks!**

onto. For example, elephants DON'T slither, and cows DON'T hop. Praising the interaction between listener and reader that Davis's book inspires, *Booklist* contributor Susan Dove Lempke called *Who Hops?* a book that will make "a toddler's story hour dream come true," while in *Publishers Weekly* the book was praised as "silly" and "entertaining."

Who Hoots? is a sequel of sorts to *Who Hops?* and its lively and imaginative story is also designed for the preschool and kindergarten crowd. Featuring a reversed format, the book starts by asking the question "Who hoots?" and readers are then shown numerous animals, all *non*-hooters. When the owl is suggested, Davis's text states: "Owls don't hoot," creating questions on the part of readers who eventually figure out the book's puzzle. Marlene Gawron, reviewing *Who Hoots?* in *School Library Journal,* praised the book as "a definite winner", while Kathy Broderick stated in *Booklist* that "Davis definitely knows her audience."

In *Mabel the Tooth Fairy and How She Got Her Job* Davis once again offers young readers a unique and mesmerizing story. Mabel Becaharuvic has been a fairy

for most of her 42,364 years. Unfortunately, due to a lack of good personal hygiene, and not enough brushing or flossing, Mabel has started to lose her teeth. Her solution to avoiding toothlessness is to visit kids at night and adopt the teeth children lose naturally. Praising *Mabel the Tooth Fairy and How She Got Her Job,* critics commented in particular on the book's illustrations, which are heavily outlined in black and are bright and colorful: Davis's trademark style. The text is given a cartoon feel as well, through the use of speech balloons. While Maryann H. Owen questioned in *School Library Journal* whether young children would "warm up to a story that mentions halitosis, gingivitis, false teeth, plaque, and comprehensive dental coverage," a reviewer for *Publishers Weekly* answered in the affirmative, writing that "Davis's humor, ranging from slightly sarcastic to downright silly, gives kids of tooth-losing age an enjoyable behind-the-scenes look at a mysterious figure—and an easy-to-swallow message." A *Kirkus Reviews* contributor hailed *Mabel the Tooth Fairy and How She Got Her Job* as a "sidesplitting dental romance."

Dexter Dugan acts full of bravado even though he is actually terrified on his first day of school in *Kindergar-*

ten Rocks! Although the little boy claims to be calm, he is sure that his stuffed dog Rufus is very, very worried about the big changes ahead. Fortunately, big sister Jessie helps Dexter find a way to deal with his fears. By the time the first day of school comes to a close, Dexter is very excited about returning the next day. In *School Library Journal* Mary Elam praised *Kindergarten Rocks!* as "a gentle, humorous read to calm the anxiety of younger children" while in *Kirkus Reviews* a contributor recommended the book as "a terrific tool for those setting off on the elementary track." Praising Davis's illustrations, a *Publishers Weekly* concluded that the "buoyant vignettes" depicting Dexter happily at play in his new classroom "will reassure even the most fearful" preschooler.

In *The Curse of Addy McMahon* Davis turns to the trauma of sixth grade and a girl named Addy. Addy is sure she is cursed: her father has died, her mother's boyfriend is weird, and her best friend Jackie is not speaking to her. To make sense of things, she writes an autobiographical comic strip that gains Addy a measure of celebrity when it is published in her middle-school newspaper. Along with Addie's narrative and quirky comics, Davis weaves e-mails and instant messages, making *The Curse of Addy McMahon* "accessible to reluctant readers," according to *School Library Journal* contributor Anne Knickerbocker. Davis captures the intensity of "typical tween dilemmas," noted a *Kirkus Reviews* writer, recommending the novel as a realistic "view of a child's inner struggles and emotional growth." In *Booklist* Carolyn Phelan wrote that *The Curse of Addy McMahon* captures "the pain, poignancy, and occasional satisfaction of sixth-grade life."

In addition to her writing, Davis regularly visits elementary schools as a guest speaker. It is her hope to inspire students to become interested in reading, or even better yet, consider becoming writers themselves. While visiting she will often work with kids—sometimes up to 100 children at a time—and create, write, and illustrate a story on the spot, and her spontaneity has made her a popular speaker. Despite her success, Davis remains humbled by the more serious part of her job: kids use her books to learn how to read everyday. In advising writers of all ages, Davis told interviewer Cynthia Leitich Smith for the Children's Literature Resources Web site: "If it is your passion, don't ever give up. . . . Learn as much as possible about your genre, and go to any and all meetings/conferences/workshops where you'll meet other people who love doing this too. Camaraderie is essential to keeping the spirit up in this very tough business. And read as many books as possible!"

Biographical and Critical Sources

PERIODICALS

Booklist, September 15, 1998, Susan Dove Lempke, review of *Who Hops?,* p. 234; October 1, 2000, Kathy Broderick, review of *Who Hoots?,* p. 344.

Good Housekeeping, February, 2003, Ellen Welty, "Writing Their Own Fairy Tale," p. 85; July 1, 2008, Carolyn Phelan, review of *The Curse of Addy McMahon,* p. 61.

Kirkus Reviews, October 1, 2001, review of *Scared Stiff,* p. 1421; September 15, 2002, review of *Party Animals,* p. 1387; September 15, 2003, review of *Mabel the Tooth Fairy and How She Got Her Job,* p. 1173; June 15, 2005, review of *Kindergarten Rocks!,* p. 681; April 1, 2008, review of *The Curse of Addy McMahon.*

Publishers Weekly, August 24, 1998, review of *Who Hops?,* p. 55; August 23, 1999, review of *I Hate to Go to Bed,* p. 57; September 24, 2001, review of *Scared Stiff,* p. 92; December 9, 2002, review of *Party Animals,* p. 21; October 13, 2003, review of *Mabel the Tooth Fairy and How She Got Her Job,* p. 79; July 11, 2005, review of *Kindergarten Rocks!,* p. 92.

Record-Review (Westchester County, NY), January 25, 2002, Ellen S. Best, "What's All the Hoot about Katie Davis?," p. 17.

School Library Journal, September, 1998, Adele Greenlee, review of *Who Hops?,* p. 171; March, 2000, Ginny Gustin, review of *I Hate to Go to Bed,* p. 194; December, 2000, Marlene Gawron, review of *Who Hoots?,* p. 107; September, 2001, Sarah O'Neal, review of *Scared Stiff,* p. 187; December, 2002, Sheilah Kosco, review of *Party Animals,* p. 86; January, 2004, Maryann H. Owen, review of *Mabel the Tooth Fairy and How She Got Her Job,* p. 96; September, 2005, Mary Elam, review of *Kindergarten Rocks!,* p. 168; July, 2008, Anne Knickerbocker, review of *The Curse of Addy McMahon,* p. 96.

ONLINE

Children's Literature Resources Web site, http://www. cynthialeitichsmith/com/ (September, 2000), interview with Davis.

Katie Davis Home Page, http://www.katiedavis.com (November 15, 2009).

*   *   *

DAWSON, Willow 1975-

Personal

Born 1975, in Vancouver, British Columbia, Canada; daughter of Clif Dawson (an artist); married Ray Cammaert (a musician and songwriter for the band Pink Moth). *Education:* Ontario College of Art and Design, diploma. *Hobbies and other interests:* Gardening, hiking, singer and saw player in band Pink Moth (formerly Little Brown Bat).

Addresses

Home—Toronto, Ontario, Canada. *E-mail*—jarsofhoney @willowdawson.com.

Career

Illustrator and graphic novelist. Member, RAID Studio.

Member

Writers' Union of Canada.

Awards, Honors

Best Bet for Junior Nonfiction Award, Ontario Library Association, 2008, and Cybils Graphic-Novel Award nomination, Joe Shuster Comics for Kids Award nomination, *ForeWord* Book of the Year Award nomination, and Norma Fleck Award for Canadian Children's Nonfiction nomination, all 2009, all for *No Girls Allowed*.

Writings

SELF-ILLUSTRATED

The Innumerable Obsessions of Purl McGee (children's book), privately published (Toronto, Ontario, Canada), 2006.

Lila and Ecco's Do-It-Yourself Comics Club (graphic novel), Kids Can Press (Toronto, Ontario, Canada), 2011.

Author and illustrator of *100 Mile House* (ongoing autobiographical comic), published by topshelfcomix.com. Contributor of comic "Ella and Squid's Top Five March Break Favourites" to *Owl* magazine. Contributor to anthologies, including *The Beguiling's Comics Festival*, Legion of Evil Press, 2009; *Girls Who Bite Back: Witches, Mutants, Slayers, and Freaks,* Sumach Press, 2004; and *Drawing the Line*, DTL Press, 2004.

ILLUSTRATOR

Susan Hughes, *No Girls Allowed: Tales of Daring Women Dressed as Men for Love, Freedom, and Adventure* (graphic novel), Kids Can Press (Toronto, Ontario, Canada), 2008.

Pamela Cross, *A Girl's Guide to Knowing Her Rights,* YWCA Canada (Toronto, Ontario, Canada), 2009.

Also illustrator of comic book *Mother May I,* by Sarrah Young, 2003, and comic-book series "Violet Miranda: Girl Pirate," by Emily Pohl-Weary, Kiss Machine Presents (Toronto, Ontario, Canada), 2004-07. Illustrator of comics essay, "The Problem with Villains," by Mariko Tamaki, Trinity Square Video, 2010. Contributor of illustrated segments for television film *Let's Talk about It,* directed by Deepa Mehta, Omni TV, 2005.

Sidelights

Based in Toronto, Canadian artist and illustrator Willow Dawson is a graphic novelist with a strong graphic style who works sequentially in India ink or as a painter in acrylics on cardboard. Raised in a creative household—her father is also an artist—Dawson had immersed herself in comix culture by the late 1990s, publishing 'zines and mini-comics. From there she gradually took on larger projects, some funded by the Ontario Arts Council and the Canadian Council for the Arts, and earned increasing recognition within the Toronto arts community. Dawson's online comic and soon-to-be graphic novel "100 Mile House" is a chronicle of her childhood experiences at her family's cabin in the woods of 100 Mile House, British Columbia.

While Dawson was still completing her illustration diploma at the Ontario College of Art and Design, her work with writer Emily Pohl-Weary on the comic-book/graphic novella "Violet Miranda: Girl Pirate" attracted the attention of an editor at Kids Can Press. Soon she was working alongside writer Susan Hughes on the graphic novel *No Girls Allowed: Tales of Daring Women Dressed as Men for Love, Freedom, and Adventure.*

Geared for preteens, *No Girls Allowed* includes stories about seven women who, because of the circumstances of their own time in history, found it necessary to dress as men. Ranging from ancient Egypt to the U.S. Civil War, Hughes and Dawson bring to life Egyptian Queen Hatshepsut, Chinese warrior Mu Lan, ninth-century

Willow Dawson contributes the comic-book-style art to Susan Hughes unusual and grrrl-friendly graphic novel No Girls Allowed. (Illustration © 2008 by Willow Dawson. Used by permission of Kids Can Press Ltd., Toronto.)

Scandinavian pirate Alfhild, and escaped slave Ellen Craft, among others. Reviewing the work for *Quill & Quire*, Sara Forsyth described Dawson's "stark images" as "full of detail," while Benjamin Russell asserted in *School Library Journal* that the book's "bold art clearly depicts each account" and injects the volume with "visual flair." In *Kirkus Reviews* a writer recommended *No Girls Allowed* as an "uniquely themed offering"; its "simple" text and "clean . . . ink drawing" share a "no-nonsense" approach that will make the book useful to students of women's history, the critic asserted.

In her interview with Robin Brenner for the *School Library Journal* Web log, Dawson gave encouragement to budding comic artists, particularly young women considering the field. "Keep drawing, writing, and exposing yourself to new ideas and new kinds of storytelling," she recommended. "And watch good movies. Watch how they set up shots, establish scenes and use perspective and point-of-view. These are some of the things movies and comics have in common and they are important devices for making comics communicate effectively." "The best way [to jump-start your career] is to self-publish and distribute your own work to start, even if you're photocopying little comic 'zines and stapling them together by hand," Dawson added. "But I think the most important thing is to always take yourself seriously. Self-confidence is attractive and people will want to work with you."

Biographical and Critical Sources

PERIODICALS

Kirkus Reviews, August 1, 2008, review of *No Girls Allowed: Tales of Daring Women Dressed as Men for Love, Freedom, and Adventure.*
Kliatt, September, 2008, Claire Rosser, review of *No Girls Allowed*, p. 37.
Quill & Quire, October, 2008, Sara Forsythe, review of *No Girls Allowed.*
School Library Journal, September, 2008, Benjamin Russell, review of *No Girls Allowed*, p. 215.

ONLINE

Boing Boing Web site, http://boingboing.net/ (May 26, 2009), Cory Doctorow, review of *No Girls Allowed.*
Jazma Web site, http://www.jazmaonline.com/ (July 22, 2009), Richard Vasseur, interview with Dawson.
School Library Journal Web log, http://www.schoollibraryjournal.com/blog/ (September 30, 2008), Robin Brenner, interview with Dawson.
Top Shelf Productions Web site, http://www.topshelfcomix.com/ (November 9, 2009), Willow Dawson, "100 Mile House."
Willow Dawson Home Page, http://www.willowdawson.com (November 15, 2009).

DONER, Kim 1955-

Personal

Born July 21, 1955, in Tulsa, OK; daughter of Otto (a sales engineer) and Elizabeth Jane Doner; married (divorced); married Dennis England, 2004; children: (first marriage) Sophie Alison Wieczorek, Lucy Amanda Wieczorek. *Education:* University of Tulsa, B.A. (medical illustration), 1976, and graduate study.

Addresses

Office—P.O. Box 702724, Tulsa, OK 74170-2724. *E-mail*—kim@kimdoner.com.

Career

Illustrator and portrait artist. Portraitist, beginning 1984; illustrator, 1992—; photographer and fused glass artist. Speaker at schools. *Exhibitions:* Work exhibited in solo show at Museum of Nebraska Art, 2006, and in "This Is Our Land" diplomacy project, sponsored by US Department of State.

Member

International Reading Association, Society of Children's Book Writers and Illustrators, Center for Poets and Writers.

Awards, Honors

Oklahoma Book Award for best illustrated book, Center for the Book, 1995, for *Green Snake Ceremony;* Best Children's Book designation, *ForeWord* magazine, 1997 for *Buffalo Dreams;* named Oklahoma illustrator, 2006.

Writings

SELF-ILLUSTRATED

Buffalo Dreams, WestWinds Press (Portland, OR), 1999.
On a Road in Africa, afterword by Chryssee Perry Martin, Tricycle Press (Berkeley, CA), 2008.

ILLUSTRATOR

Sherrin Watkins, *White Bead Ceremony*, Council Oak Books (Tulsa, OK), 1994.
Sherrin Watkins, *Green Snake Ceremony*, Council Oak Books, 1995.
Molly Levite Griffis, *The Buffalo in the Mall*, Eakin Press (Austin, TX), 1996.
David M. Schwartz, *Q Is for Quark: A Science Alphabet Book*, Tricycle Press (Berkeley, CA), 2001.
Christopher Philips, *The Philosophers' Club*, Tricycle Press (Berkeley, CA), 2001.
Edith Hope Fine, *Cryptomania!: Teleporting into Greek and Latin with the CryptoKids*, Tricycle Press (Berkeley, CA), 2004.

Kim Doner (Reproduced by permission.)

Sidelights

Illustrator Kim Doner was inspired to begin writing her own picture-book texts by her love of animals. Describing the home she shares with her husband as a "zoo" due to the presence of the succession of wild animals she has rescued and nursed back to health over the years, the Oklahoma-based animal lover found a kindred spirit in Chryssee Perry Martin. Martin, who grew up in Tulsa, Oklahoma, was appointed honorary warden of an animal orphanage in Nairobi, Kenya. In *On a Road in Africa* Doner inspires young children with Martin's story and also supports her work: a portion of the book's sales benefitted Martin's Nairobi Animal Orphanage.

Beginning her illustration career in the mid-1990s, Doner has created art for books that include Sherrin Watkins' *White Bead Ceremony* and *Green Snake Ceremony*, *Q Is for Quark: A Science Alphabet* by David M. Schwartz, and *The Philosophers' Club* by Christopher Phillips. Her first original self-illustrated book, *Buffalo Dreams*, was released in 1999 and recounts the experiences of Sarah, a Native-American girl, as she and her family make a pilgrimage to the cave of a rare white buffalo calf and she learns the extent of her own bravery and strength. While Linda Perkins wrote in *Booklist* that Doner's story moves slowly, the ending of her tale "is exciting and emotionally moving," and her "dramatic" illustrations feature "a variety of perspectives." In *Publishers Weekly* a reviewer noted the nov-

el's "spiritual" focus and added that *Buffalo Dreams* is brought to life in "realistic artwork" highlighted by "engaging [visual] touches."

In a text that introduces several Swahili words, *On a Road in Africa* describes the daylong journey of Martin (known in the book as "Mama Orphanage" or "Mama O") as she travels to surrounding villages to gather food for the animals cared for at the Nairobi Animal Orphanage. Traveling from stores to schools and agencies, Mama O also encounters a wide range of African wildlife as well as a diverse range of people. In *School Library Journal* Kathy Piehl praised Doner's ability to bring to life "a vibrant, modern country where water buffalo share the roads" and communities come together "to care for wildlife." Although a *Kirkus Reviews* critic found Doner's rhyming text to be somewhat "awkward," the critic exclaimed upon "the genuine love special people give to wild animals [that] leaps from the page." In *Booklist* Gillian Engberg praised *On a Road in Africa* as an "upbeat picture book" that treats readers to a "rhyming, chiming, singsong" text. As a visiting author at schools, Doner shows sketches and slides from the book, and also performs the story with a djembe and accompanying drumbeat.

One of Doner's first illustration projects, *White Bead Ceremony*, was undertaken after she was approached by Council Oak Books. "*Green Snake Ceremony* is the story of a Shawnee family searching for a green snake to use in an empowering ceremony they perform for their children," Doner once explained to *SATA*. "Part of the ceremony involves putting the snake in the mouth of a child. The family never finds a green snake—they buy a garter snake and wrap it in green cloth to use. The snake is later released at a nearby nature center. The little girl misinterprets the description of the ceremony and (of course) doesn't want a snake in her mouth. When I read the story, I thought, 'I wouldn't want to be *her . . . or* the snake.' Then I thought, 'What if there is a green snake? What if he lives under the house, and hears they are looking for him? And what if he manages to never get caught?' A whole second, humorous story was added through illustrations of this mythical little guy avoiding capture. It was a blast to do, and received the award of Best Illustrated Book of 1995 in Oklahoma."

"Many acquaintances in my life have teased me about 'What do you want to be when you grow up?,'" Doner once told *SATA*, "and I have had a question in return: 'Can't I just BE when I grown up?' [In my current career] . . . I don't have to grow up. I can immerse myself in my favorite profession (art), my favorite pastime (stories), my favorite people (kids, including those who still think like them), and my favorite hobby (communication in all forms), and have the whole enchilada. What a deal!

"I work every day with such a variety of jobs that it's hard to say how many hours and where: I draw, paint, write, do scheduling, plan tours, balance the books, research, do presentations, and teach. My vision of my work is broad: I hope that each and every book enriches as many lives as possible through humor or meaning or education or entertainment. My advice: If you *know* you have found what you love, DON'T EVER QUIT. Join critique groups, work hard, stay disciplined, ask questions, volunteer services, stay open, and nurture your dreams. Life is too short to sink into a 'life of quiet desperation,' and creating is tantamount to breathing.

"I've found a secret to all of this, too. I am no longer aging. Through connecting with imagination and humor and creativity and kids, I am 'younging'. Sometime next year, I'll probably turn ten years old and get to start trick or treating again. Watch out!"

Biographical and Critical Sources

PERIODICALS

Booklist, January 1, 2000, Linda Perkins, review of *Buffalo Dreams,* p. 935; February 15, 2008, Gillian Engberg, review of *On a Road in Africa,* p. 92.

Kirkus Reviews, April 15, 2008, review of *On a Road in Africa.*

Publishers Weekly, November 15, 1999, review of *Buffalo Dreams,* p. 66.

School Library Journal, November, 2001, Linda M. Kenton, review of *Q Is for Quark: A Science Alphabet Book,* p. 184; December, 2001, Lynn Dye, review of *The Philosophers' Club,* p. 170; November, 2004, Lynda Ritterman, review of *Cryptomania!: Teleporting into Greek and Latin with the Crypto Kids,* p. 143; April, 2008, Kathy Piehl, review of *On a Road in Africa,* p. 130.

Doner's expressive views of animals and nature are a highlight of her picture book On a Road in Africa.

Tulsa World, May 9, 2008, James D. Watts, Jr., "Local Author's Book Captures Essence of Africa."

ONLINE

Kim Doner Home Page, http://www.kimdoner.com (November 15, 2009).

*   *   *

DUNN, Carolyn 1965-
(Carolyn Dunn Anderson)

Personal

Born 1965, in Los Angeles, CA; married James Anderson; has children. *Education:* Earned B.A.; M.A.; doctoral studies at University of Southern California.

Addresses

Home—Southern CA.

Career

Journalist, educator, playwright, poet, and musician. Former radio producer and host, including of *American Indian Airwaves;* voice-over artist for film and television. Instructor at Humboldt State University, Four Winds Indian School, Chico, CA, and California Polytechnic State University, Pomona; California State University, Long Beach, lecturer in American Indian Studies program. Member of board of directors, Red Nation Celebration (nonprofit); member of advisory board, Interstitial Arts Foundation. Musician, performing with the Mankillers (all-woman Native drum group) and Red Hawk (rock band); director of stated readings.

Awards, Honors

Wordcraft Circle of Storytellers and Writers Year's Best Short Story, 1999, for "Salmon Creek Road Kill," and Book of the Year for Poetry award, 2002, for *Outfoxing Coyote;* James Irvine Foundation fellow, University of Southern California Center for American Studies and Ethnicity, 2005; awards (with others) from Native American Music Awards and Humboldt Area Foundation.

Writings

(Editor with Carol Comfort) *Through the Eye of the Deer: An Anthology of Native American Women Writers,* illustrated by Willow Dawson, Aunt Lute Books (San Francisco, CA), 1999.

(Editor with Paula Gunn Allen) *Hozho: Walking in Beauty: Native-American Stories of Inspiration, Humor, and Life,* illustrated by Willow Dawson, Contemporary Books (Chicago, IL), 2001.

Outfoxing Coyote (poetry collection), Painted Horse Press, 2002.

(With Ari Berk) *Coyote Speaks: Wonders of the Native American World,* Abrams Books for Young Readers (New York, NY), 2008.

Sidelights

A Native American poet and playwright, Carolyn Dunn is also an award-winning storyteller who has been honored for her writing and her music. Her work, with its woman-centered focus, draws on Dunn's experiences living in the Southwestern United States and encompasses college-level teaching, radio and theatre productions, and writing. Her published work includes the edited anthologies *Through the Eye of the Deer: An Anthology of Native American Women Writers* and *Hozho: Walking in Beauty: Native-American Stories of Inspiration, Humor, and Life,* the poetry collection *Outfoxing Coyote,* and *Coyote Speaks: Wonders of the Native American World,* a book coauthored with folklorist Ari Berk that shares Native American traditions through a mix of art and prose. Praising Dunn's verses in *Outfoxing Coyote,* Charles de Lint commented in the *Magazine of Fantasy and Science Fiction* that she "hits the mark so often, and writes with such confidence of the shadowy world of the spirits, that you find yourself wondering if she's entirely of this world herself."

In *Coyote Speaks* Dunn and Berk pair images depicting artifacts of various tribes with accounts of the myths and legends from those indigenous cultures throughout the Americas. They organize their work by topics that include trickster tales, stories of hunting, myths of little people, and modern stories. The coauthors present original retellings of dozens of stories and then provide information on the explanation and history behind each tale. Citing the book's visual appeal, a *Kirkus Reviews* writer went on to praise *Coyote Speaks* as "arresting in its presentation," and a *Children's Bookwatch* contributor maintained that the volume "encourages better understanding of Native American cultures . . . through word and image." In *Booklist* Hazel Rochman recommended Dunn and Berk's volume as a "comprehensive" resource featuring a diversity of Indian peoples as well as "a rich collection of exciting art and story that keeps the past alive," and Riva Pollard concluded her *School Library Journal* review by hailing *Coyote Speaks* as "outstanding for its art and artifact pictures."

Biographical and Critical Sources

PERIODICALS

Booklist, July 22, 2008, Hazel Rochman, review of *Coyote Speaks: Wonders of the Native American World.*
Children's Bookwatch, November, 2008, review of *Coyote Speaks.*
Kirkus Reviews, July 15, 2008, review of *Coyote Speaks.*

Magazine of Fantasy and Science Fiction, October-November, 2002, Charles de Lint, review of *Outfoxing Coyote,* p. 57.

Publishers Weekly, December 20, 1999, review of *Through the Eye of the Deer,* p. 56.

School Library Journal, October, 2008, Riva Pollard, review of *Coyote Speaks,* p. 164.

ONLINE

Carolyn Dunn Home Page, http://www.carolyndunn.com (December 1, 2009).

Carolyn Dunn Web log, http://realhollywoodindian. blogspot.com (December 1, 2009).*

E-F

EECKHOUT, Emmanuelle 1976-

Personal
Born 1976, in Charleroi, Belgium.

Addresses
Home—Nivelles, Belgium. *E-mail*—emmanuelle@eeckhout-emmanuelle.be.

Career
Writer, illustrator, and librarian.

Awards, Honors
Prix de Jeunes Lecteurs de la Ville de Nanterre, 2007, for *Trop la honte* by Ludovic Flavant.

Writings

SELF-ILLUSTRATED, EXCEPT AS NOTED

La vengeance de Germaine, L'école des loisirs (Brussels, Belgium), 2002.

Une histoire d'amour à crrroquer!, L'école des loisirs (Brussels, Belgium), 2003.

La tortue, le lièvre, L'école des loisirs (Brussels, Belgium), 2004.

Un papa à domicile, L'école des loisirs (Brussels, Belgium), 2005.

Au revoir, Papa, illustrated by Emile Jadoul, L'école des loisirs (Brussels, Belgium), 2006.

Le loup, la fouine et l'oeuf, illustrated by Catherine Pineur, L'école des loisirs (Brussels, Belgium), 2007.

Les fantômes, ça n'existe pas!, L'école des loisirs (Brussels, Belgium), 2008, translated as *There's No Such Things as Ghosts!,* Kane/Miller Books (La Jolla, CA), 2008.

Robert, L'école des loisirs (Brussels, Belgium), 2008.

Le requin du bocal, L'école des loisirs (Brussels, Belgium), 2009.

ILLUSTRATOR

Maurice Guillaume, *Gontran, le prince qui s'ennuyait,* L'école des loisirs (Brussels, Belgium), 2004.

Ludovic Flamant, *Chafi,* L'école des loisirs (Brussels, Belgium), 2005.

Ludovic Flamant, *Trop la honte,* L'école des loisirs (Brussels, Belgium), 2007.

Biographical and Critical Sources

PERIODICALS

Horn Book, January-February, 2009, Jennifer M. Brabander, review of *There's No Such Things as Ghosts!*, p. 77.

Kirkus Reviews, September 1, 2008, review of *There's No Such Things as Ghosts!*

School Library Journal, November, 2008, Marge Loch Wouters, review of *There's No Such Things as Ghosts!*, p. 87.

ONLINE

Emmanuelle Eeckhout Home Page, http://www.eeckhout-emmanuelle.be (November 15, 2009).*

* * *

ELLIOT, David 1952-

Personal
Born November 10, 1952, in Ashburton, New Zealand; son of Robert (an insurance salesman) and Joy (a homemaker) Elliot; married Gillian Whitehead (a librarian),

David Elliot (Photograph by Otago Daily Times/Allied Press Ltd. Reproduced by permission.)

May 10, 1986, children: Mhairi, Jess. *Education:* Wellington Polytechnic, stage-1 graphics, 1971; University of Canterbury, fine arts diploma (painting), 1976; Christchurch College of Education, teaching diploma, 1986.

Addresses

Home—Port Chalmers, Dunedin, Otago, New Zealand. *E-mail*—david@davidelliot.org.

Career

Author and illustrator. Hutt Valley High School, New Zealand, assistant art teacher, 1987-88; Queens High School, Dunedin, New Zealand, art teacher, 1989-93, head of art department, 1994-97, part-time tutor in painting and drawing for adults, beginning 1998; freelance illustrator, 1986—. Worked variously as a zoo gatekeeper, dishwasher, and interior designer. Dunedin College of Education, writer-in-residence, 2000.

Member

New Zealand Society of Authors, New Zealand Book Council, Children's Literature Foundation of New Zealand.

Awards, Honors

Russell Clark Illustration Award, New Zealand Library Association, 1989, for *Arthur and the Dragon;* Queen Elizabeth II Arts Council/Unilever/Choysa Award, 1991, and Russell Clark Illustration Award finalist, 1995, both for *Dragon Tangle;* International TV Association New Zealand, best interactive illustration title, 1995, for CD-ROM *Mungo: The Only Pirate Left;* Honour designation, *New Zealand Post* Children's Book Awards, 2000, for *Sydney and the Seamonster;* Spectrum Print Book Design Award Highly Commended designation, 2001, for *Sydney and the Whalebird;* Russell Clark Illustration Award finalist, and *New Zealand Post* Children's Picture Book Awards Best Book designation, both 2003,

both for *Pigtails the Pirate;* Spectrum Print Book Design Award for Best Children's Book, and Spectrum Design Awards Best Book Award runner up, both 2006, both for *Mona Minim and the Smell of the Sun; New Zealand Post* Children's Book Award finalist, 2009, for *Chicken Feathers.*

Writings

FOR CHILDREN

Arthur's Star, Whitcoulls (Christchurch, New Zealand), 1986.

Dragon Tangle, Ashton Scholastic (Auckland, New Zealand), 1994.

Sydney and the Seamonster, Random House (Auckland, New Zealand), 1999.

Sydney and the Whalebird, Random House (Auckland, New Zealand), 2000.

Pigtails the Pirate, Random House (Auckland, New Zealand), 2002.

The Adventures of Sydney Penguin, Random House (Auckland, New Zealand), 2007.

ILLUSTRATOR

Pauline Cartwright, *Arthur and the Dragon,* Nelson Price Milburn (Petone, New Zealand), 1989, Steck-Vaughn (Austin, TX), 1990.

Anna Kenna, *A Close Call,* Learning Media (Wellington, New Zealand), 1998.

Anna Kenna, *The Bad Dad List,* Learning Media (Wellington, New Zealand), 1998.

Janice Marriott, *The Curse of Being Pharaoh,* Learning Media (Wellington, New Zealand), 1998.

Jo Noble, editor, *One Hundred New Zealand Poems for Children,* Random House (Auckland, New Zealand), 1999.

Pauline Cartwright, *Annie and Rufus,* Bridgehill (Alexandra, New Zealand), 1999.

Susan Brocker and Elizabeth Hookings, *Legendary Places,* Lands End Publishing (Auckland, New Zealand), 2000.

Mandy Hager, *Stumpy's Secret,* Learning Media (Wellington, New Zealand), 2000.

Jo Noble, editor, *Thirty New Zealand Stories for Children,* Random House (Auckland, New Zealand), 2000.

Rachel McAlpine, editor, *Another One Hundred New Zealand Poems for Children,* Random House (Auckland, New Zealand), 2001.

Feana Tuéakoi, *Cooped Up,* Learning Media (Wellington, New Zealand), 2001.

Barbara Else, editor, *Another Thirty New Zealand Stories for Children,* Random House (Auckland, New Zealand), 2002.

Jack Lasenby, *Aunt Effie,* Longacre Press (Dunedin, New Zealand), 2002.

Jack Lasenby, *Aunt Effie's Ark,* Longacre Press (Dunedin, New Zealand), 2003.

Janet Frame, *Mona Minim and the Smell of the Sun,* Random House (Auckland, New Zealand), 2005.

Lewis Carroll, *The Hunting of the Snark: An Agony, in Eight Fits,* Otakau Press (Dunedin, New Zealand), 2006.

Donald Kerr, *The Smell of Powder: A History of Duelling in New Zealand,* 2006.

T.A. Barron, *The Eternal Flame,* Philomel Books (New York, NY), 2006.

Jeffrey Kluger, *Nacky Patcher and the Curse of the Dry Land Boats,* Philomel (New York, NY), 2007.

Joy Cowley, *Chicken Feathers,* Philomel Books (New York, NY), 2008.

Tessa Duder, editor, *The Word Witch: The Magical Verse of Margaret Mahy,* HarperCollins (Auckland, New Zealand), 2009.

Illustrator of book covers and CD-ROM *Mungo: The Only Pirate Left,* 1995. Contributor of illustrations to periodicals.

ILLUSTRATOR; "REDWALL" NOVEL SERIES

Brian Jacques, *Triss,* Philomel Books (New York, NY), 2002.

Brian Jacques, *Loamhedge,* Philomel Books (New York, NY), 2003.

Illustration by David Elliot of the Jubjub Bird, for a new edition of Lewis Carroll's **The Hunting of the Snark.** (Illustration courtesy of David Elliot.)

Brian Jacques, *Mossflower,* Philomel Books (New York, NY), 2004.

Brian Jacques, *Rakkety Tam,* Philomel Books (New York, NY), 2004.

Brian Jacques, *High Rhulain,* Philomel Books (New York, NY), 2005.

Brian Jacques, *Eulalia,* Philomel Books (New York, NY), 2007.

Brian Jacques, *Doomwyte,* Philomel Books (New York, NY), 2008.

ILLUSTRATOR; "GREAT TREE OF AVALON" NOVEL SERIES

T.A. Barron, *Child of the Dark Prophecy,* Philome Books (New York, NY), 2004.

T.A. Barron, *Shadows on the Stars,* Philome Books (New York, NY), 2005.

T.A. Barron, *The Eternal Flame,* Philome Books (New York, NY), 2006.

ILLUSTRATOR; "CASTAWAYS" NOVEL SERIES

Brian Jacques, *The Angel's Command: A Tale from the Castaways of the Flying Dutchman,* Philomel Books (New York, NY), 2003.

Brian Jacques, *Voyage of Slaves: A Tale from the Castaways of the Flying Dutchman,* Philomel Books (New York, NY), 2006.

Sidelights

New Zealand artist and author David Elliot came to illustration in an unusual way. After studying fine art, he found a job as a gatekeeper at Scotland's Edinburgh Zoo. As he once recalled to *SATA,* "The Zoo was a wonderful stimulus, especially after the gates were closed and the animals were more relaxed." He passed time on the job doing pencil sketches of animals, honing the detailed illustration style that he has brought to his more-recent children's-book projects, such as creating the intricate spot art for Brian Jacques' popular "Redwall" fantasy series as well as texts by Jack Lasenby, Janet Frame, Joy Cowley, T.A. Barron, and Margaret Mahy. Reviewing Elliot's images for Cowley's chapter book *Chicken Feathers, Booklist* contributor Thom Barthelmess concluded that the artist's "warm, evocative pencil sketches" pair nicely with the author's "rich storytelling voice," and Miriam Lang Budin wrote in her *School Library Journal* review that the artist's "personality-laden . . . illustrations extend readers' sense of Cowley's characters."

Although he worked for the next eight years as a high-school art teacher after returning to New Zealand, Elliot also took on small-scale illustration projects for magazines and book covers. In 1998, with his younger daughter now in school and his partner working full time, he made the shift to full-time illustrating and his first works included artwork for *One Hundred New Zealand Poems for Children* and his original picture book *Sydney and the Seamonster. Magpies* reviewer Frances Plumpton

Elliot's illustration projects include creating illustrations for Brian Jacques' High Rhulain. (Illustration copyright © 2005 by David Elliot. Reproduced by permission of Firebird, a division of Penguin Putnam Books for Young Readers.)

found much to like about *One Hundred New Zealand Poems for Children,* which contains works written for and by children. Calling Elliot's black pencil illustrations for this work "a treat," Plumpton added that "his witty illustrations underpin, but do not overwhelm, the poetry" and demonstrate the illustrator's "versatility interpreting a variety of moods."

In *Sydney and the Seamonster* a penguin named Sydney is an inventor whose experiments wreck havoc on his island home. A reviewer for *Reading Times* praised Elliot's picture book highly, describing it as a "great story with superb visual skills" that contains "visual excitement and humour." As is the case with *Sydney and the Seamonster,* Elliot likes to make his illustrations meaty with subtext. "I've always liked fantasy that has an edge and a darkness to it," the illustrator admitted to *Otago Daily Times* interviewer Charmian Smith. "If I have the chance I will try and give an image that quality. It makes the images more important and gives them a strength and gravity that you feel belongs to it." Elliot's amusing penguin character returns in *Sydney and the Whalebird* and *The Adventures of Sydney Penguin.*

"I love drawing!," Elliot once told *SATA.* "Through it my imagination materialises before me and continues to sprout ideas as I draw. Things grow out of the paper; characters, places, situations take on lives of their own, and it often becomes a race to nail them down, before they wander off, or meander into untieable knots. I have found through experience that the best nail is a good story, something that pins [my ideas], squealing and squirming though they may be, firmly to the plot. It is then just a matter of helping them be what they want to be, to the best of my ability. I hope what I am able to find in the paper reflects the enjoyment I have had in the search."

Biographical and Critical Sources

BOOKS

Chris Gaskin, *Picture Book Magic: Chris Gaskin interviews Nine Leading New Zealand Children's Illustrators,* Reed Children's Books (Auckland, NZ), 1996.

PERIODICALS

Booklist, September 1, 2005, Kay Weisman, review of *High Rhulain,* p. 134; May 15, 2008, Thom Barthelmess, review of *Chicken Feathers,* p. 42.
Horn Book, January-February, 2006, Anita L. Burkham, review of *High Rhulain,* p. 82.
Junior Bookshelf, December, 1994, review of *Dragon Tangle,* p. 202.
Kirkus Reviews, April 15, 2008, review of *Chicken Feathers.*
Magpies, November, 1999, Frances Plumpton, "A Look at *One Hundred New Zealand Poems for Children*"; March 2001, Raymond Huber, interview with Elliot, New Zealand supplement, p. 1.
Otago Daily Times (New Zealand), April 4, 2000, Charmian Smith, "Fantasy: Elliot Drawn to the Edge," p. B13.
Reading Times, November, 1999, review of *Sydney and the Seamonster,* p. 41.
School Librarian, November, 1994, Peter Andrews, review of *Dragon Tangle,* p. 145.
School Library Journal, September, 2004, Christine McGinty, review of *Rakkety Tam,* p. 208; April, 2008, Miriam Lang Budin, review of *Chicken Feathers,* p. 104.

ONLINE

David Elliot Home Page, http://www.davidelliot.org (December 1, 2009).

*   *   *

FERRAIOLO, Jack D.

Personal

Married; children: two.

Addresses

Home—MA. *Agent*—Donald Maass Literary Agency, 121 W. 27th St., Ste. 801, New York, NY 10001.

Career

Author and director, editor, and producer of animated films. Scholastic Media Soup2Nuts entertainment division, producer and director of cartoon series *O'Grady, Science Court, Home Movies,* and *WordGirl,* then development executive, beginning 2009.

Awards, Honors

Emmy Award for Best Writing in Animation, Academy of Television Arts and Sciences, 2008, for *WordGirl.*

Writings

The Big Splash, Amulet Books (New York, NY), 2008.

Sidelights

In addition to working on a variety of children's animated series for television, Jack D. Ferraiolo is also the author of a novel for young readers titled *The Big Splash*. Written in the style of a detective story, *The Big Splash* introduces readers to the students of Franklin Middle School, an institution controlled by Vinny Bigglo and his juvenile gangster accomplices. Nicknamed "Biggs," Vinny maintains control of the underground market of forged parental signatures, contraband candy, and stolen copies of upcoming tests. Those who decide to challenge the young leader's authority quickly find themselves the target of squirt-gun shooters who aim a urine-colored liquid directly under their victim's waistline, leading to humiliating accusations of self-soiling and permanent social exclusion by fellow students. When a hired gun named Nikki Fingers decides to break with Vinny's gang, she finds herself the target of such an attack. Upset by the incident, both Vinny and Nikki's sister hire seventh-grader Matt Stevens to discover the perpetrator.

School Library Journal critic Riva Pollard wrote that in *The Big Splash* "Ferraiolo cleverly adapts hard-boiled whodunit roles to a slightly cartoonish middle school arena." A *Kirkus Reviews* contributor remarked that the author's "first-person present-tense narration carries in it echoes of Marlowe," giving further attention to "crafty twists and turns" of his novel's plot. Writing in *Publishers Weekly,* a reviewer highlighted the book's "crisp prose and surprisingly poignant moments," while *New York Times Book Review* contributor Rich Cohen described *The Big Splash* as "entertaining and thrilling" as it humorously captures the transitioning of "the happy, dumb and unsuspecting from the safe world of lower school to the grim and ghastly terror of high school."

Biographical and Critical Sources

PERIODICALS

Kirkus Reviews, August 1, 2008, review of *The Big Splash.*
Kliatt, September, 2008, Claire Rosser, review of *The Big Splash,* p. 10.
New York Times Book Review, October 12, 2008, Rich Cohen, review of *The Big Splash,* p. 22.
Publishers Weekly, September 15, 2008, review of *The Big Splash,* p. 67.
School Library Journal, November, 2008, Riva Pollard, review of *The Big Splash,* p. 120.

ONLINE

Jack D. Ferraiolo Home Page, http://www.jackferraiolo. com (November 14, 2009).*

* * *

FINN, Mary

Personal

Born in Ireland; children: one son.

Addresses

Home—Dublin, Ireland. *Agent*—Sarah Manson, 6 Totnes Walk, London N2 0AD, England.

Career

Journalist and novelist. Radio Telefís Éireann (now RTÉ), Dublin, Ireland, journalist and reviewer for print and online publications; freelance writer.

Writings

The Adventure Guide to Dublin, illustrated by Francis Hyland, Wolfhound Press (Dublin, Ireland), 1984, 3rd edition, Merlin Publishing, 1992.

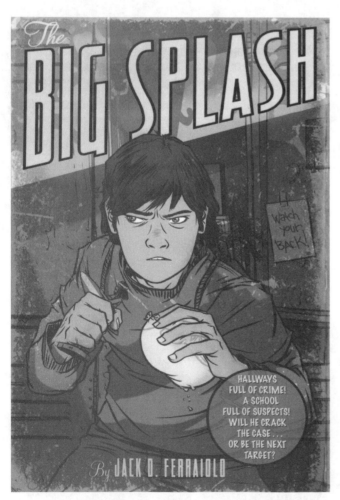

Cover of Jack D. Ferraiolo's middle-grade novel The Big Splash, *featuring cover art by Nathan Fox.* (Amulet Books, 2008. Illustration © by Nathan Fox. Reproduced by permission.)

Anila's Journey, Candlewick Press (Cambridge, MA), 2008.

Sidelights

A resident of Dublin, Ireland, Mary Finn worked as a journalist for Irish broadcaster Radio Telefís Éireann, writing articles and reviewers for the company's print publication *RTÉ* before turning to fiction writing. Finn's novel *Anila's Journey* was inspired by her interest in the story behind the eighteenth-century painting. "An Indian Lady (Indian bibi Jemdanee)," a work by Irish artist Thomas Hickey that hangs in the National Gallery of Ireland.

In *Anila's Journey* Finn transports readers back to the late 1700s, during the British colonization of India, as a fourteen-year-old mixed-race girl determines to make art her career. With the whereabouts of her Irish businessman father unknown and her Bengali mother now dead of a broken heart, Anila Tandy realizes that she is on her own. Although Indian society does not support women who must work, Anila is encouraged by a friend, the painter Thomas Hickey, to believe that she can make her way in the world through her art. With Hickey's help, she meets a British naturalist who hires her to paint the birds he discovers during his expedition from Calcutta up the Ganges river. As the girl is exposed to new experiences, as well as to adversity, she is also haunted by her own past, and the trip becomes a test of the young woman's own determination.

Finn's story "will captivate patient readers," Geri Diorio wrote in *School Library Journal,* the critic adding that *Anila's Journey* features "characters . . . as vibrant as their surroundings." Describing the novel as "layered" and "atmospheric," Gillian Engberg went on to further praise Finn's fiction debut, writing in *Booklist* that the author's "cinematic descriptions" of her Indian setting combine with information about colonial life to add "lyricism" to the "well-told" story. In *Kliatt* Claire Rosser maintained that Finn's narrative, "rich with visual images," is "all the more exotic because of the vivid colors and beauty of colonial India." While praising the many details that bring to life the story's exotic setting, Rosser concluded that "the drama of the plot and the characters" will transfix what she described as an "exceptionally fine historical novel," and a *Kirkus Reviews* writer wrote that in *Anila's Journey* Finn sensitively captures "a heartwarming, rich, believable coming-of-age."

Cover of Mary Finn's historical novel Anila's Journey, *which follows the adventures of a creative young woman dedicated to her art.* (Illustrations © 2008 by Dorling Kindersley/Getty Images (bird); © 2008 by Academy of Natural Sciences of Philadelphia/Corbis (flowers); © by Neil Fletcher and Matthew Ward/Getty Images (branches). Photographs © 2008 by Robert Bremec/iStockphoto (boat); © 2008 by Frank van Haalen/iStockphoto (water); © 2008 by Jyothi Joshi/Dreamstime.com (fabric). Reproduced by permission of the publisher, Candlewick Press, Inc., Cambridge, MA.)

Biographical and Critical Sources

PERIODICALS

Booklist, October 1, 2008, Gillian Engberg, review of *Anila's Journey,* p. 36.
Guardian (London, England), February 2, 2008, Mary Hoffman, review of *Anila's Journey.*
Kirkus Reviews, September 15, 2008, review of *Anila's Journey.*
Kliatt, November, 2008, Claire Rosser, review of *Anila's Journey,* p. 10.
School Library Journal, January, 2009, Geri Diorio, review of *Anila's Journey,* p. 100.*

G

GANNIJ, Joan
(Joan Levine Gannij)

Personal

Born in New York, NY; immigrated to Netherlands, 1987; daughter of Adele Gannij (a photographer); children: Geoff.

Addresses

Home—Amsterdam, Netherlands.

Career

Writer, photojournalist, and educator. Worked variously as a disc jockey, photojournalist, and talk-show host until 1987; freelance writer.

Writings

FOR CHILDREN

Elusive Moose, illustrated by Clare Beaton, Barefoot Books (Cambridge, MA), 2006.
Hidden Hippo, illustrated by Clare Beaton, Barefoot Books (Cambridge, MA), 2008.

OTHER

Flying Visits: Scandinavia (travel guide), Cadogan Guides, 2004.
Flying Visits: Iceland, Finland, and the Baltic (travel guide), Cadogan Guides, 2005.

Author of poetry chapbooks, including *Wounds of Change;* author of *The Cruelty of Loveless Love: A Collector's Monograph of Portraits of Charles Bukowski* (photographs). Contributor to periodicals, including *Vrij Nederland.*

Sidelights

Joan Gannij was raised in a household where creativity was valued, and her mother's work as a professional photographer in Hollywood inspired Gannij to follow a similar career path. In the early 1970s she worked as a writer and photographer as well as hosting her own radio show. Gradually shifting to writing as her primary focus, the American-born Gannij immigrated to the Netherlands in the late 1980s. In addition to publishing several poetry chapbooks, she has produced travel books focusing on Scandinavia, Iceland, and Finland as well as producing several picture books for children.

Gannij collaborates with textile artist Clare Beaton on the "hide-and-seek" picture books *Hidden Hippo* and *Elusive Moose.* In *Hidden Hippo* a young narrator describes her journey through the African grasslands, as she encounters a variety of animals, birds, and plants, while in *Elusive Moose* the geography shifts to a northern latitude where boreal forests and alpine regions are the focus. In *Kirkus Reviews* a critic praised *Hidden Hippo* as a "rhyming, interactive safari romp" featuring a "succinct, informative" text enlivened by Gannij's "simple, easily recited verse." The author's "clever rhyming" text and Beaton's "signature fabric appliqué collages" combine to produce a "visually stunning" picture book suitable for budding conservationists, wrote *School Library Journal* critic Linda Ludke in a review of the same book. Beaton's unique appliquéd art, "accented with tiny sequins, buttons, and beads, make a cozy . . . backdrop for [Gannij's] . . . "humorous, winning" narrative about a young traveler's wish to see a stately forest creature, wrote Connie Fletcher in reviewing *Elusive Moose* for *Booklist,* and in *School Library Journal* Martha Simpson dubbed the picture book "a cozy fall-turns-to-winter story to share with budding nature lovers."

Joan Gannij's picture book Elusive Moose *gains a puzzle-like element through Clare Beaton's clever applique-and-collage illustrations.* (Barefoot Books, 2007. Illustration copyright © 2006 by Clare Beaton. Reproduced by permission.)

Biographical and Critical Sources

PERIODICALS

Booklist, November 15, 2006, Connie Fletcher, review of *Elusive Moose,* p. 53.

Kirkus Reviews, August 15, 2008, review of *Hidden Hippo.*

School Library Journal, November, 2006, Martha Simpson, review of *Elusive Moose,* p. 94; October, 2008, Linda Ludke, review of *Hidden Hippo,* p. 131.

ONLINE

Laterna Magica Web site, http://www.laterna.net/ (November 20, 2009), "Joan Gannij."*

*   *   *

GANNIJ, Joan Levine
See GANNIJ, Joan

*   *   *

GARCIA, Cristina 1958-

Personal

Born July 4, 1958, in Havana, Cuba; immigrated to United States, c. 1960; daughter of Frank M. and Hope Lois Garcia; married Scott Brown, December 8, 1990; children: Pilar Akiko. *Education:* Barnard College, B.A., 1979; Johns Hopkins University, M.A., 1981. *Politics:* Democrat. *Hobbies and other interests:* Contemporary dance, music, travel, foreign languages.

Addresses

Home—Los Angeles, CA. *Agent*—Lavin Agency, 222 3rd St., Ste. 1130, Cambridge, MA 02142. *E-mail*—pinkhydrangea@hotmail.com.

Career

Journalist and author. *Time* (magazine), New York, NY, reporter and researcher, 1983-85, correspondent, 1985-90, bureau chief in Miami, FL, 1987-88.

Cristina Garcia (Photograph by Jerry Bauer. Reproduced by permission.)

Member

Amnesty International, PEN American Center.

Awards, Honors

National Book Award finalist, National Book Foundation, 1992, for *Dreaming in Cuban;* Hodder fellowship, Princeton University, 1992-93; Cintas fellowship, 1992-93; Whiting Writers Award, 1996.

Writings

FOR CHILDREN

The Dog Who Loved the Moon, illustrated by Sebastía Serra, Atheneum Books for Young Readers (New York, NY), 2008.
I Wanna Be Your Shoebox (middle-grade adult novel), Simon & Schuster Books for Young Readers (New York, NY), 2008.

FOR ADULTS

Dreaming in Cuban (novel), Knopf (New York, NY), 1992.
Cars of Cuba (essay), created by D.D. Allen, photographs by Joshua Greene, Abrams (New York, NY), 1995.
The Aguero Sisters (novel), Knopf (New York, NY), 1997.
Monkey Hunting (novel), Knopf (New York, NY), 2003.

(Editor and author of introduction) *Cubanismo! The Vintage Book of Contemporary Cuban Literature,* Vintage (New York, NY), 2003.
La caida del cielo, Ediciones Vigia (Matanzas, Cuba), 2003.
(Editor and author of introduction) *Bordering Fires: The Vintage Book of Contemporary Mexican and Chicano/a Literature,* Vintage (New York, NY), 2006.
A Handbook to Luck, Knopf (New York, NY), 2007.

Author's work has been translated into Spanish.

Sidelights

A former journalist, Cuban-born author Cristina Garcia became a finalist for the National Book Award on the strength of her first novel, *Dreaming in Cuban.* As her writing career has continued, Garcia has broadened her audience, addressing teens in *I Wanna Be Your Shoebox* and younger children in the picture book *The Dog Who Loved the Moon.* As Michiko Kakutani remarked in the *New York Times* on the 1982 publication of *Dreaming in Cuban,* Garcia's fiction debut "announces the debut of a writer blessed with a poet's ear for language, a historian's fascination with the past and a musician's intuitive understanding of the ebb and flow of emotion."

Dreaming in Cuban chronicles three generations of a Cuban family. The matriarch, Celia, falls in love with a married Spaniard and writes him letters for twenty-five years. Despite this long-distance affair, Celia marries a man she does not love, and the couple has two daughters, Lourdes and Felicia, and a son, Javier. Celia also becomes enamored of the Cuban Revolution and its leader, Fidel Castro. Lourdes, however, is raped by a revolutionary, and carries her hatred of the revolution with her when she moves to New York City with her husband and opens two successful bakeries. Felicia stays in Cuba with her mother, marries a sailor who gives her syphilis, and eventually meets a tragic end. Javier becomes a scientist and immigrates to Czechoslovakia, only to return a bitter alcoholic. As for the next generation, Thulani Davis explained in the *New York Times Book Review,* "Celia's grandchildren can only be described as lost and abandoned by the obsessions of the parents. Richard Eder, writing in the *Los Angeles Times,* called *Dreaming in Cuban* "poignant and perceptive," noting that "the realism is exquisite," and Davis dubbed it "a jewel of a first novel."

The Aguero Sisters introduces Constancia and Reina, sisters who have been separated for thirty years. Constancia is married to Heberto, who has recently retired from his cigar business. They have moved from New York City to Key Biscayne, Florida, and Constancia has become a successful businesswoman and entrepreneur with her own line of homemade, natural body and face creams. Heberto soon disappears from the main plot as he embarks on a new career as a counterrevolutionary and becomes embroiled in a Bay of Pigs-like plot to overthrow the Cuban government. Meanwhile, Reina still lives in Cuba as a traveling electrician. When the two sisters are reunited in Miami, they work to strip away the lies that constitute their lives, and this process extends to their respective daughters, the artist Isabel and former volleyball coach-turned-prostitute Dulce. The primary element that connects all four women, aside from their kinship per se, is the quest to learn the truth about the death of Constancia and Reina's mother, Blanca Mestre de Aguero, whose brutal murder at the hands of her husband is shrouded in mystery and lies. According to *Time* reviewer Pico Iyer: "Both Aguero sisters share something deep as blood: a matter-of-fact commitment to the magic of their island of honey and rum. Constancia makes spells for women in the form of the 'luscious unguents' she markets; Reina casts spells over men."

Reviewing *The Aguero Sisters* in Chicago's *Tribune Books*, Ruth Behar praised the novel as a "gorgeously written, . . . flamboyant feminist vision of Cuban and American history, women's lives, memory and desire." Kakutani noted "the force of Ms. Garcia's powerfully imagined characters" and "the magic of her prose," while *Nation* critic Ilan Stavans cited Garcia's "astonishing literary style and dazzling attention to telling detail." Describing Garcia as "a wise and generous storyteller," Iyer concluded that the novelist "has crafted a beautifully rounded work of art as warm and wry and sensuous as the island she clearly loves."

Monkey Hunting is a multigenerational saga that focuses on a family of mixed Chinese and Cuban descent. Garcia's tale begins with Chen Pan, who travels from his homeland in China to Cuba in the 1850s, where he is at first enslaved and forced to work in the sugarcane fields. However, Chen surmounts this challenge to become a successful Havana businessman, then falls in love with a mulata named Lucrecia and finds happiness as a family man. The experiences of his descendants vary widely: son Lorenzo becomes a physician; daughter Chen Fang lives in China, where she becomes a teacher and counterrevolutionary; and grandson Domingo Chen ends up in New York City, where he encounters racism and ends up a soldier fighting in Vietnam.

Mary Margaret Benson, writing in *Library Journal*, called *Monkey Hunting* "a brilliantly conceived work—and it's also delightful reading." Although a *Publishers Weekly* reviewer maintained that some characters are undeveloped, the work stands as "a richly patterned mini-epic, a moving chorus of distinct voices." In the opinion of *Atlantic Monthly* critic Margot Livesey, *Monkey Hunting* combines "gorgeous writing" with extraordinary empathy and understanding.

Although Garcia intended her novel *A Handbook to Luck* for older readers, Claire Rosser maintained in *Kliatt* that the work "will resonate with YA readers able to handle it." Garcia's story focuses on three individuals who are struggling to find their way in three different corners of the world. Enrique Florit is a precocious nine

year old from Cuba whose mother has recently died in an accident during his father's magic act. He and his father move to Las Vegas to get a fresh start, but the lure of the gambling life soon reels Enrique in. Meanwhile, in El Salvador, young Marta Claros sells used clothing to help support her family, while her little brother escapes one form of brutality only to witness another. Marta, too, hopes to find a better life by escaping to the United States, where she works as a nanny without gaining citizenship. In Tehran, Iran, Leila Rezvani is part of a well-off family, but she feels isolated from both her family and the world around her. Following these three characters, Garcia tangles their lives together in an intriguing story. As a *Publishers Weekly* critic remarked, the author "lovingly portrays her characters grappling with misfortune and luck in unfamiliar surroundings," and *Booklist* critic Donna Seaman noted of *A Handbook to Luck* that Garcia "writes rhapsodically of nature's beauty, [as] life emerges as a cosmic game of chance under luck's misrule."

Eighth-grader Yumi Ruiz-Hirsch is the main character in *I Wanna Be Your Shoebox*, a novel that highlights Garcia's "exceptional ability to channel a range of voices," according to a *Publishers Weekly* critic. Yumi's heritage is a patchwork quilt: her mom is Cuban, her Brooklyn-born dad is a mix of Jewish and Japanese. In addition to her cultural heritage, Yumi also has a creative one: her mom is a novelist and her father is a songwriter and musician in a punk band. Yumi loves music too, and when her southern California middle school decides to cut orchestra, she worries that her clarinet-playing days are over. Bigger changes are in store, however, when her beloved grandpa is diagnosed with cancer and her mom decides to remarry and move north. Garcia's novel about a preteen dealing with change was praised by *School Library Journal* critic Maria B. Salvadore as a "fast, funny, and surprisingly plausible" tale featuring a "likeable" cast of characters. Also reviewing *I Wanna Be Your Shoebox*, Hazel Rochman concluded in *Booklist* that Garcia's story is a "celebration of ordinariness in all its rich diversity."

Featuring artwork by Sebastía Serra, *The Dog Who Loved the Moon* also features a child growing up in a musical family. For Pilar, her birthday gift of pink satin ballet slippers and a puppy is the answer to her dream: not only can she now dance like a ballerina, but she will now have a dancing partner! Unfortunately, Paco the puppy has other ideas, and would rather sing to the moon than dance with Pilar. Fortunately, Pilar's uncle finds a way to unite the dog's need to sing and the girl's need to dance. A *Kirkus Reviews* critic described *The Dog Who Loved the Moon* as "a fanciful story" that features computer-enhanced, retro-styled art that "are rich with texture and detail." In *Booklist* Shelle Rosenfeld also praised Serra's art and dubbed Garcia's picturebook debut an "upbeat tale that celebrates community, family traditions, . . . and the joyful rewards of music and dance."

In addition to her fiction, Garcia has edited *Cubanismo! The Vintage Book of Contemporary Cuban Literature*, a collection of stories, poetry, and nonfiction that provides a broad overview of the creative writing coming from the island nation while also confronting the stereotypes associated with the region. Another editing project, *Bordering Fires: The Vintage Book of Contemporary Mexican and Chicano/a Literature*, address how the boundary between the United States and Mexico has affected the works of writers working near that divide, addressing issues of immigration, racism, and cultural assimilation, among others.

Biographical and Critical Sources

BOOKS

Contemporary Literary Criticism, Volume 76, Gale (Detroit, MI), 1993.

Contemporary Novelists, 7th edition, St. James (Detroit, MI), 2001.

Notable Hispanic American Women, 2nd edition, Gale (Detroit, MI), 1998.

PERIODICALS

Atlantic Monthly, May, 2003, Margot Livesey, "Time Travel," p. 123.

Booklist, October 15, 2006, Donna Seaman, review of *Bordering Fires: The Vintage Book of Contemporary Mexican and Chicano/a Literature*, p. 16; February 1, 2007, Donna Seaman, review of *A Handbook to Luck*, p. 31; April 15, 2008, Shelle Rosenfeld, review of *The Dog Who Loved the Moon*, p. 49; August 1, 2008, Hazel Rochman, review of *I Wanna Be Your Shoebox*, p. 70.

Contemporary Literature, summer, 2007, Ylce Irizirry, interview with Garcia, p. 175.

Kirkus Reviews, March 15, 2003, review of *Cubanismo! The Vintage Book of Contemporary Cuban Literature*, p. 427; March 1, 2008, review of *The Dog Who Loved the Moon*.

Kliatt, July, 2008, Claire Rosser, review of *A Handbook to Luck*, p. 23.

Library Journal, March 15, 1997, Barbara Hoffert, review of *The Aguero Sisters*, p. 88; April 1, 2003, Mary Margaret Benson, review of *Monkey Hunting*, p. 128; June 15, 2003, Ron Ratliff, review of *Cubanismo!*, p. 71; September 15, 2006, Nedra Crowe Evers, review of *Bordering Fires*, p. 58.

Los Angeles Times, March 12, 1992, Richard Eder, review of *Dreaming in Cuban*, p. E10.

MELUS, fall, 2000, Katherine Payant, "From Alienation to Reconciliation in the Novels of Cristina Garcia," p. 163.

Nation, May 19, 1997, Ilan Stavans, review of *The Aguero Sisters*, p. 32.

New York Times, February 25, 1992, Michiko Kakutani, review of *Dreaming in Cuban*, p. C17; May 27, 1997, Michiko Kakutani, review of *The Aguero Sisters*, p. C16; June 24, 2003, Michiko Kakutani, review of *Monkey Hunting*, p. E6.

New York Times Book Review, May 17, 1992, Thulani Davis, review of *Dreaming in Cuban*, p. 14; May 18, 2003, Jennifer Schuessler, "Fantasy Island," p. 11.

Publishers Weekly, January 13, 1992, review of *Dreaming in Cuban*, p. 46; March 10, 1997, review of *The Aguero Sisters*, p. 48; April 7, 2003, review of *Monkey Hunting*, p. 48; January 8, 2007, review of *A Handbook to Luck*, p. 29; July 28, 2008, review of *I Wanna Be Your Shoebox*, p. 75.

Review of Contemporary Fiction, fall, 1997, Jane Juffer, review of *The Aguero Sisters*, p. 243.

School Library Journal, April, 2008, Madeline Walton-Hadlock, review of *The Dog Who Loved the Moon*, p. 108; October, 2008, Maria B. Salvadore, review of *I Wanna Be Your Shoebox*, p. 144.

Time, May 12, 1997, Pico Ayer, review of *The Aguero Sisters*, p. 88.

Tribune Books (Chicago, IL), June 8, 1997, Ruth Behar, review of *The Aguero Sisters*, sec. 14, p. 1.

Washington Post Book World, March 1, 1992, Alan West, review of *Dreaming in Cuban*, p. 9; July 13, 1997, Nina King, review of *The Aguero Sisters*, p. 1.

World Literature Today, winter, 1998, Ana Maria Hernandez, review of *The Aguero Sisters*, p. 134; winter, 2000, Rocio G. Davis, "Back to the Future: Mothers, Languages, and Homes in Cristina Garcia's *Dreaming in Cuban*," p. 60; May-June, 2008, Catherine Rendon, review of *A Handbook to Luck*, p. 60.*

*   *   *

GARLAND, Michael 1952-

Personal

Born 1952, in New York, NY; son of a police officer; married; wife's name Peggy; children: Katie, Alice, Kevin. *Education:* Pratt Institute, B.F.A., 1974. *Hobbies and other interests:* Painting landscapes.

Addresses

Home—Patterson, NY. *E-mail*—garlandmp@comcast.net.

Career

Author and illustrator of children's books. Formerly worked as a janitor in a nursing home and as a cab driver.

Awards, Honors

Certificates of merit, Society of Illustrators, 1981-88, 1990-92; *Booklist* Editor's Choice designation, and National Council on Social Studies/Children's Book Council Notable Children's Trade Book designation, both c.

1989, both for *My Cousin Katie;* California State Young Readers Award; Delaware State Reading Award; Texas Armadillo Reader's Choice Award; two silver medals, Society of Illustrators.

Writings

SELF-ILLUSTRATED

My Cousin Katie, T.Y. Crowell (New York, NY), 1989.

Circus Girl, Dutton Children's Books (New York, NY), 1993.

Dinner at Magritte's, Dutton Children's Books (New York, NY), 1995.

Mouse before Christmas, Dutton Children's Books (New York, NY), 1995.

Angel Cat, Boyds Mills Press (Honesdale, PA), 1998.

An Elf for Christmas, Dutton Children's Books (New York, NY), 1999.

The Big Stone, Millbrook Press (Brookfield, CT), 1999.

Icarus Swinebuckle, Albert Whitman (Morton Grove, IL), 2000.

Christmas Magic, Dutton Children's Books (New York, NY), 2001.

Last Night at the Zoo, Boyds Mills Press (Honesdale, PA), 2001.

Mystery Mansion: A Look-Again Book, Dutton Children's Books (New York, NY), 2001.

The President and Mom's Apple Pie, Dutton Children's Books (New York, NY), 2002.

Christmas City: A Look-Again Book, Dutton Children's Books (New York, NY), 2002.

Miss Smith's Incredible Storybook, Dutton Children's Books (New York, NY), 2003.

The Great Easter Egg Hunt: A Look-Again Book, Dutton Children's Books (New York, NY), 2005.

Miss Smith Reads Again!, Dutton Children's Books (New York, NY), 2006.

Hooray José!, Marshall Cavendish Children (Tarrytown, NY), 2007.

How Many Mice?, Dutton Children's Books (New York, NY), 2007.

King Puck, HarperCollins (New York, NY), 2007.

Americana Adventure: A Look-Again Book, Dutton Children's Books (New York, NY), 2008.

Miss Smith and the Haunted Library, Dutton Children's Books (New York, NY), 2009.

ILLUSTRATOR

Lucille Clifton, *Sonora the Beautiful,* Dutton (New York, NY), 1981.

Dale Carlson, *The Frog People,* Dutton (New York, NY), 1982.

Washington Irving, *The Legend of Sleepy Hollow: Found among the Papers of the Late Diedrich Knickerbocker,* Caroline House (Honesdale, PA), 1992.

Max Lucado, *Alabaster's Song: Christmas through the Eyes of an Angel,* Word Publications (Dallas, TX), 1996.

Elizabeth Friedrich, *Leah's Pony,* Boyds Mills Press (Honesdale, PA), 1996.

Corinne Demas Bliss, *Electra and the Charlotte Russe,* Boyds Mills Press (Honesdale, PA), 1997.

Marlene Targ Brill, *Diary of a Drummer Boy,* Millbrook Press (Brookfield, CT), 1998.

Ann Tompert, *Saint Patrick,* Boyds Mills Press (Honesdale, PA), 1998.

Ann Tompert, *Saint Nicholas,* Boyds Mills Press (Honesdale, PA), 2000.

Holy Bible: Children's Illustrated Edition, Nelsonword (Nashville, TN), 2001.

Debbie Bertram and Susan Bloom, *The Best Place to Read,* Random House (New York, NY), 2003.

Ann Tompert, *Joan of Arc: Heroine of France,* Boyds Mills Press (Honesdale, PA), 2003.

Stu Smith, *Goldilocks and the Three Martians,* Dutton Children's Books (New York, NY), 2004.

James Patterson, *SantaKid,* Little, Brown (New York, NY), 2004.

Kimberly Wagner Klier, *Firefly Friend,* Children's Press (New York, NY), 2004.

Gloria Estefan, *The Magically Mysterious Adventures of Noelle the Bulldog,* Rayo (New York, NY), 2005.

Steven Kroll, *Pooch on the Loose: A Christmas Adventure,* Marshall Cavendish Children (New York, NY), 2005.

Debbie Bertram and Susan Bloom, *The Best Time to Read,* Random House (New York, NY), 2005.

Gloria Estefan, *Noelle's Treasure Tale: A New Magically Mysterious Adventure,* Rayo (New York, NY), 2006.

Margery Cuyler, *That's Good! That's Bad! In Washington, DC,* Henry Holt (New York, NY), 2007.

Debbie Bertram and Susan Bloom, *The Best Place to Read,* Dragonfly Books (New York, NY), 2007.

Debbie Bertram and Susan Bloom, *The Best Book to Read,* Random House Children's Books (New York, NY), 2008.

Carole Roberts, *Beth's Job,* Sandpiper (Boston, MA), 2009.

Margery Cuyler, *That's Good! That's Bad! on Santa's Journey,* Henry Holt (New York, NY), 2009.

Adaptations

Miss Smith's Incredible Storybook was adapted for video, Spoken Arts, 2006.

Sidelights

Michael Garland began his career as an illustrator of children's books and he now both writes and illustrates works in a number of areas, including biography, picture books, and puzzle-and-story combinations. Both as an author and illustrator, Garland's work is known for its imagination, charm, and energy. His illustrations were described as "a slick fusion of soft and razor-edged computer images that sport electric coloring and quirky shading" by a *Kirkus Reviews* contributor in appraising Garland's work for Debbie Bertram and Susan Bloom's *The Best Place to Read.* Reviewing *Joan of Arc: Heroine of France* in *Publishers Weekly,* the artist "blend[s] mostly flat, postmodern perspectives with photo-collage elements and a spectrum of styles, from painterly to folk-like to . . . almost puckish," in bringing to life Ann Tompert's picture-book biography.

Michael Garland creates inspired illustrations to bring to life Max Lucado's picture book **Alabaster's Song.** (Tommy Nelson, a division of Thomas Nelson, Inc., 1996. Illustration © 1996 by Michael Garland. Reproduced by permission.)

Garland suspected from a very young age that he would grow up to be an artist. "I wasn't the smartest one in my class or the best athlete in any sport," he recalled on the Penguin Group USA Web site, "but when they passed out the paper and crayons, it was my time to shine." Drawing was a frequent feature of Garland's early work, as well as painting; he is particularly respected for his skill in acrylic painting. *Electra and the Charlotte Russe* was his first foray into computer-assisted illustration, a technique for which he has also become well known. He continues to use both traditional methods—painting and drawing—as well as computer techniques in his art.

My Cousin Katie, Garland's debut as an author/illustrator, is the story of a young child and her life on a farm. During the visit of a cousin, all of the farm activities are depicted both visually and by means of the text, and the reader sees Katie as a real participant in the life of the farm. Garland employs a simple vocabulary to depict this experience, making the story appropriate for young children. *School Library Journal* reviewer Janet DiGianni called attention to the illustrator's technique of rendering scenes and objects from a child's perspective, thus reinforcing Katie's view of the scale of life. Critics have commented on Garland's use of a realistic style imbued with a certain idealism that conveys a romantic vision of rural farm life.

Like *My Cousin Katie, Circus Girl* presents a child's life that is substantially different from the more-familiar urban or suburban model. The author has imagined, in book form, the life of an extended family of circus performers. Father performs as a clown, while mother is a tightrope walker. Alice, the circus girl, and the rest of the family are all involved in the work that makes the show possible. There is no plot, but rather a group of scenes depicting everyday activities that make up life in the circus. Garland again employed a realistic style, with a bright palette of acrylic paints. Carolyn Phelan, writing in *Booklist* praised the fanciful final scene where the father, in full clown regalia, reads a bedtime story to Alice and cages full of enthralled wild animals.

One of many original, self-illustrated books by Garland, *Dinner at Magritte's* was inspired by the artist/author's long-held interest in surrealism. In the *New York Times Book Review,* the book was complimented for its wit and value as sophisticated entertainment. Garland's other books frequently feature the same fanciful quality; *The President and Mom's Apple Pie,* a tale of President William Howard Taft's legendary appetite, *Icarus Swinebuckle, Hooray José!,* and *King Puck* have all been recognized for their charm and humor.

In *The President and Mom's Apple Pie* Garland imagines what might have happened if Taft had gotten distracted on a trip to a small town in 1909. A small boy narrates how the 300-pound president came to his town to dedicate a new flagpole, but instead set off in search of the source of a wonderful smell. Taft's quest takes him to an Italian restaurant, a barbeque joint, and Mrs. Wong's Hunan Palace before he finds the source: an apple pie cooling on the boy's own windowsill. "The colorful, playful illustrations capture the energy of the comical situation," wrote a *Kirkus Reviews* contributor, and in *Booklist* Connie Fletcher wrote that Garland's "bold, eye-popping artwork fairly leaps off the page."

A little mouse with a love of sports is the star of *Hooray José!,* a picture book that features Garland's colorful, computer-enhanced art and a "buoyant, rhyming text [that] keeps the plot moving quickly," according to *School Library Journal* critic Joy Fleishhacker. In the story, José is never asked to play during pick-up basketball games, but he practices his on-court technique anyway, hoping for his big break. Finally, the little mouse gets his chance to shine, when he is called from the bench during a championship face-off between the Mice and the Rats.

A fanciful tale that is based on an Irish legend, *King Puck* takes readers to Ireland, where Seamus the farmer and his goat Finny live a quiet, simple life. It is also a lonely life, however, but when Seamus wishes for someone to talk with, his wish is granted and Finny begins to speak. The goat's talents are eventually heralded far and wide, when the goat wins a festival in the town of Killorglin and becomes king for a day. As a reward, both man and goat are treated to regular visits from a Killorglin librarian, who keeps them supplied with entertaining books to read and discuss. Predicting that young people will enjoy the book's "lively, colorful pictures," Lee Bock added in his *Booklist* review that *King Puck* "is a simple, silly story that youngsters will enjoy."

Garland's self-illustrated stories include *Miss Smith's Incredible Storybook,* the first in a series of books that feature a second grader named Zack and Zack's very unusual teacher. Miss Smith styles her bright, orange-red hair in spikes and wears a leather jacket, but to the students in her class, the most unusual thing about her is her magical, leather-bound storybook. When she opens this book and reads aloud, the characters emerge to roam the classroom, which itself is transformed into a forest or pirate ship or whatever else is featured in the tale. At story's end, the book closes and everything returns to normal. One day, when Miss Smith is late in arriving at school, the principal opens the magic book to read—and promptly flees in terror when a dragon emerges from the pages. The students in Zack's class

Garland captures viewer attention with playful perspectives in his illustrations for Corinne Demas Bliss's **Electra and the Charlotte Russe.** (Boyd's Mill Press, 1997. Illustration copyright © 1997 by Michael Garland. Reproduced by permission.)

add to the chaos, reading the beginnings of more and more stories but never finishing any of them, causing characters from the Cowardly Lion to the Mad Hatter to crowd into the school. In characteristic fashion, Garland's "lively, bright illustrations have a glossy, computer-generated quality . . . that young readers will appreciate," Catherine Threadgill remarked in her review of *Miss Smith's Incredible Storybook* for *School Library Journal.*

Miss Smith returns in *Miss Smith Reads Again!* and *Miss Smith and the Haunted Library,* both of which find the carrot-topped teacher turning the pages of her magical storybook. In *Miss Smith and the Haunted Library* she chooses a tale that allows all manner of frights to invade Zack's class, while in *Miss Smith Reads Again!* the children are taken to a prehistoric jungle during their teacher's reading of Arthur Conan Doyle's *The Lost World.* When Zack changes the plot, and their teacher is carried aloft to a pterodactyl's nest, he and his fellow students find themselves at the mercy of a hungry T-Rex until the boy makes a plot correction and deals with the dinosaur threat. Reviewing *Miss Smith Reads Again! School Library Journal* contributor Maura Bresnahan maintained that Garland's focus on one story combines with his story's "nonstop action" to "win an even larger audience of fans" than he did with Miss Smith's first picture-book outing. In *Kirkus Reviews* a contributor concluded that Garland's mix of "glossy, elaborately detailed" artwork, likeable characters, and "exciting adventures" will "draw" young readers.

Garland has also produced several "search-and-find" combination story-and-puzzle books. *Christmas Magic: A Look-Again Book, Mystery Mansion: A Look-Again Book, Christmas City: A Look-Again Book, The Great Easter Egg Hunt: A Look-Again Book,* and *Americana Adventure: A Look-Again Book* are structured around a boy named Tommy and Tommy's Aunt Jeanne. The aunt uses rhymed clues to lead Tommy on mysterious searches through fantastic landscapes—*The Great Easter Egg Hunt,* for example, features a ten-foot-tall chocolate bunny and a Fifth Avenue Easter parade that has been crashed by Santa Claus, a Halloween witch, and a leprechaun, while *Americana Adventure* finds Tommy on a U.S. history tour to commemorate Independence Day, guided by his aunt's cryptic notes. At the end of each hunt is a lovely surprise.

Garland's hunts are complex—over four hundred animals are hidden in the illustrations for *Mystery Mansion,* for example—and this makes finding the hidden objects all a challenge that will keep puzzle-loving kids coming back. The "Look-Again" books have received favorable notice for their opulent and complex illustrations and have been recognized for presenting challenges both to the intellect and the imagination; reviewing *Americana,* Martha Topol wrote in *School Library*

Journal that the book "takes the search-and-find game to a new level" by "providing a fun entry into history" for its readers. A reviewer for *Publishers Weekly* noted of *Mystery Mansion* that Garland's digital art adds considerably to the attractiveness of the book and the experience it evokes, while Linda L. Walkins, reviewing *The Great Easter Egg Hunt* for *School Library Journal,* called the artwork "vibrant" and "eye-catching." "Garland . . . pulls out all the digital stops" in *Christmas City,* according to Phelan, the *Booklist* critic adding that the author/illustrator creates "an ornately detailed, architectural fantasy of a grand metropolis."

Biographical and Critical Sources

PERIODICALS

Booklist, September 1, 1989, Denise Wilms, review of *My Cousin Katie,* p. 70; November 1, 1992, Carolyn Phelan, review of *The Legend of Sleepy Hollow: Found among the Papers of the Late Diedrich Knickerbocker,* p. 513; June 1, 1993, Carolyn Phelan, review of *Circus Girl,* p. 1856; March 1, 1996, Susan Dove Lempke, review of *Leah's Pony,* p. 1187; October 15, 1997, Julie Corsaro, review of *The Mouse before Christmas,* p. 414; February 1, 1998, Ilene Cooper, review of *Saint Patrick,* p. 916; November 1, 1999, Kathy Broderick, review of *An Elf for Christmas,* p. 538; February 15, 2000, John Peters, review of *Icarus Swinebuckle,* p. 1117; July, 2001, Connie Fletcher, review of *Last Night at the Zoo,* p. 2019; September 1, 2001, Catherine Andronik, review of *Christmas Magic,* p. 120; March 1, 2002, Connie Fletcher, review of *The President and Mom's Apple Pie,* p. 1140; October 1, 2002, Carolyn Phelan, review of *Christmas City: A Look-Again Book,* p. 335; February 15, 2005, Julie Cummins, review of *The Great Easter Egg Hunt: A Look-Again Book,* p. 1084; March 15, 2005, Julie Cummins, review of *The Best Time to Read,* p. 1662; September 1, 2005, Ilene Cooper, review of *Pooch on the Loose: A Christmas Adventure,* p. 144; June 1, 2007, Shelle Rosenfeld, review of *How Many Mice?,* p. 80; April 15, 2008, Shelle Rosenfeld, review of *The Best Books to Read,* p. 48; May 15, 2008, Bina Williams, review of *Americana Adventure: A Look-again Book,* p. 45.

Bulletin of the Center for Children's Books, April, 1993, review of *Circus Girl,* p. 247; April, 1995, review of *Dinner at Magritte's,* p. 273; November, 2001, review of *Christmas Magic,* p. 102.

Catholic Library World, March, 1999, Charlotte Decker, review of *Angel Cat,* p. 48.

Childhood Education, fall, 2001, Valerie Deysher, review of *Last Night at the Zoo,* p. 49.

***Garland combines his original story with his colorful art in the picture book* Americana Adventure.** (Illustration © 2008 by Michael Garland. All rights reserved. Reproduced by permission of Dutton Children's Books, a division of Penguin Putnam Books for Young Readers.)

Children's Book Review Service, winter, 1990, review of *My Cousin Katie,* p. 62; January, 1999, review of *Angel Cat,* p. 50; April, 1999, review of *The Big Stone,* p. 104.

Horn Book, July-August, 1995, Mary M. Burns, review of *Dinner at Magritte's,* p. 450.

Kirkus Reviews, October 15, 1998, review of *Angel Cat,* p. 1531; September 15, 1999, review of *An Elf for Christmas,* p. 1499; April 1, 2000, review of *Icarus Swinebuckle,* p. 474; May 1, 2002, review of *The President and Mom's Apple Pie,* p. 653; November 1, 2002, review of *Christmas City,* p. 1618; December 1, 2002, review of *The Best Place to Read,* p. 1766; June 1, 2003, review of *Miss Smith's Incredible Storybook,* p. 803; December 15, 2004, review of *The Great Easter Egg Hunt,* p. 1201; July 1, 2005, review of

The Best Time to Read, p. 731; June 1, 2006, review of *Miss Smith Reads Again!,* p. 571; December 15, 2006, review of *King Puck,* p. 1267; April 1, 2007, review of *How Many Mice?;* July 1, 2007, review of *That's Good! That's Bad! In Washington, DC;* April 15, 2008, review of *Americana Adventure;* May 1, 2008, review of *The Best Book to Read.*

New York Times Book Review, September 24, 1995, review of *Dinner at Magritte's,* p. 29; June 16, 2002, Rebecca Boggs Roberts, review of *The President and Mom's Apple Pie,* p. 20.

Publishers Weekly, May 31, 1993, review of *Circus Girl,* p. 54; May 22, 1995, review of *Dinner at Magritte's,* p. 59; October 6, 1997, review of *The Mouse before Christmas,* p. 54; January 26, 1998, review of *Saint Patrick,* p. 86; September 27, 1999, review of *An Elf*

for Christmas, p. 55; March 6, 2000, review of *Icarus Swinebuckle,* p. 111; September 25, 2000, review of *Saint Nicholas,* p. 113; January 22, 2001, review of *Last Night at the Zoo,* p. 324; July 2, 2001, review of *Mystery Mansion: A Look-Again Book,* p. 75; September 24, 2001, review of *Christmas Magic,* p. 50; March 25, 2002, review of *The President and Mom's Apple Pie,* p. 63; February 10, 2003, review of *Joan of Arc: Heroine of France,* p. 187; June 9, 2003, review of *Miss Smith's Incredible Storybook,* p. 51; September 26, 2005, review of *Pooch on the Loose,* p. 86.

School Library Journal, November, 1989, Janet DiGianni, review of *My Cousin Katie,* p. 80; November, 1992, Andrew W. Hunter, review of *The Legend of Sleepy Hollow,* p. 94; December, 1993, Louise L. Sherman, review of *Circus Girl,* pp. 86-87; March, 1996, Liza Bliss, review of *Leah's Pony,* p. 173; October, 1997, Carolyn Jenks, review of *Electra and the Charlotte Russe,* p. 88; March, 1998, Patricia Pearl Dole, review of *Saint Patrick,* p. 207; May, 1998, Jackie Hechtkopf, review of *Diary of a Drummer Boy,* p. 107; October, 1998, Patricia Pearl Dole, review of *Angel Cat,* p. 100; June, 1999, Jackie Hechtkopf, review of *The Big Stone,* p. 95; October, 1999, review of *An Elf for Christmas,* p. 67; October, 2000, review of *Saint Nicholas,* p. 63; May, 2001, Blair Christolon, review of *Last Night at the Zoo,* p. 115; September, 2001, John Peters, *Mystery Mansion,* p. 188; October, 2001, review of *Christmas Magic,* p. 65; June, 2002, Alicia Eames, review of *The President and Mom's Apple Pie,* p. 94; October, 2002, Maureen Wade, review of *Christmas City,* p. 59; March, 2003, Ann Welton, review of *Joan of Arc,* p. 225; May, 2003, Kathie Meizner, review of *The Best Place to Read,* p. 108; October, 2003, Catherine Threadgill, review of *Miss Smith's Incredible Storybook,* p. 125; February, 2005, Linda L. Walkins, review of *The Great Easter Egg Hunt,* p. 97; July, 2006, Maura Bresnahan, review of *Miss Smith Reads Again!,* p. 78; February, 2007, Lee Bock, review of *King Puck,* p. 86; May, 2007, Joy Fleishhacker, review of *Hooray José!,* p. 97; June, 2007, Jessica Lamarre, review of *How Many Mice?,* p. 97; September, 2007, Wendy Lukehart, review of *That's Good! That's Bad! In Washington, DC,* p. 161; June, 2008, Lee Bock, review of *The Best Book to Read,* p. 95, and Martha Topol, review of *Americana Adventure,* p. 123.

Wilson Library Bulletin, November, 1992, Frances Bradburn, review of *The Legend of Sleepy Hollow,* p. 74.

ONLINE

Boyds Mills Press Web site, http://www.boydsmillspress.com/ (November 20, 2009), "Authors and Illustrators: Michael Garland."

Michael Garland Home Page, http://www.garlandpicturebooks.com (November, 20, 2009).

Penguin Group USA Web site, http://us.penguingroup.com/ (January 26, 2006), "Michael Garland."*

GIOVANNI, Nikki 1943-
(Yolande Cornelia Giovanni, Yolande Cornelia Giovanni, Jr.)

Personal

Born Yolande Cornelia Giovanni, Jr., June 7, 1943, in Knoxville, TN; daughter of Gus Jones (a probation officer) and Yolande Cornelia (a social worker) Giovanni; children: Thomas Watson. *Education:* Fisk University, B.A. (with honors), 1967; postgraduate studies at University of Pennsylvania School of Social Work and Columbia University School of Fine Arts, 1968.

Addresses

Office—Department of English, Virginia Tech, 403 Shanks Hall, Blacksburg, VA 24061.

Career

Poet, writer, activist, educator, commentator, reviewer, critic, and lecturer. Queens College of the City University of New York, Flushing, NY, assistant professor of black studies, 1968; Rutgers University, Livingston College, New Brunswick, NJ, associate professor of English, 1968-72; College of Mount St. Joseph on the Ohio, Mount St. Joseph, OH, professor of creative writing, 1985-87; Virginia Tech, Blacksburg, VA, professor of English, 1987-99, Gloria D. Smith Professor of Black Studies, 1997-99, university distinguished professor, 1999—. Ohio State University, Columbus, visiting professor of English, 1984; Texas Christian University, visiting professor in humanities, 1991; University of Oregon, Martin Luther King, Jr., visiting professor, 1992; University of Minnesota, Hill visiting professor, 1993; Indiana University, Kokomo, visiting professor, 1995; Fisk University, visiting distinguished professor, 2007. Philadelphia Clef Club of Jazz and Performing Arts, artist in residence, 1996-97; Walt Whitman Birthplace, poet-in-residence, 2004-05. Founder of publishing firm, NikTom Ltd., 1970; participated in "Soul at the Center," Lincoln Center for the Performing Arts, 1972; co-chair, Literary Arts Festival for State of Tennessee Homecoming, 1986; appointed to Ohio Humanities Council, 1987; director, Warm Hearth Writer's Workshop, 1988—; member of board of directors, Virginia Foundation for Humanities and Public Policy, 1990-93, and Mill Mountain Theatre, 2001—; member of national advisory board, National Underground Museum and Freedom Center, 1997—, and member of multimedia advisory panel for Virginia Museum of Fine Arts, 2002—; participant in Appalachian Community Fund, 1991-93, and Volunteer Action Center, 1991-94; featured poet, International Poetry Festival, Utrecht, Holland, 1991. Has given numerous poetry readings and lectures worldwide and appeared on numerous television talk shows, including *Soul!* and *Tonight Show.*

Member

National Council of Negro Women (recipient of life membership and Scroll), Society of Magazine Writers,

Nikki Giovanni (Reproduced by permission.)

National Black Heroines for PUSH, Winnie Mandela Children's Fund Committee, PEN, Delta Sigma Theta (honorary member), Phi Beta Kappa.

Awards, Honors

Grants from Ford Foundation, 1967, National Endowment for the Arts, 1968, and Harlem Cultural Council, 1969; named among Ten Most Admired Black Women, *Amsterdam News,* 1969; named Woman of the Year, *Ebony,* 1970; outstanding achievement award, *Mademoiselle,* 1971; Omega Psi Phi Fraternity Award, 1971, for outstanding contribution to arts and letters; Meritorious Plaque for Service, Cook County Jail, 1971; Prince Matchabelli Sun Shower Award, 1971; National Association of Radio and Television Announcers Award for Best Spoken-Word Album, 1972, for recording *Truth Is on Its Way;* Woman of the Year Youth Leadership Award, *Ladies' Home Journal,* 1972; National Book Award nomination, 1973, for *Gemini;* Best Books for Young Adults citation, American Library Association (ALA), 1973, for *My House;* Woman of the Year citation, Cincinnati Chapter of YWCA, 1983; elected to Ohio Women's Hall of Fame, 1985; Outstanding Woman of Tennessee citation, 1985; Post-Corbett Award, 1986; Distinguished Recognition Award, Detroit City Council, 1986; Ohioana Book Award, 1988; Silver Apple Award, Oakland Museum Film Festival, 1988, for *Spirit to Spirit;* named Woman of the Year, National Association for the Advancement of Colored People (NAACP; Lynchburg chapter), 1989; Tennessee Writer's Award, *Nashville Banner,* 1994; Jeanine Rae Award for the Advancement of Women's Culture, 1995; Langston Hughes Award, 1996; Image Award, NAACP, 1998, for *Love Poems,* and 2000, for *Blues;* Tennessee Governor's Award, 1998; inducted into National Literary Hall of Fame for Writers of African Descent, 1998-99; Appalachian Medallion Award, 1998-99; Virginia Governor's Award for the Arts, 2000; Certificate of Commendation, U.S. Senate, 2000; SHero Award for Lifetime Achievement, 2002; Rosa Parks Woman of Courage Award, 2001; Black Caucus Award for nonfiction, ALA, and NAACP Image Award for Outstanding Literary Work, both 2003, both for *Quilting the Black-eyed Pea;* Grammy Award nomination, 2003, for *The Nikki Giovanni Poetry Collection;* East Tennessee Writers Hall of Fame Award for Poetry, 2004-05; John Henry "Pop" Lloyd Humanitarian Award, 2004-05; HUES Leadership Network for Women of Color Award, University of Virginia Women's Center, 2006; Oppenheim Toy Portfolio Best Book Award, *Child* magazine Best Children's Book of the Year Award, and Caldecott Honor Book designation, all 2006, all for *Rosa;* Carl Sandburg Literary Award, Chicago Public Library Foundation, 2007; Gwendolyn Brooks/John O. Killens Award, 2007; Notable Social Studies Trade Book for Young People, National Council for the Social Studies/Children's Book Council, 2008, for *On My Journey Now;* Sankofa Freedom Award, African American Resource Center, 2008; Women of Power Legacy Award, Black Enterprise, 2008; NAACP Image Award for Poetry, 2008, for *Acolytes;* National Parenting Publications Gold Award, 2008, and NAACP Image Award, 2009, both for *Hip Hop Speaks to Children;* American Book Award, 2008, for *The Collected Poetry of Nikki Giovanni: 1968-1998;* Alumni Award for Outreach Excellence, Virginia Tech, 2009; Reverend Martin Luther King, Jr. Award, Lehigh University, 2009; selected to recite poetry at presidential inauguration and Lincoln Bicentennial, both Washington, DC, 2009. Recipient of honorary degrees from Wilberforce University, 1972, University of Maryland (Princess Anne campus), 1974, Ripon University, 1974, Smith College, 1975, College of Mount St. Joseph on the Ohio, 1985, Mount Saint Mary College, 1987, Fisk University, 1988, Indiana University, 1991, Otterbein College, 1992, Rockhurst College, 1993, Widener University, 1993, Albright College, 1995, Cabrini College, 1995, Allegheny College, 1997, Delaware State University, 1998, Martin University, 1999, Wilmington University, 1999, Manhattanville College, 2000, State University of West Georgia, 2001, Central State University, 2001, Pace University, 2002, West Virginia University, 2003, Florida A&M University, 2003, and Dillard University, 2009. Recipient of keys to numerous cities, including Dallas, TX, New York, NY, Cincinnati, OH, Miami, FL, New Orleans, LA, Baltimore, MD, Mobile, AL, St. Petersburg, FL, Saginaw, MI, and Los Angeles, CA.

Writings

POETRY

Black Feeling, Black Talk (also see below), Broadside Press (Detroit, MI), 1968, 3rd edition, 1970.

Black Judgment (also see below), Broadside Press (Detroit, MI), 1968.

Black Feeling, Black Talk/Black Judgment (omnibus), Morrow (New York, NY), 1970, selection published as *Knoxville, Tennessee,* illustrated by Larry Johnson, Scholastic (New York, NY), 1994.

Re: Creation, Broadside Press (Detroit, MI), 1970.

Poem of Angela Yvonne Davis, Afro Arts (New York, NY), 1970.

My House, foreword by Ida Lewis, Morrow (New York, NY), 1972.

The Women and the Men, Morrow (New York, NY), 1975.

Cotton Candy on a Rainy Day, introduction by Paula Giddings, Morrow (New York, NY), 1978.

Those Who Ride the Night Winds, Morrow (New York, NY), 1983.

The Selected Poems of Nikki Giovanni, 1968-1995, Morrow (New York, NY), 1996.

Love Poems, Morrow (New York, NY), 1997.

Blues: For All the Changes—New Poems, Morrow (New York, NY), 1999.

Quilting the Black-eyed Pea: Poems and Not Quite Poems, Morrow (New York, NY), 2002.

Prosaic Soul of Nikki Giovanni, HarperCollins (New York, NY), 2003.

The Collected Poetry of Nikki Giovanni: 1968-1998, Morrow (New York, NY), 2003.

The Girls in the Circle, illustrated by Cathy Ann Johnson, Scholastic (New York, NY), 2004.

Acolytes, William Morrow (New York, NY), 2007.

Bicycles: Love Poems, Morrow (New York, NY), 2009.

FOR CHILDREN

Spin a Soft Black Song: Poems for Children, illustrated by Charles Bible, Hill & Wang (New York, NY), 1971, illustrated by George Martins, Lawrence Hill (Westport, CT), 1985, revised edition, Farrar, Straus (New York, NY), 1987.

Ego-Tripping and Other Poems for Young People, illustrated by George Ford, Lawrence Hill (Chicago, IL), 1973.

Vacation Time: Poems for Children, illustrated by Marisabina Russo, Morrow (New York, NY), 1980.

The Genie in the Jar, illustrated by Chris Raschka, Holt (New York, NY), 1996.

The Sun Is So Quiet, illustrated by Ashley Bryant, Holt (New York, NY), 1996.

Rosa, illustrated by Bryan Collier, Henry Holt (New York, NY), 2005.

The Grasshopper's Song: An Aesop's Fable Revisited, illustrated by Chris Raschka, Candlewick Press (Cambridge, MA), 2008.

Lincoln and Douglass: An American Friendship, illustrated by Bryan Collier, Henry Holt (New York, NY), 2008.

(Editor) *Hip Hop Speaks to Children: A Celebration of Poetry with a Beat,* Sourcebooks/Jabberwocky (Naperville, IL), 2008.

SOUND RECORDINGS

Truth Is on Its Way (album), Atlantis, 1971.

Like a Ripple on a Pond (album), Collectibles, 1973.

The Way I Feel (album), Atlantic, 1975.

Legacies—The Poetry of Nikki Giovanni (album), Folkways, 1976.

The Reason I Like Chocolate (and Other Children's Poems) (album), Folkways, 1976.

Cotton Candy on a Rainy Day (album), Folkways, 1978.

Nikki Giovanni and the New York Community Choir (album), Collectibles, 1993.

In Philadelphia (album), Collectibles, 1997.

Stealing Home: For Jack Robinson (album), Sony, 1997.

Our Souls Have Grown Deep like the Rivers (compilation), Rhino, 2000.

The Nikki Giovanni Poetry Collection (CD), HarperAudio, 2002.

OTHER

(Editor) *Night Comes Softly: An Anthology of Black Female Voices,* Medic Press (Newark, NJ), 1970.

Gemini: An Extended Autobiographical Statement on My First Twenty-five Years of Being a Black Poet, Bobbs-Merrill (Indianapolis, IN), 1971.

(With James Baldwin) *A Dialogue: James Baldwin and Nikki Giovanni,* Lippincott (Philadelphia, PA), 1973.

(With Margaret Walker) *A Poetic Equation: Conversations between Nikki Giovanni and Margaret Walker,* Howard University Press (Washington, DC), 1974, revised edition, 1983.

(Author of introduction) Adele Stephanie Sebastian, *Intro to Finé* (poems), Woman in the Moon, 1985.

Sacred Cows . . . and Other Edibles (essays), Morrow (New York, NY), 1988.

(Editor, with C. Dennison) *Appalachian Elders: A Warm Hearth Sampler,* Pocahontas Press (Blacksburg, VA), 1991.

(Author of foreword) *The Abandoned Baobob: The Autobiography of a Woman,* Chicago Review Press (Chicago, IL), 1991.

Racism 101 (essays), Morrow (New York, NY), 1994.

(Editor) *Grand Mothers: Poems, Reminiscences, and Short Stories about the Keepers of Our Traditions,* Holt (New York, NY), 1994.

(Editor) *Shimmy Shimmy Shimmy like My Sister Kate: Looking at the Harlem Renaissance through Poems,* Holt (New York, NY), 1995.

(Editor) *Grand Fathers: Reminiscences, Poems, Recipes, and Photos of the Keepers of Our Traditions,* Holt (New York, NY), 1999.

(Author of foreword) Margaret Ann Reid, *Black Protest Poetry: Polemics from the Harlem Renaissance and the Sixties,* Peter Lang (New York, NY), 2001.

On My Journey Now: Looking at African-American History through the Spirituals, foreword by Arthur C. Jones, Candlewick Press (Cambridge, MA), 2007.

Contributor to books and anthologies, including *The Black Woman: An Anthology,* edited by Toni Cade, New American Library (New York, NY), 1970; *Brothers and Sisters,* edited by Arnold Adoff, Macmillan (New York, NY), 1970; *Black Women Writers, 1950-1980: A Critical Evaluation,* edited by Mari Evans, Anchor/Doubleday (New York, NY), 1984; *Lure and Loathing: The Ambivalence of Assimilation,* edited by Gerald Early, Viking/Penguin (New York, NY), 1991; *African American Literature: An Anthology of Nonfiction, Fiction, Poetry, and Drama,* edited by Demetrice Worley and Jesse Perry, Jr., National Textbook Company (Lincolnwood, IL), 1993; *I Know What the Red Clay Looks Like: The Voice and Vision of Black Women Writers,* edited by Rebecca Carroll, Crown (New York, NY), 1994; *My Soul Is a Witness: African-American Women's Spirituality,* edited by Gloria Wade-Gayles, Beacon Press (Boston, MA), 1995; *I Am the Darker Brother: An Anthology of Modern Poems by African Americans,* edited by Arnold Adoff, Simon & Schuster (New York, NY), 1997; *How to Make Black America Better,* compiled and edited by Tavis Smiley, Doubleday (New York, NY), 2000; *Out of the Rough: Women's Poems of Survival and Celebration,* edited by Dorothy Perry Thompson, Novello Festival Press (Charlotte, NC), 2001; *In Praise of Our Teachers,* edited by Gloria Wade-Gayles, Beacon Press, 2003; and *Breaking the Silence: Inspirational Stories of Black Cancer Survivors,* edited by Karin Stanford, Hilton Publishing Company (Chicago, IL), 2005.

Contributor to periodicals, including *Black Creation, Black World, Ebony, Essence, Freedom Ways, Journal of Black Poetry, Negro Digest, Conversation, Black Graphics International, Afro-American Woman Magazine, Black Works, Encore, Saturday Review of Education, International Educational and Cultural Exchange, New York Times, New Yorker, Journal of Blacks in Higher Education, Literary Cavalcade, San Francisco Examiner, Career Insights, Ohioana Quarterly, Catalyst, Black Collegian, Georgia Review, Proteus, Cincinnati Enquirer, New York Times Magazine, Roanoke Times, Tennessee English Journal, Vibe, Umbra,* and *O, the Oprah Magazine.*

Contributor to *Voices of Diversity: The Power of Book Publishing* (videotape), Diversity Committee of the Association of American Publishers/Kaufman Films, 2002. Editorial consultant, Encore American and Worldwide News.

A selection of Giovanni's public papers is housed at Mugar Memorial Library, Boston University.

Adaptations

Many of Giovanni's poems have been recorded to audiocassette and compact disc.

Sidelights

One of the most prominent poets to emerge from the black literary movement of the late 1960s, Nikki Giovanni is famous for strongly voiced poems that testify to her evolving awareness and experience: as a daughter and young girl, a black woman, a revolutionary in the civil rights movement, and a mother. Giovanni's poetry explores a full range of themes—from womanhood to slavery to romantic love—and draws images and rhythms from sources as varied as the Bible, hymns, jazz, popular music, and colloquial speech. Her informal style makes her work accessible to both adults and children. In addition to collections such as *Re: Creation* and *Acolytes,* Giovanni has published several acclaimed books for children, including *Ego Tripping and Other Poems for Young People, The Genie in the Jar,* and *Rosa.* Like her adult works, "Giovanni's poems for children . . . exhibit a combination of casual energy and sudden wit," wrote Nancy Klein in the *New York Times Book Review.*

According to Andrea King Collier in *Writer,* Giovanni's "work stands as a history lesson and a window on the future of our culture. She has become a literary rock star, drawing grandparents, parents and high school kids chanting 'Nikki, Nikki' to her readings. Her work is edgy, honest and politically aware; some call her viewpoints radical. But Giovanni clearly sees herself as a writer and artist, not an activist. It is her interest in understanding the past that helps her make sense of the future." In the introduction to *Cotton Candy on a Rainy Day,* Paula Giddings praised the poet's commitment to her work: "Giovanni is a witness. Her intelligent eye has caught the experience of a generation and dutifully recorded it. . . . I have never known anyone who cares so much and so intensely about the things she sees around her as Nikki."

The author was born Yolande Cornelia Giovanni in 1943 in Knoxville, Tennessee, a city nestled in the Smoky Mountains. Her family life was a happy one, and the strong-willed and independent Giovanni was particularly close to both her older sister Gary, who studied music, and her maternal grandmother, Louvenia Terrell Watson. Her grandmother—an outspoken women—instilled in the young Nikki an intense admiration and appreciation for her race. Other members of her family influenced her in the oral tradition of poetry. "I come from a long line of storytellers," she once commented. "My grandfather was a Latin scholar and he loved the myths, and my mother is a big romanticist, so we heard a lot of stories growing up. . . . I appreciated the quality and the rhythm of the telling of the stories, and I know when I started to write that I wanted to retain that—I didn't want to become the kind of writer that was stilted or that used language in ways that could not be spoken."

When Giovanni was still young, she moved with her family to a suburb of Cincinnati, Ohio, but she remained close to her grandmother and spent several of her teen years in Knoxville. As a teenager, she was conservative in her outlook—a supporter of Republican presidential candidate Barry Goldwater and a follower of writer Ayn Rand, who was famous for her philosophy of objectivism. In 1960, at the age of seventeen, Giovanni enrolled in Nashville's all-black Fisk University. There, her independent nature caused her to abide by her own rules, and she was eventually asked by school officials to leave. She returned to Fisk in 1964, however, and became a dedicated student—one focused on both political and literary activities. She edited a campus literary magazine, *Elan,* and also participated in writing workshops. Politically awakened to the changes occurring on the American social scene in the 1960s, Giovanni helped restore Fisk's chapter of the SNCC (Student Non-Violent Coordinating Committee) at a time when SNCC was pressing the concept of "black power" to bring about social and economic reform. In 1967, Giovanni graduated from Fisk with an honors degree in history and a commitment to become a poet and a voice for the black movement.

Giovanni's first published volume of poetry grew out of her response to the assassinations of Martin Luther King, Jr., Malcolm X, Medgar Evers, and Robert Kennedy. *Black Feeling, Black Talk* and *Black Judgment* display a strong, almost militant African-American perspective as Giovanni recounts her growing political and spiritual awareness. These early books, which were followed by *Re: Creation,* quickly established Giovanni as a prominent new African American voice. *Black Feeling, Black Talk* sold more than 10,000 copies in its first year alone, making its author an increasingly visible and popular figure on the reading and speaking circuit. Because of Giovanni's overt activism, her fame as a personality almost preceded her critical acclaim as a poet. She gave the first public reading of her work at Birdland, a trendy New York City jazz club, to a standing-room-only audience. Mitchell described the poems Giovanni produced between 1968 and 1970 as "a kind of ritualistic exorcism of former nonblack ways of thinking and an immersion in blackness. Not only are they directed at other black people whom [Giovanni] wanted to awaken to the beauty of blackness, but also at herself as a means of saturating her own consciousness."

Giovanni's first three volumes of poetry were enormously successful, considering the relatively low public demand for contemporary poetry. *Black Judgment* alone sold 6,000 copies in three months, almost six times the typical sales for a book of its type. As she traveled to speaking engagements at colleges around the country, Giovanni was often hailed as one of the leading black poets of the new black renaissance. The prose poem "Nikki-Rosa," Giovanni's reminiscence of her childhood in a close-knit African-American home, which was first published in *Black Judgment.* As it became her most beloved and most anthologized work, "Nikki-Rosa" expanded her appeal to an audience well beyond fans of her more activist poetry.

In 1969, Giovanni took a teaching position at Rutgers University. That year she also gave birth to her son, Thomas. Her decision to bear a child out of wedlock was understandable to anyone who knew her. Even as a young girl she had determined that the institution of marriage was not hospitable to women and would never play a role in her life. Despite her success as a poet of the black revolution, Giovanni's work exhibited a shift in focus after the birth of her son. Her priorities had expanded and now encompassed providing her child with the security of a stable home life. As she remarked to an interviewer for *Harper's Bazaar,* "To protect Tommy there is no question I would give my life. I just cannot imagine living without him. But I can live without the revolution." During this period Giovanni produced a collection of autobiographical essays and two poetry collections for adults. She also made several recordings of her poetry set against a gospel music backdrop. Reviewing these works, Mitchell commented that "we see evidence of a more developed individualism and greater introspection, and a sharpening of her creative and moral powers, as well as of her social and political focus and understanding."

In addition to writing her own poetry, Giovanni sought exposure for other African American women writers through NikTom, Ltd., a publishing cooperative she founded in 1970. Gwendolyn Brooks, Margaret Walker, Carolyn Rodgers, and Mari Evans were among those who benefited from Giovanni's efforts. Travels to other parts of the world, including the Caribbean, also filled much of the poet's time and contributed to the evolution of her work. As she broadened her perspective, Giovanni began to review her own life. Her introspection led to *Gemini: An Extended Autobiographical Statement on My First Twenty-five Years of Being a Black Poet,* which earned a nomination for the National Book Award. *Gemini* is a combination of prose, poetry, and other "bits and pieces." In the words of a critic writing in *Kirkus Reviews,* it is a work in which "the contradictions are brought together by sheer force of personality."

Giovanni's sophistication and maturity are evident in *My House.* Her viewpoint, still firmly seated in black revolutionary consciousness, balances a wide range of social concerns. Her rhymes are more pronounced, more lyrical, more gentle. The themes of family love, loneliness, and frustration, which Giovanni had raged over in her earlier works, find softer expression in this collection. "*My House* is not just poems," commented Kalumu Ya Salaam in *Black World.* "*My House* is how it is, what it is to be a young, single, intelligent Black woman with a son and no man. It is what it is to be a woman who has failed and is now sentimental about some things, bitter about some things, and generally always frustrated, always feeling frustrated on one of various levels or another." In a review for *Contemporary Women Poets,* Jay S. Paul called the book "a poetic tour through . . . a place rich with family remembrance, distinctive personalities, and prevailing love."

During the early 1970s, Giovanni began to compose verse for children. Among her published volumes for young readers are *Spin a Soft Black Song, Ego-Tripping and Other Poems for Young People,* and *Vacation Time.* Written for children of all ages, Giovanni's poems are unrhymed incantations of childhood images and feelings. *Spin a Soft Black Song,* which she dedicated to her son Tommy, covers a wealth of childhood interests, such as basketball games, close friends, moms, and the coming of spring. "Poem for Rodney" finds a young man contemplating what he wants to be when he grows up. "If" reflects a young man's daydreams about what it might have been like to participate in a historic event. In a *New York Times Book Review* article on *Spin a Soft Black Song,* Klein noted that Giovanni "explores the contours of childhood with honest affection, side-stepping both nostalgia and condescension."

Ego-Tripping and Other Poems from Young People contains several poems previously published in *Black Feeling, Black Talk.* Focusing on African-American history, the collection explores issues and concerns specific to black youngsters. In "Poem for Black Boys," for ex-

Cover of Giovanni's Ego-Tripping and Other Poems for Young People, *featuring cover art by George Ford.* (Illustration © 1973, 1993, by George Ford. Reproduced by permission of Lawrence Hill Books, an imprint of Chicago Review Press, Inc.)

ample, Giovanni wonders why young boys of color do not play runaway slave or Mau-Mau, thereby identifying with the brave heroes of their own race rather than the white cowboys of the Wild West. "Revolutionary Dreams" and "Revolutionary Music" speak to the racial strife of the 1960s and 1970s and look toward an end to racial tension. Commenting on *Ego-Tripping,* a *Kirkus Reviews* contributor claimed: "When [Giovanni] grabs hold . . . it's a rare kid, certainly a rare black kid, who could resist being picked right up."

Vacation Time contrasts with Giovanni's two earlier poetry collections for children by being "a much more relaxed and joyous collection which portrays the world of children as full of wonder and delight," according to Kay E. Vandergrift in *Twentieth-Century Children's Writers.* In *Vacation Time* Giovanni uses more traditional rhyme patterns than in *Spin a Soft Black Song.* Reviewing the work for the *Bulletin of the Center for Children's Books,* Zena Sutherland noted that the rhythms often seem forced and that Giovanni uses "an occasional contrivance to achieve scansion." Yet other critics praised the poet's themes. "In her singing lines, Giovanni shows she hadn't forgotten childhood adventures in . . . exploring the world with a small person's sense of discovery," wrote a *Publishers Weekly* reviewer. Mitchell, too, claimed: "One may be dazzled by the smooth way [Giovanni] drops all political and personal concerns [in *Vacation Time*] and completely enters the world of the child and brings to it all the fanciful beauty, wonder, and lollipopping."

Giovanni's other works for children include *Knoxville, Tennessee, The Genie in the Jar,* and *The Sun Is So Quiet.* The first work, a free-verse poem originally published in *Black Feeling, Black Talk/Black Judgment,* celebrates the pleasures of summer. The illustrated work, with art by Larry Johnson, recalls the simple pleasures and comfortable life that Giovanni experienced as she spent her summers growing up in Knoxville. She describes listening to inspiring gospel music; eating barbecue and homemade ice cream; enjoying the warm summer weather; and spending time with loving family and friends. In Giovanni's work, "Knoxville represents the home of heart, where everyone is welcome," remarked *Booklist* contributor Ilene Cooper. The author's poem evoking "summertime in the rural South makes for a sunny picture book," commented a *Publishers Weekly* contributor. In a *Horn Book* review, Ellen Fader deemed *Knoxville, Tennessee* "a celebration of African-American family life for all families."

As Giovanni moved through her middle years, her works continued to reflect her changing concerns and perspectives. *The Selected Poems of Nikki Giovanni, 1968-1995,* which spans the first three decades of her career, was heralded by *Booklist* critic Donna Seaman as a "rich synthesis [that] reveals the evolution of Giovanni's voice and charts the course of the social issues that are her muses, issues of gender and race." Two later volumes, *Blues: For All the Changes—New Poems and Quilting the Black-eyed Pea: Poems and Not Quite Poems,* mark the crossover from the twentieth to the twenty-first century with poetry that is "socially conscious, outspoken, and roguishly funny," according to Seaman. "Giovanni makes supple use of the irony inherent in the blues, writing tough, sly, and penetrating monologues that both hammer away at racism and praise the good things in life." *The Collected Poetry of Nikki Giovanni: 1968-1998* contains the complete contents of the first seven of Giovanni's poetry collections, as well as other uncollected works published since then, with notes and an afterword by Giovanni herself. In assessing Giovanni's influence over her career, a *Publishers Weekly* reviewer observed that her "outspoken advocacy, her consciousness of roots in oral traditions, and her charismatic delivery place her among the forbearers of present-day slam and spoken-word scenes."

The Genie in the Jar, published in 1996, is "basically a celebration of creativity and community," in which a young African-American girl is encouraged to dance, move, and create as she forms the substance of her world around her, observed Susan Dove Lempke in *Booklist.* The poem also stresses the joys of family, as the girl, the "genie" of the title, places her trust in her mother, the "jar" that holds limitless love for her, noted a *Publishers Weekly* critic. Also published in 1996, *The Sun Is So Quiet* is a collection of thirteen poems, rang-ing in topics from snowflakes to bedtime to missing teeth. "The poems," wrote a *Publishers Weekly* reviewer, "hover like butterflies, darting in to make their point and then fluttering off."

Giovanni examines one of the famous acts of civil disobedience in United States history in *Rosa,* a picture-book biography of Rosa Parks, best known for refusing to give up her bus seat to a white patron in Montgomery, Alabama, in 1955. The narrative focuses not only on Parks's action but also the response of the Women's Political Council, which organized a boycott of the bus system. *Rosa* was described as "a handsome and thought-provoking introduction" to the civil-rights movement by Margaret Bush in *School Library Journal.* A *Publishers Weekly* contributor called the work "a fresh take on a remarkable historic event and on Mrs. Parks's extraordinary integrity and resolve." *On My Journey Now: Looking at African-American History through the Spirituals,* a title for young adults, contains Giovanni's thoughts on more than forty songs, including "Go Down, Moses" and "Ain't Got Time to Die," and their unique place in American history. According to a *Kirkus Reviews* critic, the author "focuses on the triumph over extreme adversity inherent in both the lyrics and the African-American experience itself," and *Booklist* contributor Hazel Rochman noted that Giovanni "tracks a tradition that runs from the spirituals all the way to rhythm and blues and then hip-hop and rap."

Christopher Raschka's unique gestured paintings serve as a backdrop for Giovanni's dynamic verse in **The Genie in the Jar.** (Henry Holt, 1996. Reproduced by permission of Christopher Raschka.)

In *The Grasshopper's Song: An Aesop's Fable Revisited,* Giovanni offers her version of the familiar tale "The Ant and the Grasshopper." When Nestor and Abigail Ant deny Jimmy Grasshopper a share of their harvest, he hires a law firm to sue them, claiming that his soothing songs helped the ants perform their arduous chores during the long summer. As the case goes to trial, the book's "focus shifts from the value of hard work to the important place that art holds in our lives," Joan Kindig observed in *School Library Journal.* A *Publishers Weekly* contributor applauded "Giovanni's detailed and insightful prose" and called *The Grasshopper's Song* "a shrewd evaluation of the value of art."

Giovanni also served as the editor of *Hip Hop Speaks to Children: A Celebration of Poetry with a Beat,* an anthology containing works by Langston Hughes, Eloise Greenfield, and Kanye West, among others. The collection "highlights the use of rhythm and vernacular in hip-hop, rap, and African-American poetry," Lauralyn Persson commented in *School Library Journal,* and *Booklist* reviewer John Peters remarked that the work, which is accompanied by a CD, "will be fun for families to share as they get their groove on."

Giovanni continues to look back on her contributions to American literature with pride. "My job as a writer is to say things in the way that makes sense to me, which is what I do and have always done," she told Collier in a *Writer* interview. "My integrity as a writer means a lot to me," she added. "This is a career that's over 30 years old. And if you had asked anybody back then if they thought I'd still be here, writing and being read, everybody would have said 'no.' I don't look back like that because it has been a good and solid writing career." The prolific author and educator shows no signs of slowing down. As Giovanni remarked to Rohan Preston in the Minneapolis *Star-Tribune,* "All I've ever had is a brain and a body and a voice. . . . I am happy to use them to make a contribution. It's fun to be alive."

Giovanni's rhymes in The Sun Is So Quiet *are brought to life in Ashley Bryan's colorful paintings.* (Illustration copyright © 1996 by Ashley Bryan. Reprinted by arrangement with Henry Holt and Company, LLC.)

Biographical and Critical Sources

BOOKS

Children's Literature Review, Gale (Detroit, MI), Volume 6, 1984, Volume 73, 2002.

Contemporary Authors Autobiography Series, Volume 6, Gale (Detroit, MI), 1988.

Contemporary Black Biography, Volume 39, Gale (Detroit, MI), 2003.

Contemporary Literary Criticism, Gale (Detroit, MI), Volume 2, 1974, Volume 4, 1975, Volume 19, 1981, Volume 64, 1991, Volume 177, 1999.

Contemporary Poets, 7th edition, St. James Press (Detroit, MI), 2001.

Contemporary Southern Writers, St. James Press (Detroit, MI), 1999.

Contemporary Women Poets, St. James Press (Detroit, MI), 1998.

Dictionary of Literary Biography, Gale (Detroit, MI), Volume 5: *American Poets since World War II,* 1980, Volume 41: *Afro-American Poets since 1955,* 1985.

Evans, Mari, editor, *Black Women Writers, 1950-1980: A Critical Evaluation,* Doubleday (New York, NY), 1984.

Fowler, Virginia, *Nikki Giovanni,* Twayne (Boston, MA), 1992.

Fowler, Virginia, editor, *Conversations with Nikki Giovanni,* University Press of Mississippi (Jackson, MS), 1992.

Giovanni, Nikki, *Gemini: An Extended Autobiographical Statement on My First Twenty-five Years of Being a Black Poet,* Bobbs-Merrill (Indianapolis, IN), 1971.

Giovanni, Nikki, and James Baldwin, *A Dialogue: James Baldwin and Nikki Giovanni,* Lippincott (Philadelphia, PA), 1973.

Giovanni, Nikki, and Margaret Walker, *A Poetic Equation: Conversations between Nikki Giovanni and Margaret Walker,* Howard University Press (Washington, DC), 1974.

Giovanni, Nikki, *Cotton Candy on a Rainy Day,* introduction by Paula Giddings, Morrow (New York, NY), 1978.

Giovanni, Nikki, *My House,* introduction by Ida Lewis, Morrow (New York, NY), 1972.

Inge, Tonette Bond, editor, *Southern Women Writers: The New Generation,* University of Alabama Press (Tuscaloosa, AL), 1990.

Giovanni captures the story of civil-rights activist Rosa Parks in her picture book Rosa, *which features artwork by Bryan Collier.* (Illustration copyright © 2005 by Bryan Collier. Reprinted by arrangement with Henry Holt and Company, LLC.)

Josephson, Judith P., *Nikki Giovanni: Poet of the People,* Enslow Publishers (Berkeley Heights, NJ), 2003.

Lee, Don L., *Dynamite Voices I: Black Poets of the 1960s,* Broadside Press (Detroit, MI), 1971.

Mitchell, Felicia, editor, *Her Words: Diverse Voices in Contemporary Appalachian Women's Poetry,* University of Tennessee Press (Knoxville, TN), 2002.

St. James Guide to Children's Writers, 5th edition, St. James Press (Detroit, MI), 1999.

St. James Guide to Young-Adult Writers, 2nd edition, St. James Press (Detroit, MI), 1999.

Tate, Claudia, editor, *Black Women Writers at Work,* Crossroads Publishing (New York, NY), 1983.

PERIODICALS

American Visions, February-March, 1998, Monica Dyer-Rowe, review of *Love Poems,* p. 30; October, 1999, Denolynn Carroll, review of *Blues: For All the Changes—New Poems,* p. 34.

Black Collegian, February, 2000, Crystal Kimpson Roberts, "Poet Laureate Shares Her Views on Carving out a Successful Career," p. 155.

Black Issues Book Review, November 1, 2002, "From the Editor-in-Chief," p. 1; November 1, 2002, review of *Quilting the Black-eyed Pea: Poems and Not Quite Poems,* p. 32; March-April, 2004, Jadi Keambiroiro, review of *The Collected Poetry of Nikki Giovanni: 1968-1998,* p. 24.

Black Issues in Higher Education, October 28, 1999, Michele N-K Collison, "The Perks and Perils of Recruiting Academic Superstars," p. 30.

Black World, July, 1974, Kalumu Ya Salaam, review of *My House,* p. 64.

Booklist, December 1, 1993, Donna Seaman, review of *Racism 101,* p. 658; February 15, 1994, Ilene Cooper, review of _Knoxville, Tennessee,_ p. 1084; September 15, 1994, Carolyn Phelan, review of _Grand Mothers: Poems, Reminiscences, and Short Stories about the Keepers of Our Traditions,_ p. 122; December 15, 1995, Donna Seaman, review of _The Selected Poems of Nikki Giovanni, 1968-1995,_ p. 682; April 1, 1996, Susan Dove Lempke, review of _The Genie in the Jar,_ p. 1367; June 1, 1999, Hazel Rochman, review of _Grand Fathers: Reminiscences, Poems, Recipes, and Photos of the Keepers of Our Traditions,_ p. 1807; December 15, 2003, Donna Seaman, review of _The Collected Poetry of Nikki Giovanni,_ p. 721; December 1, 2006, Janet St. John, review of _Acolytes,_ p. 11; February 1, 2007, Hazel Rochman, review of _On My Journey Now,_ p. 56; September 15, 2008, John Peters, review of _Hip Hop Speaks to Children: A Celebration of Poetry with a Beat,_ p. 54.

Bulletin of the Center for Children's Books, October, 1980, Zena Sutherland, review of _Vacation Time,_ p. 31.

Christian Science Monitor, April 17, 2007, Elizabeth Lund, "Nikki Giovanni and Charles Bukowski: New Collections from Poetry's Icons," review of _Acolytes,_ p. 13; April 23, 2009, Elizabeth Lund, review of _Bicycles,_ p. 25.

Chronicle of Higher Education, February 6, 2004, Michael Arnone, "Grammy and the Professor."

Ebony, February, 1972, Peter Bailey, "Nikki Giovanni: I Am Black, Female, Polite," pp. 48-50; January, 2007, review of _Acolytes,_ p. 32.

English Journal, April, 1973, John W. Conner, review of _My House,_ p. 650.

Essence, March, 1994, Elsie B. Washington, "Nikki Giovanni: Wisdom for All Ages," p. 67; May, 1999, Evelyn C. White, "The Poet and the Rapper," interview with Giovanni, p. 122.

Harper's Bazaar, July, 1972, Gwen Mazer, "Nikki Giovanni," p. 50.

Horn Book, September-October, 1994, Ellen Fader, review of _Knoxville, Tennessee,_ p. 575.

Houston Chronicle, March 3, 2004, Teresa Wiltz, "For Poet Giovanni, a State of Grace," profile of Giovanni, p. 8; October 1, 2007, "Virginia Tech; Tragedy Teaches Professor a Lesson," p. 2.

Instructor, January 1, 2005, Liza Charlesworth, "The Poetry of Nikki Giovanni: Celebrate the Season and Black History Month with a Frosty Gem by Nikki Giovanni," p. 59.

Jet, May 25, 1972, Cordell M. Thompson, "Nikki Giovanni: Black Rebel with Power in Poetry," pp. 18-24; May 22, 1995, "Nikki Giovanni Bounces Back after Cancer Forces Partial Removal of Her Lung and Ribs," p. 65.

Journal of Negro History, summer, 2000, Jennifer Walters, "Nikki Giovanni and Rita Dove: Poets Redefining," p. 210.

Kirkus Reviews, September 15, 1971, review of _Gemini: An Extended Autobiographical Statement on My First Twenty-five Years of Being a Black Poet,_ p. 1051; January 1, 1974, review of _Ego-Tripping and Other Poems,_ p. 11; February 15, 2007, review of _On My Journey Now;_ September 15, 2008, review of _Lincoln and Douglass: An American Friendship,_

Library Journal, January, 1996, Ellen Kaufman, review of _The Selected Poems of Nikki Giovanni, 1968-1995,_ p. 103; February 1, 1997, Frank Allen, review of _Love Poems,_ p. 84; May 1, 1999, Louis McKee, review of _Blues,_ p. 84; November 1, 2002, Ann Burns, review of _Quilting the Black-eyed Pea,_ p. 114; November 15, 2002, Rochelle Ratner, review of _Quilting the Black-eyed Pea,_ p. 76; February 1, 2003, Rochelle Ratner, review of _The Nikki Giovanni Poetry Collection,_ p. 136; March 1, 2004, Ellen Kaufman, review of _The Collected Poetry of Nikki Giovanni,_ p. 81; January 1, 2007, Louis McKee, review of _Acolytes,_ p. 113.

New Orleans Times-Picayune, March 10, 1996, Susan Larson, "Poet Princess: Between the Lines with a Teller of Tales," p. D1.

New York Times, August 1, 1996, Felicia R. Lee, "At Home with Nikki Giovanni: Defying Evil and Mortality," p. C9; May 14, 2000, "Poet Gives Concrete Advice at Manhattanville College," p. 40.

New York Times Book Review, November 28, 1971, Nancy Klein, "Americana, City-Style and Country Style: _Spin a Soft Black Song,_" p. 8; May 5, 1974, Nancy Rosenberg, "A Tree Grows in Print," p. 38.

Philadelphia Tribune, January 9, 1996, Susan Levy, "Oh, Nikki! Poet Nikki Giovanni Celebrates Twenty-five Years in Print with the Publication of _The Selected Poems of Nikki Giovanni,_" p. 1D.

Publishers Weekly, May 23, 1980, review of _Vacation Time,_ p. 77; December 13, 1993, review of _Racism 101,_ p. 54; January 24, 1994, review of _Knoxville, Tennessee,_ p. 54; August 8, 1994, review of _Grand Mothers,_ p. 450; December 18, 1995, review of _The Selected Poems of Nikki Giovanni, 1968-1995,_ pp. 51-52; February 19, 1996, review of _The Genie in the Jar,_ p. 214; October 21, 1996, review of _The Sun Is So Quiet,_ p. 83; June 28, 1999, Calvin Reid, "Nikki Giovanni: Three Decades on the Edge," interview with Giovanni, p. 46; July 12, 1999, review of _Grand Fathers,_ p. 96; November 17, 2003, review of _The Collected Poetry of Nikki Giovanni,_ p. 59; August 29, 2005, review of _Rosa,_ p. 56; December 18, 2006, review of _Acolytes,_ p. 44; April 7, 2008, review of _The Grasshopper's Song: An Aesop's Fable Revisited,_ p. 59.

School Library Journal, April, 1994, Judy McCoy, review of _Knoxville, Tennessee,_ p. 119; October, 1994, Ruth K. MacDonald, review of _Grand Mothers,_ p. 152; May, 1996, Ruth K. MacDonald, review of _Shimmy Shimmy Shimmy like My Sister Kate: Looking at the Harlem Renaissance through Poems,_ p. 103; January, 1997, Ronald Jobe, review of _The Sun Is So Quiet,_ p. 100; July, 1999, Patricia Lothrop-Green, review of _Grand Fathers,_ p. 107; November 17, 2003, review of _The Collected Poetry of Nikki Giovanni,_ p. 59; February, 2005, Catherine Callegari, review of _The Girls in the Circle,_ p. 97; September, 2005, Margaret Bush, review of _Rosa,_ p. 192; March, 2007, Denise Ryan, review of _On My Journey Now: Looking at African-American History through the Spirituals,_ p. 228; October, 2008, Lauralyn Persson, review of _Hip Hop Speaks to Children,_ p. 169; June, 2008, Joan Kindig, review of _The Grasshopper's Song,_ p. 102.

Star-Tribune (Minneapolis, MN), Rohan Preston, "Poet Nikki Giovanni Writes of a Love Supreme: The Legendary Wordsmith Responds to Tragedy and Bad News with a Flurry of Sensual, Exultant Poems."

USA Today, March 16, 1994, Anita Manning, "Poet Nikki Giovanni Tilting at Academia," p. 4D.

Washington Post Book Review, February 14, 1988, Marita Golden, review of *Sacred Cows . . . and Other Edibles,* p. 3; February 13, 1994, Phyllis Crockett, "A Free Spirit of the '60s," p. X4.

Writer, October, 2005, Andrea King Collier, interview with Giovanni, p. 22.

Writer's Digest, February, 1989, Lois Rosenthal, "Writing as Breathing: Nikki Giovanni," pp. 30-34.

ONLINE

Nikki Giovanni Home Page, http://www.nikki-giovanni. com (November 1, 2009).

Bill Moyers Journal Web site, http://www.pbs.org/moyers/ journal/ (February 13, 2009), transcript of interview with Giovanni.

OTHER

Spirit to Spirit: The Poetry of Nikki Giovanni (television special), PBS, 1987.*

* * *

GIOVANNI, Yolande Cornelia
See GIOVANNI, Nikki

* * *

GIOVANNI, Yolande Cornelia, Jr.
See GIOVANNI, Nikki

* * *

GOEDE, Irene 1966-

Personal

Born 1966, in Landsmeer, Netherlands. *Education:* D' Witte Leli (Amsterdam, Netherlands), education degree, 1989; Constantijn Huygens (Kampen, Netherlands), illustration degree, 1992.

Addresses

Home—Netherlands. *Office*—Koewegje 4, 8021 AG Zwolle, Netherlands. *E-mail*—info@irenegoede.nl.

Career

Illustrator. Has also worked as an art teacher.

Illustrator

Margaret Wise Brown, *De kleine indiaan,* Lemniscaat (Rotterdam, Netherlands), 1994.

Huis op z'n kop, Averroès (Amsterdam, Netherlands), 1995.

Walter Menkveld, *Boerderij in bedrijf,* Cantecleer (Baarn, Netherlands), 2002.

Mariken Jongman, *Wasbeer en Otter vinden een doos,* SGO (Hoevelaken, Netherlands), 2003.

Mariken Jongman, *Wasbeer en Otter vieren kerst,* SGO (Hoevelaken, Netherlands), 2004.

Petra Cremers, *Adres onbekend,* Holland (Haarlem, Netherlands), 2004.

Gerbrand Fenijn, *Misja het mandenverkopertje,* Callenbach (Kampen, Netherlands), 2004.

Mieke van Hooft, *Zwijgplicht,* Holland (Haarlem, Netherlands), 2004.

Rik Hoogendoorn, *Mark en het mysterie van het Boze Meertje,* Van Goor (Amsterdam, Netherlands), 2004.

Vrouwke Klapwijk, *Bas op het ijs,* Callenbach (Kampen, Netherlands), 2004.

Hans Post, *Kriebelpoten,* Lemniscaat (Rotterdam, Netherlands), 2005, translated by Nancy Forest-Flier as *Creepy Crawlies,* Front Street/Lemniscaat (Asheville, NC), 2006.

Hans Post and Kees Heij, *Mus,* Lemniscaat (Rotterdam, Netherlands), 2007, translated as *Sparrows,* Lemniscaat (Honesdale, PA), 2008.

Rian Visser, *Het grote bouwwerk: de tijd van de jagers en boeren,* Delubas (Drunen, Netherlands), 2008.

Joke Reijnders, *Problemen op de palts: de tijd van monniken en ridders 500-1000: Karel de Grote,* Delubas (Drunen, Netherlands), 2008.

Also illustrator of other children's books.

Sidelights

A prolific illustrator in her native Netherlands, artist Irene Goede expanded her audience to the United States when her work appeared in a book by Dutch author Hans Post. Initially published as *Kriebelpoten,* Post's *Creepy Crawlies* follows a young cat as it tours her house and garden, searching for insects, birds, and small rodents. Post and Goede feature a number of common creatures, from mice to cockroaches to fleas, showing readers how many unsavory bugs actually live in close proximity to human dwellings. Writing in *Kirkus Reviews,* a contributor wrote that Goede "depicts each creature with casual naturalism," while a *Children's Bookwatch* critic complimented the artist's "lovely and realistic color drawings" for *Creepy Crawlies.*

Another work by Goede and Post, *Sparrows* is a 2008 translation of the book *Mus.* Joined by author Kees Heij, Goede and Post trace the development of a family of birds over the course of a year, beginning with the flock of young hatchlings that comes to life in the spring. Over the next three seasons, the young sparrows learn to fly, build a nest, and avoid being eaten by predators. By the following spring, the cycle of life continues as these birds begin preparing for their new role as parents, mating with other sparrows and starting families of their own. Several reviewers offered favorable comments about Goede's artwork, *School Library Journal* critic Ellen Fader noting that her "attention-grabbing watercolor illustrations accurately depict the

Irene Goede's illustration projects include creating the nature-themed art for **Sparrows** *by* **Hans Post.** (Lemniscaat, 2008. Illustration copyright © 2006 by Irene Goede. Reproduced by permission.)

life of a house sparrow." Writing in *Kirkus Reviews,* a critic maintained that the illustrator's "stunning artwork" deserves extra attention from readers, noting that her inclusion of "realistic details, colors and textures . . . make the images pop off the pages."

Biographical and Critical Sources

PERIODICALS

Booklist, August 1, 2008, Hazel Rochman, review of *Sparrows,* p. 75.

Children's Bookwatch, June, 2006, review of *Creepy Crawlies.*

Horn Book, September-October, 2008, Danielle J. Ford, review of *Sparrows,* p. 613.

Kirkus Reviews, April 1, 2006, review of *Creepy Crawlies,* p. 354; July 15, 2008, review of *Sparrows.*

School Library Journal, October, 2008, Ellen Fader, review of *Sparrows,* p. 135.

ONLINE

Irene Goede Home Page, http://www.irenegoede.nl (November 20, 2009).*

GOSCHKE, Julia 1973-

Personal

Born 1973, in Hamburg, Germany. *Education:* Fachhochschul für Gestaltung (Hamburg, Germany), degree, 2000.

Addresses

Home—Hamburg, Germany.

Career

Author and illustrator. Layout artist for periodicals, beginning 1998; freelance author and illustrator.

Writings

SELF-ILLUSTRATED

Schlappi, Minedition (Salzburg, Germany), 2006, translated by Charise Myngheer as *Langley Longears,* Penguin (New York, NY), 2006.

ILLUSTRATOR

Christian Pletz, *Tüt-tüt, das kleinie Nilpferd,* Buch Verlag Kempen (Kempen, Germany), 2005.

(And adaptor) Paul Auster, *Timbuktu,* Minedition (New York, NY), 2008.

Biographical and Critical Sources

PERIODICALS

Publishers Weekly, July 28, 2008, review of *Timbuktu,* p. 74.

School Library Journal, July, 2006, Linda Ludke, review of *Langley Longears,* p. 78.

ONLINE

Julia Goschke Home Page, http://www.juliagoschke.com (November 22, 2009).*

H

HAGER, Jenna Bush
See BUSH, Jenna

*　　*　　*

HAHN, Mary Downing 1937-

Personal

Born December 9, 1937, in Washington, DC; daughter of Kenneth Ernest (an automobile mechanic) and Anna Elisabeth (a teacher) Downing; married William F. Hahn, October 7, 1961 (divorced, 1977); married Norman Pearce Jacob (a librarian), April 23, 1982; children: (first marriage) Katherine Sherwood, Margaret Elizabeth. *Education:* University of Maryland at College Park, B.A., 1960, M.A., 1969, doctoral study, 1970-74. *Politics:* Democrat. *Hobbies and other interests:* Reading, walking, travel, photography, bicycling.

Addresses

Home—Columbia, MD. *E-mail*—mdh12937@aol.com.

Career

Novelist and artist. Art teacher at junior high school in Greenbelt, MD, 1960-61; Hutzler's Department Store, Baltimore, MD, clerk, 1963; correspondence clerk for Navy Federal Credit Union, 1963-65; homemaker and writer, 1965-70; English instructor, University of Maryland, 1970-75; freelance artist for *Cover to Cover,* WETA-TV, 1973-75; Prince George's County Memorial Library System, Laurel Branch, Laurel, MD, children's librarian associate, 1975-91; full-time writer, 1991—.

Member

Society of Children's Book Writers and Illustrators, Washington Children's Book Guild.

Awards, Honors

American Library Association (ALA) Reviewer's Choice designation, Library of Congress Children's Books honor, and *School Library Journal* Best Books

Mary Downing Hahn (Reproduced by permission.)

citations, all 1983, Child Study Association of America Children's Books of the Year designation, and National Council of Teachers of English Teachers' Choice citation, both 1984, and William Allen White Children's Choice Award, 1986, all for *Daphne's Book;* Dorothy Canfield Fisher Award, 1988, and Maud Hart Lovelace Award, both for *Wait till Helen Comes;* Child Study Association Book Award, 1989, Jane Addams Children's Book Award Honor Book designation, 1990, and California Young Reader's Medal, 1991, all for *December Stillness;* ALA Books for Reluctant Readers designation, 1990, and Maud Hart Lovelace Award, both for *The Dead Man in Indian Creek;* Mark Twain Award, for *The Doll in the Garden;* ALA Notable Book citation, Scott O'Dell Award for Historical Fiction, and Joan G. Sugarman Award, all 1992, and Hedda Seisler Mason Award, 1993, all for *Stepping on the Cracks;* Best Book for Young Adults citation, Young Adult Library Services Association (YALSA), 1993, and New York Public Library Books for the Teen Age citation, 1994, both for *The Wind Blows Backward;* YALSA pick, 2001, for *Look for Me by Moonlight;* numerous child-selected awards.

Writings

FOR CHILDREN

The Sara Summer, Clarion (Boston, MA), 1979.

The Time of the Witch, Clarion (New York, NY), 1982.

Daphne's Book, Clarion (New York, NY), 1983.

The Jellyfish Season, Clarion (New York, NY), 1985.

Wait till Helen Comes: A Ghost Story, Clarion (New York, NY), 1986, reprinted, 2008.

Tallahassee Higgins, Clarion (New York, NY), 1987.

December Stillness, Clarion (New York, NY), 1988.

Following the Mystery Man, Clarion (New York, NY), 1988.

The Doll in the Garden, Clarion (New York, NY), 1989, reprinted, 2007.

The Dead Man in Indian Creek, Clarion (New York, NY), 1990.

The Spanish Kidnapping Disaster, Clarion (New York, NY), 1991.

Stepping on the Cracks, Clarion (New York, NY), 1991.

The Wind Blows Backward (young-adult novel), Clarion (New York, NY), 1993.

Time for Andrew: A Ghost Story, Clarion (New York, NY), 1994.

Look for Me by Moonlight, Clarion (New York, NY), 1995.

The Gentleman Outlaw and Me—Eli: A Story of the Old West, Clarion (New York, NY), 1996.

Following My Own Footsteps, Clarion (New York, NY), 1996.

As Ever, Gordy, Clarion (New York, NY), 1998.

Anna All Year Round, illustrated by Diane de Groat, Clarion (New York, NY), 1999.

Promises to the Dead, Clarion (New York, NY), 2000.

Anna on the Farm, illustrated by Diane de Groat, Clarion (New York, NY), 2001.

Hear the Wind Blow, Clarion (New York, NY), 2003.

The Old Willis Place: A Ghost Story, Clarion (New York, NY), 2004.

Janey and the Famous Author, Clarion (New York, NY), 2005.

Witch Catcher, Clarion (New York, NY), 2006.

Deep and Dark and Dangerous, Clarion Books (New York, NY), 2007.

All the Lovely Bad Ones: A Ghost Story, Clarion Books (New York, NY), 2008.

Closed for the Season: A Mystery, Clarion Books (Boston, MA), 2009.

Contributor to anthologies, including *Don't Give up the Ghost,* 1993, *Bruce Coville's Book of Ghost Stories,* 1994, and *Bruce Coville's Book of Nightmares,* 1995.

Hahn's books have been translated into Danish, Swedish, Italian, German, Japanese, and French.

Sidelights

A former librarian and artist, Mary Downing Hahn is best known for writing novels that combine fantasy and the supernatural, often setting these stories in her home state of Maryland. In addition to her fantasy and ghost tales, Hahn also draw upon her memories of childhood to write closely detailed stories that explore themes such as the loss of a parent or loved one, the struggle for identity and acceptance, and the blending of families. Hahn's award-winning novels, which include *Daphne's Book*, *Wait till Helen Comes: A Ghost Story*, *The Jellyfish Season*, *Stepping on the Cracks*, and *Look for Me by Moonlight,* have earned her a large and loyal readership whom she regularly visits on her school speaking tours. As she once told *SATA,* she strives to create "real life" in her novels. "Like the people I know, I want my characters to be a mixture of strengths and weaknesses, to have good and bad qualities, to be a

Hahn's elementary-grade novel **Daphne's Book** *deals with her characteristic coming-of-age themes.* (Used by permission of Bantam Books, an imprint of Random House Children's Books, a division of Random House, Inc.)

little confused and unsure of themselves." As in real life, a happy ending is not always guaranteed. "At the same time, however," Hahn remarked, "I try to leave room for hope."

Reading to her own daughters gave Hahn the encouragement she needed to try her hand at writing. When her first attempts were rejected, she took some graduate courses and then got a job in a library. Working around books, Hahn once again began writing for children. Her first book, *The Sara Summer,* was published in 1979 after three years of writing and revision.

The story of a twelve year old who feels uncomfortable in the world around her, *The Sara Summer* exhibits an "intimate knowledge of subteens and a well-tuned ear," according to a *Publishers Weekly* contributor. The work centers on the developing friendship between Emily, who is often teased about her height, and Sara, a new neighbor who is even taller than Emily. Unfortunately, Sara's brash, independent demeanor has a cruel side, exhibited in her treatment of her younger sister. Through a confrontation over this issue, Sara and Emily come to a new understanding of each other and themselves. Although Cyrisse Jaffee, writing in *School Library Journal,* faulted the book's "lack of plot," she noted that "kids will find [*The Sara Summer*] easy to read and relate to." "The vivid characterizations of the two girls make the author's first novel a worthwhile venture," Richard Ashford concluded in *Horn Book.*

The Jellyfish Season "is a very realistic look at family stress and the permanent changes it can make," wrote a *Bulletin of the Center for Children's Books* reviewer. When her father loses his job, thirteen-year-old Kathleen, together with her mother and her three younger sisters, must move in with relatives living in another town. *Horn Book* critic Mary M. Burns commented that the story's "well-defined characters are the key ingredients in an appealing, first-person narrative which ably conveys the tensions created by economic hardships." Although a reviewer in *Publishers Weekly* stated that Kathleen sometimes expresses herself "in words too adult for belief," *School Library Journal* writer Marjorie Lewis praised Hahn's resolution of "almost insurmountable problems in a most satisfying, realistic and reassuring way" and predicted that *The Jellyfish Season* "should be a favorite among young teens."

Hahn's young characters often live in unusual family situations. In *Tallahassee Higgins,* for example, Talley must move in with her childless aunt and uncle when her irresponsible mother takes off for Hollywood in search of stardom. *Bulletin of the Center for Children's Books* critic Zena Sutherland praised the novel's "strong characters, good pace, and solid structure," while *Voice of Youth Advocates* contributor Dolores Maminski described *Tallahassee Higgins* as "sad, humorous, believable and readable." In *Following the Mystery Man* Hahn's young protagonist convinces herself that her grandmother's new tenant is the father she has never

known. She then finds herself in a heap of trouble when she discovers he is really a criminal. While Elizabeth S. Watson, writing in *Horn Book,* found that "there are no really frightening moments in this rather gentle, occasionally sad story," *School Library Journal* contributor Elizabeth Mellett called *Following the Mystery Man* "a suspenseful book that will keep readers interested and entertained until the last page."

In *Stepping on the Cracks,* Hahn takes readers back to World War II as two patriotic twelve-year-old girls risk the wrath of their parents and the ostracism of their community when they befriend a conscientious objector. A *Kirkus Reviews* writer called the novel "suspenseful, carefully wrought, and thought-provoking—a fine achievement." While acknowledging these strengths, Sutherland added in her *Bulletin of the Center for Children's Books* review that "what makes [the novel] outstanding is the integrity of the plot and the consistency of the characterization." In *Horn Book* Maeve Visser Knoth similarly concluded of *Stepping on the Cracks* that "the engrossing story handles the wide range of issues with grace and skill."

Writing in the *Bulletin of the Center for Children's Books* Roger Sutton described Hahn's young-adult novel *The Wind Blows Backward* as "a lavishly romantic novel, with all the moody intensity anyone could want." In the story, Lauren's middle-school crush on Spencer is revived in their senior year of high school. However, Spencer is haunted by his father's suicide and Lauren worries that he now seems tempted to follow in his father's footsteps. In portraying Lauren's relationships, a *Publishers Weekly* critic commented, "Hahn makes excellent use of contrasting family situations to illustrate her theme of perseverance." Although *Booklist* critic Stephanie Zvirin found the plot to be "predictable," Gerry Larson wrote in *School Library Journal* that "YA readers will identify with the pressures, conflicts, and concerns facing these teens." In *Voice of Youth Advocates,* Marilyn Bannon praised Hahn's handling of the subject of teen suicide, noting that "because [Hahn] has crafted such interesting, well rounded characters, her message is delivered effectively."

The first of Hahn's novels to include elements of the supernatural, *The Time of the Witch* centers on a young girl's desire for her parents to stay together. "Sulky and opinionated, Laura is not a particularly attractive character," wrote Ann A. Flowers in *Horn Book;* nevertheless, "her problems are real and understandable." In her quest to halt the divorce of her parents, Laura seeks help from a local witch, who uses the opportunity to settle an old score with the unsuspecting family. Barbara Elleman, writing in *Booklist,* described the witch as one "readers won't soon forget," and *School Library Journal* contributor Karen Stang Hanley remarked that the "elements of mystery, suspense and the occult are expertly balanced against the realistic dimensions" of Hahn's story.

Cover of Hahn's suspenseful novel **All the Lovely Bad Ones,** *featuring cover art by Greg Spalenka.* (Illustration © 2008 by Greg Spalenka. Reproduced by permission of Houghton Mifflin Company.)

The supernatural is also an element of *Wait till Helen Comes,* a tale Cynthia Dobrez described in Chicago's *Tribune Books* as "suspenseful and often terrifying." Molly and her brother move with their mother into a converted church near a graveyard. They are joined by their new stepfather and his daughter, Heather, whose troublemaking includes her increasingly ominous friendship with a ghost. *Wait till Helen Comes* was widely praised for its effective pacing, realistic characterizations, and convincing supernatural elements. While Watson characterized the novel's opening as "rather slow," she added that Hahn "has written a gripping and scary ghost story that develops hauntingly." Judy Greenfield concluded in *School Library Journal: Wait till Helen Comes* "is a powerful, convincing, and frightening tale" that should produce "a heavy demand from readers who are not 'faint at heart.'"

Hahn returns to ghost stories with *The Doll in the Garden,* a work Sutton dubbed "not as straight-ahead-scary" as *Wait till Helen Comes,* but which nonetheless benefits from "a direct style and smooth storytelling." After the death of her father, Ashley and her mother move into an apartment in a house owned by a hostile woman. Ashley and a new friend discover a doll buried in the garden and then encounter the ghost of a dying child that leads them back in time where they discover the landlady's secret. Although *Horn Book* critic Ethel R. Twichell found the ending "a little too pat," she nonetheless concluded that "Ashley's intriguing although never really scary experiences" in *The Doll in the Garden* "should hold most readers' attention to the end."

Time for Andrew is a similarly spooky time-travel story. While spending the summer with relatives in Missouri, twelve-year-old Drew becomes switched in time with his namesake, Andrew, who lived in the house eighty years before. When Andrew refuses to return to his own time for fear he will die of diphtheria, the two boys must join forces to change their family history. While Virginia Golodetz, writing in *School Library Journal,* characterized Hahn's ending as "humorous but somewhat contrived," Sutton dubbed *Time for Andrew* an "assured work from a deservedly popular writer, who, while gifted with the instincts of a storyteller, doesn't let her narrative get away from her characters."

In *Look for Me by Moonlight* Hahn creates a supernatural romance for teen readers. In this "deliciously spine-tingling story," as it was described by a reviewer for *Publishers Weekly,* Hahn spins the tale of sixteen-year-old Cynda as she spends some time with her father at his inn, called Underhill, on the coast of Maine. Reputedly haunted by the ghost of a woman who was murdered there many years ago, the Underhill Inn is also the place where Cynda encounters Vincent Morthanos, a guest and vampire. Cynda falls in love with the mysterious and forbidding stranger in a book that "takes the traditional elements . . . [and] places them in a setting that is alternately cozy and frightening," creating a perfect blend for readers who appreciate "danger with a dash of romance," according to *Wilson Library Bulletin* critic Linda Perkins. Similarly, a critic for *Publishers Weekly* remarked that, although some elements of the story are clichéd, "in Hahn's able hands, they add up to a stylish supernatural thriller."

Hahn branches out into adventure fiction with *The Dead Man in Indian Creek,* the story of two boys who suspect a local antique dealer of being behind the murder of the man they find in a nearby creek. Reviewers praised the fast-paced action and high suspense of this novel. Although *School Library Journal* critic Carolyn Noah found several "illogical gaps" in the plot, a *Publishers Weekly* reviewer concluded that the book's "combination of crackling language and plenty of suspense" makes *The Dead Man in Indian Creek* "likely to appeal to even the most reluctant readers."

Similar in theme, *The Spanish Kidnapping Disaster* finds three children thrown together by the marriage of their parents, whom they are unexpectedly forced to join while the adults are on their honeymoon in Spain. When one of the children lies to the wrong person about their wealth, the three are kidnapped, resulting a story containing "action, danger, and suspense," according to

Sutherland. Praising Hahn's ability to create vivid characters, a *Publishers Weekly* critic cited *The Spanish Kidnapping Disaster* as "a surprisingly understanding look at what impels people to terrorist activity."

The Old Willis Place: A Ghost Story deals with ghosts, but not in the expected way. The main character, Diana, lives with her brother in the woods behind a mansion; they have seen caretakers come and go, but they never reveal themselves to the people taking care of the property. They must never let themselves be seen and must never go into the house. Diana does not explain to readers why these are the rules; perhaps she does not know herself. However, when Lissa, a daughter of the new caretaker who is about Diana's age, arrives, the lonely girl hopes to have a friend, even though it is against the rules. As a complement to Diana's narration, readers also have access to Lissa's diary. "Hahn is a master at stretching the suspense," praised Ilene Cooper in her *Booklist* review of *The Old Willis Place,* and a critic for *Children's Bookwatch* called the novel "another satisfying ghost story." As Maria B. Salvadore noted in *School Library Journal,* Hahn's "riveting novel is a mystery and a story of friendship and of redemption," and a *Kirkus Review* critic characterized *The Old Willis Place* as "spooky, but with an underlying sweetness."

Twelve-year-old Jen is thrilled to be moving to a West Virginia estate in *Witch Catcher,* a middle-grade fantasy. When her widowed father inherits his uncle's old stone house in the mountains, Jen hopes that the move will mean a new start. However, those hopes fade when an antiques dealer named Moura begins to visit. In addition to courting Jen's dad's attention, Moura also seems obsessed with the old house and its contents, particularly its "witch catcher," an antique globe made of glass. After the globe is accidentally broken, the woman's actions become more threatening: as Jen learns, the globe was the prison of a young fairy named Kieryn. Now, the preteen must help Kieryn remain free as Moura show herself to be an evil witch who wants control over the sprite. Although Sutton wrote in *Horn Book* that Jen is "more naive than is likely," *Witch Catcher* is "an excellent start for uninitiated or unconvinced fantasy readers," and in *School Library Journal* Nicki Clausen-Grace described the book as an "engaging story" that is "sustained with page-turning suspense."

Another move that yields a mystery is the focus of *Deep and Dark and Dangerous.* Here thirteen-year-old Ali is fascinated by an old family photograph that depicts her mother and her mom's sister Dulcie as children. But there is also a third figure, someone whose image has been cut out. Why? Now, while visiting her mother's family's summer home in Maine together with her aunt Dulcie and her young cousin, Emma, Ali meets Sissy. A belligerent local girl who begins to have a bad influence on Emma, Sissy also tells about a tragic drowning that occurred years earlier and might explain the mystery of Ali's photograph. In *Booklist* Gillian

Engberg noted that *Deep and Dark and Dangerous* features "scenes that will chill readers as surely as a plunge in cold water," while in *Kliatt* Sherry Hoy assured young readers that the novel is "shivery but not gory." Noting that Hahn's novel includes "classic mystery elements," *School Library Journal* contributor Marie Orlando added that *Deep and Dark and Dangerous* is a "well-plotted story [that] mov[es] . . . along to a satisfying conclusion."

While visiting their grandmother's Vermont inn for the summer, two siblings stir up more than they can handle in *All the Lovely Bad Ones: A Ghost Story.* Twelve-year-old Travis and younger sister Corey are excited when they realize that their grandmother's bed and breakfast has a reputation for being haunted. Hoping to frighten some gullible guests, the children create several ghost-like effects. Although several guests are scared, so are some resident spirits who now come to life and reveal the inn's early history as a poorhouse. While two young ghost boys prove to be fun companions for Travis and Corey, the evil ghost of Miss Ada is far more threatening. Noting that Hahn keeps her story's creepiness at a comfort level appropriate for older elementary-grade readers, Debbie Carton wrote in *Booklist* that *All the Lovely Bad Ones* "combines chills, thrills, and poignant historical fiction." In *Publishers Weekly* a reviewer cited the novel's "genuinely spine-tingling moments" while praising Hahn for her "unique approach to a well-traversed genre," and in *School Library Journal* Terrie Dorio deemed *All the Lovely Bad Ones* a "fast-paced ghost story that readers will relish, shivering all the while."

In her novel *The Gentleman Outlaw and Me—Eli,* Hahn indulges her childhood interest in stories about the Wild West in chronicling the adventures of twelve-year-old Eliza and her dog Caesar as they make their way to Colorado in search of Eli's father. Accompanying Eli and Caesar on their quest is Calvin, a gentleman outlaw they encounter in the woods after Eli escapes her abusive guardians. At the end of many adventures, the three reach Colorado and finally locate Eli's papa, a sheriff. Lola Teubert, writing in *Voice of Youth Advocates,* characterized *The Gentleman Outlaw and Me* as a "rollicking read, full of the true flavor of the old West," while *Horn Book* reviewer Elizabeth S. Watson called it "tailor-made to satisfy a youngster's ache for high adventure." In addition to garnering praise for her storytelling abilities, Hahn once again also elicited praise for the historical background presented in the story. For example, Susan Dove Lempke was particularly impressed with the "fine job" Hahn does in "recreating the atmosphere of the days of cowboys and miners."

Known for writing about difficult subjects, Hahn tackles an abusive family situation in her series of books featuring young Gordy Smith and his family, previously introduced to readers in *Stepping on the Cracks.* In her next book featuring Gordy, titled *Following My Own Footsteps,* Hahn's young protagonist finds himself living in North Carolina with his grandmother after his father has been imprisoned for being abusive. As he adjusts to life in a new place, Gordy struggles with doubt that he will escape the violence that surrounds him, especially after his mother accepts his father's apology and decides to give the troubled man a second chance.

Praising the honest way *Stepping on the Cracks* deals with "the pain of some insoluble problems," Deborah Stevenson wrote in the *Bulletin of the Center for Children's Books* that in the novel Hahn has created a "telling and believable portrait of a boy on the cusp of major changes in his life." Maeve Visser Knoth also lauded Hahn for tackling a difficult subject, citing her deft handling of such issues as alcoholism and domestic abuse. Additionally, critics were also appreciative of Hahn's skillful re-creation of the mid-1940s. *Booklist* reviewer Susan Dove Lempke asserted that setting Gordy's story against World War II-America is a masterful touch and that Hahn presents a "terrific rendering of day-to-day life" during that era.

In the third book in Hahn's series, *As Ever, Gordy,* the young boy is beset by turmoil once again. This time the death of his grandmother forces Gordy to return to his hometown with his younger sister. As he struggles to establish a relationship with his old rival, Liz, Gordy at first relapses into his old ways, but ultimately he realizes that his father and older brother are not the best role models. Reviewing *As Ever, Gordy* for *Booklist,* Linda Perkins wrote that, although the historical background seems incidental, Hahn has done a masterful job of creating a "painfully believable adolescent" character in Gordy Smith.

In *Anna All Year Round* Hahn sets the world of eight-year-old Anna against the backdrop of pre-World War I America. Based on recollections by Hahn's own mother, *Anna All Year Round* was praised for its poignant evocation of the past, as well as the author's realistic depiction of her young protagonist. Anna is a tomboy, much to the dismay of her very proper mother, who speaks in German to Anna's aunt when the women desire to keep the girl from understanding. Anna's adventures include roller-skating down a cobblestone road and falling so that her chin requires stitches, throwing herself a "surprise" birthday party without telling her mother, learning long division, and trying to convince her mother that she should have a brightly colored coat for the winter. Stephanie Zvirin, writing in *Booklist,* noted particularly the accuracy of Hahn's research, praising the author for her skill in capturing the "flavor of [an] early 1900s setting." A reviewer for *Horn Book* noted that "all the chapters are informed by Hahn's able evocation of time and place."

In *Anna on the Farm* Hahn tells the story of one summer spent by Anna on her uncle's farm in Maryland. Unfortunately, Anna is not the only guest; her uncle's nephew, Theodore, is staying there as well. The two spark immediately, Theodore calling Anna a "city slicker" and Anna considering him a "country bumpkin"; it does not take long for pranks to start and quickly get out of hand. However, through their competition, the cousins see each other as friends. In a tale that is "rollicking fun" according to *Voice of Youth Advocates* contributor Debbie Whitbeck, Hahn provides "a great glimpse of pre-World War I America." As a *Horn Book* reviewer wrote, in *Anna on the Farm* "Hahn defies nostalgia with both the immediacy and the honesty of her up-close, present-tense telling."

Although it might sound like a ghost story, *Promise to the Dead* is actually a story about slavery at the beginning of the U.S. Civil War. Jesse makes a promise to a dying slave that he will deliver her son Perry to his aunt in Baltimore. This is complicated by the fact that Perry's aunt is white, and is the sister to the deceased slave-owner who used to own both Perry and his mother. The two boys—Jesse at age fourteen and Perry at only seven—make a desperate flight; what keeps Jesse going is that he knows he cannot break a promise to someone who is dead. Cyrisse Jaffee, writing in *School Library Journal,* called *Promise to the Dead* "an involving story that raises many of the issues that led to the Civil War," while Cooper commented in *Booklist* that although "there's a lot going on here, . . . the plot never seems too overwhelming."

With *Hear the Wind Blow,* Hahn again tackles the difficulties of war. Set, like *Promise to the Dead,* during the War between the States, the novel centers around Haswell Magruder, a teen whose father died fighting Union forces and whose brother is still out in the field. When a wounded Confederate soldier seeks to hide on the Magruder farm, the Magruders risk punishment by taking him in and attempting to nurse him back to health. Unfortunately for the compassionate family, Union troops arrive, hunt down and kill the soldier, and then raze the Magruder farm. Haswell's mother becomes ill and dies, leaving the boy to take his sister and flee to the home of their relatives. After seeing her to safety, he then travels to find his brother, discovering the realities of war along the way. In her review for *Horn Book,* Betty Carter called *Hear the Wind Blow* "a strong adventure inextricably bound to a specific time and place, but one that resonates with universal themes." "The drama of the Civil War and the fine storytelling and characterization hook readers from the outset," praised Renee Steinberg in her review for *School Library Journal,* while a reviewer for *Publishers Weekly* noted that, "with his bravery and his honest grapplings with complex issues, Haswell will win readers' interest and sympathy from the outset."

Biographical and Critical Sources

PERIODICALS

Booklist, October 15, 1982, Barbara Elleman, review of *The Time of the Witch,* p. 311; May 1, 1993, Stephanie Zvirin, review of *The Wind Blows Backward,* pp.

1580, 1582; April 1, 1994, Stephanie Zvirin, review of *Time for Andrew: A Ghost Story*, p. 1446; March 15, 1995, Ilene Cooper, review of *Look for Me by Moonlight*, p. 1322; April 1, 1996, Susan Dove Lempke, review of *The Gentleman Outlaw and Me—Eli*, p. 1364; September 15, 1996, Susan Dove Lempke, review of *Following My Own Footsteps*, p. 240; May 1, 1998, Linda Perkins, review of *As Ever, Gordy*, p. 1518; March 15, 1999, Stephanie Zvirin, review of *Anna All Year Round*, p. 1329; April 1, 2000, Ilene Cooper, review of *Promises to the Dead*, p. 1473; February 15, 2001, Kay Weisman, review of *Anna on the Farm*, p. 1136; May 15, 2003, Hazel Rochman, review of *Hear the Wind Blow*, p. 1663; September 1, 2004, Ilene Cooper, review of *The Old Willis Place: A Ghost Story*, p. 124; December 1, 2005, Ilene Cooper, review of *Janey and the Famous Author*, p. 53; June 1, 2006, Holly Koelling, review of *Witch Catcher*, p. 70; March 15, 2007, Gillian Engberg, review of *Deep and Dark and Dangerous*, p. 47; May 1, 2008, Debbie Carton, review of *All the Lovely Bad Ones*, p. 86.

Book Report, January, 2001, Michele Baker, review of *Promises to the Dead*, p. 57.

Bulletin of the Center for Children's Books, February, 1986, review of *The Jellyfish Season*, p. 108; April, 1987, Zena Sutherland, review of *Tallahassee Higgins*, p. 146; September, 1988, Roger Sutton, review of *December Stillness*, p. 9; March, 1989, Roger Sutton, review of *The Doll in the Garden*, p. 171; May, 1991, Zena Sutherland, review of *The Spanish Kidnapping Disaster*, p. 218; December, 1991, Zena Sutherland, review of *Stepping on the Cracks*, p. 91; May, 1993, Roger Sutton, review of *The Wind Blows Backward*, pp. 281-282; April, 1994, Roger Sutton, review of *Time for Andrew*, pp. 259-260; October, 1996, Deborah Stevenson, review of *Following My Own Footsteps*, p. 61.

Children's Bookwatch, December, 2004, review of *The Old Willis Place*.

Horn Book, October, 1979, Richard Ashford, review of *The Sara Summer*, p. 534; February, 1983, Ann A. Flowers, review of *The Time of the Witch*, p. 44; March-April, 1986, Mary M. Burns, review of *The Jellyfish Season*, p. 201; November-December, 1986, Elizabeth S. Watson, review of *Wait till Helen Comes*, pp. 744-745; July-August, 1988, Elizabeth S. Watson, review of *Following the Mystery Man*, p. 493; November-December, 1988, Nancy Vasilakis, review of *December Stillness*, pp. 786-787; May-June, 1989, Ethel R. Twichell, review of *The Doll in the Garden*, p. 370; November-December, 1991, Maeve Visser Knoth, review of *Stepping on the Cracks*, p. 736; September, 1996, Maeve Visser Knoth, review of *Following My Own Footsteps*, pp. 595-596; September, 1996, Elisabeth S. Watson, review of *The Gentleman Outlaw and Me—Eli*, p. 596; July, 1999, review of *Anna All Year Round*, p. 465; May, 2001, review of *Anna on the Farm*, p. 324; May-June, 2003, Betty Carter, review of *Hear the Wind Blow*, pp. 346-347; July-August, 2006, Roger Sutton, review of *Witch Catcher*, p. 442; May-June, 2008, Roger Sutton, review of *All the Lovely Bad Ones*, p. 312.

Kirkus Reviews, October 15, 1991, review of *Stepping on the Cracks*, p. 1343; April 1, 1995, review of *Look for Me by Moonlight*, p. 468; June 15, 1996, review of *Following My Own Footsteps*, p. 899; May 15, 2003, review of *Hear the Wind Blow*, p. 751; September 1, 2004, review of *The Old Willis Place*, p. 866; July 15, 2005, review of *Janey and the Famous Author*, p. 790; June 1, 2006, review of *Wind Catcher*, p. 573; May 1, 2007, review of *Deep and Dark and Dangerous*.

Kliatt, July, 2003, Claire Rosser, review of *Hear the Wind Blow*, p. 12; November, 2008, Sherry Hoy, review of *Deep and Dark and Dangerous*, p. 29.

New York Times Book Review, October 23, 1983, Barbara Cutler Helfgott, review of *Daphne's Book*, p. 34.

Publishers Weekly, November 19, 1979, review of *The Sara Summer*, p. 79; August 5, 1983, review of *Daphne's Book*, p. 92; December 6, 1985, review of *The Jellyfish Season*, p. 75; February 9, 1990, review of *The Dead Man in Indian Creek*, p. 62; March 1, 1991, review of *The Spanish Kidnapping Disaster*, p. 73; November 1, 1991, review of *Stepping on the Cracks*, p. 81; April, 26, 1993, review of *The Wind Blows Backward*, pp. 80-81; April 10, 1995, review of *Look for Me by Moonlight*, p. 63; July 8, 1996, review of *Following My Own Footsteps*, p. 84; April 19, 1999, review of *Anna All Year Round*, p. 74; April 17, 2000, review of *Promises to the Dead*, p. 81; May 19, 2003, review of *Hear the Wind Blow*, p. 75; March 10, 2008, review of *All the Lovely Bad Ones*, p. 82.

School Library Journal, December, 1979, Cyrisse Jaffee, review of *The Sara Summer*, p. 86; November, 1982, Karen Stang Hanley, review of *The Time of the Witch*, p. 84; October 1983, Audrey B. Eaglen, review of *Daphne's Book*, p. 168; October, 1985, Marjorie Lewis, review of *The Jellyfish Season*, p. 172; October, 1986, Judy Greenfield, review of *Wait till Helen Comes*, p. 176; April, 1988, Elizabeth Mellett, review of *Following the Mystery Man*, p. 100; April, 1990, Carolyn Noah, review of *The Dead Man in Indian Creek*, p. 118; May, 1993, Gerry Larson, review of *The Wind Blows Backward*, p. 124; May, 1994, Virginia Golodetz, review of *Time for Andrew*, p. 114; July 8, 1996, review of *Following My Own Footsteps*, p. 84; May, 1999, Linda Bindner, review of *Anna All Year Round*, p. 90; June, 2000, Cyrisse Jaffee, review of *Promises to the Dead*, p. 146; March, 2001, Debbie Whitbeck, review of *Anna on the Farm*, p. 209; May, 2003, Renee Steinberg, review of *Hear the Wind Blow*, pp. 152-153; December, 2004, Maria B. Salvadore, review of *The Old Willis Place*, p. 146; August, 2006, Nicki Clausen-Grace, review of *Witch Catcher*, p. 121; May, 2007, Marie Orlando, review of *Deep and Dark and Dangerous*, p. 134; May, 2008, Terrie Dorio, review of *All the Lovely Bad Ones*, p. 124.

Tribune Books (Chicago, IL), April 5, 1987, Cynthia Dobrez, review of *Wait till Helen Comes*, sec. 14, p. 4.

Voice of Youth Advocates, August, 1993, Marilyn Bannon, review of *The Wind Blows Backward*, p. 152; June, 1987, Dolores Maminski, review of *Tallahassee Higgins*, p. 78; June, 1996, Lola Teubert, review of *The Gentleman Outlaw and Me—Eli*, pp. 95-96; March, 2001, Debbie Whitbeck, review of *Anna on the Farm*, p. 209.

Wilson Library Bulletin, June, 1995, Linda Perkins, review of *Look for Me by Moonlight,* p. 135.

ONLINE

Mary Downing Hahn Home Page, http://www.hmbooks. com (November 15, 2009).

OTHER

A Visit with Mary Downing Hahn (video), Kit Morse Productions, Houghton Mifflin (New York, NY), 1994.*

* * *

HALFMANN, Janet 1944-

Personal

Born April 18, 1944, in St. Johns, MI; daughter of a farmer and a homemaker; married Thomas Halfmann (an artist and a teacher), 1966; children: four. *Education:* Michigan State University, B.A. (English and Spanish education), 1967, B.A. (journalism), 1979.

Addresses

Home—South Milwaukee, WI. *E-mail*—janet@janet halfmann.com.

Career

Writer. Daily newspaper reporter, Wichita, KS; *Country Kids,* Greendale, WI, managing editor; Golden Books, Racine, WI, manager, editor, and writer of coloring and activity books; freelance children's book author, 1997—.

Member

Society of Children's Book Writers and Illustrators.

Awards, Honors

Parents' Choice Approved designation, 2004, for *Red Bat at Sleepy Hollow Lane,* 2005, for *Canada Goose at Cattail Lane,* and 2006, for *Polar Bear Horizon;* National Science Teachers Association Recommended designation, 2007, for *Canada Goose at Cattail Lane;* President's Awards for Best Overall Book and Best Picture Book, both Florida Publishers Association, both 2008, and Teacher's Choice Award, *Learning* magazine, 2009, all for *Little Skink's Tail;* Honor Book designation, Society of School Librarians International, 2008, Best Children's Books of the Year designation, Bank Street College of Education, and Honor Book designation, Paterson Prize for Books for Young People, both 2009, Land of Enchantment Book Award masterlist inclusion, New Mexico Library Association, 2009-10, and Beehive Book Awards nomination, Children's Literature Association of Utah, 2010, all for *Seven Miles to Freedom.*

Janet Halfmann (Reproduced by permission.)

Writings

"BUGS" SERIES; NONFICTION

Dragonflies, photographs by Blair Nikula, Smart Apple Media (Mankato, MN), 1999.

Grasshoppers, Smart Apple Media (Mankato, MN), 1999.

Ants, photographs by Dan L. Perlman, Smart Apple Media (Mankato, MN), 1999.

(With Adele Richardson) *Bugbook,* Smart Apple Media (Mankato, MN), 1999.

Fireflies, photographs by James E. Lloyd, Smart Apple Media (Mankato, MN), 1999.

"DESIGNING THE FUTURE" SERIES; NONFICTION

Mosques, Creative Education (Mankato, MN), 2000.

Greek Temples, Creative Education (Mankato, MN), 2000.

Theaters, Creative Education (Mankato, MN), 2000.

"LIFEVIEWS" SERIES; NONFICTION

Life in the Sea, photographs by Tom Stack and Associates, Creative Education (Mankato, MN), 2000.

Life in a Garden, photographs by David Liebman, Creative Education (Mankato, MN), 2000.

Life in a Tree, photographs by David Liebman, Creative Education (Mankato, MN), 2001.

Life in a Pond, photographs by David Liebman, Creative Education (Mankato, MN), 2001.

Life in a Tide Pool, photographs by Tom Stack and Associates, Creative Education (Mankato, MN), 2001.

Life under a Stone, photographs by David Liebman, Creative Education (Mankato, MN), 2001.

"LET'S INVESTIGATE" SERIES; NONFICTION

Peanuts, Creative Education (Mankato, MN), 2002.
Spiders, Creative Education (Mankato, MN), 2002.

"NATURE'S PREDATORS" SERIES; NONFICTION

Scorpions, Kidhaven Press (San Diego, CA), 2003.
Lizards, Kidhaven Press (San Diego, CA), 2004
Mongoose, Kidhaven Press (San Diego, CA), 2005.

"SMITHSONIAN BACKYARD" SERIES; NONFICTION

Red Bat at Sleepy Hollow Lane, illustrated by Thomas Buchs, Soundprints (Norwalk, CT), 2004.

Canada Goose at Cattail Lane, illustrated by Daniel J. Stegos, Soundprints (Norwalk, CT), 2005.

Alligator at Saw Grass Road, illustrated by Lori Anzalone, Soundprints (Norwalk, CT), 2006.

Little Black Ant on Park Street, illustrated by Kathleen Rietz, Soundprints (Norwalk, CT), 2009.

Garter Snake at Willow Creek Lane, Soundprints (Norwalk, CT), 2010.

"SMITHSONIAN OCEANIC" SERIES; NONFICTION

Pelican's Catch, illustrated by Bob Dacey and Debra Bandelin, Soundprints (Norwalk, CT), 2004.

Dolphin's Rescue: The Story of a Pacific White-sided Dolphin, illustrated by Steven James Petruccio, Soundprints (Norwalk, CT), 2005.

Polar Bear Horizon, illustrated by Adrian Chesterman, Soundprints (Norwalk, CT), 2006.

Hermit Crab's Home: Safe in a Shell, illustrated by Bob Dacey and Debra Bandelin, Soundprints (Norwalk, CT), 2007.

Narwhal: Unicorn of the Sea, illustrated by Steven James Petruccio, Soundprints (Norwalk, CT), 2008.

JUVENILE NONFICTION

Skyscrapers, Smart Apple Media (Mankato, MN), 2003.
Plant Tricksters, F. Watts (New York, NY), 2003.
The Tallest Building, Kidhaven Press (San Diego, CA), 2004.

Seven Miles to Freedom: The Robert Smalls Story, illustrated by Duane Smith, Lee & Low Books (New York, NY), 2008.

Contributor to children's magazines, including *Ranger Rick, Boys' Life,* and *National Geographic World.*

JUVENILE FICTION

Little Skink's Tail, illustrated by Laurie Allen Klein, Sylvan Dell Publishing (Mount Pleasant, SC), 2007.

Little Black Ant on Park Street, illustrated by Kathleen Rietz, Soundprints (Norwalk, CT), 2009

Good Night, Little Sea Otter, Star Bright Books (Long Island City, NY), 2010.

Fur and Feathers, illustrated by Laurie Allen Klein, Sylvan Dell Publishing (Mount Pleasant, SC), 2010.

Sidelights

Janet Halfmann started her writing career as a daily newspaper reporter, then became the managing editor for *Country Kids* magazine and worked at Golden Books, creating coloring and activity books for young children. Now a freelance children's author, Halfmann has published dozens of children's nonfiction titles, including her multi-award-winning U.S. Civil War-era picture book biography *Seven Miles to Freedom: The Robert Smalls Story.* She has also moved into fiction with her award-winning picture book *Little Skink's Tail,* which has received several honors.

Part of Creative Education's "Lifeviews" series, Halfmann's *Life in the Sea* features photographs by Tom Stack. The book covers the smallest creatures in the

Halfmann recounts an exiting but little-known story from Civil-war history in **Seven Miles to Freedom,** *a story illustrated by Duane Smith.*
(Illustration copyright © 2008 by Duane Smith. Reproduced by permission of Lee & Low Books, Inc.)

oceans, describing their interdependence and unique concepts, such as bioluminescence. Kathryn Kosiorek, reviewing *Life in the Sea* in *School Library Journal,* commented that "stunning photographs in vibrant color" bring to life the undersea world in all its complexity. A companion volume, *Life in a Garden,* features photographs by David Liebman. Here Halfmann introduces the smaller creatures found in common gardens, including nematodes, fungi, beetles, slugs, snails, and aphids.

Halfmann's nonfiction picture book *Canada Goose at Cattail Lane,* a National Science Teachers Association Recommended title, follows two Canada geese as they hatch and raise their goslings on a small pond. Another nature-related nonfiction title, *Plant Tricksters,* "came about because I have always been fascinated by the amazing things plants and animals do to survive," Halfmann explained, "such as an orchid looking like a female bee to attract a male bee pollinator. That fascination led me to propose a series of books on plant and animal tricksters to Franklin Watts. While I didn't get a go-ahead for the series, I did get a contract for *Plant Tricksters* as part of a 'Plants and Fungi' series. As a farmer's daughter, avid gardener, and nature watcher, researching *Plant Tricksters* was more entertainment than work."

Illustrated by Duane Smith, Halfmann's *Seven Miles to Freedom* tells the story of how a group of slaves working on a Confederate gunboat managed to steal that ship and escape through Charleston harbor with their families during the first years of the U.S. Civil War. Robert Smalls, the head of that effort, eventually became the first African-American captain of a U.S. ship and also had a distinguished political career. Reviewing *Seven Miles to Freedom* in *School Library Journal,* Lucinda Snyder Whitehurst praised Halfmann's "detailed" text and Smith's "artistically beautiful" illustrations. In *Booklist* Hazel Rochman observed that "the strongly impressionistic art, largely in shades of brown and blue, will appeal . . . to older children." A critic writing in *Kirkus Reviews* remarked that "page turns and textual pacing combine to relate the actual escape with pulse-pounding excitement." The same critic called the book "a triumph."

"I was inspired to write *Seven Miles to Freedom* while doing research on African Americans in the Civil War," Halfmann explained. "'What a gripping adventure!' I thought, as I read about how Robert Smalls stole a Confederate steamboat right from under the noses of the Confederates and delivered it to the Union Navy. I was sure young readers would be as spellbound by his daring escape as I was. And at the same time, they would learn the story of an important African-American hero who is seldom found in history books. After his escape, Smalls worked as a civilian pilot for the Union and went on to serve five terms in Congress. He devoted his entire life to improving the lives of all people, especially African Americans."

Halfmann was inspired to write *Little Skink's Tail* while researching a book about lizards. "I was fascinated by young skinks, which often have bright blue tails," she once explained. "To escape an enemy, the skink can snap off its tail—and it keeps on wiggling. And the tail grows back! The inspiration to have Little Skink daydream about wearing the tails of other animals came from watching my children—and now my grandchildren—play dress-up and pretend. As I wrote the story, I pictured my granddaughter dancing about, showing off each tail."

Illustrated by Laurie Allen Klein, *Little Skink's Tail* introduces a skink who loses her tail to a hungry crow. She then goes on to imagine replacing her tail with that of other animals. Soon enough she realizes that her own tail has grown back. Susan E. Murray, writing in *School Library Journal,* cited the story's mix of humor and fact, pointing out that the "nature activities Halfmann includes in her story make *Little Skink's Tail* "attractive" as a teaching tool.

Another picture-book story, this time a work of nonfiction, *Hermit Crab's Home: Safe in a Shell,* is brought to life in artwork by Bob Dacey and Debra Bandelin. In a simple text, Halfmann follows the life of a hermit crab, from its start as an egg, through its challenges against predators and its development as a mature crab growing into a larger shell. A contributor to the *Midwest Book Review* called *Hermit Crab's Home* "a fascinating children's picturebook," and added that Dacey and Bandelin's "artwork adds the perfect touch" to Halfmann's text.

In another work of nonfiction, *Narwhal: Unicorn of the Sea,* Halfmann takes young readers to the Arctic. In a text that pairs with illustrations by Steven James Petruccio, children can follow the adventures of the narwhal, a whale with a long, unicorn-like tooth jutting out from his jaw. As A.E. Jaskiewicz wrote in *Front Street Reviews* online, *Narwhal* "is educational, but told in a way that will make kids enjoy learning about this unusual creature." "Add in the beautiful and realistic pictures," Jaskiewicz continued, and *Narwhal* is "an all around winner."

Halfmann once noted: "I began writing for children when my children were young. I had some success, selling a few articles to children's magazines, such as *Ranger Rick.* But I wanted to make a living writing, so I went back to college and got a second degree in journalism (my first degrees were in English and Spanish with plans to become a teacher). The journalism degree led to careers as a daily newspaper reporter in Wichita, Kansas; managing editor of a national children's magazine called *Country Kids* in Greendale, Wisconsin; a manager, editor, and writer of coloring and activity books for Golden Books in Racine, Wisconsin. When Golden Books moved its headquarters to New York City in 1997 . . . I began my career as a full-time freelance children's writer, my original dream.

"Many of my books are on animals and nature. I grew up on a farm in mid-Michigan, and I got my love of nature from my parents, especially my dad who was what I call a 'farmer's farmer.' He loved animals and the land and that love rubbed off on me.

"I do a tremendous amount of research, even for my fiction picture books. I want to know as much as possible about the person, animal, habitat, etc. that I am writing about so I can make the story come alive for the reader. I try to convey the wonder and excitement that I feel to my readers. I hope they enjoy reading my books as much as I enjoy writing them.

"Not only do I love to write, but I feel privileged to be a children's writer because I feel reading is so important for kids. Parents and other caregivers can give children so much by reading to them from a young age. Reading opens up so many possibilities and is a wonderful bonding experience between caregiver and child. A child who is read to is more likely to become a reader. And a child who can read well is likely to have an easier time in school.

"For aspiring writers, I advise them to read, read, read; write, write, write; and revise, revise, revise until every word shines. Once the manuscript is finished, the writer should study publishers to see who does that kind of book, and send it out. After mailing the manuscript, the writer should forget about it and move on to a new project (most writers have a huge file of rejection letters). I also would strongly advise aspiring writers to join writers groups, such as the Society of Children's Book Writers and Illustrators, especially their state chapter. There is so much to be learned from other writers' experiences."

Biographical and Critical Sources

PERIODICALS

Booklist, June 1, 2008, Hazel Rochman, review of *Seven Miles to Freedom: The Robert Smalls Story,* p. 98.

Kirkus Reviews, April 1, 2008, review of *Seven Miles to Freedom.*

Library Media Connection, January 2008, Jennifer MacKay, review of *Little Skink's Tail,* p. 64; January-February, 2009, Susan Boatwright, review of *Seven Miles to Freedom,* p. 81.

Midwest Book Review, January 1, 2008, review of *Hermit Crab's Home: Safe in a Shell.*

Multicultural Review, spring, 2009, Linda C. Jolivet, review of *Seven Miles to Freedom,* p. 74.

School Library Journal, August 1, 2000, Kathryn Kosiorek, review of *Life in a Garden,* p. 199; August 1, 2000, Kathryn Kosiorek, review of *Life in the Sea,* p. 200; October 1, 2005, Be Astengo, review of *Dolphin's Rescue: The Story of a Pacific White-Sided Dolphin,* p. 115; January 1, 2008, Susan E. Murray,

review of *Little Skink's Tail,* p. 87; July, 2008, Lucinda Snyder Whitehurst, review of *Seven Miles to Freedom,* p. 112.

ONLINE

Front Street Reviews Online, http://www.frontstreetreviews. com/ (January 1, 2010), A.E. Jaskiewicz, review of *Narwhal: Unicorn of the Sea.*

Janet Halfmann Home Page, http://www.janethalfmann. com (January 1, 2010).

*   *   *

HARLEY, Bill 1954-

Personal

Born July 1, 1954, in Greenville, OH; son of Max (a law editor) and Ruth (an editor and writer) Harley; married Debbie Block (an artist manager), June 7, 1980; children: Noah, Dylan. *Education:* Hamilton College, B.A., 1977. *Religion:* Society of Friends (Quaker). *Hobbies and other interests:* Sailing, gardening.

Addresses

Home—Seekonk, MA. *Office*—Round River Productions, Inc., 301 Jacob St., Seekonk, MA 02771.

Career

American Friends Service Committee, Syracuse, NY, social worker, 1977-80; storyteller, author, songwriter, and musical performer with the Troublemakers, beginning 1980. Founder, Providence Learning Connection; co-founder, Stone Soup Coffeehouse, Providence, RI; vice president and board member, Pokanoket Watershed Alliance. Speaker at schools, festivals, conferences and workshops; performer on numerous recordings; commentator, *All Things Considered,* National Public Radio, beginning 1991.

Member

National Storytelling Association, Authors Guild, Authors League of America, Children's Music Network, National Storytelling Network (member, Circle of Excellence, 2001).

Awards, Honors

National Association of Independent Record Distributors and Manufacturers Award (NAIRD) honorable mention, 1984, for *Monsters in the Bathroom;* Gold Choice awards, *Parents* magazine, 1987, for *Fifty Ways to Fool Your Mother,* 1989, for *You're in Trouble* and (with Peter Alsop) for *Peter Alsop and Bill Harley: In the Hospital,* 1990, for *I'm Gonna Let It Shine,* 1992, for *Who Made This Mess?,* 2003, for *The Town around the Bend,* 2005, for *Blah Blah Blah;* Choice Silver Award, *Par-*

Bill Harley (Photograph by Susan Wilson. Reproduced by permission.)

ents magazine, 1987, for *Cool in School,* 1990, for both *Grownups Are Strange* and *Come on out and Play,* 1995, for *Wacka Wacka Woo and Other Stuff* and *From the Back of the Bus,* 2008, for *Yes to Running!;* NAIRD Indie Award, 1987, for *Dinosaurs Never Say Please,* 1990, both for *Come on out and Play* and *Grownups Are Strange;* American Library Association Notable Recording designation, 1990, for *I'm Gonna Let It Shine;* National Association of Performing Arts Award, 1992, for *Who Made This Mess?,* 1993, for *Big Big World;* *Storytelling World* award, 1995, for both *Wacka Wacka Woo, and Other Stuff* and *From the Back of the Bus,* 2001, for *The Town around the Bend,* 2003, for *The Town around the Bend,* 2004, for *The Teachers' Lounge,* 2005, for *One More Time* and *Blah Blah Blah;* Choice Award, *Parents* magazine, 1995, for *Wacka Wacka Woo and Other Stuff;* Pick of the Lists designation, American Bookseller Association, 1996, for *Sitting Down to Eat;* Grammy Award finalist, 1998, for *Weezie and the Moonpies,* 1999, for *The Battle of the Mad Scientists,* 2007, for *I Wanna Play,* and award, 2005, for *Blah Blah Blah,* 2008, for *Yes to Running;* National Parenting Publications Association (NAPPA) Gold award, 1996, for *Big Big World,* 1997, for *There's a Pea on My Plate,* 2001, for *Down in the Backpack,* 2004, for *The Teachers' Lounge,* 2007, for *I Wanna Play,* 2008, for *Yes to Running!;* Best Children's Book designation, Bank Street School of Education, and William Allen White Children's Book AWard, both 2006, both for *The Amazing Flight of Darius Frobisher;* National Green Earth Book Award for Best Environmental Book of the Year in Children's Fiction category, 2009, for *Night of the Spadefoot Toads;* NAPPA Honor designation, 2008, and Oppenheim Toy Portfolio Gold award, and Just Plain Folks Music Award for Children's Storytelling, both 2009, all for *Yes to Running!*

Writings

FOR CHILDREN

Carna and the Boots of Seven Strides, Riverbank Press (Berkeley, CA), 1994.

Nothing Happened (picture book), illustrated by Ann Miya, Tricycle Press (Berkeley, CA), 1995.

Sarah's Story (picture book) Tricycle Press (Berkeley, CA), 1996.

Sitting down to Eat (picture book), August House (Little Rock, AR), 1996.

Bear's All-night Party (picture book), illustrated by Melissa Ferreira, August House (Little Rock, AR), 2001.

Dear Santa: The Letters of James B. Dobbins (picture book) HarperCollins (New York, NY), 2005.

The Amazing Flight of Darius Frobisher (chapter book), Peachtree (Atlanta, GA), 2006.

Dirty Joe, the Pirate: A True Story (picture book) illustrated by Jack E. Davis, HarperCollins (New York, NY), 2008.

Night of the Spadefoot Toads (chapter book), Peachtree Press (Atlanta, GA), 2008.

Contributor to books, including *Ready-to-Tell Tales,* edited by David Holt and Bill Mooney, August House (Little Rock, AR), 1994. Author of *Flyboy* (serialized online novel), 2006; author of songbooks published by Hal Leonard, including *I'm Gonna Let It Shine Musical Revue,* 1996, *Big Big World Musical Revue,* 2000, and *Do It Together,* 2006.

RECORDINGS

Monsters in the Bathroom, Round River Records (Seekonk, MA), 1984.

Fifty Ways to Fool Your Mother, Round River Records (Seekonk, MA), 1986.

Coyote, Round River Records (Seekonk, MA), 1987.

(With Peter Alsop) *Peter Alsop and Bill Harley: In the Hospital,* Round River Records (Seekonk, MA), 1989.

Cool in School: Tales from 6th Grade, Round River Records (Seekonk, MA), 1990.

Grownups Are Strange, Round River Records (Seekonk, MA), 1990.

Come on out and Play, Round River Records (Seekonk, MA), 1990.

I'm Gonna Let It Shine: A Gathering of Voices for Freedom, Round River Records (Seekonk, MA), 1990.

Who Made This Mess? (DVD), A & M Records, 1992.

You're in Trouble, A & M Records, 1992.

Dinosaurs Never Say Please, A & M Records, 1992.

Big Big World, A & M Records, 1993.

Already Someplace Warm (for adults), Round River Records (Seekonk, MA), 1994.

From the Back of the Bus: Completely True Stories, Round River Records (Seekonk, MA), 1995.

Wacka Wacka Woo and Other Stuff, Round River Records (Seekonk, MA), 1995.

Sitting on My Hands: A Collection of Commentaries as Aired on National Public Radio's "All Things Considered," Round River Records (Seekonk, MA), 1995.

Lunchroom Tales: A Natural History of the Cafetorium, Round River Records (Seekonk, MA), 1996.

Weezie and the Moon Pies, Round River Records (Seekonk, MA), 1998.

The Battle of the Mad Scientists, and Other Tales of Survival Round River Records (Seekonk, MA), 2000.

Down in the Backpack, Round River Records (Seekonk, MA), 2002.

Mistakes Were Made—Live (for adults), Round River Records (Seekonk, MA), 2002.

The Town around the Bend: Bedtime Stories and Songs, Round River Records (Seekonk, MA), 2003.

The Teachers' Lounge, Round River Records (Seekonk, MA), 2005.

I Wanna Play, Round River Records (Seekonk, MA), 2006.

Blah Blah Blah: Stories about Clams, Swamp Monsters, Pirates, and Dogs, Round River Records (Seekonk, MA), 2007.

Yes to Running: Bill Harley Live (DVD), Round River Records (Seekonk, MA), 2008.

There's a Pea on My Plate, Round River Records (Seekonk, MA), 2009.

First Bird Call (for adults), Round River Records (Seekonk, MA), 2009.

Also featured in video *Bill Harley: Who Made This Mess?,* 1992.

Sidelights

"If Calvin, of *Calvin and Hobbes* fame, were to grow up, he'd be Bill Harley," Catherine Cella stated in *Billboard,* describing the popular children's author, storyteller, and musician. A full-time performer since 1980, Harley has made the rounds—everywhere from elementary school gymnasiums to outdoor festivals and concert stages—entertaining audiences of adults and children alike with his delightfully humorous and universally recognizable vignettes about growing up. While interacting with his audiences, he usually likes to let people arrive at their own conclusions. "Giving someone a story because they need it, and not because you love it, is a rock my ship tries to avoid," he once explained regarding his ongoing work with children. "After having spent so much time listening to kids' interests and concerns, and spent so much time wandering around in my own memories and past, I think it's possible to speak seriously (and humorously!) about issues that matter to children."

Many of Harley's performance pieces for children have been produced as award-winning recordings, among them *Wacka Wacka Woo and Other Stuff, Blah Blah Blah: Stories about Clams, Swamp Monsters, Pirates, and Dogs, The Teachers' Lounge,* and *Yes to Running: Bill Harley Live.* In *Blah Blah Blah,* his Grammy Award-winning recording, Harley demonstrates that "he knows how to spring laughs," according to *Booklist* critic Paul Shackman, while in *The Teachers' Lounge* he treats fans to what Dan Keding described in *Sing Out!* as "another wonderful CD that explores the wonders of growing up."

Recounted in what *Booklist* contributor Kristi Beavin described as a "voice . . . as elastic and entertaining as bubble gum," Harley's snicker-inducing sagas draw on the rich legacies of folk music and storytelling tradi-

tions, while other tales lapse into lunacy while touching on more modern absurdities. Such surface silliness does not mask Harley's message, however. "I've got a lot of concerns that this world we're leaving our kids is not in real good shape," he told Michael J. Vieira for Rhode Island's *Providence Journal.* One of the insights he tries to leave behind with children and their parents is where their own—and each other's—feelings are coming from, so that they can relate to each other more fairly and understand their own actions better. "There is a child in each of us," Harley told Alexis Magner Miller in the *Providence Sunday Journal,* "and we'd all be a little healthier if we could honor that part of ourselves."

In addition to his work as a performer, Harley also entertains through books, capturing the spirit of his most popular routines in *Carna and the Boots of Seven Strides, Nothing Happened, Bear's All-Night Party,* and *Dirty Joe, the Pirate: A True Story,* among others. "My mother writes for children," Harley once explained to *SATA,* in discussing his move into publishing, "[and] some of the stories I made up as a kid ended up in basal readers. I suppose my development as an author

Harley's folksy storytelling style is a feature of **Big Big World,** *featuring artwork by Frank Bolle.* (Illustration by Frank Bolle © 1993 by A & M Records, Inc. Reproduced by permission.)

is only coming full circle. In between, though, I developed an interest in oral traditions and have done most of my work live, as a storyteller and singer and on tape. I am fascinated by the spoken word and the connection between story and song."

Transforming the energy and physical humor from stage performances into equally entertaining books provided Harley with a fresh challenge when he began *Carna and the Boots of Seven Strides.* "As a storyteller or songwriter, there is constant feedback from the audience about what is working," Harley explained. "It's in performance that I discover what the story is about—if I'm listening, the audience will tell me things about the story I don't know." In his writing Harley has relied on an audience composed of friends and family that he counts on for an honest opinion—as well as the advice of his editor. "Writing for children or adults, I'm still writing for myself," he confided. "I try to keep this thought in front of me when I'm working." "Of course," he added, "I'd like to have some fun while I'm doing it. I enjoy bringing adults up short—calling attention to their behavior, as well as honoring the kid's perspective."

Originally narrated on Harley's recording *Blah Blah Blah,* the fun-filled picture-book version of *Dirty Joe, the Pirate* features cartoon artwork by Jack E. Davis. As Harley tells it, the story follows on a mean pirate who trolls the high seas in search of dirty socks. When he spies the ship of fellow pirate Stinky Annie, Dirty Joe and his crew attack, but ultimately come out the losers. Not only do Stinky Annie and her pirate band fight barefoot, they also win the battle and make off with their favorite collectible: the crew's underwear. "Clever rhyming . . . hoist[s] the audience appeal" of *Dirty Joe, the Pirate* "to the tiptop of the mast," quipped a *Kirkus Reviews* writer in a review of Harley's humorous picture book.

Harley turns to older readers in the chapter books *The Amazing Flight of Darius Frobisher* and *Night of the Spadefoot Toads.* In *The Amazing Flight of Darius Frobisher* eleven-year-old Darius suddenly finds himself alone: his widowed father took off in a hot-air balloon and never returned, and now the courts are declaring the man dead. Sent to live with his taciturn aunt Inga, Darius finds a new friend in Daedalus, an eccentric neighbor of Inga's who rebuilds bicycles and may have even found a way to make a bicycle fly. Another relocated middle-schooler, Ben Moroney, is the focus of *Night of the Spadefoot Toads,* and in Ben's case he has moved from the Arizona desert to the wooded, rolling hills of New England. Guided by a friendly science teacher, Ben discovers that some reptiles and amphibians can be found nearby, and he ultimately focuses his energy on preserving the home of an endangered toad species. In *School Library Journal* Walter Minkel described *The Amazing Flight of Darius Frobisher* as a "pleasant blend of melodrama and fantasy," while Melinda Piehler wrote in the same periodical that Harley casts *Night of the Spadefoot Toads* with a "well-developed, realistic 'child hero.'"

Harley's amusing story in **Dirty Joe the Pirate** *is brought to life by cartoon artist Jack E. Davis.* (Illustration © 2008 by Jack E. Davis. Used by permission of HarperCollins Children's Books, a division of HarperCollins Publishers.)

In addition to books and performances, Harley further connects with audiences through his work on National Public Radio's program *All Things Considered,* where he entertains listeners with regular commentaries. "Almost invariably, the ones that get the strongest response are the ones that have to do with memories or issues of childhood," he once explained to *SATA.* "And that's from a bunch of grownups."

Even with a touring schedule that sometimes keeps him away from his own family for weeks at a time, Harley considers himself to be fortunate. "While the hardest thing for me to do is to sit down and write with no one making me do it, it is also very satisfying. I am fascinated by the stuff that comes out. And when I'm not doing that, I get to take a guitar and a handful of songs and stories and hang out with people who want to hear me. . . . Stories help us understand and make sense of the world. When you have a lot of stories inside, you can make your own. That's what I do."

Biographical and Critical Sources

PERIODICALS

Billboard, February 22, 1992, Catherine Cella, "Talent 4 Children."

Booklist, April 15, 1995, Mary Harris Veeder, review of *Nothing Happened,* p. 1506; November 1, 1995, Kristi Beavin, reviews of *Wacka Wacka Woo and Other Stuff* and *From the Back of the Bus,* p. 491; December 15, 1996, John Sigwald, review of *Lunchroom Tales: A Natural History of the Cafetorium,* p. 739; March 15, 1998, Rob Reid, review of *There's a Pea on My Plate,* p. 1256; November 1, 1998, John Sigwald, review of *Weezie and the Moonpies,* p. 516; September 15, 2000, Jean Hatfield, review of *The Battle of the Mad Scientists, and Other Tales of Survival,* p. 258; February 1, 2005, Kristi Jemtegaard, review of *The Teachers' Lounge,* p. 988; April 1, 2007, Paul Shackman, review of *Blah Blah Blah: Stories about Clams, Swamp Monsters, Pirates, and Dogs,* p. 85; November 1, 2008, Paul Shackman, review of *Yes to Running: Bill Harley Live,* p. 63.

Kirkus Reviews, April 15, 2008, review of *Dirty Joe the Pirate: A True Story;* September 1, 2008, review of *Night of the Spadefoot Toads.*

Providence Journal, December 27, 1990, Michael J. Vieira, "Silliness Is Serious Business for Singer of Children's Songs."

Providence Sunday Journal, April 14, 1991, Alexis Magner Miller, "A Class Clown with a Message Youngsters Can Understand," pp. HZ1-2.

Publishers Weekly, February 20, 1995, review of *Nothing Happened,* p. 205; September 8, 1997, review of *There's a Pea on My Plate,* p. 32; June 15, 1998, review of *Weezie and the Moon Pies,* p. 21; December 13, 1999, review of *The Battle of the Mad Scientists, and Other Tales of Survival,* p. 31; November 12, 2001, review of *Down in the Backpack,* p. 22; November 10, 2003, review of *The Town around the Bend,* p. 23; March 12, 2007, review of *I Wanna Play,* p. 62.

School Library Journal, September, 2002, Kirsten Martindale, review of *Down in the Backpack,* p. 81; January, 2004, Beverly Bixler, review of *The Town around the Bend,* p. 70; December, 2006, Walter Minkel, review of *The Amazing Flight of Darius Frobisher,* p. 143; April, 2007, Stephanie Bange, review of *I Wanna Play,* p. 78; May, 2008, Marge Loch-Wouters, review of *Dirty Joe, the Pirate,* p. 100; March, 2009, Melinda Piehler, review of *Night of the Spadefoot Toads,* p. 144.

Sing Out!, spring, 2005, Dan Keding, review of *The Teachers' Lounge,* p. 150.

Toledo Blade, February 26, 1993, David Yonke, "Tales That Touch the Entire Family"; October, 2001, Judith Constantinides, review of *Bear's All-Night Party,* p. 119.

ONLINE

Bill Harley Home Page, http://www.billharley.com (November 20, 2009).

*   *   *

HAYES, Sarah 1945-

Personal

Born 1945, in England; married; children: Felix, two other children.

Addresses

Home—Powys, Wales.

Career

Author and illustrator of books for children.

Awards, Honors

Nestlé Smarties Book Prize shortlist, 1986, for *Happy Christmas, Gemma.*

Writings

FOR CHILDREN

(Reteller) *Beauty and the Beast; The Musicians of Bremen; The Three Sillies,* illustrated by David Scott, Walker Books (London, England), 1985, Crown (New York, NY), 1986.

(Reteller) *Cinderella; Lazy Jack; Queen of the Bees,* illustrated by Gill Tomblin, Walker Books (London, England), 1985, Crown (New York, NY), 1986.

(Reteller) *Hansel and Gretel; The Gingerbread Man; The Six Swans,* illustrated by Colin Hadley, Walker Books (London, England), 1985.

(Reteller) *Puss in Boots; Toads and Diamonds; The Donkey, the Table, and the Stick; The Three Wishes,* illustrated by David Scott, Walker Books (London, England), 1985.

(Reteller) *Little Red Riding Hood; The Three Bears; The Emperor's New Clothes; The King of the Cats,* illustrated by Gerrard McIvor, Walker Books (London, England), 1985.

(Reteller) *Jack and the Beanstalk; The Little Red Hen; The Elves and the Shoemaker; The Princess and the Pea,* illustrated by Gerald McIvor, Walker Books (London, England), 1985.

(Reteller) *Book of Fabulous Beasts,* illustrated by Gerrard McIvor, Walker Books (London, England), 1985, published as *Enchanted Beasts,* Crown (New York, NY), 1986.

(Reteller) *Book of Giants,* illustrated by Chris Riddell, Walker Books (London, England), 1985, published as *Gruesome Giants,* Crown (New York, NY), 1986.

(Reteller) *Sleeping Beauty; The Wolf and the Seven Little Kids; The Fisherman and His Wife; The Magic Porridge Pot,* illustrated by Gill Tomblin, Walker Books (London, England), 1985, Crown (New York, NY), 1986.

(Reteller) *Snow White and the Seven Dwarfs; The Old Woman in Luck; The Three Billy Goats Gruff,* illustrated by Caroline Anstey, Walker Books (London, England), 1985, Crown (New York, NY), 1986.

(Reteller) *The Three Little Pigs; The Frog Prince; The Sultan's Daughter; The Enormous Turnip,* illustrated by Colin Hadley, Walker Books (London, England), 1985, Crown (New York, NY), 1986.

A Bad Start for Santa, illustrated by Jamie Charteris, Atlantic Monthly Press (Boston, MA), 1986.

Happy Christmas, Gemma, illustrated by Jan Ormerod, Lothrop, Lee & Shepard (New York, NY), 1986.

This Is the Bear, illustrated by Helen Craig, Lippincott (New York, NY), 1986.

(Reteller) *Away in a Manger,* illustrated by Inga Moore, Little Simon (New York, NY), 1987.

Bad Egg: The True Story of Humpty Dumpty, illustrated by Charlotte Voake, Joy Street Books (Boston, MA), 1987.

The Boot Gang's Christmas Caper, illustrated by Juan Wijingaard, Walker Books (London, England), 1988.

(Selector) *Clap Your Hands: Finger Rhymes,* illustrated by Toni Goffe, Lothrop, Lee & Shepard (New York, NY), 1988.

Eat Up, Gemma, illustrated by Jan Ormerod, Lothrop, Lee & Shepard (New York, NY), 1988.

(Selector) *Stamp Your Feet: Action Rhymes,* illustrated by Toni Goffe, Lothrop, Lee & Shepard (New York, NY), 1988.

This Is the Bear and the Picnic Lunch, illustrated by Helen Craig, Joy Street Books (Boston, MA), 1988.

(Reteller) *Robin Hood,* illustrated by Patrick Benson, Henry Holt (New York, NY), 1989.

Crumbling Castle, illustrated by Helen Craig, Walker Books (London, England), 1989, Candlewick Press (Cambridge, MA), 1992.

Mary, Mary, illustrated by Helen Craig, Margaret K. McElderry Books (New York, NY), 1990.

(Self-illustrated) *Nine Ducks Nine,* Walker Books (London, England), 1990.

The Grumpalump, illustrated by Barbara Firth, Clarion Books (New York, NY), 1990.

This Is the Bear and the Scary Night, illustrated by Helen Craig, Walker Books (London, England), 1991, Joy Street Books (Boston, MA), 1992.

(Self-illustrated) *The Cats of Tiffany Street,* Candlewick Press (Cambridge, MA), 1992.

(Reteller) *The Candlewick Book of Fairy Tales,* illustrated by P.J. Lynch, Candlewick Press (Cambridge, MA), 1993, published as *Favourite Fairy Tales,* Walker Books (London, England), 1997.

Easy Peasy, illustrated by John Bendall-Brunello, Walker Books (London, England), 1994.

This Is the Bear and the Bad Little Girl, illustrated by Helen Craig, Candlewick Press (Cambridge, MA), 1995.

Sound City: A Guided Tour for Beginning Readers, illustrated by Margaret Chamberlin, Walker Books (London, England), 1998.

Lucy Anna and the Finders, Candlewick Press (Cambridge, MA), 2000.

Dog Day, illustrated by Hannah Broadway, Farrar Straus & Giroux (New York, NY), 2008.

Teeny Tiny Tales, Mathew Price (Denton, TX), 2010.

Adaptations

This Is the Bear was adapted as a play by Vivian French.

Sidelights

A British writer, Sarah Hayes is the author and illustrator of dozens of books for young children, among them retellers of traditional fairy and folk tales, rhyme collections, and original stories such as *Happy Christmas, Gemma, Dog Day,* and her beloved picture book *This Is the Bear.* Hayes began her career in children's books in the mid-1980s by producing a number of illustrated story anthologies, and she also teamed with illustrators

Sarah Hayes' picture book Dog Day ***features endearing cartoon art by Hannah Broadway.*** (Illustration copyright © 2008 by Hannah Broadway. Used by permission of Farrar Straus & Giroux, LLC.)

to produce the *Book of Fabulous Beasts* and *Book of Giants*. In 1986 Hayes produced some of her best-known stories, among them the Smarties Book Award-nominated *Happy Christmas, Gemma, A Bad Start for Santa,* and *This Is the Bear,* the last a collaboration with artist Helen Craig that led to three more picture books. Reviewing one of Hayes' self-illustrated picture books, the counting story *Nine Ducks Nine,* a *Publishers Weekly* critic wrote that her "pastoral watercolors" mesh with the author's "lighthearted" tale.

In *This Is the Bear* Hayes uses a sing-song rhyming text to introduce young readers to a stuffed toy on the verge of an exciting adventure. One fateful day, Fred the toy bear is gathered up with the family trash and soon finds himself at the town dump. Fortunately, the bear's human companion and the family dog are hot on his trail, and Hayes ends her story on an up note. Fred returns in *This Is the Bear and the Picnic Lunch, This Is the Bear and the Scary Night,* and *This Is the Bear and the Bad Little Girl,* all of which feature Craig's ink-and-watercolor art. Praising *This Is the Bear and the Bad Little Girl,* which finds Fred abducted by a pudgy-fingered young toynapper during a dinner at a restaurant, Carolyn Phelan wrote in *Booklist* that Hayes' "simple" text pairs with Craig's "delicate" images to produce a picture book with "visual humor and narrative charm."

Other picture books by Hayes include *Dog Day,* a story about Ben and Ellie, two children who arrive at school only to discover that their new teacher is Rif the dog! Brought to life in Hannah Broadway's digitized art, *Dog Day* was described by a *Publishers Weekly* critic as a "cheerful comedy" with "lots of visual interest." In *School Library Journal* Carolyn Janssen also praised the picture book, predicting that the author's "simple to read" story will inspire "repeated readings" at storytime. "Broadway's charmingly simple" art brings to life the children's "joyful curiosity," noted a *Kirkus Reviews* writer, the critic adding that the "playful" interactive story in *Dog Day* "will have young readers in stitches."

Biographical and Critical Sources

PERIODICALS

Booklist, November 15, 1995, Carolyn Phelan, review of *This Is the Bear and the Bad Little Girl,* p. 564; December 15, 2000, Kelly Milner Halls, review of *Lucky Anna and the Finders,* p. 827.

Horn Book, November-December, 1995, Martha V. Parravano, review of *This Is the Bear and the Bad Little Girl,* p. 760.

Kirkus Reviews, July 1, 2008, Sarah Hayes, review of *Dog Day.*

New York Times Book Review, December 7, 1986, review of *Happy Christmas, Gemma,* p. 77; November 29,

1987, Peter F. Neumeyer, review of *Bad Egg: The True Story of Humpty Dumpty,* p. 28; November 28, 1993, review of *The Candlewick Book of Fairy Tales,* p. 22.

Publishers Weekly, August 31, 1990, review of *Mary Mary,* p. 66; October 12, 1990, review of *Nine Ducks Nine,* p. 61; January 25, 1991, review of *The Grumpalump,* p. 58; November 9, 1992, review of *The Cats of Tiffany Street,* p. 84; November 20, 2000, review of *Lucy Anna and the Finders,* p. 68; July 28, 2008, review of *Dog Day,* p. 73.

School Library Journal, December, 2000, JoAnn Jonas, review of *Lucy Anna and the Finders,* p. 109; July, 2008, Carolyn Janssen, review of *Dog Day,* p. 74.*

       *   *   *

HENDRIX, John 1976-

Personal

Born 1976, in St. Louis, MO; married; wife's name Andrea; children: Jack, Anneli. *Education:* Attended University of Kansas; School of Visual Arts, graduate degree, 2003.

Addresses

Home—St. Louis, MO. *E-mail*—mail@johnhendrix.com.

Career

Illustrator and author. Washington University, St. Louis, MO, instructor in illustration; Parsons School of Design, New York, NY, instructor; *New York Times,* New York, NY, assistant art director. *Exhibitions:* Work exhibited at Society of Illustrators shows and at Subterranean Books Gallery, St. Louis, MO.

Awards, Honors

Silver Medal, Society of Illustrators, 2006.

Writings

SELF-ILLUSTRATED

(Self-illustrated) *John Brown: His Fight for Freedom,* Harry Abrams (New York, NY), 2009.

ILLUSTRATOR

Sid Fleischman, *The Giant Rat of Sumatra; or, Pirates Galore,* Greenwillow (New York, NY), 2005.

Mary Elizabeth Hanson, *How to Save Your Tail: If You Are a Rat Nabbed by Cats Who Really Like Stories about Magic Spoons, Wolves with Snout-Warts, Big, Hairy Chimney Trolls—and Cookies Too,* Schwartz & Wade (New York, NY), 2007.

John Hendrix (Photograph by Jay Fram. Reproduced by permission.)

Deborah Hopkinson, *Abe Lincoln Crosses a Creek: A Tall Thin Tale (Introducing His Forgotten Frontier Friend)*, Schwartz & Wade (New York, NY), 2008.

Contributor of illustrations to a variety of periodicals, including *Sports Illustrated, Wall Street Journal, Esquire, Vanity Fair, New Yorker, Rolling Stone,* and *Newsweek.*

Sidelights

A graduate of the School of Visual Arts, illustrator John Hendrix began his career as an artist in New York City, teaching at Parsons School of Design and working in the art department at the *New York Times.* After relocating to his hometown of St. Louis, Missouri, Hendrix continued to work in the publishing industry, creating book jackets, commissioned illustrations for national periodicals, and eventually books for children.

After providing artwork for Sid Fleischman's 2005 novel *The Giant Rat of Sumatra; or, Pirates Galore,* the artist teamed with author Mary Elizabeth Hanson to produce the whimsically titled *How to Save Your Tail: If You Are a Rat Nabbed by Cats Who Really Like Stories about Magic Spoons, Wolves with Snout-Warts, Big, Hairy Chimney Trolls—and Cookies Too.* Published in 2007, *How to Save Your Tail* features an unusual rat who loves not only reading but also baking. Captured and held in a castle by cats of the queen, the clever rodent talks his way out of trouble by crafting a series of fanciful adaptations of traditional children's fairy tales.

Writing in *Kirkus Reviews,* a critic wrote that Hendrix's "pen-and-ink drawings spice up the humor and flavor the delicious wordplay," an observation echoed by *School Library Journal* contributor Debbie Lewis O'Donnell, who predicted that the same illustrations "will captivate even the most reluctant of young readers."

Hendrix teams up with Deborah Hopkinson on *Abe Lincoln Crosses a Creek: A Tall Thin Tale (Introducing His Forgotten Frontier Friend),* a picture book about a near-drowning incident that occurred during the sixteenth president's childhood. While attempting to cross a swollen body of water with his friend Austin Gollaher, the young Lincoln falls into the raging waters. Only the actions of his quick-thinking companion save the seven-year-old Abe, and this effort is never forgotten, even when the boy grows up and becomes president of the United States. "Hendrix's illustrations have a naive and rustic flavor that's in perfect harmony with the gravelly, homespun narrator's voice," wrote Kathy Krasniewicz in her *School Library Journal* review of the book. The artist's contributions also earned favorable attention from Barbara Auerbach, who wrote in the same periodical that *Abe Lincoln Crosses a Creek* is a "clever collaboration" that offers readers "a rip-roaring adventure with hilarious watercolors and pen-and-ink illustrations."

In his first solo effort, *John Brown: His Fight for Freedom,* Hendrix turns to the life of the famous abolitionist. Beginning his biography with a brief overview of the

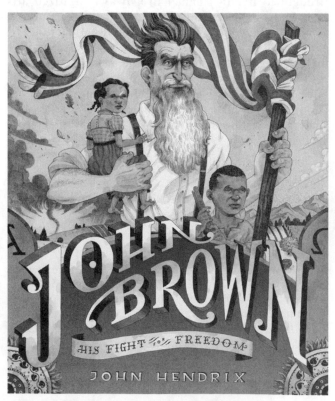

Cover of Hendrix's picture book **John Brown.** (Illustration courtesy of John Hendrix.)

Deborah Hopkinson's folksy story **Abe Lincoln Crosses a Creek** *is enriched by Hendrix's art.* (Illustration copyright © 2008 by John Hendrix. Used by permission of Schwartz & Wade Books, an imprint of Random House Children's Books, a division of Random House, Inc.)

debate over slavery just prior to the start of the U.S. Civil War, the author/illustrator explains how John Brown began helping slaves as a conductor on the Underground Railroad. Eventually, Brown became convinced that only armed struggle would end the institution of slavery in the United States and he led an attack in Kansas on pro-slavery settlers. Three years later, Brown and his small band of followers attempted to gain armaments for their cause by launching an attack on a federal military arsenal in Harpers Ferry, Virginia. Unsuccessful in his attempt, Brown faced a hangman's noose on December 2, 1859, and was martyred by abolitionists in subsequent years.

In *John Brown* Hendrix presents young readers with "a strong introduction to Brown's controversial legacy," claimed a *Publishers Weekly* critic, while *School Library Journal* contributor Margaret Bush described the author/illustrator's "colorful and blunt" narrative as a "thought-provoking presentation of the man and his time." While suggesting that the author's topic might be more suited to older readers, *Booklist* reviewer Ian Chipman predicted that the "attention-commanding art-

work" in *John Brown* will attract children "resistant to reading about historical figures" and provide "fertile ground for discussion about motivations and repercussions."

Hendrix told *SATA:* "As both an artist and writer, I am a believer in speaking up to your audience, especially children. Some of the great books for children, do this of course. The brilliant *The Invention of Hugo Cabret* by Brian Selznick and even silly books like the classics from Dr. Seuss use complex narratives and complex visual language. Why can't children of a certain age also manage moral complexity? The life of John Brown is a great vessel to discuss the vital skill of discernment. We all know that slavery was not just wrong, but an intolerable horror. But, how far should we go to oppose evil that plants itself on our doorstep? Based on what we all learned in history class, John Brown seems like such an unwieldy figure to present in a picture-book format. I think part of the initial appeal of *John Brown.* is a kind of skeptical curiosity. But, once you really examine his life, what he believed, and the circumstances he was placed in, the final judgement on Old Man Brown is not so clear.

"If the election of President Barack Obama indeed sparks an era of change, perhaps we can begin to think differently of John Brown the abolitionist, and honor the narrative of the black community. Might we see in John Brown not a fanatic, murderer, and terrorist, but a freedom fighter as well as a father desperate to protect his family and a humanitarian who refused to enjoy his own freedom when his darker brethren were denied theirs? However flawed, we should admire his unwillingness to make a truce with repression. His desire to act, at great risk to himself and his family, in the face of injustice on behalf of a group of people to which he did not belong is the very best part of the American character. It is something we would wish for ourselves and for our children."

Biographical and Critical Sources

PERIODICALS

Booklist, February 1, 2005, Michael Cart, review of *The Giant Rat of Sumatra; or, Pirates Galore,* p. 957; April 1, 2007, John Peters, review of *How to Save*

Hendrix's illustration projects include cover art for Jean-Claude Mourlevat's award-winning novel **The Pull of the Ocean.** (Illustration copyright © 2006 by John Hendrix. Used by permission of Delacorte Press, an imprint of Random House Children's Books, a division of Random House, Inc.)

Your Tail: If You Are a Rat Nabbed by Cats Who Really Like Stories about Magic Spoons, Wolves with Snout-Warts, Big, Hairy Chimney Trolls—and Cookies Too, p. 57; September 15, 2008, Carolyn Phelan, review of *Abe Lincoln Crosses a Creek: A Tall Thin Tale (Introducing His Forgotten Frontier Friend),* p. 52; October 15, 2009, Ian Chipman, review of *John Brown: His Fight for Freedom,* p. 50.

Horn Book, March-April, 2005, Betty Carter, review of *The Giant Rat of Sumatra,* p. 200; September-October, 2008, Betty Carter, review of *Abe Lincoln Crosses a Creek,* p. 569; November-December, 2009, Betty Carter, review of *John Brown,* p. 693.

Kirkus Reviews, February 1, 2005, review of *The Giant Rat of Sumatra,* p. 176; April 1, 2007, review of *How to Save Your Tail;* August 15, 2008, review of *Abe Lincoln Crosses a Creek.*

Kliatt, January, 2005, Paula Rohrlick, review of *The Giant Rat of Sumatra,* p. 8.

Publishers Weekly, February 21, 2005, review of *The Giant Rat of Sumatra,* p. 176; October 19, 2009, review of *John Brown,* p. 53.

School Library Journal, January, 2005, Steven Englefried, review of *The Giant Rat of Sumatra,* p. 130; June, 2007, Debbie Lewis O'Donnell, review of *How to Save Your Tail,* p. 107; October, 2008, Barbara Auerbach, review of *Abe Lincoln Crosses a Creek,* p. S12; September, 2008, Kathy Krasniewicz, review of *Abe Lincoln Crosses a Creek,* p. 149; November, 2009, Margaret Bush, review of *John Brown,* p. 132.

ONLINE

John Hendrix Home Page, http://www.johnhendrix.com (November 21, 2009).

John Hendrix Web Log, http://johnhendrix.blogspot.com (November 21, 2009).

*   *   *

HIAASEN, Carl 1953-

Personal

Born March 12, 1953, in Fort Lauderdale, FL; son of K. Odel (a lawyer) and Patricia Hiaasen; married Constance Lyford (a registered nurse and attorney), November 12, 1970 (divorced 1996); married 1999; second wife's name Fenia; children: (first marriage) Scott Andrew; (second marriage) two sons. *Education:* Attended Emory University, 1970-72; University of Florida, B.S., 1974.

Addresses

Home—Vero Beach, FL. *Office*—Miami Herald, One Herald Plaza, Miami, FL 33132. *Agent*—Lavin Agency, 222 Third St., Ste. 1130, Cambridge, MA; gagnon thelavinagency.com. *E-mail*—chiaasen@MiamiHerald. com.

Carl Hiaasen (Photograph by John Sciulli/Wire Image/Getty Images. Reproduced by permission.)

Career

Novelist, journalist, columnist, and environmentalist. *Cocoa Today,* Cocoa, FL, reporter, 1974-76; *Miami Herald,* Miami, FL, reporter, 1976—, columnist, 1985—. Barry College, professor, 1978-79.

Member

Authors Guild, Authors League of America.

Awards, Honors

National Headliners Award, distinguished service medallion, Sigma Delta Chi, public service first-place award, Florida Society of Newspaper Editors, Clarion Award, Women in Communications, Heywood Broun Award, Newspaper Guild, and Pulitzer Prize finalist in public-service reporting, all 1980, all for newspaper series about dangerous doctors; Green Eyeshade Award, Sigma Delta Chi, first-place award for in-depth reporting, Florida Society of Newspaper Editors, grand prize for investigative reporting, Investigative Reporters and Editors, and Pulitzer Prize finalist in special local reporting, all 1981, all for newspaper series on drug-smuggling industry in Key West; Silver Gavel Award, American Bar Association, 1982; Newbery Honor Book, American Library Association, 2003, and Rebecca Cau-

dill Young Readers' Book Award, 2005, both for *Hoot;* Damon Runyon Award, Denver Press Club, 2004; Green Earth Book Award, Newton Marasco Foundation, 2006, for *Flush.*

Writings

YOUNG-ADULT NOVELS

Hoot, Knopf (New York, NY), 2002.
Flush, Knopf (New York, NY), 2005.
Scat, Knopf (New York, NY), 2009.

ADULT NOVELS

(With William D. Montalbano) *Powder Burn,* Atheneum (New York, NY), 1981.
(With William D. Montalbano) *Trap Line,* Atheneum (New York, NY), 1982.
(With William D. Montalbano) *A Death in China,* Atheneum (New York, NY), 1984.
Tourist Season, Putnam (New York, NY), 1986.
Double Whammy, Putnam (New York, NY), 1987.
Skin Tight, Putnam (New York, NY), 1989.
Native Tongue, Knopf (New York, NY), 1991.
Strip Tease, Knopf (New York, NY), 1993.
Stormy Weather, Knopf (New York, NY), 1995.
Naked Came the Manatee, Putnam (New York, NY), 1996.
Lucky You, Knopf (New York, NY), 1997.
Sick Puppy, Knopf (New York, NY), 2000.
Basket Case, Knopf (New York, NY), 2002.
Skinny Dip, Knopf (New York, NY), 2004.
Nature Girl, Knopf (New York, NY), 2006.

OTHER

Team Rodent: How Disney Devours the World (nonfiction), Ballantine (New York, NY), 1998.
Kick Ass: Selected Columns, University Press of Florida (Gainesville, FL), 1999.
Paradise Screwed: Selected Columns, Putnam (New York, NY), 2001.
(Editor, and author of introduction) *The Best American Mystery Stories 2007,* Houghton Mifflin (Boston, MA), 2007.
The Downhill Lie: A Hacker's Return to a Ruinous Sport, Knopf (New York, NY), 2008.

Contributor to magazines and newspapers, including *Rolling Stone, Penthouse, Us, Playboy,* and *Esquire.*

Adaptations

Strip Tease was adapted for a film, written and directed by Andrew Bergman, starring Demi Moore and Armand Assante, Castle Rock Entertainment, 1996; *Hoot* was adapted for a film, directed by Wil Shriner, New Line Cinema, 2006; many of Hiaasen's titles are available as audiobooks.

Sidelights

As an award-winning investigative reporter and columnist for the *Miami Herald,* Carl Hiaasen has written about dangerous doctors and drug smuggling, unscrupulous developers, among other subjects. Both his columns and his fictional works, such as *Tourist Season, Stormy Weather,* and *Nature Girl,* reflect his outrage over Florida's social and environmental ills. Hiaasen's novels have been described by *Book* essayist Robert Brookman as "rollicking satires that paint the Sunshine State as a paradise lost, a bizarre cesspool of greed, corruption, environmental neglect and gun-toting stupidity."

Hiaasen is also the author of *Hoot, Flush,* and *Scat,* a trio of critically acclaimed young-adult novels that also examine environmental issues. "These are real simple stories, stories about kids making a difference," Hiaasen remarked in an *OnEarth,* interview. The serious messages in these books are not lost on his audience. As Hiaasen told *Booklist* contributor Sue-Ellen Beauregard, "To a kid, there is no ambiguity about whether it is right or wrong. You don't run a bulldozer over another living creature. And that's what they did when I was a kid. Watching that with my friends made us very angry and still provides the fuel for what I write about today."

A native of South Florida, Hiaasen grew up with dual interests. He wanted to be a writer, but he also enjoyed the outdoors and especially savored Florida's unspoiled wilderness areas. He graduated from the University of Florida in 1974, and by 1976 had earned a position with the *Miami Herald* as a reporter. He soon became a member of the newspaper's investigative team, and he continues to write two columns a week that take aim at corruption in every level of government and business. Hiaasen began his fiction-writing career with coauthor William D. Montalbano and then struck out on his own. As Polly Paddock put it in the *Charlotte Observer:* "Underneath all Hiaasen's hijinks, there is the righteous indignation that marks both his journalistic and novelistic work. Hiaasen hates hypocrisy, pretension, corporate greed, political corruption and the rape of the environment. He won't let us forget that."

Hiaasen has turned his righteous indignation into humorous satire in which heroes and villains alike exhibit farcical quirks and an attachment to creative forms of violence. The good guys are often eco-terrorists seeking to preserve the ever-dwindling plots of undeveloped land; the bad guys wallow in greed as they pursue the rape of the state. According to Joe Queenan in the *New York Times Book Review,* Hiaasen "has made a persuasive case that the most barbaric, ignorant and just plain awful people living in this country today reside, nay flourish, in the state of Florida." Desmond Ryan cited Hiaasen in the *Philadelphia Inquirer* for "his customary pungency, wit and flair," adding that the novelist "has a way of leaving the reprobates and sleazebags that infest the land of the hanging chad flattened like roadkill."

Tourist Season, a tongue-in-cheek account of terrorists who bully Miami tourists in order to depress the tourism industry, received considerable acclaim. Tony Hillerman noted in the *New York Times Book Review* that *Tourist Season* "is full of . . . quick, efficient, understated little sketches of the sort of subtle truth that leaves you grinning." In *Double Whammy* a news photographer turned private eye tangles with a host of bizarre characters, including a former governor of Florida who lives on road kill and a murderer with the head of a pit bull attached to his arm. "The writing style is macabre-funny," noted Walter Walker in a *New York Times Book Review* of the novel, "and it delivers the plot's myriad twists and turns with breathtaking speed."

Greedy plastic surgeons, sensationalistic television personalities, and money-grubbing lawyers are the targets of *Skin Tight,* another fast-paced mix of satire and thriller. The hero, Mick Stranahan, a former Florida state investigator, is threatened by an old feud with a corrupt plastic surgeon suspected of murder. In self-defense, Stranahan keeps a trained barracuda under his stilt house. In one incident the barracuda eats the hand of a hit man trying to murder Stranahan, but the hit

Hiaasen's first middle-grade novel, Hoot, *finds Roy trying to save endangered owls in his Florida town.* (Cover art © MMV New Line Cinema Productions, Inc. and Walden Media, LLC. All rights reserved. Used by permission of Yearling, an imprint of Random House Children's Books, a division of Random House, Inc.)

man gets a weed trimmer as a prosthesis—and then comes after Stranahan again. In the *New York Times Book Review,* Katherine Dunn observed that while Hiaasen's tone in *Skin Tight* does not hold the same warmth toward its subjects as did *Tourist Season*, it is still fascinating and impressive. "No one has ever designed funnier, more terrifying bad guys," she added, "or concocted odder ways of doing away with them."

In *Stormy Weather* Hiaasen uses the aftermath of a devastating hurricane to once again skewer the greedy and corrupt in South Florida. Characters include Edie Marsh, a con woman who has tried in vain to blackmail the Kennedys but who recognizes a new opportunity for enrichment when the hurricane blows through; an advertising executive who ends his honeymoon at Disneyland to venture to Miami to videotape the storm's damage; and a recurring Hiaasen bit player, the one-eyed former governor of Florida who now lives in the swamp, sustaining himself with road kill. *Chicago Tribune Books* reviewer Gary Dretzka noted: "Hiaasen writes with the authority of a documentary filmmaker. . . . He displays no mercy for anyone perceived as being responsible for defiling his home environment." Calling *Stormy Weather* "caustic and comic," *Time* critic John Skow explained the author's use of villains in his literary formula: "turn over a rock and watch in glee and honest admiration as those little rascals squirm in the light."

An eco-terrorist with an anger-management problem serves as the hero in *Sick Puppy.* After seeking revenge on a litterbug, Twilly Spree discovers that the target of his revenge is also a big-time lobbyist involved in expediting the illegal sale of an untouched barrier island. Twilly kidnaps the man's dog and wife in the hope of using them as leverage to save the island. In the meantime, the lobbyist enlists the help of an unscrupulous developer and his sadistic sidekick to put an end to Twilly. A *Publishers Weekly* reviewer deemed *Sick Puppy* "a devilishly funny caper" in which Hiaasen "shows himself to be a comic writer at the peak of his powers." Bill Ott observed in *Booklist* that "Hiaasen's brand of apocalyptic surrealism is nothing if not distinctive."

The publication of *Basket Case* marked a departure for Hiaasen. The novel is narrated in the first person by a principled journalist named Jack Tagger, and among the villains is the newspaper industry itself. Tagger, an obituary writer, investigates the suspicious death of a former rock star, the lead singer of Jimmy and the Slut Puppies. Jimmy's silly lyrics are offered for the reader's perusal, set within a story dealing with Tagger's obsession with death and with the decline of serious reportage in newspapers. Ott, in a review for *Booklist,* applauded Hiaasen for venturing beyond "his unique brand of apocalyptic surrealism" to produce "a rip-roaringly entertaining tale." *Orlando Sentinel* reviewer William McKeen declared that *Basket Case* "is what loyal readers have come to expect from the guy—an intelligent,

Another eco-thriller geared for middle graders, Hiaasen's Scat *sets its suspenseful story in a Florida swamp.* (Illustration © 2009 by Alfred A. Knopf. Used by permission of Alfred A. Knopf, an imprint of Random House Children's Books, a division of Random House, Inc.)

funny, deeply moral book about the decline of Western Civilization." McKeen was particularly delighted with Tagger, declaring him "probably one of Hiaasen's most endearing fictional characters."

Skinny Dip tells the tale of Chaz Perrone, an incompetent and greedy marine scientist who is helping a tycoon to illegally dump fertilizer into the Everglades. Perrone attempts to kill his wife, Joey, after she finds out about his illegal doings. Joey survives, however, and with the help of former cop Mick Stranahan she begins to haunt and taunt her husband in a comic romp that has its roots in the current events of the Sunshine State. Another novel, *Nature Girl,* takes elements of two Shakespearian comedies—*A Midsummer's Night Dream* and *As You Like It*—and transports them to modern-day Florida in the middle of the Ten Thousand Islands, a region of wilderness that stands in for the Forest of Arden. A group of lovers find themselves wandering through this wilderness along with a series of characters that includes a Seminole Indian and a fishmonger who is stalking them. Rather than focusing on the environment, in *Nature Girl* Hiaasen tackles the subject of how people treat each other. Henrietta Clancy, reviewing the novel for *New Statesman,* remarked that "Hiaasen's satirical wizardry is constantly entertaining."

Hoot, Hiaasen's debut work for young adults, tells the story of Roy Eberhardt, a middle-school student who moves into Coconut Cove with his family and tries to adjust to life in South Florida. Before long, he is dealing with a bully, a mysterious boy called Mullet Fingers, and a protest group hoping to stop a construction project that threatens the habitat of owls. In a review for *School Library Journal,* Miranda Doyle called *Hoot* "entertaining but ultimately not very memorable," while a *Publishers Weekly* contributor predicted that "characteristically quirky characters and comic twists will surely gain the author new fans." Bill Ott, writing for *Booklist,* praised Hiaasen for letting "his inner kid run rampant" in *Hoot* and added that the book "is full of offbeat humor, buffoonish yet charming supporting characters, and genuinely touching scene of children enjoying the wildness of nature." Not only did *Hoot* earn praise from both readers and reviewers, but it was awarded a Newbery honor designation, one of the highest awards in the world of children's books.

Another mystery that centers on the ecosystems of his home state of Florida, *Flush* follows the adventures of Paine Underwood and his children Noah and Abbey as they attempt to stop Dusty Muleman, the owner of a local floating casino, from dumping sewage into area waters. Paine goes so far as to sink the *Coral Queen,* an act that gets him thrown in jail, and has his wife talking about divorce. Noah and Abbey, however, are far more understanding of their father's determination, and they throw their support behind Paine's efforts. Stephanie Zvirin, writing for *Booklist,* opined that "the sparkle that catapulted *Hoot* into the limelight isn't quite as brilliant here." However, Betty Carter, in a review for *Horn Book,* remarked that "Hiaasen hits his stride" with *Flush*, adding that "it is the multidimensional characters who give the novel its vitality." A reviewer for *Publishers Weekly* wrote that, "while much of this adventure . . . is predictable, Hiaasen creates enough interesting plot twists to keep the pages turning." Joel Shoemaker, reviewing the novel for *School Library Journal,* pointed out a few flaws in the overall plot, but concluded that Hiaasen's "environmental story is front and center and readers will be hooked as the good guys try to do the right thing."

In *Scat* Hiaasen introduces Nick Waters, a fourteen year old who decides to mount his own search for Mrs. Starch, a science teacher who disappeared while on a class field trip to the Everglades. With the help of a feisty sidekick, Marta Gonzalez, Nick discovers that an endangered Florida panther patrols the swamp, a fact that threatens to sink the plans of some crooked businessmen who have started an illegal oil drilling operation in the area. "With his trademark rapid-fire style," wrote *Christian Science Monitor* reviewer Augusta Scattergood, "Hiaasen fills this novel with suspense, humor, and oddball characters, human and animal." Josh Lacey,

reviewing the novel in the London *Guardian,* stated that, "Whatever your political alignment, you'll find nothing dreary or didactic about Hiaasen's writing; *Scat* is a funny and furiously fast-moving novel populated by engaging characters and fuelled by a strong sense of moral outrage."

In addition to his adult novels and children's books, Hiaasen has also published several volumes of his collected columns, as well as *Team Rodent: How Disney Devours the World,* a scathing critique of the Walt Disney Corporation. *Atlanta Journal-Constitution* writer Mike Williams observed that in his nonfiction, "Hiaasen wastes no time. He sets his tone to rapid-fire acerbic, squeezes off a few rounds to clear his muzzle, then goes on full automatic, like Rambo taking on the world." In the *Sarasota Herald Tribune,* David Grimes remarked that "reading a collection of Carl Hiaasen's newspaper columns reveals a frightening truth about his loopy novels: They're not that big an exaggeration." *Southern Cultures* reviewer David Zucchino maintained that when "Hiaasen opens fire . . . he is pitiless. He

An infusion of sewage into the Florida Keys inspires public protest and a mystery in Flush, *another middle-grade thriller by Hiaasen.* (Illustration © 2005 by Alfred A. Knopf. Used by permission of Alfred A. Knopf, an imprint of Random House Children's Books, a division of Random House, Inc.)

savages the men and institutions he believes are turning his beloved Miami and South Florida into a crass, violent, drug-soaked strip mall." A *Publishers Weekly* critic felt that Hiaasen "writes with an old-time columnist's sense of righteous rage and an utterly current and biting wit."

In the words of *January* magazine contributor Linda Richards, "Hiaasen's humor is his trademark: it's a wry humor, certainly, and he seems to stand arms akimbo as he creates his worlds: Worlds where the shenanigans of various South Florida hoods and hoodwinkers are par for the course." Discussing the satirical nature of his books, Hiaasen remarked in an essay on his home page, "I've got to be mad about something in order to be funny, which means all my books are going to deal with issues that are important to me—the trashing of the environment, political corruption, racial injustice, whatever." He concluded, "I would consider myself a deeply concerned member of the human race. I would like my children and grandchildren to be able to grow up in a place where they can always see a bald eagle or a manatee or a school of dolphins—or a pair of little burrowing owls, for that matter."

Biographical and Critical Sources

PERIODICALS

Contemporary Literary Criticism, Volume 238, Gale (Detroit, MI), 2007.

PERIODICALS

Atlanta Journal-Constitution, June 14, 1998, Mike Williams, "Hiaasen Tackles 'Rodent' That Ate Florida," p. L11; January 2, 2000, Phil Kloer, "Hiaasen's 'Sick' Tale a Fun Ride," p. K12.

Book, January-February, 2002, Robert Brookman, "Excitable Boy," p. 27.

Booklist, November 1, 1999, Bill Ott, review of *Sick Puppy,* p. 483; May 1, 2001, Bill Ott, "Hiaasen's People," p. 1704; September 15, 2001, David Pitt, review of *Paradise Screwed: Selected Columns,* p. 184; November 1, 2001, Bill Ott, review of *Basket Case,* p. 444; October 15, 2002, Bill Ott, review of *Hoot,* p. 405; May 1, 2006, Sue-Ellen Beauregard, interview with Hiaasen, p. 53; December 1, 2006, Bill Ott, review of *Nature Girl,* p. 5; February 15, 2008, Bill Ott, review of *The Downhill Lie: A Hacker's Return to a Ruinous Sport,* p. 4; November 1, 2008, Ian Chipman, review of *Scat,* p. 41.

Charlotte Observer, January 16, 2002, Polly Paddock, review of *Basket Case;* August, 2005, Stephanie Zvirin, review of *Flush,* p. 2028.

Chicago Tribune, January 23, 2002, Patrick T. Reardon, review of *Basket Case.*

Christian Science Monitor, February 17, 2009, Augusta Scattergood, review of *Scat,* p. 25.

Entertainment Weekly, January 18, 2002, Bruce Fretts, "Sunny Delight," p. 72.

Fort Worth Star-Telegram, January 9, 2002, Jeff Guinn, review of *Basket Case.*

Guardian (London, England), October 17, 2009, Josh Lacey, review of *Scat.*

Horn Book, September-October, 2005, Betty Carter, review of *Flush,* p. 579; January-February, 2009, Betty Carter, review of *Scat,* p. 94.

Houston Chronicle, January 16, 2000, Jim Barlow, "Carl Hiaasen: The Kinky Friedman of Thriller Writers," p. 17.

January, January, 2002, Linda Richards, interview with Hiaasen.

Library Journal, February 15, 2008, Steven Silkunas, review of *The Downhill Lie,* p. 111.

Los Angeles Times Book Review, October 13, 1991, Jack Viertel, review of *Native Tongue,* p. 9.

Maclean's, January 17, 2002, Paula Friedman, review of *Basket Case,* p. 2.

New Statesman, January 29, 2007, Henrietta Clancy, "Modern Manners" review of *Nature Girl,* p. 67.

New York Times, June 14, 1998, Deborah Stead, review of *Team Rodent: How Disney Devours the World,* p. B9; January 6, 2000, Christopher Lehmann-Haupt, "Lots of Bad-natured Floridians and One Good-natured Dog," p. B10; January 3, 2002, Janet Maslin, "An Obit Writer's Renewed Zest for Life," p. B13; May 19, 2008, Janet Maslin, review of *The Downhill Lie,* p. E8.

New York Times Book Review, March 16, 1986, Tony Hillerman, review of *Tourist Season,* p. 23; March 6, 1988, Walter Walker, review of *Double Whammy,* p. 20; October 15, 1989, Katherine Dunn, review of *Skin Tight,* p. 42; January 9, 2000, Joe Queenan, "Everything Is Rotten in the State of Florida," p. 10; March 25, 2001, Scott Veale, review of *Sick Puppy,* p. 28; December 3, 2006, John Leland, review of *Nature Girl,* p. 10; June 29, 2008, Holly Brubach, review of *The Downhill Lie,* p. 12; February 15, 2009, David Pogue, review of *Scat,* p. 14.

OnEarth, fall, 2006, "Drowning in Corruption; Crooked Politicians, Sleazy Developers, and Governors Who Eat Roadkill: Welcome to Carl Hiaasen's Florida."

Orlando Sentinel, January 16, 2002, William McKeen, review of *Basket Case.*

People, May 15, 2000, Christina Cheakalos, "Hurricane Hiaasen," p. 139.

Philadelphia Inquirer, January 16, 2002, Desmond Ryan, review of *Basket Case.*

Publishers Weekly, October 25, 1999, review of *Kick Ass: Selected Columns of Carl Hiaasen,* p. 61; November 8, 1999, review of *Sick Puppy,* p. 49; November 12, 2001, review of *Basket Case,* p. 36; June 24, 2002, review of *Hoot,* p. 58; June 27, 2005, review of *Flush,* p. 64; September 18, 2006, review of *Nature Girl,* p. 32; March 3, 2008, review of *The Downhill Lie,* p. 41; October 27, 2008, review of *Scat,* p. 55.

Sarasota Herald Tribune, September 2, 2001, David Grimes, "More Florida Bad Guys in Carl Hiaasen Collection," p. E5.

School Library Journal, September 1, 2005, Joel Shoemaker, review of *Flush,* p. 204.

Southern Cultures, fall, 2000, David Zucchino, review of *Kick Ass,* p. 73.

Sun-Sentinel (Ft. Lauderdale, FL), November 15, 2006, Oline H. Cogdill, review of *Nature Girl.*

Time, August 14, 1995, John Skow, review of *Stormy Weather,* p. 70.

Times Literary Supplement, November 5, 1993, Karl Miller, review of *Strip Tease,* p. 12.

Tribune Books (Chicago, IL), August 13, 1995, Gary Dretzka, review of *Stormy Weather,* p. 5.

Variety, July 13, 1998, Andrew Paxman, review of *Team Rodent,* p. 6.

Writer, June, 2003, "Carl Hiaasen (How I Write)," p. 66.

ONLINE

BookPage Web site, http://www.bookpage.com/ (January 27, 2002), Jay Lee MacDonald, "Carl Hiaasen Takes a Bite out of Crimes against the Environment."

Carl Hiaasen Home Page, http://www.carlhiaasen.com (November 1, 2009).

Miami Herald Web site, http://www.miamiherald.com/ (November 1, 2009), "Carl Hiaasen."

Powells.com, http://www.powells.com/ (September 29, 2005), Dave Weich, "A Kinder, Gentler Carl Hiaasen, Still Pissing People Off."*

I

ICHIKAWA, Satomi 1949-

Personal

Born January 15, 1949, in Gifu, Japan; immigrated to Paris, France, 1971; daughter of Harumi (a teacher) and Nobuko Ichikawa. *Education:* Attended college in Japan. *Hobbies and other interests:* Collecting dolls (used), piano, dance.

Addresses

Home—Paris, France.

Career

Author and illustrator of books for children, 1974—. *Exhibitions:* Work exhibited at Gallery Printemps Ginza, Japan, 1984.

Awards, Honors

Prix Critici in Erba special mention, Bologna Children's Book Fair, 1978, for *Suzette et Nicolas au marché;* Kodansha prize (Japan), 1978, for illustrations in *Sun through Small Leaves;* Sankei prize (Japan), 1981, for illustrations in *Keep Running, Allen!;* Notable Book selection, American Library Association, for *Dance, Tanya.*

Satomi Ichikawa (Photograph by Marianne Veron. Reproduced by permission.)

Writings

SELF-ILLUSTRATED

A Child's Book of Seasons (poetry), Heinemann (London, England), 1975, Parents' Magazine Press (New York, NY), 1976.

Friends, Heinemann (London, England), 1976, Parents' Magazine Press (New York, NY), 1977.

Suzette et Nicolas dans leur jardin, Gautier-Languereau (Paris, France), 1976, translated by Denise Sheldon as *Suzanne and Nicholas in the Garden,* F. Watts (New York, NY), 1977.

Suzette et Nicolas au marché, Gautier-Languereau (Paris, France), 1977, translated by Denise Sheldon as *Suzanne and Nicholas at the Market,* F. Watts (New York, NY), 1977, translated by Robina Beckles Wilson as *Sophie and Nicky Go to Market,* Heinemann (London, England), 1984.

Let's Play, Philomel (New York, NY), 1981.

Children through Four Seasons, Kaisei-sha (Tokyo, Japan), 1981.

Angels Descending from the Sky, Kaisei-sha (Tokyo, Japan), 1983.

Children in Paris (two volumes), Kaisei-sha (Tokyo, Japan), 1984.

Furui oshiro no otomodachi, Kaisei-sha (Tokyo, Japan), 1984, translated as *Nora's Castle,* Philomel (New York, NY), 1986.

Beloved Dolls, Kaisei-sha (Tokyo, Japan), 1985.

Nora's Stars, translated from the Japanese, Philomel (New York, NY), 1989.

Nora's Duck, translated from the Japanese, Philomel (New York, NY), 1991.

Nora's Roses, translated from the Japanese, Philomel (New York, NY), 1993.

(With Patricia Lee Gauch) *Fickle Barbara,* Philomel (New York, NY), 1993.

Nora's Surprise, translated from the Japanese, Philomel (New York, NY), 1994.

Please Come to Tea!, Heinemann (London, England), 1994.

Isabela's Ribbons, Philomel (New York, NY), 1995.

Y a-t-il des ours en Afrique?, L'école de Loisirs (Paris, France), 1998, translation published as *The First Bear in Africa!,* Philomel (New York, NY), 2001.

La robe de Nöel, L'école des Loisirs (Paris, France), 1999, translated as *What the Little Fir Tree Wore to the Christmas Party,* Philomel (New York, NY), 2001.

Mon cochon Amarilla: une histoire du Guatemala, L'école de Loisirs (Paris, France), 2003, translated as *My Pig Amarillo: A Tale from Guatemala,* Philomel (New York, NY), 2003.

La La Rose, Philomel (New York, NY), 2003.

Baobonbon, L'école de Loisirs (Paris, France), 2004.

Le magasin de mon père, L'école de Loisirs (Paris, France), 2004, translated as *My Father's Shop,* Kane/Miller (La Jolla, CA), 2006

Ma chèvre Karam-Karam, L'école de Loisirs (Paris, France), 2005.

I Am Pangoo the Penguin, Philomel (New York, NY), 2006

Le papillon de Boun, L'école de Loisirs (Paris, France), 2006.

Dalla-dalla, L'école de Loisirs (Paris, France),2007.

Come Fly with Me, Philomel (New York, NY), 2008.

ILLUSTRATOR

Elaine Moss, compiler, *From Morn to Midnight* (poetry), Crowell (New York, NY), 1977.

Clyde R. Bulla, *Keep Running, Allen!,* Crowell (New York, NY), 1978.

Marie-France Mangin, *Suzette et Nicolas et l'horloge des quatre saisons,* Gautier-Languereau (Paris, France), 1978, translated as *Suzanne and Nicholas and the Four Seasons,* F. Watts (New York, NY), 1978, translated by Joan Chevalier as *Suzette and Nicholas and the Seasons Clock,* Philomel (New York, NY), 1982, translated by Robina Beckles Wilson as *Sophie and Nicky and the Four Seasons,* Heinemann (London, England), c. 1985.

Cynthia Mitchell, *Playtime* (poetry), Heinemann (London, England), 1978, Collins (New York, NY), 1979.

Cynthia Mitchell, compiler, *Under the Cherry Tree* (poetry), Collins (New York, NY), 1979.

Michelle Lochak and Marie-France Mangin, *Suzette et Nicolas et le cirque des enfants,* Gautier-Languereau (Paris, France), 1979, translated by Joan Chevalier as *Suzanne and Nicholas and the Sunijudi Circus,* Philomel (New York, NY), 1980.

Marcelle Vérité, *Suzette et Nicolas aiment les animaux,* Gautier-Languereau (Paris, France), 1980.

Marcelle Vérité, *Suzette et Nicolas au zoo,* Gautier-Languereau (Paris, France), 1980.

Robina Beckles Wilson, *Sun through Small Leaves: Poems of Spring,* Collins (New York, NY), 1980.

Marcelle Vérité, *Shiki no kodomotachi,* Kaisei-sha (Tokyo, Japan), 1981.

Martine Jaureguiberry, *La joyeuse semaine de Suzette et Nicolas,* Gautier-Languereau (Paris, France), 1981, translation by Joan Chevalier published as *The Wonderful Rainy Week: A Book of Indoor Games,* Philomel (New York, NY), 1983.

Resie Pouyanne, *Suzette et Nicolas: L'année en fetes,* Gautier-Languereau (Paris, France), 1982.

Robina Beckles Wilson, *Merry Christmas! Children at Christmastime around the World,* Philomel (New York, NY), 1983.

Resie Pouyanne, *Suzette et Nicolas font le tour du monde,* Gautier-Languereau (Paris, France), 1984.

Cynthia Mitchell, editor, *Here a Little Child I Stand: Poems of Prayer and Praise for Children,* Putnam (New York, NY), 1985.

Marie-France Mangin, *Sophie bout de chou,* Gautier-Languereau (Paris, France), 1987.

Elizabeth Laird, *Happy Birthday!: A Book of Birthday Celebrations,* Philomel (New York, NY), 1988.

Sylvia Clouzeau, *Butterfingers,* translated from the French by Didi Charney, Aladdin Books (New York, NY), 1988.

Marie-France Mangin, *Sophie and Simon,* Macmillan (New York, NY), 1988.

Patricia Lee Gauch, *Dance, Tanya* (also see below), Philomel (New York, NY), 1989.

Elizabeth Laird, *Rosy's Garden: A Child's Keepsake of Flowers,* Philomel (New York, NY), 1990.

Patricia Lee Gauch, *Bravo, Tanya,* Philomel (New York, NY), 1992.

Patricia Lee Gauch, *Fickle Barbara,* Philomel (New York, NY), 1993.

Patricia Lee Gauch, *Tanya and Emily in a Dance for Two* (also see below), Philomel (New York, NY), 1994.

Patricia Lee Gauch, *Tanya Steps Out,* Philomel (New York, NY), 1996.

Patricia Lee Gauch, *Tanya and the Magic Wardrobe,* Philomel (New York, NY), 1997.

Eiko Kadono, *Grandpa's Soup,* Eerdmans (Grand Rapids, MI), 1999.

Janet Taylor Lisle, *The Lost Flower Children,* Puffin (New York, NY), 1999.

Patricia Lee Gauch, *Presenting Tanya, the Ugly Duckling* (also see below), Philomel (New York, NY), 2000.

Maryann K. Cusimano Love, *You Are My I Love You,* Philomel (New York, NY), 2001.

Patricia Lee Gauch, *Tanya and the Red Shoes,* Philomel (New York, NY), 2002.

Patricia Lee Gauch, *The Tanya Treasury* (contains *Dance, Tanya, Tanya and Emily in a Dance for Two,* and *Presenting Tanya, the Ugly Duckling,* Philomel (New York, NY), 2002.

Maryann K. Cusimano Love, *You Are My Miracle,* Philomel (New York, NY), 2005

(With Anaïs Guéry) Catherine Legrand, *Textiles et vêtements du mond: Carnet de voyage d'une styliste,* Aubanel (Paris, France), 2007.

Maryann K. Cusimano Love, *You Are My Wish,* Philomel (New York, NY), 2010.

Sidelights

Japanese-born artist and author Satomi Ichikawa lives and works in Paris, France, where she creates books and illustrations for children. During her long career, Ichikawa has created original, self-illustrated stories such as *Isabela's Ribbons, La La Rose,* and *I Am Pangoo the Penguin* as well as books in her popular "Nora" series, while also contributing her detailed illustrations to stories by other writers. In *School Library Journal* Jacqueline Elsner called Ichikawa's illustrations "masterful," adding that each figure the artist draws, "whether animal, toy, or person, is full of life, humor, and expression in every gesture."

Unlike many prominent illustrators, Ichikawa did not have an interest in drawing as a child. "I had no idea what I wanted to become," she once told *SATA.* "I took a general course of study for women in college. Girls in Japan were usually expected to work for a few years after college and then get married." Hoping to experience life beyond her small hometown, she traveled to Italy to visit several friends, and then took a trip to France. When she explored Paris, as she recalled, "I felt at home right away. . . . Japan is beautiful, all of my

Ichikawa's detailed paintings capture the childhood delights in Patricia Lee Gauch's **Bravo, Tanya.** (Illustration copyright © 1992 by Satomi Ichikawa. Reproduced by permission of Philomel Books, a division of Penguin Putnam Books for Young Readers.)

family is there, but I grew up in the countryside where people are more conservative and where traditions tend to be restrictive." Discovering "true freedom of spirit" in Paris, Ichikawa moved there and learned to speak French while working as a live-in governess.

When Ichikawa encountered the work of illustrator Maurice Boutet de Monvel, who died in 1913, she was moved by his gentle watercolors. Inspired by Boutet de Monvel's example, she began the study of art and gradually developed her own style. "Since I had never drawn before, I started by observing real life in the gardens and in the playgrounds of Paris," she once recalled to *SATA.* "Although I am Japanese," she added, "my drawings are more European, because my awakening happened here. While I lived in Japan, I never paid much attention to its special beauty, so that it is difficult for me to draw Japanese children and scenes." What has transpired for the well-traveled artist is a bibliography that celebrates multiculturalism. She has written and illustrated books set in Guatemala, Africa, Japan, France, and England, and some of her books—especially those featuring animals—are universal in their appeal.

Locating an English publisher, Ishikawa released her first book, *A Child's Book of Seasons,* which *Horn Book* contributor Ethel L. Heins described as "charming" and "beautifully composed." Other notable early works include her "Suzanne and Nicholas" series, which begins with *Suzanne and Nicholas in the Garden.* Originally published as *Suzette et Nicolas dans leur jardin,* the book follows two children as they enjoy a summer day in the garden. When Nicholas informs Suzanne that another world exists outside the garden, Suzanne decides that the garden is big enough, at least for now. As Gayle Celizic wrote in *School Library Journal, Suzanne and Nicholas in the Garden* conveys a "sense of peace and contentment."

Ichikawa depicts further adventures of Suzanne and Nicholas in *Suzanne and Nicholas at the Market* (originally published as *Suzette et Nicolas au marché*) as well as in her illustrations for several other books in the series that are written by others. *Junior Bookshelf* critic Berna Clark described the illustrations for *Suzanne and Nicholas at the Market* as "very charming," and *School Library Journal* critic Jane F. Cullinane cited *Suzette and Nicholas and the Seasons Clock* for its "delightful pastel illustrations."

Ichikawa's "Nora" series of picture books were inspired by a summer stay in a friend's castle. As she once remembered in *SATA,* "There was no electricity, and every night I went to my room with a candle—going up and down stairs and walking along endless hallways. I stayed there for a month and a half and had no intention of working. But I was so inspired that I wrote the story of a little girl visiting this castle and in every room she discovers a presence—a king, an old piano— reminders of another life." Ichikawa especially enjoyed

The adventures of a lucky pup capture readers' imaginations in Ichikawa's self-illustrated **Come Fly with Me.** (Copyright © 2008 by Satomi Ichikawa. All rights reserved. Reproduced by permission of Philomel Books, a division of Penguin Putnam Books for Young Readers.)

the creation of *Nora's Castle,* which became her first original self-illustrated picture book. It was "a very satisfying experience," she recalled. "I have come to see that this is the best way to work."

The "Nora" books have been generally well received by critics. *Nora's Stars,* in which Nora's toys come alive at night and help her gather the stars from the sky, was described as "charming" and "cozy" by Jane Yolen in the *Los Angeles Times Book Review,* while Sally R. Dow remarked in *School Library Journal* on the "whimsical mood of this quiet bedtime fantasy." In *Nora's Duck* Nora finds a wounded duckling and takes it to Doctor John, who provides care and a home for many injured animals on his farm. Doctor John lovingly tends to the duckling, and Nora takes it back to its pond to be reunited with its mother. Ann A. Flowers wrote in *Horn Book* that the "quiet delicacy" of Ichikawa's illustrations for *Nora's Duck* "mirrors the compassion and trust of the story." A *Kirkus Reviews* writer concluded that Ichikawa's "sweet, precise style is perfect for this idyll," and Jody McCoy related in *School Library Journal* that *Nora's Duck* is an "excellent choice to encourage discussion of the humane treatment of animals."

At home with a bad cold in *Nora's Roses,* the girl is cheered by watching the passers-by enjoying her blooming rose bush. When a hungry cow robs the bush of all but one bloom, Nora preserves this flower by drawing a picture of it. Carolyn Phelan observed in *Booklist* that

Ichikawa's technique "captures . . . the beauty of a rose in bloom, and the determination of a young child," while a critic for *Quill & Quire* proclaimed that the author/illustrator's "technique is a delight." In her *School Library Journal* review, Lori A. Janick commented that *Nora's Roses* "has a gentle sweetness enhanced by exquisite watercolor illustrations."

Ichikawa sets several of her picture books far from her home in Paris. *Isabela's Ribbons* introduces a Puerto-Rican child and her verdant tropical milieu. Isabel loves colorful ribbons and playing hide-and-seek, but no other children want to play with her. Finally, when her Isabela's fantasies begin to run away with her, she finally makes new friends. A *Publishers Weekly* critic wrote that "gaily patterned watercolors packed with playful details make [*Isabela's Ribbons*] . . . a joy to behold."

Animals of the African savanna team up with a young boy to reunite a teddy bear with its owner in *The First Bear in Africa!* Meto is fascinated when a family of tourists visits his village and exhibit many things—including a teddy bear—that the boy has never seen before. When the toy bear gets left behind, Meto races across the savanna to return the stuffed animal to the family, pausing only to show the strange beast to the lion, hippo, giraffe, and elephant that he meets on the way. A *Publishers Weekly* reviewer deemed *The First Bear in Africa!* "a light, appealing caper," while in

A young boy introduces his new toy creature to the curious local wildlife in Ichikawa's self-illustrated **The First Bear in Africa!** (Philomel Books, 2001. Copyright © 1998 Lécole des loisirs, Paris. Reproduced by permission of Lécole des loisirs, and Philomel Books, a division of Penguin Putnam Books for Young Readers.)

School Library Journal Alicia Eames praised Ichikawa's picture book as "a sweet and idealized tale of universal fellowship."

Ichikawa spins another universal tale set in an exotic location in *My Pig Amarillo: A Tale from Guatemala.* Pablito is delighted when he is given a pet pig, and pig and boy quickly become fast friends. When Amarillo the pig disappears without a trace, Pablito searches endlessly and weeps into his pillow each night. It falls to Pablito's grandfather to teach the boy how to cope with grief and loss. Predicting that the sensitive story is "sure to become a classic," a *Kirkus Reviews* critic called *My Pig Amarillo* "a masterpiece of picture-book making," while in *Booklist* Ilene Cooper wrote that Ichikawa "wraps the story in universal emotions: love, longing, grief, hope."

A pink stuffed rabbit tells the story in *La La Rose,* another picture book featuring Ichikawa's unique combination of story and art. La La lives in Paris, where she is the favored friend of a girl named Clementine. When Clementine and her brother are taken to play in Luxembourg Gardens, La La is lost, and her path back to her young companion is marked by a fall down stairs, a tussle with a crow, a swim in a pond, and her discovery by a caring child. Praising the simple tale, Cooper maintained that it is given resonance by Ichikawa's paintings, with their "wonderful mix of action and thoughtfulness, sweetness and subtlety." A *Kirkus Reviews* writer dubbed *La La Rose* a "lush retelling of the familiar lost-and-found tale," adding that it benefits from the author/illustrator's "inspired use of light and shadow," while in *School Library Journal* Catherine Threadgill described the book as "a beautifully illustrated tale of friendship."

Another stuffed toy takes center stage in *I Am Pangoo the Penguin,* but unlike La La's dilemma, Pangoo the stuffed penguin becomes separated from his human companion by his own choice. Young Danny takes his favorite stuffed penguin everywhere, and Pangoo enjoys his special place in Danny's life. However, a new birthday brings a new selection of stuffed toys, and Pangoo finds himself relegated to a shelf rather than curled up in Danny's bed. Sad, he decides to join the real penguins he has seen on his many trips to the local zoo, even though an icy home and a diet of raw fish brings no happiness to Pangoo. Praising *I Am Pangoo the Penguin* as a "charming story," a *Publishers Weekly* added that Ichikawa's gentle watercolor images capture the toy's "unconditional love for his toddler owner." In *School Library Journal* Lauralyn Persson described the book's text as "smoothly and concisely written" while the accompanying illustrations effectively "use . . . line and color to convey character and atmosphere."

In *Come Fly with Me* a wooden toy plane named Cosmos dreams of the time it can take to the skies that it can see from the playroom window. Together with a toy dog named Woggy, Cosmos escapes, and the two toys quickly encounter a series of adventures in their aerial

Ichikawa employs loose pen-and-watercolor art to animate her original story in **My Pig Amarillo.** (Philomel Books, 2002. Reproduced by permission of Philomel Books, a division of Penguin Putnam Books for Young Readers.)

trip around Paris. In *Booklist* Cooper wrote that Ichikawa gears her story to a younger child by showing that "trouble and turbulence are endured with bravery that leads to a happy resolution," while a *Publishers Weekly* reviewer praised the artist's visual tour of the Paris skyline as shown from the "perspective" of "a wooden propeller plane and a stuffed dog who are best friends." In *School Library Journal* Martha Simpson cited the book's "beautifully drawn aerial views" and called *Come Fly with Me* a "soaring selection [that] will spark the imaginations" of toddlers with adventurous spirits.

Although Ichikawa enjoys illustrating her own texts, she still finds time to illustrate stories by other authors. *You Are My I Love You,* a story by Maryann K. Cusimano Love, explores the love between a mother and child teddy bear as they share a day together, and the collaboration between author and illustrator continues in *You Are My Miracle* and *You Are My Wish.* A *Publishers Weekly* reviewer noted that the text and illustrations for *You Are My I Love You* work together by "instantly communicating all that the reader needs to know about the wonders of loving and being loved," and a *Kirkus Reviews* writer deemed *You Are My Miracle* a gentle Christmas-themed story enhanced by "watercolors [that] are a delight." *Grandpa's Soup,* a story by Eiko Kadono, finds a grieving widower hoping to rejoin life by trying over and over to re-create his late wife's meatball soup. The story made its debut in Japan, but according to Marta Segal in *Booklist,* its "gentle lessons on coping with grief are applicable to any culture."

Ichikawa's collaboration with writer P.L. Gauch in the "Tanya" series have been a particular joy for the artist. "This is the first time that my love for dance and my drawing have joined," she once told *SATA.* When readers first meet Tanya in *Dance, Tanya,* the preschooler loves to dance and wishes she could join her older sister at dancing class and on stage at recitals. After attending her sister's recital, Tanya beguiles her family by dancing her own version of "Swan Lake." Her reward comes soon after: her own leotard and dancing slippers, and lessons at her sister's school. Reviewing *Dance, Tanya* in *Booklist,* Denise Wilms concluded that "Gauch's sweet story gains strength from Ichikawa's soft watercolor paintings."

Tanya's adventures continue in *Bravo, Tanya, Tanya and the Red Shoes, Tanya and Emily in a Dance for Two, Presenting Tanya, the Ugly Duckling,* and *Tanya Steps Out,* each of which share the love of classical ballet and the frustrations and challenges of studying a demanding art. In *Tanya and the Red Shoes,* Tanya gets the pointe shoes she has longed for—and the blisters, calluses, and clumsiness that goes with them. *Tanya and Emily in a Dance for Two* describes the budding friendship between Tanya and Emily, the best dancer in the class. The girls find inspiration from each other when Tanya teaches Emily to dance like the animals at the zoo, and Emily helps Tanya to perfect her *cabriolet.* *Bravo, Tanya* was commended by a *Kirkus Reviews* contributor, who wrote that "Ichikawa captures the joy and energy of the dance in her sensitive paintings." In her *Horn Book* review of *Tanya and Emily in a Dance for Two,* Hanna B. Zeiger noted that Tanya's escapades provide "a delight for the dancer hidden in all of us."

Biographical and Critical Sources

BOOKS

Children's Literature Review, Volume 62, Gale (Detroit, MI), 2000.
Ichikawa, Satomi, *Suzanne and Nicholas in the Garden,* F. Watts (New York, NY), 1977.

PERIODICALS

Booklist, September 1, 1989, Denise Wilms, review of *Dance, Tanya,* pp. 70-71; March 15, 1993, Carolyn Phelan, review of *Nora's Roses,* p. 1360; December 1, 1999, Marta Segal, review of *Grandpa's Soup,* p. 712; September 1, 2001, GraceAnne A. DeCandido, review of *What the Little Fir Tree Wore to the Christmas Party,* p. 120; April 1, 2003, Ilene Cooper, review of *My Pig Amarillo: A Tale from Guatemala,* p. 1396; January 1, 2004, Ilene Cooper, review of *La La Rose,* p. 858; February 15, 2006, GraceAnne A. DeCandido, review of *My Father's Shop,* p. 102; February 1, 2008, Ilene Cooper, review of *Come Fly with Me,* p. 44.

Five Owls, September-October, 1994, review of *Nora's Surprise,* p. 12.
Horn Book, June, 1976, Ethel L. Heins, review of *A Child's Book of Seasons,* pp. 280-281; April, 1979, Michael Patrick Hearn, "Satomi Ichikawa," p. 180; March, 1992, Ann A. Flowers, review of *Nora's Duck,* p. 191; November-December, 1994, Hanna B. Zeiger, review of *Tanya and Emily in a Dance for Two,* p. 718; May, 1999, review of *The Lost Flower Children,* p. 333.
Junior Bookshelf, April, 1978, Berna Clark, review of *Suzanne and Nicholas at the Market,* p. 89.
Kirkus Reviews, May 1, 1989, review of *Nora's Stars,* p. 693; November 1, 1991, review of *Nora's Duck,* p. 1404; April 1, 1992, review of *Bravo, Tanya,* p. 464; May 1, 2003, review of *My Pig Amarillo,* p. 678; January 1, 2004, review of *La La Rose,* p. 37; November 1, 2005, review of *You Are My Miracle,* p. 1195; March 15, 2006, review of *My Father's Shop,* p. 292; August 1, 2006, review of *I Am Pangoo the Penguin,* p. 788; February 15, 2008, review of *Come Fly with Me.*
Los Angeles Times Book Review, June 4, 1989, Jane Yolen, review of *Nora's Stars,* p. 11.
Publishers Weekly, June 7, 1993, Herbert R. Lottman, "In the Studio with Satomi Ichikawa," p. 19; August 21, 1995, review of *Isabela's Ribbons,* p. 65; April 12, 1999, review of *The Lost Flower Children,* p. 75; November 8, 1999, review of *Grandpa's Soup,* p. 66; March 12, 2001, review of *The First Bear in Africa!,* p. 90; April 9, 2001, review of *You Are My I Love You,* p. 73; May 12, 2003, review of *My Pig Amarillo,* p. 66; February 23, 2004, review of *La La Rose,* p. 76; October 23, 2006, review of *I Am Pangoo the Penguin,* p. 50; January 14, 2008, review of *Come Fly with Me,* p. 56.
Quill & Quire, April, 1993, Joanne Schott, review of *Nora's Roses,* p. 36.
School Library Journal, April, 1983, Jane F. Cullinane, review of *Suzette and Nicholas and the Seasons Clock,* p. 104; March, 1987, Gayle Celizic, review of *Suzette and Nicholas in the Garden,* p. 146; July, 1989, Sally R. Dow, review of *Nora's Stars,* pp. 66-67; November, 1991, Jody McCoy, review of *Nora's Duck,* p. 1404; June, 1993, Lori A. Janick, review of *Nora's Roses,* pp. 77-78; May, 1994, Jacqueline Elsner, review of *Nora's Surprise,* p. 96; September, 1994, Cheri Estes, review of *Tanya and Emily in a Dance for Two,* p. 184; June, 1999, Susan Pine, review of *Presenting Tanya, the Ugly Duckling,* pp. 95-96; June, 2001, Alicia Eames, review of *The First Bear in Africa!,* p. 118; October, 2001, review of *What the Little Fir Tree Wore to the Christmas Party,* p. 66; May, 2003, Marge Loch-Wouters, review of *My Pig Amarillo,* p. 122; February, 2004, Catherine Threadgill, review of *La La Rose,* p. 114; October, 2006, Lauralyn Persson, review of *I Am Pangoo the Penguin,* p. 113; April, 2008, Martha Simpson, review of *Come Fly with Me,* p. 112.

ONLINE

Kaisei-Sha Web site, http://www.kaiseisha.net/ (November 15, 2009), "Satomi Ichikawa."*

J-K

JANGO-COHEN, Judith 1955-

Personal

Born 1955. *Education:* B.S. (biology); earned K-8 teaching certification. *Hobbies and other interests:* Reading, travel, hiking, singing, folk dancing, theatre.

Addresses

Home—MA. *E-mail*—jangocohen@mac.com.

Career

Author, speaker, naturalist, and photographer. Worked previously as a science teacher.

Member

Society of Children's Book Writers and Illustrators, Massachusetts Reading Association, Massachusetts Library Association, Greater Boston Reading Council (member of board).

Awards, Honors

Notable Social Studies Trade Books for Young People selection, National Council for the Social Studies/ Children's Book Council (CBC), 2006, for *Chinese New Year;* Children's Choices Reading List inclusion, International Reading Association/CBC, 2008, for *Real-life Sea Monsters.*

Writings

Going Wild in the Ocean, McClanahan (New York, NY), 1999.

Going Wild with Bugs, McClanahan (New York, NY), 1999.

Digging Armadillos, Lerner (Minneapolis, MN), 1999.

First Hidden Pictures (activity book), McClanahan (New York, NY), 2000.

Judith Jango-Cohen (Photograph by Eliot Cohen. Reproduced by permission.)

Clinging Sea Horses ("Pull Ahead" series), Lerner (Minneapolis, MN), 2001.

Crocodiles, Benchmark Books (New York, NY), 2001.

Desert Iguanas, Lerner (Minneapolis, MN), 2001.

Penguins ("Animals, Animals" series), Benchmark Books (New York, NY), 2002.

Giraffes ("Animals, Animals" series), Benchmark Books (New York, NY), 2002.

Fire Trucks, Lerner (Minneapolis, MN), 2003.

The Bald Eagle ("Pull Ahead" series), Lerner (Minneapolis, MN), 2003.

Crocodiles ("Animals, Animals" series), Benchmark Books (New York, NY), 2003.

(And photographer with Eliot Cohen) *Dump Trucks,* Lerner (Minneapolis, MN), 2003.

Freshwater Fishes, Benchmark Books (New York, NY), 2003.

Hungry Ladybugs, Lerner (Minneapolis, MN), 2003.

Hovering Hummingbirds, Lerner (Minneapolis, MN), 2003.

Gorillas, Benchmark Books (New York, NY), 2003.

The American Flag, Lerner (Minneapolis, MN), 2004.

Flying Squirrels, Lerner (Minneapolis, MN), 2004.

Armadillos, Lerner (Minneapolis, MN), 2004.

The Liberty Bell, Lerner (Minneapolis, MN), 2004.

Mount Rushmore, Lerner (Minneapolis, MN), 2004.

Octopuses ("Animals, Animals" series), Benchmark Books (New York, NY), 2004.

Camels ("Animals, Animals" series), Benchmark Books (New York, NY), 2005.

Rhinoceroses ("Animals, Animals" series), Benchmark Books (New York, NY), 2005.

Librarians, Lerner (Minneapolis, MN), 2005.

Ellis Island, Children's Press (New York, NY), 2005.

Chinese New Year ("On My Own Holidays" series), illustrated by Jason Chin, Carolrhoda (Minneapolis, MN), 2005.

The Respiratory System, Lerner (Minneapolis, MN), 2005.

Ben Franklin's Big Shock ("On My Own Science" series), Millbrook Press (Minneapolis, MN), 2006.

Porcupines ("Animals, Animals" series), Marshall Cavendish Benchmark (New York, NY), 2006.

The History of Food ("Major Inventions through History" series), Twenty-first Century Books (Minneapolis, MN), 2006.

Why Does It Rain?, illustrated by Tess Feltes, Millbrook Press (New York, NY), 2006.

Kangaroos, Marshall Cavendish Benchmark (New York, NY), 2006.

Bionics ("Cool Science" series), Lerner (Minneapolis, MN), 2007.

Hippopotamuses ("Animals, Animals" series), Marshall Cavendish Benchmark (New York, NY), 2007.

Bees ("Animals, Animals" series), Marshall Cavendish Benchmark (New York, NY), 2007.

Real-life Sea Monsters ("On My Own Science" series), illustrated by Ryan Durney, Millbrook Press (Minneapolis, MN), 2008.

Let's Look at Iguanas, Lerner (Minneapolis, MN), 2010.

Contributor to children's periodicals, including *Science World, SuperScience,* and *Science Spin.*

Author's works have been translated into Spanish.

BOARD BOOKS

Terrence the Turtle, Joshua Morris (Westport, CT), 1996.

Katy the Crocodile, Joshua Morris (Westport, CT), 1996.

Freddy the Frog, Joshua Morris (Westport, CT), 1996.

A School Bus Adventure, Joshua Morris (Westport, CT), 1997.

Freddie's Forest Pals, Joshua Morris (Westport, CT), 1998.

Sidelights

After working as a science teacher for nearly a decade, Judith Jango-Cohen started writing children's nonfiction books in the late 1990s, establishing a career that has expanded to include over forty works. Over the years, Jango-Cohen has penned numerous titles in the "Animals, Animals" series, initially published by Benchmark Books and later by Marshall Cavendish Benchmark. Disparate creatures, such as penguins, hippos, octopuses, giraffes, bees, and crocodiles, are scrutinized by the author, with *Hippopotamuses* earning particular praise from *Booklist* critic Jennifer Mattson for providing "an engaging look" at the oversized animal. Reviewing *Giraffes* and *Penguins* in *School Library Journal,* Sandra Welzenbach predicted that both works will "delight readers" and "be a hit with animal lovers and report writers."

Jango-Cohen has also contributed to other series published by Millbrook Press, including her book *Real-life Sea Monsters,* which is included in the publisher's "On My Own Science" series. In this work, the author recounts traditional tales about mythical sea creatures and then offers modern-day explanations about what animals might have inspired these stories. For instance, after sharing information about the fictional sea terror called the Kracken, Jango-Cohen suggests that the origins of this imaginary creature likely come from the giant squid, a cephalopod known to be over fifty-five feet in length. According to a contributor to *Kirkus Reviews, Real-life Sea Monsters* "makes science feel as mysterious and exciting as science fiction."

"My favorite book as a child was *Harriet the Spy,* by Louise Fitzhugh," Jango-Cohen explained to *SATA.* "Harriet wants to know everything about the world. She carries around a notebook in which she records her observations. If you are a curious person, then writing may be a perfect profession for you. It is for me!"

Jango-Cohen's picture book Real-life Sea Monsters *features the fantastic detailed artwork of Ryan Durney.* (Illustration copyright © 2008 by Lerner Publishing Group, Inc. Reproduced by Millbrook Press, a division of Lerner Publishing Group.)

Biographical and Critical Sources

PERIODICALS

Booklist, January 1, 2005, Carolyn Phelan, review of *Chinese New Year,* p. 866; January 1, 2007, Jennifer Mattson, review of *Hippopotamuses,* p. 86.

Kirkus Reviews, July 1, 2008, review of *Real-life Sea Monsters.*

School Library Journal, January, 2001, Patricia Manning, review of *Clinging Sea Horses,* p. 118; February, 2002, Sandra Welzenbach, reviews of *Giraffes* and *Penguins,* p. 122; February, 2003, Pam Spencer Holly, review of *Crocodiles,* p. 132; January, 2004, Edward Sullivan, review of *The Bald Eagle,* p. 112; May, 2004, Cynthia M. Sturgis, review of *Octopuses,* p. 133; February, 2005, Cynde Suite, reviews of *Camels* and *Rhinoceroses,* p. 118; February, 2006, Lynn K. Vanca, review of *Porcupines,* p. 118, and Eldon Younce, review of *The History of Food,* p. 146; May, 2006, Kate Kohlbeck, review of *Ben Franklin's Big Shock,* p. 113; March, 2007, Maren Ostergard, review of *Bionics,* p. 231; May, 2007, Karey Wehner, review of *Bees,* p. 118; September, 2007, Nancy Call, review of *Real life Sea Monsters,* p. 183.

ONLINE

Judith Jango-Cohen Home Page, http://www.jangocohen. com (November 29, 2009).

Judith Jango-Cohen Photography Page, http://www.agpix. com/cohen (November 29, 2009).*

*   *   *

KIMMEL, Eric A. 1946-

Personal

Born October 30, 1946, in Brooklyn, NY; son of Morris N. (a certified public accountant) and Anne (an elementary school teacher) Kimmel; married Elizabeth Marcia Sheridan (a professor of education), April 7, 1968 (divorced 1975); married Doris Ann Blake, June 16, 1978; children: Bridgett (stepdaughter). *Education:* Lafayette College, A.B. (English literature), 1967; New York University, M.A., 1969; University of Illinois, Ph.D. (education), 1973. *Politics:* Democrat. *Religion:* Jewish.

Addresses

Home and office—2525 NE 35th Ave., Portland, OR 97212-5232. *E-mail*—kimmel@comcast.net.

Career

Writer. Indiana University at South Bend, assistant professor of education, 1973-78; Portland State University, Portland, OR, professor of education, 1978-94, then emeritus. Full-time writer, 1994—.

Eric A. Kimmel (Photograph by Michael Wilhelm. Reproduced by permission.)

Member

International Reading Association, Authors Guild, Authors League of America, Society of Children's Book Writers and Illustrators, PEN Northwest, Phi Beta Kappa, Phi Delta Kappa, Kappa Delta Pi.

Awards, Honors

Juvenile Book Merit Award, Friends of American Writers, 1975, for *The Tartar's Sword;* Ten Best Books of 1989, Association of Booksellers for Children, for *Anansi and the Moss-covered Rock;* Present Tense—Joel A. Cavior Award for Notable Children's Book, National Council of Teachers of English, 1990, and Caldecott Medal Honor designation, both for *Hershel and the Hanukkah Goblins;* Sydney Taylor Picture Book Award, Association of Jewish Libraries, 1990, and National Jewish Book Award nomination, both for *The Chanukkah Guest;* Notable Children's Trade Book in the Field of Social Studies, Children's Book Council/National Council for the Social Studies (CBC/NCSS), 1992, for *The Greatest of All;* Notable Children's Trade Book in the Field of Social Studies, CBC/NCSS, 1992, and Aesop Prize, Children's Folklore Section of the American Folklore Society, 1993, both for *Days of Awe;* Parents' Choice Award, 1994, for *The Three Princes;* Paul A. Witty Short Story Award, International Reading Association (IRA), for *Four Dollars and Fifty Cents;* Anne Izard Storytellers' Choice Award, for *The Spotted Pony;*

Irma and James H. Black Award, Bank Street College of Education, for *Three Sacks of Truth;* Sydney Taylor Book Award, National Jewish Picture Book Award finalist, Zena Sutherland Award, University of Chicago Lab School, Notable Children's Book selection, American Library Association, Best Children's Books of 2000 selection, *Publishers Weekly,* and One Hundred Titles for Reading and Sharing selection, New York Public Library, 2000, all for *Gershon's Monster;* Best Children's Books selection, Bank Street College of Education, 2001, for *The Runaway Tortilla;* Notable Book selection, for *The Jar of Fools;* White House Easter Egg Roll featured book, 2001, for *The Birds' Gift;* Sydney Taylor Award Honor Book designation, 2001, for *A Cloak for the Moon.* Several of Kimmel's books have been nominated or won state awards from organizations in Colorado, Georgia, Nebraska, Nevada, Oregon, Utah, Kentucky, Pennsylvania, and Washington, and have been named to numerous "best books," "children's choice," and "teachers' choice" lists of organizations including the New York Public Library, American Booksellers Association, and IRA/CBC.

Writings

FOR CHILDREN

The Tartar's Sword (novel), Coward, 1974.
(Reteller) *Mishka, Pishka, and Fishka, and Other Galician Tales,* illustrated by Christopher J. Spollen, Coward, 1976.
Why Worry?, illustrated by Elizabeth Cannon, Pantheon (New York, NY), 1979.
Nicanor's Gate, illustrated by Jerry Joyner, Jewish Publication Society, 1979.
Hershel of Ostropol, illustrated by Arthur Friedman, Jewish Publication Society, 1981.
(With Rose Zar) *In the Mouth of the Wolf,* Jewish Publication Society, 1983.
(Reteller) *Anansi and the Moss-covered Rock,* illustrated by Janet Stevens, Holiday House (New York, NY), 1988.
The Chanukkah Tree, illustrated by Giora Carmi, Holiday House (New York, NY), 1988.
Charlie Drives the Stage, illustrated by Glen Rounds, Holiday House (New York, NY), 1989.
Hershel and the Hanukkah Goblins, illustrated by Trina Schart Hyman, Holiday House (New York, NY), 1989.
The Chanukkah Guest, illustrated by Giora Carmi, Holiday House (New York, NY), 1990.
Four Dollars and Fifty Cents, illustrated by Glen Rounds, Holiday House (New York, NY), 1990.
(Reteller) *Nanny Goat and the Seven Little Kids,* illustrated by Janet Stevens, Holiday House (New York, NY), 1990.
I Took My Frog to the Library, illustrated by Blanche Sims, Viking (New York, NY), 1990.
(Reteller) *Baba Yaga: A Russian Folktale,* illustrated by Megan Lloyd, Holiday House (New York, NY), 1991.

(Adapter) *Bearhead: A Russian Folktale,* illustrated by Charles Mikolaycak, Holiday House (New York, NY), 1991.
(Reteller) *The Greatest of All: A Japanese Folktale,* illustrated by Giora Carmi, Holiday House (New York, NY), 1991.
(Adapter) *Days of Awe: Stories for Rosh Hashanah and Yom Kippur,* illustrated by Erika Weihs, Viking (New York, NY), 1991.
(Reteller) *Anansi Goes Fishing,* illustrated by Janet Stevens, Holiday House (New York, NY), 1992.
(Reteller) *Boots and His Brothers: A Norwegian Tale,* illustrated by Kimberly Bulcken Root, Holiday House (New York, NY), 1992.
(Adapter) *The Four Gallant Sisters,* illustrated by Tatiana Yuditskaya, Holt (New York, NY), 1992.
(Adapter) *The Old Woman and Her Pig,* illustrated by Giora Carmi, Holiday House (New York, NY), 1992.
(Reteller) *The Spotted Pony: A Collection of Hanukkah Stories,* illustrated by Leonard Everett Fisher, Holiday House (New York, NY), 1992.
(Reteller) *The Tale of Aladdin and the Wonderful Lamp,* illustrated by Ju-Hong Chen, Holiday House (New York, NY), 1992.
(Adapter) *Three Sacks of Truth: A Story from France,* illustrated by Robert Rayevsky, Holiday House (New York, NY), 1993.
(Adapter) *The Witch's Face: A Mexican Tale,* illustrated by Fabricio Vanden Broeck, Holiday House (New York, NY), 1993.
Asher and the Capmakers: A Hanukkah Story, illustrated by Will Hillenbrand, Holiday House (New York, NY), 1993.
(Reteller) *The Gingerbread Man,* illustrated by Megan Lloyd, Holiday House (New York, NY), 1993.
(Reteller) *Anansi and the Talking Melon,* illustrated by Janet Stevens, Holiday House (New York, NY), 1994.
One Good Tern Deserves Another (novel), Holiday House (New York, NY), 1994.
(Adapter) *I-Know-Not-What, I-Know-Not-Where: A Russian Tale,* illustrated by Robert Sauber, Holiday House (New York, NY), 1994.
(Adapter) *Iron John: A Tale from the Brothers Grimm,* illustrated by Trina Schart Hyman, Holiday House (New York, NY), 1994.
(Reteller) *Bernal and Florinda: A Spanish Tale,* illustrated by Robert Rayevsky, Holiday House (New York, NY), 1994.
(Reteller) *The Three Princes: A Tale from the Middle East,* illustrated by Leonard Everett Fisher, Holiday House (New York, NY), 1994.
(Reteller) *The Valiant Red Rooster: A Story from Hungary,* illustrated by Katya Arnold, Holt (New York, NY), 1994.
(Reteller) *The Goose Girl: A Story from the Brothers Grimm,* illustrated by Robert Sauber, Holiday House (New York, NY), 1995.
(Adapter) *Rimonah of the Flashing Sword: A North African Tale,* illustrated by Omar Rayyan, Holiday House (New York, NY), 1995.
Bar Mitzvah: A Jewish Boy's Coming of Age, Viking (New York, NY), 1995.

(Reteller) *The Adventures of Hershel of Ostropol,* illustrated by Trina Schart Hyman, Holiday House (New York, NY), 1995.

Billy Lazroe and the King of the Sea: A Tale of the Northwest, illustrated by Michael Steirnagle, Harcourt (San Diego, CA), 1996.

(Reteller) *Count Silvernose: A Story from Italy,* illustrated by Omar Rayyan, Holiday House (New York, NY), 1996.

The Magic Dreidels: A Hanukkah Story, illustrated by Katya Krenina, Holiday House (New York, NY), 1996.

One Eye, Two Eyes, Three Eyes, illustrated by Dirk Zimmer, Holiday House (New York, NY), 1996.

The Tale of Ali Baba and the Forty Thieves: A Story from the Arabian Nights, illustrated by Will Hillenbrand, Holiday House (New York, NY), 1996.

Onions and Garlic: An Old Tale, illustrated by Katya Arnold, Holiday House (New York, NY), 1996.

(Adapter) *Sirko and the Wolf: A Ukrainian Tale,* illustrated by Robert Sauber, Holiday House (New York, NY), 1997.

(Adapter) *Squash It!: A True and Ridiculous Tale,* illustrated by Robert Rayevsky, Holiday House (New York, NY), 1997.

(Reteller) *Ten Suns: A Chinese Legend,* illustrated by Yong-Sheng Xuan, Holiday House (New York, NY), 1998.

(Reteller) *Seven at One Blow: A Tale from the Brothers Grimm,* illustrated by Megan Lloyd, Holiday House (New York, NY), 1998.

When Mindy Saved Hanukkah, pictures by Barbara McClintock, Scholastic (New York, NY), 1998.

(Reteller) *Be Not far from Me: The Oldest Love Story: Legends from the Bible,* illustrated by David Diaz, Simon & Schuster (New York, NY), 1998.

(Editor) *A Hanukkah Treasury,* illustrated by Emily Lisker, Holt (New York, NY), 1998.

(Reteller) *Easy Work!: An Old Tale,* illustrated by Andrew Glass, Holiday House (New York, NY), 1998.

(Reteller) *The Birds' Gift: A Ukrainian Easter Story,* illustrated by Katya Krenina, Holiday House (New York, NY), 1999.

(Reteller) *The Rooster's Antlers: A Story of the Chinese Zodiac,* illustrated by Yong Sheng Xuan, Holiday House (New York, NY), 1999.

(Adaptor) *Sword of the Samurai: Adventure Stories from Japan,* Harcourt (New York, NY), 1999.

The Runaway Tortilla, illustrated by Randy Cecil, Winslow (Delray Beach, FL), 2000.

(Reteller) *Gershon's Monster: A Story for the Jewish New Year,* illustrated by Jon J. Muth, Scholastic (New York, NY), 2000.

(Adaptor) *The Jar of Fools: Eight Hanukkah Stories from Chelm,* illustrated by Mordecai Gerstein, Holiday House (New York, NY), 2000.

Grizz!, illustrated by Andrew Glass, Holiday House (New York, NY), 2000.

Montezuma and the Fall of the Aztecs, illustrated by Daniel San Souci, Holiday House (New York, NY), 2000.

(Reteller) *The Two Mountains: An Aztec Legend,* illustrated by Leonard Everett Fisher, Holiday House (New York, NY), 2000.

Zigazak: A Hanukkah Story, illustrated by Jon Goodell, Random House (New York, NY), 2001.

(Reteller) *A Cloak for the Moon,* illustrated by Katya Krenina, Holiday House (New York, NY), 2001.

Website of the Warped Wizard (chapter book), illustrated by Jeff Shelly, Dutton (New York, NY), 2001.

(Reteller) *Anansi and the Magic Stick,* illustrated by Janet Stevens, Holiday House (New York, NY), 2001.

Robin Hook, Pirate Hunter!, illustrated by Michael Dooling, Scholastic (New York, NY), 2001.

Pumpkinhead, illustrated by Steve Haskamp, Winslow Press (Delray Beach, FL), 2001.

Website of the Cracked Cookies (chapter book), illustrated by Jeff Shelly, Dutton (New York, NY), 2001.

Why the Snake Crawls on Its Belly, illustrated by Allen Davis, Pitspopany Press (New York, NY), 2001.

(Reteller) *The Erie Canal Pirates,* illustrated by Andrew Glass, Holiday House (New York, NY), 2002.

The Brass Serpent, illustrated by Joanna Miller, Pitspopany Press (New York, NY), 2002.

(Reteller) *Three Samurai Cats: A Story from Japan,* illustrated by Mordicai Gerstein, Holiday House (New York, NY), 2003.

Brother Wolf, Sister Sparrow: Stories about Saints and Animals, illustrated by John Winch, Holiday House (New York, NY), 2003.

(And compiler) *Wonders and Miracles: A Passover Companion,* Scholastic (New York, NY), 2004.

(Reteller) *Hayyim's Ghost* (based on a story by Beatrice Silverman Weinreich), illustrated by Ari Binus, Pitspopany Press (New York, NY), 2004.

(Reteller and adaptor) *Don Quixote and the Windmills* (based on the novel by Miguel de Cervantes Saavedra), illustrated by Leonard Everett Fisher, Farrar & Straus (New York, NY), 2004.

(Reteller) *The Castle of the Cats,* illustrated by Katya Krenina, Holiday House (New York, NY), 2004.

Cactus Soup, illustrated by Phil Huling, Marshall Cavendish (New York, NY), 2004.

(Reteller) *The Spider's Gift: A Ukranian Christmas Story,* illustrated by Katya Krenina, Holiday House (New York, NY), 2005.

A Horn for Louis, illustrated by James Bernardin, Random House (New York, NY), 2005.

(Reteller and adaptor) *The Hero Beowulf,* illustrated by Leonard Everett Fisher, Farrar, Strauss & Giroux (New York, NY), 2005.

(Reteller) *The Lady in the Blue Cloak: Legends from the Texas Missions,* illustrated by Susan Guevara, Holiday House (New York, NY), 2006.

(Reteller) *The Frog Princess: A Tlingit Legend from Alaska,* illustrated by Rosanne Litzinger, Holiday House (New York, NY), 2006.

(Adaptor) *Blackbeard's Last Fight,* illustrated by Leonard Everett Fisher, Farrar, Strauss & Giroux (New York, NY), 2006.

(Adaptor) *The Three Cabritos* (based on the story by Peter Asbjärnsen), illustrated by Stephen Gilpin, Marshall Cavendish (New York, NY), 2007.

(Adaptor) *Rip Van Winkle's Return* (based on the story by Washington Irving), Farrar, Strauss & Giroux (New York, NY), 2007.

A Picture for Marc, illustrated by Matthew True, Random House (New York, NY), 2007.

The McElderry Book of Greek Myths, illustrated by Pep Monserrat, Margaret K. McElderry Books (New York, NY), 2007.

The Great Texas Hamster Drive: An Original Tale, illustrated by Bruce Whatley, Marshall Cavendish (New York, NY), 2007.

Anansi's Party Time, illustrated by Janet Stevens, Holiday House (New York, NY), 2008.

Little Britches and the Rattlers, illustrated by Vincent Nguyen, Marshall Cavendish (Tarrytown, NY), 2008.

Stormy's Hat: Just Right for a Railroad Man, illustrated by Andrea U'Ren, Farrar, Straus & Giroux (New York, NY), 2008.

The Fisherman and the Turtle, illustrated by Martha Aviles, Marshall Cavendish (New York, NY), 2008.

The Mysterious Guests: A Sukkot Story, illustrated by Katya Krenina, Holiday House (New York, NY), 2008.

A Spotlight for Harry, illustrated by Jim Madsen, Random House (New York, NY), 2009.

Even Higher: A Rosh Hashanah Story, illustrated by Jill Walsh, Holiday House, (New York, NY), 2009.

The Three Little Tamales, illustrated by Valeria Decampo, Marshall Cavendish, (Tarrytown, NY), 2009.

Joha Makes a Wish: A Middle Eastern Tale, illustrated by Omar Rayyan, Marshall Cavendish (Tarrytown, NY), 2010.

Kimmel's holiday-themed picture book The Chanukkah Guest *features artwork by Giora Carmi.* (Illustration copyright © by Giora Carmi. Reproduced by permission of Holiday House, Inc.)

Medio Pollito: A Spanish Tale, illustrated by Valeria Decampo, Marshall Cavendish (Tarrytown, NY), 2010.

Contributor to periodicals, including *Boy's Life, Spider, Ladybug,* and *Cricket.*

Author's works have been translated into Spanish, Greek, and Korean.

Sidelights

The award-winning author of dozens of picture books and novels, Eric A. Kimmel is well known for his adaptations or retellings of folktales from around the world, especially Yiddish tales. Kimmel blends a sardonic wit with traditional storyteller motifs such as mistaken identities, tests of courage and intelligence, wise fools, and tricksters. The result, a long list of titles which both entertain and teach, includes *Hershel and the Hanukkah Goblins, The Greatest of All: A Japanese Folktale, Anansi's Party Time, Bearhead: A Russian Folktale, Little Britches and the Rattlers, Cactus Soup,* and *The Fisherman and the Turtle. Cactus Soup,* an adaptation of the well-known folktale "Stone Soup," is an example of the author's originality; it is given new life through Kimmel's decision to set the story amid the turmoil of the Mexican Revolution. In addition to such retellings, Kimmel has also penned contemporary fiction for young readers, such as the novel *One Good Tern Deserves Another* and the chapter book *Website of the Warped Wizard,* and has retold his favorite stories in *The McElderry Book of Greek Myths.*

"I've been a storyteller for more than twenty years," Kimmel once noted. "When you stand in front of an audience of a hundred people or more, you learn very quickly what works and what doesn't. Folktales are oral stories, so it's important for the writer to be firmly rooted in oral traditions." In addition to being rooted in the oral tradition, Kimmel is also rooted in a multicultural one. Born in 1946, he was raised in an immigrant neighborhood in Brooklyn, New York, where, as he once commented, "our neighbors were Armenian, Italian, Chinese, Puerto Rican, Irish, and German. You could hear five different languages in a walk around the block." Kimmel spoke Yiddish as a child, thanks in part to the influence of his grandmother, a European immigrant and an important influence on his writing. Coming from western Ukraine and speaking five languages, she was full of stories.

More reader than athlete, as a child Kimmel was drawn to the books of Dr. Seuss, and his illustrated copy of the collected stories of the Brothers Grimm was read over and over "until it fell to pieces." "That's how I came to be a storyteller," he added, "telling other kids stories that I remembered from Grimm and from my grandmother." In college, Kimmel majored in education and taught at the college level for many years, leaving his writing and story-telling to his spare time. In 1974 he published his first book, the children's novel *The Tartar's Sword,* and two decades later he left teaching to write full time.

Kimmel's folk-tale adaptations include Anansi and the Talking Melon, *a picture book illustrated by Janet Stevens.* (Illustration copyright © 1994 by Janet Stevens. Reproduced by permission of Holiday House, Inc.)

Working as a storyteller in schools, parks, and libraries, Kimmel adapted his narration skills to his written tales. He tried to capture the experience of listening to a storyteller in his first picture books, such as *Why Worry?,* a humorous tale about a neurotic cricket and a carefree grasshopper, and *Nicanor's Gate,* a legend about the building of the Second Temple. However, as the author once noted, most of his earliest titles seemed to "sink without a trace." His big break came in the form of a request to stand in for Nobel prize-winner Isaac Bashevis Singer and write a Hanukkah story. Searching in his pile of rejections, Kimmel selected a tale based on a folkloric character, the storyteller and wanderer Hershel Ostropoler, and produced the picture book *Hershel and the Hanukkah Goblins.* Relating how Hershel gets rid of the goblins that are haunting a synagogue and keeping the locals from celebrating Hanukkah, *Hershel and the Hanukkah Goblins* "is welcome both as a Hanukkah story and as a trickster tale," noted *Horn Book* critic Hanna B. Zeiger.

Hershel and the Hanukkah Goblins has been joined on library shelves by numerous other volumes by Kimmel that explore folklore from around the world. Hershel is reprised in one of these titles, *The Adventures of Hershel of Ostropol,* which includes ten adventures of the wandering storyteller, a man described as the "Jewish first cousin of tricksters like Brer Rabbit and Till Eulenspiegel" by Rodger Kamenetz in the *New York Times Book Review.* "Kimmel has a good ear, makes clever use of repetition and knows how to structure a story that has a good joke, with a hearty punch line," Kamenetz concluded.

The Chanukkah Guest, one of several holiday books by Kimmel, features a story of mistaken identity in which a bear is mistaken for a rabbi by a nearsighted woman. "Festivity, generosity and cooperation are all celebrated in this wintry holiday tale that children of all religions will enjoy," wrote a *Publishers Weekly* reviewer. A more unusual Hannukah story is the focus of *A Horn for*

Louis, which melds the childhood of noted jazz musician Louis Armstrong with the Jewish holiday to create what a *Kirkus Reviews* writer deemed a "warm Hanukkah tale with a whiff of old New Orleans." In *A Hanukkah Treasury,* Kimmel brings together a potpourri of holiday information and tales and poems that a contributor for *Publishers Weekly* praised for including "more than enough material to keep a family going for eight days and nights." *Wonders and Miracles: A Passover Companion* contains songs, poems, and stories compiled by Kimmel that "gloriously celebrates the Passover Seder, an evening of observances, history, remembrances, and family sharing," according to *School Library Journal* contributor Susan Pine.

In *The Jar of Fools: Eight Hanukkah Stories from Chelm* Kimmel transports readers to the legendary Yiddish town of fools, resulting in a "true gem," according to a reviewer for *School Library Journal.* A kindhearted fool is also the focus of *Onions and Garlic: An Old Tale,* adapted from a Jewish folktale about the poor merchant Getzel, who ultimately makes good while his acquisitive older brothers are left short. A contributor for *Kirkus Reviews* observed that Kimmel "retells the Jewish folktale . . . with lively dialogue and a comic twist at the end."

Gershon's Monster, a story celebrating the Jewish New Year, is based on a Hasidic legend concerning Rosh Hashanah, while *The Mysterious Guests: A Sukkot Story* focuses on a less-familiar Jewish holiday. In *Gershon's Monster* Gershon the baker finally repents his wicked ways when his sins threaten the lives of his beloved twin children. "The story will achieve its full impact when children, with adult help, begin to understand why it is so important to recognize the wrongs they've

Megan Lloyd contributes her engaging cartoon art to Kimmel's humorous retelling **The Gingerbread Man.** (Illustration copyright © 1993 by Megan Lloyd. Reproduced by permission of Holiday House, Inc.)

The folk-tale roots of Kimmel's **The Frog Princess** *are reflected in Rosanne Litzinger's stylized art.* (Illustration © 2006 by Rosanne Litzinger. Reproduced by permission of Holiday House, Inc.)

committed and try to right them," wrote *Booklist* critic Ilene Cooper. The biblical patriarchs Jacob, Isaac, and Abraham cloak themselves as strangers and show their gratitude to those who give them food and shelter in *The Mysterious Guests,* an "entertaining tale [that] contains important values . . . applicable year-round and in every tradition," according to Heidi Estrin in *School Library Journal.*

Inspired by his grandmother's stories, many of Kimmel's retellings take place in Eastern Europe. In *Baba Yaga* he retells a well-known Russian folktale replete with an evil stepmother and the sweet stepdaughter who outwits both her and the local witch, Baba Yaga. "This engrossing story is both fanciful and suspenseful," wrote a *Publishers Weekly* reviewer. Kimmel presents another Russian folktale in *Bearhead,* about a half man/half bear who is raised by a human and grows into the wise fool of popular folk legend. "Kimmel's lively text plays up the broad, almost slapstick humor of the story," remarked Denise Anton Wright in a review of *Bearhead*

for *School Library Journal.* In *The Castle of the Cats,* a story from Latvia, the youngest son of a farmer gives up his contest for the family lands in favor of true love. Reviewing the picture book in *School Library Journal,* Grace Oliff noted that, due to his "true storyteller's voice," Kimmel "keeps the action moving at an energetic pace without sacrificing images or details."

In *Billy Lazroe and the King of the Sea: A Tale of the Northwest* Kimmel transplants a Russian folktale to his own part of the world, setting his retelling in Oregon at the turn of the twentieth century. "Kimmel's lyrical text . . . has a strong sense of frontier adventure," noted *Booklist* contributor Hazel Rochman, while a *Publishers Weekly* reviewer wrote that Kimmel "lets the creative juices flow in his Oregonian version of an old Russian seafaring tale."

One Eye, Two Eyes, Three Eyes was originally told to Kimmel by his grandmother; it is the story of a young girl, cast into slavery, who, with the help of a magic goat, is finally freed to marry a prince. Further Ukrainian influences are found in *The Birds' Gift,* an Easter story that deals with the origin of the intricate process of decorating eggs for the spring holiday. "Filled with warmth, the story is illustrated with charming folk-art paintings," commented Patricia Pearl Dole in her *School Library Journal* review of *One Eye, Two Eyes, Three Eyes.* "Kimmel reserves the full force of his storytelling for folkloric rather than religious elements," noted a reviewer for *Publishers Weekly.*

Kimmel's beloved Brothers Grimm have provide him with a deep well of potential retellings. In *The Four Gallant Sisters* he adapts "The Four Artful Brothers" into a story that is "real reading pleasure," according to Linda Boyles in *School Library Journal,* the critic adding that Kimmel "couches his adaptation in the strong direct language of a master storyteller." His retelling of another Grimm story in *The Goose Girl* is "polished," according to *Booklist* reviewer Janice Del Negro. Similarly, *Iron John: A Tale from the Brothers Grimm* is a "seamless" retelling, as a reviewer for *Publishers Weekly* described the picture book. According to another reviewer from that magazine, Kimmel's dramatic retelling "flows from scene to scene with a clear sense of adventure and romance and an underlying sense of mystery." In *School Library Journal,* Grace Oliff dubbed Kimmel's *Seven at One Blow: A Tale from the Brothers Grimm* a "thoroughly enjoyable retelling of a traditional tale" that includes "only minor deviations from the original Grimm story."

Three Sacks of Truth: A Story from France employs the familiar motif of a suitor who must pass tests to win the hand of the fair princess. "In this crisp and sprightly interpretation, storyteller Kimmel takes full advantage of the plot's sly humor," wrote Penny Kaganoff in a review for *Publishers Weekly.* Other European tales retold by Kimmel include the Hungarian folktale *The Valiant Red Rooster, Count Silvernose: A Story from Italy, Squash It!: A True and Ridiculous Tale,* from Spain, and *Easy Work!: An Old Tale,* a Norwegian folktale transplanted to America. In *Count Silvernose,* ugly Assunta comes to the rescue of her beautiful sisters, using her skill of cleverness in a story that *Booklist* reviewer Susan Dove Lempke noted "combines humor and suspense, pitting good against evil and delivering a magnificently satisfying conclusion." Reviewing *Squash It!,* Kimmel's adaptation of a Spanish tale of a flea and a royal louse, a contributor for *Kirkus Reviews* wrote that the story is peppered with "judiciously chosen details" and "is good for reading aloud to kids who relish a bit of grossness in their story-hour diet." In addition to European folktales, Kimmel mines literature in *Don Quixote and the Windmills,* which is based on Miguel Cervantes' famous novel, and *The Hero Beowulf,* his retelling of the ancient Anglo-Saxon epic.

Other published books by Kimmel range ever farther afield, drawing from Middle-Eastern, African, Asian, Mexican, and South American folklore. Turning to Asia,

Kimmel features a mouse living in Japan's imperial palace in *The Greatest of All* and presents tales of Japanese derring-do in both *Sword of the Samurai: Adventure Stories from Japan* and *Three Samurai Cats: A Story from Japan.* He also adapts a story from the Chinese zodiac in *The Rooster's Antlers,* which follows the Jade Emperor as he selects twelve animals to represent the years in his calendar. "Reluctant readers looking for a short book of high adventures will be especially pleased," noted Karen Morgan in a *Booklist* review of *Sword of the Samurai,* while Barbara Scotto wrote in *School Library Journal* that readers "who delight in stories of knights will be happy to discover" Kimmel's Asian tales.

Enhanced by animé-style illustrations by Mordicai Gerstein, *Three Samurai Cats* brings to life a Zen-inspired tale about a rapacious rodent and three warriors. "Humor, wisdom and excitement make this offbeat tale a winner," wrote a *Publishers Weekly* contributor of Kimmel's entertaining story. In his *Ten Suns: A Chinese Legend,* in which "narrative and the dramatic illustrations . . . work wonderfully together to create a beautiful tale of Chinese gods, misuse of power, and heroism that restores the faith of a people," according to *Booklist* contributor Helen Rosenberg.

U.S. history and folklore have been a rich resource for Kimmel, and many of his books are set in the American southwest. In the title tale from *The Lady in the Blue Cloak: Legends of the Texas Missions* he focuses on a female figure known to appear to the Tejas Indians living near the location of the Mission of San Francisco de los Tejas in the late seventeenth century; other stories recount the origins of other Catholic missions established by Spanish colonists in the region that is now Texas. Although Kimmel's stories feature what some might perceive as "a mostly uncritical picture of the Christian mission experience," Gillian Engberg concluded in *Booklist* that the stories collected in *The Lady in the Blue Cloak* "flow easily" and focus on a topic rarely covered in children's literature.

In *The Three Cabritos* Kimmel adapts "The Three Billy Goats Gruff" to a Mexican setting as three music-loving bearded goats must cross a bridge on their way to a local fiesta, and the fearful Chupacabra lurks below, reading to waylay all who pass by. In *School Library Journal,* Joy Fleishhacker described Kimmel's retelling as a "fun variant" on the original that features a "humorous climax" and "light tone." The story about the three little pigs comes in for a similar treatment in *The Three Little Tamales,* as three little corn-husk treats hide in the desert to avoid being eaten by Señor Lobo, the wolf. "Kimmel has . . . cooked up another traditional tale flavored with Southwestern spice," concluded Teri Markson in a favorable *School Library Journal* review of *The Three Little Tamales,* and a *Kirkus Reviews* writer cited Valeria Docampo's illustrations as "filled with southwestern colors and details."

Moving to the northeastern United States, Kimmel presents what a *Kirkus Reviews* critic characterized as a "rousing original tale of battle between canal pirates and a crew of mail carriers" in *The Erie Canal Pirates*. Based on a ballad dating from the early 1800s, his story finds a band of river pirates vanquished by Captain Flynn beneath the rushing waters of Niagara Falls. Set in the Catskill Mountains, *Rip Van Winkle's Return* retells *The Legend of Sleepy Hollow,* a famous story by Washington Irving in which a lazy man falls asleep for twenty years and awakens to a world he no longer recognizes. *The Erie Canal Pirates* was described as a "joyous and good-hearted folktale" by *Booklist* contributor Roger Leslie, and an author's note clarifies Kimmel's geographical distortions for more map-smart young readers. *Rip Van Winkle's Return* is "a shorter, more moralistic" version of the original, according to a *Kirkus Reviews* writer, and *Booklist* critic Randall Enos praised Kimmel along with illustrator Leonard Everett for making "an American literary treasure . . . accessible to young children."

A band of scraggly pirates also makes little headway in *Blackbeard's Last Fight,* which is based on a true story from North Carolina. Kimmel's version takes place in 1718 and, as narrated by a young cabin boy, follows Lieutenant Maynard's successful efforts to vanquish the troublesome Blackbeard. Animated by sword fights, musket-fire, and a chorus of hearty "arggh"s, the story

Kimmel recalls a famous story by Washington Irving in **Rip Van Winkle's Return,** *featuring artwork by Leonard Everett Fisher.* (Illustration copyright © 2007 by Leonard Everett Fisher. Used by permission of Farrar, Straus & Giroux, LLC.)

was praised as "an exciting and satisfying read" by *School Library Journal* contributor Kara Schaff Dean and "exciting fare for pirate fans—as well as a discussion-provoking case study in international relations" by a *Kirkus Reviews* writer.

"I'm always looking for good stories," Kimmel once commented. "But I have no hesitation about making changes if I feel for some reason the original doesn't work, or if I can think of a way to make it better. There is no 'authentic' version. Stories evolve over centuries as tellers add and subtract. I think of myself as one link in a long, long chain."

Biographical and Critical Sources

BOOKS

Children's Books and Their Creators, edited by Anita Silvey, Houghton, Mifflin (Boston, MA), 1995.
Tuning Up: A Visit with Eric Kimmel, Richard C. Owen (New York, NY), 2005.

PERIODICALS

Booklist, January 15, 1995, review of *Iron John: A Tale from the Brothers Grimm,* p. 863; October 15, 1995, Janice Del Negro, review of *The Goose Girl: A Story from the Brothers Grimm,* pp. 398, 400; March 15, 1996, Susan Dove Lempke, review of *Count Silvernose: A Story from Italy,* p. 1263; December 1, 1996, Carolyn Phelan, review of *The Tale of Ali Baba and the Forty Thieves: A Tale from the Arabian Nights,* p. 667; December 15, 1996, Hazel Rochman, review of *Billy Lazroe and the King of the Sea: A Tale of the Northwest,* p. 730; May 1, 1997, Helen Rosenberg, review of *Ten Suns: A Chinese Legend,* p. 1520; March 15, 1999, Karen Morgan, review of *Sword of the Samurai: Adventure Stories from Japan,* p. 329; January 1, 2000, Ilene Cooper, review of *Montezuma and the Fall of the Aztecs,* pp. 910, 914; October 1, 2000, Ilene Cooper, review of *Gershon's Monster: A Story for the Jewish New Year,* p. 362; April 15, 2004, Ilene Cooper, review of *Don Quixote and the Windmills,* p. 1446; October 15, 2002, Roger Leslie, review of *The Erie Canal Pirates,* p. 412; April 1, 2003, Ilene Cooper, review of *Brother Wolf, Sister Sparrow: Stories about Saints and Animals,* p. 1392; February 15, 2004, Ilene Cooper, review of *Wonders and Miracles: A Passover Companion,* p. 1056; September 15, 2004, Jennifer Mattson, review of *Cactus Soup,* p. 241; October 15, 2004, Julie Cummins, review of *The Castle of the Cats,* p. 410; April 15, 2005, Jennifer Mattson, review of *The Hero Beowulf,* p. 1452; February 1, 2006, Nancy Kim, review of *A Horn for Louis,* p. 68; March 1, 2006, Hazel Rochman, review of *Blackbeard's Last Fight,* p. 100; May 1, 2006, Gillian Engberg, review of *The Frog Princess: A Tlingit Legend from Alaska,* p. 86; October 1, 2006, Gillian Engberg, review of *The Lady in the Blue Cloak: Legends from the Texas Missions*, p. 65; March 1, 2007, Randall Enos, review of *Rip Van Winkle's Return*, p. 89; July 1, 2007, Ilene Cooper, review of *The Three Cabritos*, p. 63; August, 2007, Suzanne Harold, review of *A Picture for Marc*, p. 77; January 1, 2008, Gillian Engberg, review of *The McElderry Book of Greek Myths*, p. 86; April 1, 2008, Randall Enos, review of *The Fisherman and the Turtle*, p. 52; September 15, 2008, Connie Fletcher, review of *Anansi's Party Time*, p. 56, and Ian Chipman, review of *Little Britches and the Rattlers*, p. 57; March 15, 2009, Shauna Yusko, review of *The Three Little Tamales*, p. 68.

Bulletin of the Center for Children's Books, January, 1995, Roger Sutton, review of *One Good Tern Deserves Another*, p. 169; March, 2004, Betsy Hearne, review of *Wonders and Miracles*, p. 282; July-August, 2004, Karen Coats, review of *Don Quixote and the Windmills*, p. 472; June, 2006, Elizabeth Bush, review of *Blackbeard's Last Fight*, p. 459; September, 2006, Maggie Hommel, review of *The Frog Princess*, p. 20; January, 2007, Elizabeth Bush, review of *The Lady in the Blue Cloak*, p. 219.

Horn Book, January-February, 1990, Hanna B. Zeiger, review of *Hershel and the Hanukkah Goblins*, pp. 52-53; July-August, 2003, review of *Three Samurai Cats: A Story from Japan*, p. 470; January-February, 2005, Betty Carter, review of *Cactus Soup*, p. 103.

Kirkus Reviews, March 15, 1996, review of *Onions and Garlic*, p. 449; May 15, 1997, review of *Squash It!*, p. 801; September 1, 2002, review of *The Erie Canal Pirates*, p. 1312; April 15, 2003, review of *Brother Wolf, Sister Sparrow*, p. 608; January 15, 2004, review of *Wonders and Miracles*, p. 85; March 15, 2004, review of *Don Quixote and the Windmills*, p. 272; September 1, 2004, review of *Cactus Soup*, p. 868; October 15, 2004, review of *The Castle of the Cats*, p. 1008; May 1, 2005, review of *The Hero Beowulf*, p. 540; November 15, 2005, review of *A Horn for Louis*, p. 1234; March 1, 2006, review of *Blackbeard's Last Fight*, p. 232; May 1, 2006, review of *The Frog Princess*, p. 461; October 1, 2006, review of *The Lady in the Blue Cloak*, p 1017; March 1, 2007, review of *Rip Van Winkle's Return*, p. 224; August 15, 2007, review of *The Great Texas Hamster Drive;* September 1, 2007, review of *A Picture for Marc;* April 15, 2008, review of *The Little Fisherman and the Turtle;* July 15, 2008, review of *Little Britches and the Rattlers;* February 1, 2009, review of *Three Little Tamales.*

Los Angeles Times Book Review, December 6, 1998, Anne Connor, review of *A Hanukkah Treasury*, p. 4.

New York Times Book Review, December 17, 1995, Rodger Kamenetz, review of *The Adventures of Hershel of Ostropol*, p. 28.

Publishers Weekly, November 9, 1990, review of *The Chanukkah Guest*, p. 57; May 3, 1991, review of *Baba Yaga*, p. 71; April 19, 1993, Peggy Kaganoff, review of *Three Sacks of Truth*, p. 60; March 4, 1996, review of *Iron John*, p. 67; September 16, 1996, review of *The Tale of Ali Baba and the Forty Thieves*, p. 82; November 4, 1996, review of *Billy Lazroe and the King of the Sea*, p. 75; September 28, 1998, review of

A Hanukkah Treasury, p. 52; February 22, 1999, review of *The Birds' Gift*, p. 94; February 7, 2000, reviews of *Two Mountains*, p. 84, and *Montezuma and the Fall of the Aztecs*, p. 86; January 22, 2001, review of *Website of the Warped Wizard*, p. 324; February 19, 2001, review of *Robin Hook, Pirate Hunter!*, p. 90; March 17, 2003, review of *Three Samurai Cats*, p. 76; November 8, 2004, review of *Cactus Soup*, p. 54; August 28, 2006, review of *The Lady in the Blue Cloak*, p. 58; September 15, 2008, review of *The Mysterious Guests: A Sukkot Story*, p. 66.

School Library Journal, October, 1991, Denise Anton Wright, review of *Bearhead*, p. 110; May, 1992, Linda Boyles, review of *The Four Gallant Sisters*, p. 105; December, 1998, Grace Oliff, review of *Seven at One Blow*, p. 106; June, 1999, Barbara Scotto, review of *Sword of the Samurai*, p. 132; July, 1999, Patricia Pearl Dole, review of *The Birds' Gift*, p. 86; October, 2000, review of *Jar of Fools*, pp. 64-65, 148; May, 2003, Harriett Fargnoli, review of *Brother Wolf, Sister Sparrow*, p. 137; February, 2004, Susan Pine, review of *Wonders and Miracles*, p. 166; April, 2004, Ann Welton, review of *Don Quixote and the Windmills*, p. 116; October, 2004, John Sigwald, review of *Cactus Soup*, p. 144; November, 2004, Grace Oliff, review of *The Castle of the Cats*, p. 126; April, 2005, Patricia Lothrop, review of *The Hero Beowulf*, p. 154; February, 2006, Mary Elam, review of *A Horn for Louis*, p. 120; May, 2006, Kara Schaff Dean, review of *Blackbeard's Last Fight*, p. 91; June, 2006, Kirsten Cutler, review of *The Frog Princess*, p. 136; October, 2006, S.K. Joiner, review of *The Lady in the Blue Cloak*, p. 114; May, 2007, Joy Fleishhacker, review of *The Three Cabriots*, p. 119; October, 2007, review of *The Great Hamster Drive*, p. 119; September, 2008, Blair Christolon, review of *Anansi's Party Time*, p. 165; October, 2008, review of *The Mysterious Guests*, p. 114; June, 2009, review of *The Three Little Tamales*, p. 92.

Voice of Youth Advocates, April, 1995, Marian Rafal, review of *One Good Tern Deserves Another*, p. 24.

ONLINE

Author's Online Library, http://teacher.scholastic.com/ (June 12, 2001).

Eric A. Kimmel Home Page, http://ericakimmel.com (November 15, 2009).

Meet Authors and Illustrators, http://www.childrenslit. com/ (February 7, 2007), "Eric A. Kimmel."

* * *

KLIER, Kimberly Wagner

Personal

Born in IN; married; husband's name Tim; children: Chloe, David. *Education:* Attended college. *Hobbies and other interests:* Travel, walking her dogs.

Addresses

Home—Southern IN. *E-mail*—kklier@sbcglobal.net.

Kimberly Wagner Klier (Reproduced by permission.)

Career

Author and educator. Teacher of elementary school in Indiana.

Awards, Honors

Maryland Blue Crab Young-Reader Honor Book designation, 2004, for *Firefly Friend;* Amelia Bloomer List inclusion, 2009, for *You Can't Do That, Amelia!*

Writings

PICTURE BOOKS

Song of David, illustrated by Larasse Kabel, Perfection Learning (Logan, IA), 1999.
Summer of Secrets, illustrated by Dea Marks, Perfection Learning (Logan, IA), 2002.
Firefly Friend, illustrated by Michael Garland, Children's Press (New York, NY), 2004.
You Can't Do That, Amelia!, illustrated by Kathleen Kemly, Calkins Creek (Honesdale, PA), 2008.

Sidelights

"As a children's author, I enjoy sharing my love of history with young readers," Kimberly Wagner Klier explained to *SATA.* "My picture book *Song of David* captures a boy's journey on the Underground Railroad, while *You Can't Do That, Amelia!* celebrates a girl's dreams of flight. In my books, I choose characters who are facing difficult tasks in their unique places in history.

It is my hope that the stories told in my books will inspire readers to further explore the pages of American history. I love visiting schools and libraries and hope to meet many more readers in the future."

Biographical and Critical Sources

PERIODICALS

Kirkus Reviews, September 1, 2008, review of *You Can't Do That, Amelia!*
School Library Journal, October, 2008, Blair Christolon, review of *You Can't Do That, Amelia!*, p. 133.

ONLINE

Kimberly Wagner Klier Home Page, http://www.kimberly klier.com (November 15, 2009).

*   *   *

KROMMES, Beth 1956-

Personal

Born January 6, 1956, in Emmaus, PA; daughter of Frederick (businessman in the bowling and billiards industry) and Shirley Krommes; married David Rowell (a computer programmer), September 25, 1982; children: Olivia, Marguerite. *Education:* Attended St. Martin's School of Art (London, England), 1975-76; Syracuse University, B.F.A. (painting; magna cum laude), 1977; University of Massachusetts at Amherst, M.A.T. (art education), 1980. *Politics:* Democrat. *Religion:* Lutheran.

Addresses

Home and office—Peterborough, NH. *E-mail*—beth@ bethkrommes.com.

Career

Illustrator, wood engraver, and painter. Frontier Regional Junior-Senior High School, S. Deerfield, MA, art teacher, 1980; Groton Center for the Arts, Groton, CT, managing director, 1980-81; Sharon Arts Center, Sharon, NH, shop manager, 1981-83; graphic designer, beginning 1983, and art director for *80 Micro* magazine; IDG Communications, Peterborough, NH, electronic page designer, 1985-89; freelance wood engraver and illustrator, 1984—. Speaker at conferences and schools. *Exhibitions:* Works exhibited at Berkshire Museum, Pittsfield, MA, Sharon Arts Center, Peterborough, NH, Liberty Arts Center, Newport, NH, Keene State College, Keene, NH, Manchester Institute of Art and Sciences, Manchester, NH, McGowan Fine Art, Concord, NH, Chemers Gallery, Tustin, CA, Picture Book

Beth Krommes (Photograph by Olivia Krommes. Reproduced by permission.)

Festival, Seoul, South Korea, Spheris Gallery, Hanover, NH, and Art Institute of Chicago; in solo exhibition at Brattleboro Museum and Art Center, Brattleboro, VT, 2009; and in Bologna Children's Book Fair Illustrator's Exhibition, 2000, 2001, 2005, 2008, and Society of Illustrators' Original Art Show, 2003, 2007.

Member

Society of Children's Book Writers and Illustrators, Society of Wood Engravers.

Awards, Honors

Certificates of Design Excellence, *Print's Regional Design Annual,* 1985, 1986, 1987, 1988, 1990, 1991, 1994, 1999; Yankee Print Awards, League of New Hampshire Craftsmen Foundation annual juried exhibit, 1986, 1987; merit awards in printmaking, Sharon, NH, Arts Center annual regional juried exhibitions, 1986, 1989; New Hampshire State Council on the Arts individual artist fellowship, 1991; Notable Book designation, Robert Sibert Award Honor Book designation, American Library Association (ALA), Notable Social Studies Trade Book designation, and *Smithsonian* magazine Notable Book designation, all 2001, and Golden Kite Award in Illustration, Society of Children's Book Writers and Illustrators, 2002, all for *The Lamp, the Ice, and the Boat Called Fish* by Jacqueline Briggs Martin; Minnesota Book Award, 2004, for *The Hidden Folk;* ALA Notable Book designation, ASPCA Henry Bergh Award for Illustration, National Science Teachers Association Out-

standing Science Trade Book designation, and Best of the Best designation, Chicago Public Library, all 2006, all for *Butterfly Eyes, and Other Secrets of the Meadow* by Joyce Sidman; One Hundred Titles for Reading and Sharing designation, New York Public Library, Parents' Choice Approved designation, Minnesota Book Award for Children's Literature, and Randolph Caldecott Medal, ALA, all 2009, all for *The House in the Night* by Susan Marie Swanson.

Illustrator

Ruth Adams Bronz, *Miss Ruby's American Cooking,* Harper & Row (New York, NY), 1989.

Marjorie Holmes, *At Christmas the Heart Goes Home,* Doubleday (New York, NY), 1991.

James Villas, *French Country Kitchen,* Bantam (New York, NY), 1992.

Tim W. Clark and Denise Casey, compilers, *Tales of the Grizzly,* Homestead Publishing (Moose, WY), 1992.

Down Home Cooking, Reader's Digest (Pleasantville, NY), 1994.

Sandra J. Taylor, editor, *Yankee Magazine's New England Innkeepers Cookbook,* Villard (New York, NY), 1996.

Tim W. Clark and Denise Casey, compilers, *Tales of the Wolf: FIfty-one Stories of Wolf Encounters in the Wild,* Homestead Publishing (Moose, WY), 1996.

Ric Lynden Hardman, *Sunshine Rider* (young-adult novel), Bantam (New York, NY), 1998.

Phyllis Root, *Grandmother Winter* (picture book), Houghton (Boston, MA), 1999.

Jacqueline Briggs Martin, *The Lamp, the Ice, and the Boat Called Fish* (picture book), Houghton (Boston, MA), 2001.

Judith Nicholls, editor, *The Sun in Me: Poems about the Planet,* Barefoot Books (Bristol, England), 2002, Barefoot Books (Cambridge, MA), 2003.

Lise Lunge-Larsen, *The Hidden Folk: Stories of Fairies, Dwarves, Selkies, and Other Secret Beings* (picture book), Houghton Mifflin (Boston, MA), 2004.

Joyce Sidman, *Butterfly Eyes, and Other Secrets of the Meadow*, Houghton Mifflin (Boston, MA) 2006.

Susan Marie Swanson, *The House in the Night,* Houghton Mifflin (Boston, MA), 2008.

Artwork included in *ENDGRAIN: Contemporary Wood Engraving in North America,* Barbarian Press, 1994, and *An Engraver's Globe,* edited by Simon Brett, Primrose Hill Press, 2002.

Sidelights

Known for her intricate wood engravings, Beth Krommes is a Caldecott Medal-winning illustrator whose works have appeared in many exhibitions and galleries throughout New Hampshire, where she makes her home. Since the early 1990s, Krommes has also illustrated children's books using a scratchboard-and-watercolor technique, among them the picture books *Grandmother Winter* by Phyllis Root, *The Sun in Me: Poems about the Planet,* edited by Judith Nichol, *The Hidden Folk: Stories of Fairies, Dwarves, Selkies, and Other Secret*

Beings by Lise Lunge-Larsen, and *The House in the Night* by Susan Marie Swanson. Reviewing *The Sun in Me,* a *Kirkus Reviews* writer dubbed Krommes' illustrations "gorgeous," commenting on her "brilliant use of pattern and placement in space along with color that leaps from the page."

For *Grandmother Winter,* Root's lyrical tale of people's and animals' responses to the coming of winter, Krommes creates "delightful scratchboard illustrations, tinted with soft watercolors," according to *Booklist* reviewer Kay Weisman. A contributor to *Horn Book* commented on the bats, worms, frogs, fish, bears, and other creatures Krommes integrates into her images, calling them "carefully observed as well as decorative." The illustrator's work for Joyce Sidman's verse collection *Butterfly Eyes, and Other Secrets of the Meadow* also focuses on nature, in this case a pond ecosystem. "Visual clues complement the poetic suggestions in striking scratchboard scenes . . . saturated with color," wrote Margaret Bush in a *School Library Journal* review of the book, while a *Kirkus Reviews* writer dubbed *Butterfly Eyes, and Other Secrets of the Meadow* "a top-drawer blend of art and science." Calling Krommes' stylized art "splendid," *Horn Book* reviewer Joanna Rudge Long added that the pictures "reflect such precise observation that each species is easily recognizable" to young readers.

In *The Lamp, the Ice, and the Boat Called Fish* author Jacqueline Briggs Martin recounts the true story of an

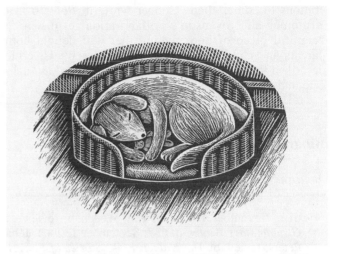

Krommes won the Caldecott Medal for her illustrations for **The House in the Night,** *a picture book by Susan Marie Swanson.* (Illustration courtesy of Beth Krommes.)

expedition that set out in 1913, led by Arctic explorer Vilhjalmur Stefansson. Hoping to prove that a continent was hidden under the Arctic ice cap, Stefansson failed in his quest when he was forced to abandon his ice-trapped fishing boat, the *Karluk*. Krommes' scratchboard art for the work was deemed "outstanding" by a *Horn Book* writer, the critic adding that "ice, artifacts, and characters are delineated in handsome black, softened with crosshatching and a limited palette." In *School Library Journal* Sue Sherif wrote that the "evocative scratchboard illustrations show many details of the cultural and physical environment" Krommes brings to light in her contribution to the award-winning picture book.

More fanciful in its focus, Lunge-Larsen's *The Hidden Folk* presents a history of magical creatures as they appear in the European folk tradition, from dwarves and flower fairies to selkies and river sprites. Noting Krommes' use of decorative borders that echo the theme of each interior illustration, *School Library Journal* contributor Harriett Fargnoli wrote that "the vivid hues and interesting textures make an eye-catching combination." John Peters concluded in his *Booklist* review of *The Hidden Folk* that Krommes' creative contribution "give[s] this gathering a suitably folktale feel," and a *Kirkus Reviews* critic asserted that the illustrator's use of "rich and brilliant color [is] at once cozy and majestic."

In 2009 Krommes was honored with the prestigious Randolph Caldecott Medal, an award given in response to her work for Swanson's *The House in the Night*. Featuring a lyrical text, the story takes readers on a nighttime ride from a quiet house through the starlit sky and up to the home of the sun and moon, then back again. In black-and-white scratchboard images highlighted with a warm, marigold yellow, Krommes "make[s] the world of the poem an enchanted place," observed *School Library Journal* critic Jayne Damron, the critic predicting that *The House in the Night* "will be loved for gen-

Krommes' detailed woodcut images are a highlight of Jacqueline Briggs Martin's picture book **The Lamp, the Ice, and the Boat Called Fish.** (Illustration copyright © 2001 by Beth Krommes. All rights reserved. Reproduced by permission of Houghton Mifflin Company.)

erations to come." Ilene Cooper wrote in *Booklist* that Krommes and Swanson's collaboration results in "a beautiful piece of bookmaking that will delight both parents and children," while a *Publishers Weekly* critic described the artist's "astonishing illustrations" as "delicate and elegant."

Biographical and Critical Sources

PERIODICALS

Booklist, November 15, 1999, Kay Weisman, review of *Grandmother Winter,* p. 637; September 1, 2004, John Peters, review of *The Hidden Folk: Stories of Fairies, Gnomes, Selkies, and Other Secret Beings,* p. 117; October 1, 2006, Gillian Engberg, review of *Butterfly Eyes, and Other Secrets of the Meadow,* p. 51; April 15, 2008, Ilene Cooper, review of *The House in the Night,* p. 46.

Horn Book, September, 1999, review of *Grandmother Winter,* p. 599; March, 2001, review of *The Lamp, the Ice, and the Boat Called Fish,* p. 198; September-October, 2006, Joanna Rudge Long, review of *Butterfly Eyes, and Other Secrets of the Meadows,* p. 603.

Kirkus Reviews, January 15, 2003, review of *The Sun in Me: Poems about the Planet,* p. 144; July 15, 2004, review of *The Hidden Folk,* p. 690; August 15, 2006, review of *Butterfly Eyes, and Other Secrets of the Meadow,* p. 852.

Natural History, December, 2002, review of *The Lamp, the Ice, and the Boat Called Fish,* p. 70.

New York Times Book Review, April 15, 2001, Heather Vogel Frederick, review of *The Lamp, the Ice, and the Boat Called Fish,* p. 25.

Publishers Weekly, September 2, 1989, Molly McQuade, review of *Miss Ruby's American Cooking,* p. 54; August 30, 1999, review of *Grandmother Winter,* p. 82; May 12, 2008, review of *The House in the Night,* p. 53.

Reading Today, April-May, 2009, interview with Krommes.

School Library Journal, July, 2001, Sue Sherif, review of *The Lamp, the Ice, and the Boat Called Fish,* p. 96; March, 2003, Kathleen Whalin, review of *The Sun in Me,* p. 222; December, 2004, Harriett Fargnoli, review of *The Hidden Folk,* p. 134; October, 2006, Margaret Bush, review of *Butterfly Eyes, and Other Secrets of the Meadow,* p. 142; April, 2008, Jayne Damron, review of *The House in the Night,* p. 123.

ONLINE

Beth Krommes Home Page, http://www.bethkrommes.com (November 21, 2009).

New Hampshire State Council on the Arts Web site, http://www.nh.gov/ (July 20, 2007), "Beth Krommes."

L

LANG, Lang 1982-

Personal

Born June 14, 1982, in Shenyang, Liaoning, China; immigrated to United States; son of Guo-Ren Lang. *Education:* Attended Central Music Conservatory (Beijing, China); attended Curtis Institute of Music (Philadelphia, PA).

Addresses

Home—New York, NY. *E-mail*—langlang@aligneg.com.

Career

Pianist and author. Has performed with international orchestras, including Vienna Philharmonic, Berlin Philharmonic, Shanghai Symphony Orchestra, and Chicago Symphony. Solo performances at venues across the globe, including at Carnegie Hall, Beijing Concert Hall, and Royal Albert Hall; performer at international events, including at 2006 World Cup, 2007 Nobel Prize concert, and 2008 Beijing Olympics. Performer in musical recordings, including *Lang Lang: Recorded in Florence Gould Auditorium First Piano Concertos, Live at Carnegie Hall, Piano Concerto No. 3,* and *Piano Concerto No. 2; Paganini Rhapsody.* Guest instructor at musical conservatories, including the Curtis Institute of Music, Juilliard School, and institutions in China. Chair, Montblanc de la Culture Arts Patronage Award Project; member, Carnegie Hall's Weill Music Institute advisory committee and artistic advisory board; founder, Lang Lang International Music Foundation. International Goodwill Ambassador to United Nations Children's Fund (UNICEF), 2004; National Academy of Recording Arts and Sciences cultural ambassador to China, 2008.

Awards, Honors

Best Instrumental Soloist nomination, Grammy Awards, and Presidential Merit Award, both National Academy of Recording Arts and Sciences, both 2007.

Writings

(With Michael French) *Lang Lang: Playing with Flying Keys,* Delacorte (New York, NY), 2008.
(With David Ritz) *Journey of a Thousand Miles: My Story,* Spiegel & Grau (New York, NY), 2008.

Sidelights

Pushed by his father, a musician whose dreams ended with the Chinese Cultural Revolution, world-renown pianist Lang Lang began receiving his first lessons on the instrument at age three and won a musical competition in his hometown two years later. Wishing his son greater success, Lang's father decided to move to Beijing with the boy, providing the child prodigy with better access to more qualified instructors. Coming to the United States in 1997 to study at the Curtis Institute of Music, Lang earned widespread praise for his impromptu performance with the Chicago Symphony, substituting for an ill André Watts. From that concert, Lang has launched a career as a pianist, entertaining audiences in music halls around the world. Becoming an international celebrity, the musician has also appeared at ceremonies for sporting events, including the 2006 World Cup soccer tournament in Germany and the 2008 Olympic Games in Beijing. He has also performed before world leaders such as U.S. president George H.W. Bush, Queen Elizabeth of England, former U.N. secretary-general Kofi Annan, and Chinese president Hu Jin-Tao.

Lang's journey to the top of the classical musical world did not come easily, as the performer recounts in two books about his life. Both published in 2008, *Journey of a Thousand Miles: My Story* relates the musician's story for adults, while *Lang Lang: Playing with Flying Keys* offers younger readers information about the high points in his life. In both books, Lang explains his struggles as a student, particularly his relationship with his demanding father. While leaving Shenyang for Beijing expanded the educational possibilities for the

Cover of pianist Lang Lang's memoir Lang Lang: Playing with Flying Keys, *featuring a photograph by Jesse Frohman.* (Jacket photograph © 2008 by Jesse Frohman. Used by permission of Delacorte Press, an imprint of Random House Children's Books, a division of Random House, Inc.)

young boy, the move also meant that he became separated from his mother, who remained behind to continue working and financing Lang's schooling. Without the reassuring presence of his loving mother, the pianist struggled to live with his obsessive father, a man who at one point suggested that Lang commit suicide after dishonoring the family name by arriving late to a piano lesson. Nonetheless, Lang remained with his father, enduring impoverished living conditions before winning several important competitions in China and Europe and eventually a scholarship at age thirteen to study in the United States. In this new country, he developed not only greater interpretive skills as a musician, but also enjoyed living like a typical American teen. Throughout both books, the performer puts his successes into context with the sacrifices he and his family endured, offering a complex portrait of the young performer.

In a review of *Journey of a Thousand Miles, Booklist* critic Ray Olson described the musician's saga as "suspenseful and engrossing." In her *New York Times Book Review* appraisal of the same book, Tara Mckelvey compared Lang's early years to a "fairy tale—though more Brothers Grimm than Disney, complete with dark and

horrific themes." Lang relates his experiences "without self-pity or bitterness," Mckelvey added, calling the work a "satisfying" autobiography. Other reviewers offered similar positive comments about *Lang Lang, Horn Book* contributor Roger Sutton calling it "a compelling and enthusiastic self-portrait." Writing in *Kirkus Reviews,* a critic noted that *Lang Lang* offers "a fascinating and engrossing portrait of a different life," while in *Booklist* Gillian Engberg predicted that the musician's "revealing, humble account may inspire readers . . . to apply themselves to their own talents."

Biographical and Critical Sources

PERIODICALS

Booklist, June 1, 2008, Ray Olson, review of *Journey of a Thousand Miles: My Story,* p. 32, and Gillian Engberg, review of *Lang Lang: Playing with Flying Keys,* p. 93.

Cosmopolitan, June, 2006, "Fun Fearless Male: Lang Lang," p. 96.

Horn Book, July-August, 2008, Roger Sutton, review of *Lang Lang,* p. 468.

Kirkus Reviews, May 15, 2008, review of *Journey of a Thousand Miles,* June 15, 2008, review of *Lang Lang.*

New York Times, September 24, 2005, Bernard Holland, "One Passionate Prodigy Takes on Another," p. B18; February 18, 2006, Anne Midgette, "Wild Piano Ride for Double 70th Birthdays," p. B10; November 7, 2008, Steve Smith, "The Flame of Beethoven, Calibrated," p. C18; June 9, 2007, Allan Kozinn, "Tortoise Meets Hare at Lincoln Center," p. B9.

New York Times Book Review, September 28, 2008, Tara Mckelvey, review of *Journey of a Thousand Miles,* p. 22.

School Library Journal, September, 2008, Nancy Menaldi-Scanlan, review of *Lang Lang,* p. 205; January, 2009, Charlotte Bradshaw, review of *Journey of a Thousand Miles,* p. 137.

ONLINE

Lang Lang Web site, http://www.langlang.com (November 25, 2009).*

*   *   *

LEE, Virginia 1976-

Personal

Born March 16, 1976, in Devon, England; daughter of Alan Lee (an illustrator and conceptual artist) and Marja Lee Kruijt (an artist). *Education:* Kingston University, degree (illustration), 1999.

Addresses

Home—Brighton, England. *E-mail*—info@virginialee. co.uk.

Virginia Lee (Reproduced by permission.)

Career

Illustrator, sculptor, and painter. Created fountains, architecture, and merchandise for *Lord of the Rings* motion-picture trilogy. Illustrator for "Storyworld" cards, including "Animal Tales" and "Stories of the Sea" sets of cards, published by Templar Publishing.

Illustrator

Antonia Barber, *The Frog Bride,* Frances Lincoln (London, England), 2007.

Sally Pomme Clayton, *Persephone,* Eerdmans (Grand Rapids, MI), 2009.

Contributor of illustrations, with others, to *The Secret History of Mermaids and Merfolk,* Candlewick Press (Somerville, MA), 2009.

Sidelights

After working as a sculptor on the fantasy movie trilogy *Lord of the Rings* in the early 2000s, British artist Virginia Lee turned her hand to children's books, illustrating two works based on traditional tales. In her first book, *The Frog Bride,* Lee provides the artwork for Antonia Barber's retelling of the Russian folk story about three princes looking for a bride. The king instructs his youngest son to shoot an arrow and find a wife near where the arrow falls. After his arrow lands in a marsh, he returns home with a frog that unexpectedly fares much better than the other princes' brides-to-be at fulfilling the queen's expectations. Upon seeing the frog bride slip out of her reptilian skin, the prince becomes enchanted with her hidden human form and sets out on a quest to make her his wife. Lee's "images draw the eye again and again," wrote a *Kirkus Reviews* critic in a review of *The Frog Bride,* describing the illustrations as "richly colored and finely designed."

Persephone, a retelling by Sally Pomme Clayton of the classic Greek myth explaining the changing of the seasons, also features artwork by Lee. Upon seeing the beautiful Persephone, Hades kidnaps the maiden, forcing her to become his goddess of the underworld. Deeply saddened by her loss, Persephone's mother Demeter allows a slow decay to spread over the land, creating an endless winter. With intervention from Zeus and the other gods from Mount Olympus, Hades eventually allows Persephone to visit her mother, bringing life back to the earth. However, since the girl consumed three pomegranate seeds while in the underworld, Persephone must return to her subterranean husband three months of the year, a move reflected by the arrival of winter in the aboveground world. Writing in *Booklist,* Carolyn Phelan described Lee's images as "impressive in their stately beauty." A *Kirkus Reviews* contributor wrote that the artist's "imaginative illustrations . . . complement the action" of Clayton's narrative, while in *School Library Journal* Joy Fleishhacker suggested that Lee "effectively use[s] color and tone to convey the characters' emotions."

"I enjoy working with a variety of media," Lee explained to *SATA,* "mainly with water-soluble oil paints or with pastels. I also like to illustrate stories which involve themes of transformation with an emotional and symbolic message at their core. I'm inspired mostly by nature, landscapes, mythology, fairy and folktales and the surreal."

Lee's illustration projects include creating artwork for Antonia Barber's **The Frog Bride.** (Illustration copyright © 2007 by Virginia Lee. Reproduced by permission.)

Lee's artwork includes "Tides of Emotion," a pastel on paper that she created in 2004. (Illustration courtesy of Virginia Lee.)

Biographical and Critical Sources

PERIODICALS

Booklist, March 15, 2009, Carolyn Phelan, review of *Persephone,* p. 61.
Children's Bookwatch, May, 2009, review of *Persephone.*
Kirkus Reviews, July 1, 2008, review of *The Frog Bride;* February 15, 2009, review of *Persephone.*
School Library Journal, May, 2009, Joy Fleishhacker, review of *Persephone,* p. 93.

ONLINE

Virginia Lee Home Page, http://www.virginialee.co.uk (November 20, 2009).

* * *

LICHTENHELD, Tom 1953-

Personal

Born 1953, in Rockford, IL; married Jan Miller. *Education:* University of Wisconsin-Madison, degree, 1979. *Hobbies and other interests:* Bicycling, swimming.

Addresses

Home—Geneva, IL. *E-mail*—tlichtenheld@ameritech. net.

Career

Art director, illustrator, and author. Fallon, Minneapolis, MN, art director, 1984-2001; freelance art director, 2001-03; Cramer Krasselt, Chicago, IL, creative director, 2004-09. Has taught advertising classes at Miami Advertising School, Minneapolis, MN, and Chicago, IL.

Awards, Honors

CLIO Award; Kelly Award finalist; named among *Adweek* magazine's "Creative All-Stars"; awards from New York Art Directors Club, British Design and Art Direction, *Communications Arts* Advertising Annual, and One Show; numerous other awards for advertising; Book of Wonder designation, *Newsweek,* 2000, for *Everything I Know about Pirates; Child* magazine best children's book designation, 2003, for *What Are YOU So Grumpy About?;* Ten Best Children's Books inclusion, *Time,* 2009, for *Duck! Rabbit!*

Writings

SELF-ILLUSTRATED

Everything I Know about Pirates: A Collection of Made-up Facts, Educated Guesses, and Silly Pictures about Bad Guys of the High Seas, Simon & Schuster (New York, NY), 2000.
Everything I Know about Monsters: A Collection of Made-up Facts, Educated Guesses, and Silly Pictures about Creatures of Creepiness, Simon & Schuster (New York, NY), 2002.
What Are YOU So Grumpy About?, Little, Brown (Boston, MA), 2003.
Everything I Know about Cars: A Collection of Made-up Facts, Educated Guesses, and Silly Pictures about Cars, Trucks, and Other Zoomy Things, Simon & Schuster Books for Young Readers (New York, NY), 2005.

Tom Lichtenheld (Photograph by Kevin White. Reproduced by permission.)

What's with This Room?, Little, Brown (New York, NY), 2005.

Bridget's Beret, Henry Holt (New York, NY), 2010.

Cloudette, Christy Ottaviano Books/Henry Holt (New York, NY), 2011.

ILLUSTRATOR

Pam Smallcomb, *Camp Buccaneer,* Simon & Schuster (New York, NY), 2002.

(And coauthor) Amy Krouse Rosenthal, *The OK Book,* HarperCollins (New York, NY), 2007.

(And coauthor) Amy Krouse Rosenthal, *It's Not Fair,* HarperCollins (New York, NY), 2008.

(And coauthor) Amy Krouse Rosenthal, *Duck! Rabbit!,* Chronicle Books (San Francisco, CA), 2009.

(And coauthor) Amy Krouse Rosenthal, *Yes Day!,* HarperCollins (New York, NY), 2009.

(And coauthor) Chris Barton, *Shark vs. Train,* Little, Brown Books for Young Readers (New York, NY), 2010.

Sidelights

Tom Lichtenheld is an award-winning art director whose clients include Ameritech, BMW, Lee Jeans, Porsche, the *Wall Street Journal,* Timex, and United Airlines. He is also the author of children's books that include *Everything I Know about Pirates: A Collection of Made-up Facts, Educated Guesses, and Silly Pictures about Bad Guys of the High Seas* and *What Are YOU So Grumpy About?* As coauthor and illustrator, he has also collaborated with writer Amy Krouse Rosenthal on a series of reassuring books for very young children that includes *Duck! Rabbit!, It's Not Fair, The OK Book,* and *Yes Day!* Praising Lichtenheld's contribution to *The OK Book, New York Times Book Review* critic Rebecca Zerkin dubbed his "understated" artwork "endearing and funny," while a *Publishers Weekly* critic wrote of *Yes Day!* that the artist's "comic-style" illustrations pair well with "the energetic vibe" of Rosenthal's story depicting a day "of irreverent (but not too crazy) fun."

Lichtenheld's career path has been an unusual one, as he revealed to Aaron Baar in an *Adweek* interview. "I grew up in Rockford, [Illinois,] this industrial town, and was this bored, artistic kid in high school. They didn't know what to do with me. They didn't think I would be able to go into college. So they decided to put me in a work-study program, and the closest thing they could find was sign painting. I really enjoyed it, being outdoors with the cows, up on a ladder, painting these big pieces of type." Lichtenheld eventually attended the University of Wisconsin—Madison, where "I basically learned to talk about art and smoke other people's cigarettes," as he recalled to Baar. "Can't say I learned how to draw. To work my way through art school, I worked at ad agencies. One day, someone needed an art director, and someone pointed at me."

Lichtenheld's career in picture books began in an equally roundabout way. Asked by his nephew to draw a pirate, Lichtenheld responded with a number of sketches, complete with humorous commentary. "When I initially sat down a lot of things came into my head," he told Debbie Long in the Arlington Heights, Illinois, *Daily Herald.* "The initial picture was actually twelve pages of nonsense and pictures of pirates, but it was a book from the start. It wasn't intended to be, it just kind of happened." It would take another three years of hard work, though, before *Everything I Know about Pirates* was accepted for publication.

In *Everything I Know about Pirates* Lichtenheld offers "a tongue-in-cheek approach to piracy," according to Cyndi Giorgis and Nancy J. Johnson in *Reading Teacher.* Based on the author's "educated guesses and made-up facts," the book unravels the many mysteries of piratedom, such as why buccaneers wear eye patches and where they get their ears pierced. Critics had praise for both the text and artwork. GraceAnne A. DeCandido noted in *Booklist* that the "illustrations . . . are suitably exaggerated and liberally, ah, salted with helpful commentary." Lichtenheld believes that part of the book's appeal stems from the drawings he originally created for his nephew. "Some of the drawings are the very same drawings I did then," he told Long. "One reason the book's been successful is the very spontaneous feeling of it—the manic energy that went into it that first day I sat down."

A companion volume, *Everything I Know about Monsters: A Collection of Made-up Facts, Educated Guesses, and Silly Pictures about Creatures of Creepiness,* is a comical guide to ghouls and fiends. Here readers learn about the various types of monsters, including "Under-the-Bed Monsters," "Attic Monsters," and "Closet Monsters," as well as the reason real monsters never appear in horror movies: they cannot act. Kathleen Kelly MacMillan, reviewing the work in *School Library Journal,* remarked that "Lichtenheld's cartoons . . . feature lots of dialogue bubbles and humorous hidden touches."

Described as another "witty compendium" by *Booklist* contributor Carolyn Phelan, Lichtenheld's *Everything I Know about Cars: A Collection of Made-up Facts, Educated Guesses, and Silly Pictures about Cars, Trucks, and Other Zoomy Things* presents a whimsical—and totally untrue—history of modern transportation in its humorous text and giggle-inducing cartoon art. Phelan praised the book as "funny and accessible," adding that *Everything I Know about Cars* "has something for everyone," from pretend-history buffs to budding car designers. "Chock full of fun fake facts," according to *School Library Journal* contributor Catherine Callegari, *Everything I Know about Cars* combines "madcap illustrations, irreverent text, and kid-friendly humor," and in *Kirkus Reviews* a critic cited the "appropriately daffy" artwork in Lichtenheld's "gassed-up laff-fest."

Illustrating Pam Smallcomb's *Camp Buccaneer* provided Lichtenheld with another opportunity to sketch pirates. In the work, a young girl's dull vacation turns into a wild adventure after she discovers a summer camp run by real pirates. Some reviewers declared Lichtenheld's illustrations to be the highlight of the tale. According to Todd Morning in *Booklist,* "the humor and appeal come less from the slight story than from Tom Lichtenheld's funny and energetic drawings," and a *Kirkus Reviews* writer cited the book's "amusing and exaggerated" art. Elaine E. Knight, writing in *School Library Journal,* also praised Lichtenheld's art in *Camp Buccaneer,* writing that the illustrator's "amusing black-and-white cartoons add to the fun."

Lichtenheld's self-illustrated *What Are YOU So Grumpy About?* catalogues the many situations that cause children to become irritable. In one instance, a child receives underwear for a birthday present, and in another, a youngster must eat "grown-up" cereal for breakfast. "Humor is everywhere," observed Nancy Menaldi-Scanlan in *School Library Journal,* "and the author clearly knows the types of traumas that can turn a child's mood sour." In *Booklist* Kay Weisman wrote that "Lichtenheld's big, bold, broadly comic art style . . . is well suited to the tone of the text and has solid child appeal," and a *Publishers Weekly* contributor noted that "each outlandish, humorously exaggerated illustration, outlined in thick black strokes to emphasize the cartoonish scenarios, make the case for the victims' foul mood."

The typical child's bedroom is given the Lichtenheld treatment in *What's with This Room?,* as the author/illustrator introduces a boy who has probably the messiest room ever. From left-over school lunches to history projects to science experiments (and a dusting of dirty laundry to boot), the items that qualify as clutter are pointed out by the boy's parents and then justified as important by the room's resident, all in a rhyming text. Lichtenheld's text "is full of humor," wrote a *Kirkus Reviews* writer, the critic adding that the author's "bright and busy" cartoon art adds to the fun, while in *School Library Journal* Rachel Vilmar dubbed *What's with This Room?* a "silly romp through the messiest mess since the Cat in the Hat came to visit."

Lichtenheld's illustrations begin as inky doodles and evolve into pen drawings in-filled with water color and colored pencil. "I get ideas by keeping my eyes and ears open, especially when I'm around kids," he explained on his home page. "Then I try to see things as a child would and write from their perspective. I always write with a specific child in mind, as if we're just having a fun conversation. I try to remember how smart kids are, which is why my books also appeal to older kids and adults."

Because writing is a lonely occupation, Lichtenheld sees many benefits to his dual career as an art director and author. "They feed off each other very nicely," he told Long in the *Daily Herald.* "After I spend three months in my studio doing a book, I'm ready to be with people," he added in his *Adweek* interview.

Biographical and Critical Sources

PERIODICALS

Adweek, November 1, 2004, Aaron Baar, interview with Lichtenheld, p. 32.

Booklist, May 15, 2000, GraceAnne A. DeCandido, review of *Everything I Know about Pirates: A Collection of Made-up Facts, Educated Guesses, and Silly Pictures about Bad Guys of the High Seas,* p. 1746; June 1, 2002, Todd Morning, review of *Camp Buccaneer,* p. 1725; March 15, 2003, Kay Weisman, review of *What Are YOU So Grumpy About?,* pp. 1332-1333; January 1, 2005, Carolyn Phelan, review of *Everything I Know about Cars: A Collection of Made-up Facts, Educated Guesses, and Silly Pictures about Cars, Trucks, and Other Zoomy Things,* p. 849; April 15, 2008, Shelle Rosenfeld, review of *It's Not Fair!,* p. 49; April 1, 2009, Ilene Cooper, review of *Duck! Rabbit!,* p. 38, and Patricia Austin, review of *Yes Day!* p. 46.

Daily Herald (Arlington Heights, IL), December 8, 2000, Debbie Long, "Geneva Man Has Scoop on Pirates," p. 1; October 22, 2002, Lisa Friedman Miner, "Hey, Kids, Everything You Wanted to Know about Monsters," p. 1.

Horn Book, May-June, 2009, Chelsey Philpot, review of *Duck! Rabbit!,* p. 286.

Kirkus Reviews, May 15, 2002, review of *Camp Buccaneer,* p. 741; April 1, 2003, review of *What Are YOU So Grumpy About?,* p. 536; January 15, 2005, review of *Everything I Know about Cars,* p. 123; September 1, 2005, review of *What's with This Room?,* p. 977; April 1, 2007, review of *The OK Book;* April 15, 2008, review of *It's Not Fair!*

New York Times Book Review, July 15, 2007, Rebecca Zerkin, review of *The OK Book,* p. 17; May 10, 2009, Bruce Handy, reviews of *Yes Day!* and *Duck! Rabbit!,* p. 20.

Publishers Weekly, May 14, 2001, review of *Everything I Know about Pirates,* p. 36; July 15, 2002, p. 75; March 31, 2003, review of *What Are YOU So Grumpy About?,* p. 65.

Reading Teacher, October, 2002, Cyndi Giorgis and Nancy J. Johnson, "Pirates," pp. 201-203; April 30, 2007, review of *The OK Book,* p. 159; March 23, 2009, review of *Duck! Rabbit!,* p. 58; May 25, 2009, review of *Yes Day!,* p. 56.

School Library Journal, June, 2002, Elaine E. Knight, review of *Camp Buccaneer,* p. 110; September, 2002, Kathleen Kelly MacMillan, review of *Everything I Know about Monsters: A Collection of Made-up Facts, Educated Guesses, and Silly Pictures about Creatures of Creepiness,* p. 215; April, 2003, Nancy Menaldi-Scanlan, review of *What Are YOU So Grumpy About?,* p. 152; May, 2005, Catherine Callegari, review of *Everything I Know about Cars,* p. 111; November, 2005, Rachael Vilmar, review of *What's with This Room?,* p. 97; July, 2007, Marge Loch-Wouters, review of *The OK Book,* p. 84; April, 2008, Jane Marino, review of *It's Not Fair!,* p. 120; May, 2009, Catherine Callegari, review of *Yes Day!,* p. 88.

ONLINE

Embracing the Child Web site, http://www.embracingthe child.org/ (March 9, 2004), "Tom Lichtenheld."

Tom Lichtenheld Home Page, http://www.tomlichtenheld. com/ (November 20, 2009).

Tom Lichtenheld Web log, http://tomlichtenheld.wordpress. com (November 20, 2009).

* * *

LINCOLN, Christopher 1952-

Personal

Born July 17, 1952, in Hartford, CT; married. *Education:* Syracuse University, B.A. (experimental design).

Addresses

Home—Excelsior, MN.

Career

Writer and art director. Formerly worked as an animator; Fallon Worldwide (advertising agency), Minneapolis, MN, art director.

Writings

FOR CHILDREN

Billy Bones: A Tale from the Secrets Closet, Little, Brown (New York, NY), 2008.

Billy Bones: The Road to Nevermore, Little, Brown (New York, NY), 2009.

Sidelights

Taking time out from his job as an art director for a Minneapolis-based advertising agency, Christopher Lincoln has also made his mark in children's publishing. Lincoln's imaginative elementary-grade novels *Billy Bones: A Tale from the Secrets Closet* and *Billy Bones: The Road to Nevermore* introduce readers to a young skeleton whose friendship with an orphaned girl draws him into the world of the living and the adventures that world holds.

Billy Bones: A Tale from the Secrets Closet is set in High Manners Manor, a large estate ruled by stern housekeeper Miss Primly and the home of the powerful Biglum family. The family's history tends toward the bad rather than the good, and it is all documented by the Bones family, skeletons that live in the manor's Secrets closet. Billy is the youngest skeleton, and when he befriends Millicent Hues, the young niece of the current Sir Biglum, he sees the manor—and his place in it—

through new eyes and gradually learns the secrets of his own past. In her *School Library Journal* review of *Billy Bones: A Tale from the Secrets Closet,* Jennifer D. Montgomery praised Lincoln's "creatively descriptive language," adding that his "delightful story moves along rapidly" while "never crossing into campy." With its "easygoing charm," the novel is "sure to amuse those . . . with a love of the mildly macabre," concluded a *Kirkus Reviews* writer in an appraisal of Lincoln's fiction debut.

Billy and Millicent return in *Billy Bones: The Road to Nevermore,* as the children venture beyond the walls of High Manners Manor. After both Millicent and Billy's uncle Grim—known to most as the Grim Reaper—are kidnapped by arch evildoer Shadewick Gloom, Billy must follow them to the shadowy world called Nevermore. While working to rescue his friend, Billy also uncovers more guilty secrets, but these secrets extend far beyond the transgression of the Biglum family. In *School Library Journal,* Beth Cuddy described *Billy Bones: The Road to Nevermore* as "action-packed and filled with colorful characters," while a *Kirkus Reviews* writer dubbed Lincoln's novel as a "madcap series of escapades."

Christopher Lincoln's ghostly middle-grade novel **Billy Bones: A Tale from the Secrets Closet** *features Avi Ofer's line drawings.* (Illustration copyright © 2008 by Avi Ofer. By permission of Little, Brown & Company.)

Biographical and Critical Sources

PERIODICALS

Bulletin of the Center for Children's Books, September, 2008, April Spisak, review of *Billy Bones: A Tale from the Secrets Closet,* p. 31.

Kirkus Reviews, July 1, 2008, review of *Billy Bones: A Tale from the Secrets Closet;* July 15, 2009, review of *Billy Bones: The Road to Nevermore.*

School Library Journal, October, 2008, Jennifer D. Montgomery, review of *Billy Bones: A Tale from the Secrets Closet,* p. 152; August, 2009, Beth Cuddy, review of *Billy Bones: The Road to Nevermore,* p. 108.

Voice of Youth Advocates, December, 2008, Courtney Wika, review of *Billy Bones: A Tale from the Secrets Closet,* p. 454.

ONLINE

Christopher Lincoln Home Page, http://www.chrislincoln. org (December 1, 2009).*

*   *   *

LISLE, Holly 1960-

Personal

Born October, 1960, in Salem, OR; children: three. *Education:* Richmond Community College, associate degree (nursing), 1982.

Addresses

Agent—Robin Rue, Writers House, 21 W. 26th St., New York, NY 10010. *E-mail*—holly@hollylisle.com.

Career

Writer. Worked variously as an advertising representative for a newspaper, singer in restaurants, guitar teacher, and commercial artist; registered nurse for ten years, primarily in emergency and critical-care units; full-time writer, 1993—. Creator of novel-writing course How to Think Sideways.

Member

Science Fiction Writers of America.

Awards, Honors

Compton Crook Award for Best First Novel, 1993; John W. Campbell Award for Best New Writer finalist, 1993, 1994; Award for Literary Excellence, 2003; Outstanding Services to Writers Award; Golden Crane Creativity Award, Creativity Portal.

Writings

FICTION

Minerva Wakes, Baen (Riverdale, NY), 1993.

(With Mercedes Lackey) *When the Bough Breaks,* Baen (Riverdale, NY), 1993.

(With S.M. Stirling) *The Rose Sea,* Baen (Riverdale, NY), 1994.

(With Chris Guin) *Mall, Mayhem, and Magic,* Baen (Riverdale, NY), 1995.

Hunting the Corrigan's Blood, Baen (Riverdale, NY), 1997.

Midnight Rain, Onyx (New York, NY), 2004.

Last Girl Dancing, Onyx (New York, NY), 2005.

I See You, Onyx (New York, NY), 2006.

Night Echoes, Signet (New York, NY), 2007.

Contributor of short stories to anthologies, including *Women at War,* edited by Lois McMaster Bujold, Tor (New York, NY), 1992; *The Enchanter Reborn,* edited by L. Sprague de Camp and Christopher Stasheff, Baen (Riverdale, NY), 1992; and *Chicks in Chainmail,* edited by Esther Friesner, Baen, 1995.

"ARHEL" NOVEL SERIES

Fire in the Mist, Baen (Riverdale, NY), 1992.

Bones of the Past, Baen (Riverdale, NY), 1993.

Mind of the Magic, Baen (Riverdale, NY), 1995.

"GLENRAVEN" NOVEL SERIES

(With Marion Zimmer Bradley) *Glenraven,* Baen (Riverdale, NY), 1996.

(With Marion Zimmer Bradley) *In the Rift,* Baen (Riverdale, NY), 1998.

"DEVIL'S POINT" NOVEL SERIES

Sympathy for the Devil, Baen (Riverdale, NY), 1996.

(With Walter Spence) *The Devil and Dan Cooley,* Baen (Riverdale, NY), 1996.

(With Ted Nolan) *Hell on High,* Baen (Riverdale, NY), 1997.

"BARD'S TALE" NOVEL SERIES

(With Aaron Allston) *Thunder of the Captains,* Baen (Riverdale, NY), 1996.

(With Aaron Allston) *Wrath of the Princes,* Baen (Riverdale, NY), 1997.

Curse of the Black Heron, Baen (Riverdale, NY), 1998.

"THE SECRET TEXTS" NOVEL SERIES

Diplomacy of Wolves, Warner Aspect (New York, NY), 1998.

Vengeance of Dragons, Warner Aspect (New York, NY), 1999.

Courage of Falcons, Warner Aspect (New York, NY), 2000.

Vincalis the Agitator, Warner Aspect (New York, NY), 2001.

"THE WORLD GATES" NOVEL SERIES

Memory of Fire, Eos (New York, NY), 2002.
The Wreck of Heaven, Eos (New York, NY), 2003.
Gods Old and Dark, Eos (New York, NY), 2004.

"THE WORLD OF KORRE" NOVEL SERIES

Talyn, Tor (New York, NY), 2005.
Hawkspar, Tor (New York, NY), 2008.

"THE MOON AND SUN" NOVEL SERIES

The Ruby Key, Orchard Books (New York, NY), 2008.
The Silver Door, Orchard Books (New York, NY), 2009.

OTHER

Also author of nonfiction works, including *How to
Think Sideways—Build Your Own Writing Career, Cre-
ate a Plot Clinic: A Step-by-Step Course for the Fiction
Writer,* and *Create a Character Clinic: A Step-by-Step
Course for the Fiction Writer.*

Sidelights

Holly Lisle is the author of dozens of novels, including
fantasy tales such as *Diplomacy of Wolves* and *The Ruby
Key,* and she has earned praise for crafting action-
packed narratives, well-developed societies, and sub-
stantive characters. "I write adventures in which strong
women and strong men are pitted against terrifying obstacles, and in which their hope and idealism and courage and faith and intelligence are their only real weap-
ons," Lisle stated on her home page. "My themes focus
on personal responsibility, the power of the individual
to effect change, and the power of love, honor, and
courage to transform."

In her first novel, *Fire in the Mist,* Lisle presents the
story of Faia, a young shepherdess living in Arhel who
exhibits a natural talent for magic. Faia joins a group of
more-advanced practitioners in order to develop her
abilities but ultimately rebels against the strict social arrangement of Arhel society, in which men and women
reside separately and are celibate. Carolyn Cushman,
reviewing *Fire in the Mist* in *Locus,* called the novel
"exceptionally well-crafted and readable," concluding
that the work is "a real page-turner that should be highly
popular with genre fans."

In *Minerva Wakes* protagonist Minerva Kiakra inadvert-
ently gains possession of a wedding ring with magical
powers, setting off a series of fantasy adventures that
include an encounter with a dragon, the abduction of
Minerva's children, and a trip to an alternate universe.
Susan E. Chmurynsky, reviewing Lisle's second novel
in *Kliatt,* called *Minerva Wakes* "a good natured and
breezy tale that moves along at a rapid clip."

In both *Bones of the Past* and *Mind of the Magic,* Lisle
returns to the saga of Faia, the protagonist of *Fire in
the Mist,* who grows into adulthood and eventually be-

Cover of Holly Lisle's fantasy novel **Mind of the Magic,** *an installment
in her "Arhel" saga, features artwork by Clyde Caldwell.* (Baen Publishing
Enterprises, 1995. Reproduced by permission.)

comes the mother of a child. *Mind of the Magic* centers
on circumstances that evolve when all the inhabitants of
the town of Arhel suddenly develop magical abilities,
then just as suddenly lose their gifts, leaving the town
in a nightmarish state of ruin. Through Faia, the community is reborn and establishes harmonious contacts
with the Klaue, nonhuman beings who cohabit the
region. Commenting on *Mind of the Magic,* Sister Avila
Lamb wrote in *Kliatt* that "there are instances of very
fine writing" and that "readers will be charmed by the
delightful characters."

Coauthored with Chris Guin, Lisle's young adult fantasy novel *Mall, Mayhem, and Magic* was published in
1995. In the story, magic wreaks havoc in a local mall
when a bookstore clerk attempts to cast a love spell on
the girl he admires. Karen S. Ellis, reviewing *Mall,
Mayhem, and Magic* in *Kliatt,* noted that coauthors Lisle
and Guin "have created an interesting combination of
fantasy, horror and humor." Ellis called the pace of the
novel "quick and exciting."

In *Sympathy for the Devil* a young woman's wish that
all those in Hell receive a second chance at redemption

brings the condemned back to earth. "Character development is well done," remarked Lesley S.J. Farmer, reviewing *Sympathy for the Devil* in *Kliatt,* "and the tone is actually light-hearted."

Glenraven, cowritten with noted fantasy writer Marion Zimmer Bradley, follows the adventures of two women who visit Glenraven, a fictitious country that harbors secrets of "Europe's mystical forgotten past." Recommending *Glenraven* in a review for *Library Journal,* a critic noted that "Bradley and Lisle expertly juxtapose contemporary women and a medieval, magical culture." In a sequel, *In the Rift,* a Wiccan who is persecuted by her neighbors finds herself hosting a quartet of otherworldly visitors. "What makes the book work is not simply the fast pace and inventive magical elements, but the characterization," Charles de Lint asserted in his review of *In the Rift* for the *Magazine of Fantasy and Science Fiction.*

Diplomacy of Wolves opens Lisle's bestselling "The Secret Texts" series, which is set in the world of Matrin. The work centers on Kait Galweigh, a noblewoman and diplomat who possesses the ability to shapeshift. *Booklist* critic Roland Green praised the "well-depicted fantasy world" Lisle creates in the novel and called *Di-plomacy of Wolves* "absorbing reading." In *Vengeance of Dragons,* the second work in the series, Kait searches for a magical artifact, the Mirror of Souls, which contains the trapped souls of powerful sorcerers. *Courage of Falcons* the conclusion to Lisle's "rousing fantasy epic," as Jackie Cassada wrote in *Library Journal,* concerns an epic battle between the Falcons, a group of renegade wizards, and the Dragons, evil necromancers who devour souls. Lisle has also written a prequel to "The Secret Texts" series titled *Vincalis the Agitator,* in which a sorcerer's apprentice discovers a horrifying secret about a utopian society. Farmer maintained that "the rich detail of the characters and subplot helps to flesh out this cautionary tale."

In *Talyn* Lisle presents a tale of warring nations. Talyn, a soldier in the Tonk Confederacy, joins forces with a rival commander from the Eastil Republic after she learns that a ceasefire engineered by Feegash diplomats is actually a plan for conquest. A critic in *Kirkus Reviews* described the novel as "an unusually thoughtful work, unsparing of detail, with characters who must solve their own problems before they save the world." A sequel, *Hawkspar,* focuses on the bond between Aaran, a slave tracker who searches for his missing sister, and a young slave girl who becomes a powerful oracle. *Talyn* is "serious, very readable fantasy," concluded *Booklist* reviewer Frieda Murray.

The Ruby Key, Lisle's first work for children, introduces "The Moon and Sun" series. Fourteen-year-old Genna and her younger brother, Danrith, are residents of Hillrush, a community of humans who, under terms of a uneasy truce, can only venture out by day; once it is dark, the land is ruled by dangerous, fairylike creatures known as nightlings. When Genna and Danrith discover that their uncle has betrayed them to Letrin, a powerful lord, they strike their own deal with the nightling ruler and embark on a dangerous quest. Krista Hurley, writing in *Booklist,* praised the author's ability to create a "complex and intriguing" world "with a complex history, well-developed societies, and a strong sense of magic."

The power of stories, especially fantasy tales, holds great significance for Lisle. As she remarked to a Teenreads.com interviewer, "Fantasy was the first genre because it let us shape the world into patterns that made sense to us and taught us how to overcome enormous obstacles with limited resources. And because it showed us that hope was not futile, that if we dared to step forward and accept the challenge, we could overcome it—sometimes alone, sometimes with a few good friends at our sides. And that is still what fantasy is about. It's also why I write it."

Lisle's middle-grade novel The Ruby Key, *part of her "Moon and Sun" series, features cover art by Joshua Middleton.* (Illustration © 2008 by Joshua Middleton. Reproduced by permission of Scholastic, Inc.)

Biographical and Critical Sources

PERIODICALS

Booklist, October 1, 1998, Roland Green, review of *Diplomacy of Wolves,* p. 313; March 15, 2002, Roland

Green, review of *Vincalis the Agitator,* p. 1219; August, 2005, Frieda Murray, review of *Talyn,* p. 2009; April 1, 2007, Maria Hatton, review of *Night Echoes,* p. 35; May 15, 2008, Frieda Murray, review of *Hawkspar,* p. 36, and Krista Hurley, review of *The Ruby Key,* p. 57.

Horn Book, May-June, 2008, Anita L. Burkam, review of *The Ruby Key,* p. 320.

Kirkus Reviews, June 1, 2005, review of *Talyn,* p. 616; April 1, 2008, review of *The Ruby Key.*

Kliatt, March, 1994, Susan E. Chmurynsky, review of *Minerva Wakes,* p. 18; September, 1995, Sister Avila Lamb, review of *Mind of the Magic,* p. 23; November, 1995, Karen S. Ellis, review of *Mall, Mayhem, and Magic,* p. 17; May, 1996, Lesley S.J. Farmer, review of *Sympathy for the Devil,* p. 18; July, 2003, Lesley S.J. Farmer, review of *Vincalis the Agitator,* p. 33.

Library Journal, August, 1996, review of *Glenraven,* p. 120; April 15, 1998, Jackie Cassada, review of *In the Rift,* p. 119; October 15, 1998, Jackie Cassada, review of *Diplomacy of Wolves,* p. 103; October 15, 1999, Jackie Cassada, review of *Vengeance of Dragons,* p. 111; August, 2000, Jackie Cassada, review of *Courage of Falcons,* p. 167.

Locus, July, 1992, Carolyn Cushman, review of *Fire in the Mist,* p. 33.

Magazine of Fantasy and Science Fiction, October-November, 1998, Charles de Lint, review of *In the Rift,* p. 36.

Publishers Weekly, February 23, 1998, review of *In the Rift,* p. 56; October 2, 2000, review of *Courage of Falcons,* p. 65; February 25, 2002, review of *Vincalis the Agitator,* p. 47; May 30, 2005, review of *Talyn,* p. 43; February 5, 2007, review of *Night Echoes,* p. 46; April 14, 2008, review of *Hawkspar,* p. 42.

School Library Journal, June, 2008, Quinby Frank, review of *The Ruby Key,* p. 145.

ONLINE

Fiction Factor Web site, http://www.fictionfactor.com/ (July 11, 2001), Lee Masterson, interview with Lisle.

Holly Lisle Home Page, http://hollylisle.com (November 1, 2009).

Scholastic Web site, http://www2.scholastic.com/ (November 1, 2009), "Holly Lisle."

Teenreads.com, http://www.teenreads.com/ (May, 2000), interview with Lisle.*

*   *   *

LUCAS, David 1966-

Personal

Born 1966, in Middlesbrough, England. *Education:* St. Martins School of Art (London, England), B.A. (with honors); Royal College of Art, M.A.

David Lucas (Photograph by Merle Moustafa. Reproduced by permission.)

Addresses

Home—Lewes, England. *E-mail*—david@davidlucas.org.uk.

Career

Author and illustrator.

Writings

SELF-ILLUSTRATED

Halibut Jackson, Andersen (London, England), 2003, Knopf (New York, NY), 2004.

Nutmeg, Andersen (London, England), 2005, Knopf (New York, NY), 2006.

Whale, Andersen (London, England), 2006, Knopf (New York, NY), 2007.

The Robot and the Bluebird, Andersen (London, England), 2007, Farrar, Straus (New York, NY), 2008.

Peanut, Candlewick Press (Somerville, MA), 2008.

The Lying Carpet, Andersen (London, England), 2008.

Something to Do, Philomel (New York, NY), 2009.

Cake Girl, Farrar, Straus (New York, NY), 2009.

ILLUSTRATOR

Hiawyn Oram, *Rubbaduck and Ruby Roo,* Boyds Mills Press (Honesdale, PA), 2005.

Sidelights

British author David Lucas published his first work for children in 2003, marking the beginning of a career that has become noted for producing unique books for young readers. Among Lucas's self-illustrated books are *Halibut Jackson, The Robot and the Bluebird, Peanut,* and *Cake Girl.*

Lucas's first self-illustrated work, *Halibut Jackson,* features an exceptionally shy character with a talent for creating clothing that allows him to blend in with his surroundings. For instance, when visiting the library, Halibut wears a special costume that looks like the spines of books on a shelf, and when he goes shopping at the grocery store, he dons a coat covered with apples to blend in at the produce department. Upon receiving an invitation to a party at the queen's palace, Halibut excitedly fashions an outfit covered in sparkling jewels and gold thread that he thinks will make him unnoticed among all the other royal attendees. His plan initially backfires, however, when he arrives at the soiree to learn that the event is being held outdoors in the garden.

Lucas pairs his quirky story with his original art in the simply titled picture book **Peanut.** (Copyright © 2008 by David Lucas. All rights reserved. Reproduced by permission of the publisher Candlewick Press, Inc., Cambridge, MA.)

However, the compliments Halibut gets from others about the beauty of his work give him the confidence to become more outgoing and begin a career as a tailor. Reviewing *Halibut Jackson* in the London *Guardian,* Julia Eccleshare deemed the book's "witty and original illustrations . . . delightfully satisfying," while *Booklist* critic Jennifer Mattson suggested that the "playful, jam-packed scenes . . . add a whimsical seek-and-find element that extends the book's appeal."

In the simply titled *Nutmeg,* Lucas puts an unusual twist on the traditional tale about being granted three wishes after freeing a bottled genie. Along with her Uncle Nicodemus and Cousin Nesbit, Nutmeg lives a bland existence, never varying from a diet of cardboard, string, and sawdust. After releasing a trapped genie, however, the diminutive creature suddenly dines on a variety of delicious treats at every meal, all served by a magic spoon. Unexpectedly, the eating implement transforms more than Nutmeg's meals, changing the family's small, humble dwelling into a boat and propelling the trio to more-exotic dining locales. Several reviewers commented favorably on the artwork in *Nutmeg, Booklist* critic GraceAnne A. DeCandido claiming that the author/illustrator makes "great things with shifting perspectives, multiple panels, and the shape-shifting cottage/boat/airship." A *Kirkus Reviews* contributor predicted of Lucas's work that "readers' imaginations will soar . . . as bursts of color transform [Nutmeg's] dreary world."

A creature stranded by a fierce storm appears in *Whale,* beginning an adventure for Joe as the young boy tries to return the lost mammal to its home. Rejecting comments from those who wish to eat the sea creature, Joe asks a series of elements for advice on how to return the beached whale to the sea. Moving from the wind to the sun to the moon, the boy finally receives an answer from the stars, which instruct him to sing for rain. Enlisting the help of his neighbors, Joe leads everyone in a chorus asking for raindrops. This request is granted, but at great cost to the village: While the rain helps float the whale to the ocean, the rising water floods Joe's village, leaving residents without homes or businesses. Determined not to let the people's good deed go unreturned, the whale enlists the help of his fellow aquatic friends to rebuild the town. Lucas reaches "just the right tone between informal, childlike story-telling and a more formal fable" in *Whale,* wrote *Booklist* contributor Carolyn Phelan. For a *Kirkus Reviews* writer, the book offers children a positive story about "young people rescuing communities threatened by unusual natural disasters."

The Robot and the Bluebird presents the author/illustrator's "most meditative work to date," according to a *Kirkus Reviews* critic. When an old robot's heart deteriorates beyond repair, it earns a trip to the junkyard because it is thought to be of no use any longer. One cold evening, a weary bluebird on its annual migration south searches for a safe place to take a night's rest and settles in the empty space in the robot's chest. Upon hearing the bird's story, the old piece of machinery decides that it can help the poor creature by carrying the bird to its southern home. The trip proves to be the last one for the kind robot, and it expires upon reaching its destination. With one final effort the robot asks the bluebird, now reunited with its flock, to make a permanent residence in its heart. "A quiet beauty permeates this old-fashioned story," maintained the *Kirkus Reviews* contributor in reviewing Lucas's gentle picturebook. In her *Booklist* review, Patricia Austin wrote that *The Robot and the Bluebird* offers a "clear message of the joys and sacrifices of enduring friendship," while a *Publishers Weekly* critic claimed that the "book's genuine sweetness will easily win over readers."

Biographical and Critical Sources

PERIODICALS

Booklist, February 1, 2004, Jennifer Mattson, review of *Halibut Jackson*, p. 982; March 1, 2005, Karin Snelson, review of *Rubbaduck and Ruby Roo*, p. 1205; August 1, 2006, GraceAnne A. DeCandido, review of *Nutmeg*, p. 90; June 1, 2007, Carolyn Phelan, review of *Whale*, p. 86; November 1, 2008, Patricia Austin, review of *The Robot and the Bluebird*, p. 50.

Guardian (London, England), October 18, 2003, Julia Eccleshare, review of *Halibut Jackson*, p. 33; October 14, 2006, Julia Eccleshare, review of *Whale*, p. 20; January 19, 2008, Julia Eccleshare, review of *The Robot and the Bluebird*, p. 20.

Kirkus Reviews, January 15, 2004, review of *Halibut Jackson*, p. 85; February 1, 2005, review of *Rubbaduck and Ruby Roo*, p. 180; August 1, 2006, review of *Nutmeg*, p. 791; May 15, 2007, review of *Whale;* October 1, 2008, review of *The Robot and the Bluebird.*

Publishers Weekly, March 7, 2005, review of *Rubbaduck and Ruby Roo*, p. 67; July 10, 2006, review of *Nutmeg*, p. 80; May 21, 2007, review of *Whale*, p. 54; October 20, 2008, review of *The Robot and the Bluebird*, p. 49.

School Library Journal, March, 2004, Marianne Saccardi, review of *Halibut Jackson*, 176; March, 2005, Be Astengo, review of *Rubbaduck and Ruby Roo*, p. 185; August, 2006, Linda L. Walkins, review of *Nutmeg*, p. 92; June, 2007, Kathy Krasniewicz, review of *Whale*, p. 114; November, 2008, Amy Lilien Harper, review of *The Robot and the Bluebird*, p. 94; March, 2009, Linda Ludke, review of *Peanut*, p. 121.

ONLINE

David Lucas Home Page, http://www.davidlucas.org.uk (November 25, 2009).

*   *   *

LY, Many 1977-

Personal

Born 1977, in Cambodia; immigrated to United States, c. 1980; married. *Education:* University of South Florida, degree.

Addresses

Home—Pittsburgh, PA. *E-mail*—many.ly@hotmail.com.

Career

Educator and writer. Former teacher of middle-grade language arts in CA; Greater Pittsburgh Literacy Council, Pittsburgh, PA, program services manager.

Awards, Honors

100 Books to Read and Share inclusion, New York Public Library, 2005, for *Home Is East;* Asian/Pacific American Award for Literature (youth category), 2009, for *Roots and Wings.*

Writings

Home Is East, Delacorte Press (New York, NY), 2005.
Roots and Wings, Delacorte Press (New York, NY), 2008.

Sidelights

Many Ly draws on her own experiences as a first-generation Cambodian American in her novels *Home Is East* and *Roots and Wings*. An infant when the Khmer Rouge ruled her birth country, Ly did not understand the violence she witnessed before she and her family left for the United States when she was three years old. "Fortunately, I was a baby and don't remember the hardship of it," she explained on her home page. "However, people older than I am (like my parents and husband) do. . . . For a long time, I did not want to recognize this part in our history. As I grew older, I learned to accept it. Now, I am beginning to embrace it—not the killings—but how my people overcame it. I don't purposely set out to write about the Khmer Rouge, though. It surfaces naturally in my stories."

Ly sets her first novel, *Home Is East*, in a Cambodian community in Florida, the state where she grew up. Her nine-year-old protagonist, Amy Lim, refuses to believe the rumors that her mom plans to leave the family. Her mother and father both grew up during the time of the Khmer Rouge, as over one-fifth of the population of Cambodia were killed, and she is convinced that her pretty young mom joined her dad in the United Stated out of love for the older man. When Amy's mother does abandon the family to start a new life, she leaves both father and daughter saddened and shocked. A move to Southern California follows, as Amy's distraught father attempts to deal with his own heartbreak. When he begins to have problems with alcohol, Amy worries, but over the next three years she learns that life changes are better accepted than fought.

Although Jennifer Mattson noted that *Home Is East* concentrates less on plot than on the preteen's emotions, she nonetheless praised Ly's novel for introducing readers "to a closely bonded immigrant commu-

Cover of Many Ly's middle-grade novel Roots and Wings, *featuring artwork by Steve Rawlings.* (Illustration © 2008 by Steve Rawlings. Used by permission of Delacorte Press, an imprint of Random House Children's Books, a division of Random House, Inc.)

nity." In *School Library Journal* Susan Oliver described the book as "a good coming-of-age story, [and] a good father-daughter story," while a *Kirkus Reviews* writer noted that Ly captures the Cambodian cultural "stoicism" that is at odds with U.S. culture. Noting the story's slow pace, Mari Li-Yan Stromquist added in her *Journal of Adolescent and Adult Literacy* review that in *Home Is East* "Ly has tenderly drawn a heartfelt story full of identifiable characters and insightful relationships."

In Ly's middle-grade novel *Roots and Wings* readers meet fourteen-year-old Grace as the Pennsylvania teen takes a trip to Florida with her single mom. Although Grace has looked forward to meeting her Cambodian relatives for many years, this trip is bittersweet: they are bringing grandmother Naree back for a Buddhist burial near her many friends in St. Petersburg. Although she is welcomed by the city's close-knit refugee community, Grace feels off balance amid the unfamiliar Cambodian traditions. Undaunted, she slowly gains information regarding her mother's past and the father she never knew, learning in the process why some things have been hidden. Ly's teen protagonist is central to "a satisfying coming-of-age story," concluded a *Kirkus Reviews* writer, while in *Booklist* Hazel Rochman noted that the novel's sometimes-overwhelming "cultural detail" contributes to an emotional journey that ends in "forgiveness and understanding." In *Kliatt* Claire Rosser recommended *Roots and Wings* as "essential reading for all those whose cultural ties go back to Southeast Asia," and *School Librar Journal* contributor Julianna M. Helt deemed the book a "beautifully written" story about a culture that is unfamiliar to many Americans.

Biographical and Critical Sources

PERIODICALS

Booklist, August, 2005, Jennifer Mattson, review of *Home Is East,* p. 1966; March 15, 2008, Hazel Rochman, review of *Roots and Wings,* p. 49.

Journal of Adolescent and Adult Literacy, April, 2006, Mari Li-Yan Stromquist, review of *Home Is East,* p. 634.

Kirkus Reviews, July 1, 2005, review of *Home Is East*; April 15, 2008, review of *Roots and Wings.*

Kliatt, July, 2008, Claire Rosser, review of *Roots and Wings,* p. 17.

School Library Journal, August, 2005, Susan Oliver, review of *Home Is East,* p. 130; July, 2008, Julianna M. Helt, review of *Roots and Wings,* p. 104.

ONLINE

Many Ly Home Page, http://manyly.com (November 20, 2009).*

M

MacHIN, Sue
See WILLIAMS, Sue

* * *

McKAY, Hilary 1959-
(Hilary Jane McKay)

Personal

Born June 12, 1959, in Boston, Lincolnshire, England; daughter of Ronald (an engineer) and Mary (a nurse) Damms; married Kevin McKay (a teacher), August 13, 1992; children: Jim, Bella. *Education:* University of St. Andrew, B.S. (botany and zoology), 1981. *Hobbies and other interests:* Reading, walking, visiting with friends.

Addresses

Home—Derbyshire, England. *Agent*—Jennifer Luithlen Agency, 88 Holmfield Rd., Liecester LE2 1SB, England.

Career

Writer. Formerly worked as a laboratory technician.

Awards, Honors

London *Guardian* Award for Children's Fiction, 1992, for *The Exiles;* Smarties Prize for Children's Literature, 1994, for *Dog Friday,* 1995, for *The Amber Cat* and *The Zoo in the Attic,* and 2002, for *Saffy's Angel; Boston Globe/Horn Book* Honor Book designation, 2002, and Whitbread Children's Book Award, 2003, both for *Saffy's Angel.*

Writings

FOR CHILDREN

The Exiles ("Exiles" trilogy; also see below), Victor Gollancz (London, England), 1991, Margaret K. McElderry Books (New York, NY), 1992.

Hilary McKay (Photograph by Wildsmith-Towle. Reproduced by permission.)

The Exiles at Home ("Exiles" trilogy; also see below), Victor Gollancz (London, England), 1993, Margaret K. McElderry Books (New York, NY), 1994.

Dog Friday ("Dog Friday" trilogy; also see below), Victor Gollancz (London, England), 1994, Margaret K. McElderry Books (New York, NY), 1995.

The Amber Cat ("Dog Friday" trilogy; also see below), Victor Gollancz (London, England), 1995, Margaret K. McElderry Books (New York, NY), 1997.

Happy and Glorious, illustrated by Hilda Offen, Hodder & Stoughton (London, England), 1996.

Practically Perfect, illustrated by Hilda Offen, Hodder & Stoughton (London, England), 1996.

Why Didn't You Tell Me?, illustrated by John Eastwood, Piccadilly (London, England), 1996.

The Exiles in Love ("Exiles" trilogy; also see below), Victor Gollancz (London, England), 1996, Margaret K. McElderry Books (New York, NY), 1998.

Strange Bear, illustrated by Alex Ayliffe, Hodder & Stoughton (London, England), 1998.

Where's Bear?, illustrated by Alex Ayliffe, Margaret K. McElderry Books (New York, NY), 1998.

The Birthday Wish ("Pudding Bag School" series), illustrated by David Melling, Hodder & Stoughton (London, England), 1998.

Cold Enough for Snow ("Pudding Bag School" series), illustrated by David Melling, Hodder & Stoughton (London, England), 1998.

Dolphin Luck ("Dog Friday" trilogy), Hodder & Stoughton (London, England), 1998, Margaret K. McElderry Books (New York, NY), 1999.

The Exiles ("Exiles" trilogy omnibus; contains *The Exiles, The Exiles at Home,* and *The Exiles in Love*), Hodder & Stoughton (London, England), 1998.

A Strong Smell of Magic ("Pudding Bag School" series), illustrated by David Melling, Hodder & Stoughton (London, England), 1999.

Pirates Ahoy!, illustrated by Alex Ayliffe, Hodder & Stoughton (London, England), 1999, Margaret K. McElderry Books (New York, NY), 2000.

Was That Christmas?, illustrated by Amanda Harvey, Hodder & Stoughton (London, England), 2001, Margaret K. McElderry Books (New York, NY), 2002.

There's a Dragon Downstairs, illustrated by Amanda Harvey, Hodder Children's Books (London, England), 2003, Margaret K. McElderry Books (New York, NY), 2005.

Swop!, illustrated by Kirstin Holbrow, Barrington Stoke (Edinburgh, Scotland), 2005.

Dragon!, illustrated by Mike Philips, Barrington Stoke (Edinburgh, Scotland), 2006.

The Story of Bear, illustrated by Serena Riglietti, Hodder Children's Books (London, England), 2007.

Amazing!, illustrated by Mike Philips, Barrington Stoke (Edinburgh, Scotland), 2008.

Wishing for Tomorrow (sequel to *A Little Princess* by Frances Hodgeson Burnett), Hodder Children's Books (London, England), 2009, Margaret K. McElderry Books (New York, NY), 2010.

"PARADISE HOUSE" SERIES

The Zoo in the Attic, illustrated by Tony Kenyon, Victor Gollancz (London, England), 1995.

The Treasure in the Garden, illustrated by Tony Kenyon, Victor Gollancz (London, England), 1995.

The Echo in the Chimney, illustrated by Tony Kenyon, Victor Gollancz (London, England), 1996.

The Magic in the Mirror, illustrated by Tony Kenyon, Victor Gollancz (London, England), 1996.

The Surprise Party, illustrated by Tony Kenyon, Hodder & Stoughton (London, England), 2000.

Keeping Cotton Tail, illustrated by Tony Kenyon, Hodder & Stoughton (London, England), 2000.

"BEETLE AND FRIENDS" SERIES

Beetle and the Hamster, illustrated by Lesley Harker, Scholastic Children's Books (London, England), 2002.

Beetle and the Bear, illustrated by Lesley Harker, Scholastic Children's Books (London, England), 2002.

Beetle and Lulu, illustrated by Lesley Harker, Scholastic Children's Books (London, England), 2002.

Beetle and the Big Tree, illustrated by Lesley Harker, Scholastic Children's Books (London, England), 2002.

"CASSON FAMILY" YOUNG-ADULT NOVEL SERIES

Saffy's Angel, Hodder & Stoughton (London, England), 2001, Margaret K. McElderry Books (New York, NY), 2002.

Indigo's Star, Hodder Children's Books (London, England), 2003, Margaret K. McElderry Books (New York, NY), 2004.

Permanent Rose, Hodder Children's Books (London, England), 2005, Margaret K. McElderry Books (New York, NY), 2006.

Caddy Ever After, Margaret K. McElderry Books (New York, NY), 2006.

Forever Rose, Hodder Children's Books (London, England), 2007, Margaret K. McElderry Books (New York, NY), 2008.

"CHARLIE" SERIES

Charlie and the Great Escape, illustrated by Sam Hearn, Scholastic (London, England), 2007.

Charlie and the Tooth Fairy, illustrated by Sam Hearn, Scholastic (London, England), 2007.

Charlie and the Birthday Bash, illustrated by Sam Hearn, Scholastic (London, England), 2007.

Charlie and the Big Snow, illustrated by Sam Hearn, Scholastic (London, England), 2007.

Charlie and the Cat Flap, illustrated by Sam Hearn, Scholastic (London, England), 2007.

Charlie and the Haunted Tent, illustrated by Sam Hearn, Scholastic (London, England), 2008.

Charlie and the Rocket Boy, illustrated by Sam Hearn, Scholastic (London, England), 2008.

Charlie and the Cheese and Onion Crisps, illustrated by Sam Hearn, Scholastic (London, England), 2008.

OTHER

(With Rita Cheminais) *Inclusion and School Improvement,* David Fulton Publishers (London, England), 2002.

Adaptations

Several of McKay's books, including *Dog Friday, Dolphin Luck, Happy and Glorious, Practically Perfect, Saffy's Angel, The Amber Cat, The Birthday Wish, The Exiles, Permanent Rose,* and *Indigo's Star* have all been adapted for audio cassette.

Sidelights

Writing stories that she herself would like to read, British author Hilary McKay has charmed young readers with books that include *The Exiles, Dog Friday,* the "Charlie" books, and her popular series of young-adult novels in the "Casson Family" series, which includes *Saffy's Angel* and *Caddy Ever After.* Noted for their realistic plots, likable characters, and humorous highlights, McKay's stories have won her numerous fans in both her native England and the United States. "I don't believe in writing down to children and am not conceited enough to desire to inflict my own opinions on other people," the author once noted. "I can't stand Good Cause books!" In 2009 McKay pleased her many fans while also sparking renewed interest in a childhood classic when she produced *Wishing for Tomorrow,* a sequel to Frances Hodgeson Burnett's beloved 1905 children's novel *A Little Princess.*

Before she began her writing career, McKay earned a bachelor's degree in science and worked as a laboratory technician. She began to write "as an extension of reading," as she once noted in an essay for *Something about the Author Autobiography Series* (SAAS). "I have read thousands of books. They influence my writing in the same way as the weather and as people I trust do. They are part of my landscape."

Despited her roundabout route to a writing career, McKay shares a childhood love of books with many of her fellow writers. Without a television in her home, she looked to reading as recreation. "In my family we read like starving dogs eat, huge, indiscriminate, barely chewed gulps," she recalled in *SAAS.* "Anything, ancient damp relics from the six-penny secondhand bookstall on the market, books scrounged from neighbors, books from the town library (blessed place), books that belonged to bookshops . . . we raced through whole paperbacks at a time." McKay's favorite authors included Enid Blyton, E. Nesbit, Arthur Ransome, L.M. Montgomery, Marjorie Kinnan Rawlings, Mark Twain, Eleanor Farjeon, and Louisa May Alcott.

McKay shared her books with her three sisters: Bridget, Robin, and Lorna, and the four girls spent their days much like the girls in McKay's "Exiles" trilogy, which includes *The Exiles, The Exiles at Home,* and *The Exiles in Love.* When not in school, the sisters spent a great deal of time reading. They quarreled and kidded one another. They earned pocket money by harvesting produce and working on a farm. As McKay recalled of those days working on the farm in *SAAS,* "It was a

lovely place. We would never have gone home given half a chance. I had never been so happy, or so dirty, or so exhausted."

McKay studied zoology and botany at the University of St. Andrew in Scotland, then married Kevin McKay and moved to Cumbria, England. "In Cumbria we lived in great poverty and cheerfulness in a haunted seventeenth-century cottage," she recalled. "Kevin taught maths, and I worked in the local pub and cleaned holiday cottages and painted pictures to sell to tourists, and all our St. Andrew's friends came to stay, especially Isabel, who said, 'I don't see why you don't write a book. You know what books are and you can write letters. Sometimes they are quite amusing. And you might get some money.'"

At Isabel's urging, McKay wrote the book that was eventually published as *The Exiles.* After it was completed, she and her husband moved to Derbyshire, where she worked as a chemist during the day and wrote at night. With the birth of her first child, McKay decided to stay home with her growing family and become a full-time writer.

The Exiles begins when the four Conroy sisters learn that their father has received an inheritance. At first, the

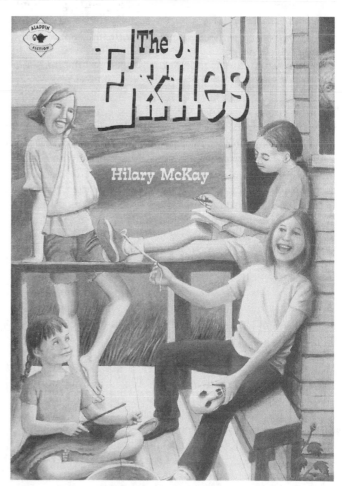

Cover of McKay's middle-grade novel The Exiles, *featuring artwork by* ***Caty Bartholomew.*** (Aladdin Paperbacks, 1996. Reproduced by permission of Caty Bartholomew.)

sisters—Ruth, Naomi, Rachel, and Phoebe—are excited about the money, but when they learn that their parents plan to use the inheritance to remodel their house, sending them to stay with their grandmother for the summer, they become upset. To make matters worse, when the sisters arrive at their grandmother's house in Cumbria, they find that she has few books to read. Rather than reading, "Big Grandma," as they call her, expects the girls to exercise, explore nature in the Lake District, seek adventure, and help out around the house. In desperation, the "exiled" girls read cookbooks and the complete works of Shakespeare (the only books they can find). They also begin to enjoy the activities Grandma forces upon them and even begin to appreciate and understand the older woman. "Like the writings of Beverly Cleary and Lois Lowry, this warm-hearted first novel provides an ample supply of chuckles," commented a *Publishers Weekly* reviewer in a review of *The Exiles,* while a critic for *Kirkus Reviews* described the work as "delightful," and concluded that "McKay has a real gift for amusing dialogue and descriptions."

In *The Exiles at Home* the four sisters are back at home with their parents. When Ruth secretly pledges ten pounds each month to help educate a boy in Africa, her sisters pitch in to help her fulfill the obligation because she cannot make enough money baby-sitting. Naomi gardens for an elderly couple and Rachel and Phoebe sell food to their classmates. Although the girls manage to get into trouble in the process, they enjoy writing to their new African friend. Soon Big Grandma finds out about the pledge and the girls' determination to meet it; at the end of the story, an elderly neighbor bequeaths enough money for the African boy's education as well as a trip to Africa for the girls and Big Grandma. Patricia J. Morrow noted in *Voice of Youth Advocates* that although *The Exiles* finds the sisters engaged in "some . . . actions [that] were dangerous," in *The Exiles at Home* they are "more entrepreneurial though still shortsighted." The book's conclusion, wrote A.R. Williams in *Junior Bookshelf,* "should awake a glow of satisfaction in readers," and *Booklist* critic Carolyn Phelan deemed *The Exiles at Home* refreshing "for its wit and emotional candor."

In *The Exiles in Love* older sisters Ruth and Naomi brood over new romantic interests, while younger siblings Rachel and Phoebe occupy themselves in other ways, Rachel in gaining recognition as May queen, and Phoebe in preparing for a future career as an international spy. When the girls exhibit a fascination for a French visitor named Philippe, Big Grandma offers to take all four to France for a holiday. "Part of the appeal" of McKay's "Exiles" novels "is the light, amusing style, the warmth and accuracy (exaggerated but believable) of the portrayal of the girls' feelings, and the way such basically good-hearted characters never become dull," commented a *Junior Bookshelf* contributor.

Like the "Exiles" books, many of McKay's stories are organized into multi-book series. Part of a trilogy that

McKay's compelling middle-grade novel Saffy's Angel *features cover art by John Collier.* (Illustration © 2002 by John Collier. Reproduced by permission.)

includes *The Amber Cat* and *Dolphin Luck, Dog Friday* follows the story of Robin, a ten year old who has been afraid of dogs ever since one attacked him at the beach. Robin must also deal with his father's death and with the fact that his mother's bed-and-breakfast business is not faring well. When he meets Old Blanket, the dog next door, and the children who own him Robin begins to recover his courage, and even makes a canine friend of his own when he encounters a stray dog and rescues it. Describing *Dog Friday* as "poignant," *School Library Journal* contributor Ann M. Burlingame explained that it is about "honesty and the complexities of friendship."Phelan concluded in her *Booklist* review that McKay's "distinctive and refreshing" story possesses "sharply realized characters, [a] fast-paced story, and witty dialogue," while a *Junior Bookshelf* critic predicted of *Dog Friday* that "children will be greatly entertained by this rollicking story."

A fairy tale with the author's trademark stamp of humor, *Practically Perfect* introduces a ten-year-old queen who alleviates her boredom by creating her own royal racecourse and ultimately rides the Royal Donkey to victory. As the story progresses and the years pass, the queen's ladies-in-waiting grow increasingly anxious to have their restive adolescent mistress marry. The headstrong young queen dismisses suitor after suitor before she decides to marry her childhood friend: the gardener's boy. McKay tells another imaginative story in *There's a Dragon Downstairs,* which finds Sophie convinced by noises she hears that a dragon creeps into her house every evening and melts into the deepening shadows as night falls. At first the girl tries a succession of disguises in the hopes of vanquishing the beast, but when she realizes that she enjoys its presence she can at last meet and befriend the magical creature. "With her natural sweetness and genuine curiosity, Sophie may remind young readers of their own shadowy adventures," maintained Jake Coburn in appraising the picture book for the *New York Times Book Review.* In *Booklist* Phelan called *There's a Dragon Downstairs* a "carefully structured" story that gains interest from Amanda Harvey's "crosshatched pencil drawings" tinted with water-color wash, and a *Publishers Weekly* critic dubbed it a "charming and comforting read-aloud."

McKay introduces her popular "Casson Family" novels in the award-winning *Saffy's Angel,* and the family's story plays out in *Indigo's Star, Permanent Rose, Caddy Ever After,* and *Forever Rose.* According to *Booklist* critic Gillian Engberg, in *Saffy's Angel* readers meet an "eccentric, irresistible family" whose members live in a rundown house outside of London. At age eight, Saffron discovered that she was adopted into the family only five years before, after her biological mother (her adoptive mother's twin sister) died in a car accident in Italy. Still feeling cut off from the rest of the family due to her adoption, thirteen-year-old Saffy now learns that her grandfather in Italy left her an angel, although what kind and where this angel is she knows not. Because the teen believes that the angel is central to her understanding of who she truly is, she travels to Italy in search of her inheritance, aided by her family members and a new friend. A critic for *Kirkus Reviews* wrote that Saffy's little sister Rose is a particularly vivid character who is central to "some very funny scenes," while the eccentricity of other family members adds to the story's warmth and humor. B. Allison Gray wrote in *School Library Journal* that "delicious phrasing and a wonderfully descriptive style add further to the sense of British eccentricity" in *Saffy's Angel,* and a *Publishers Weekly* reviewer predicted that the story's "especially entertaining subplots" and "droll dialogue will keep readers chuckling."

The annals of the Casson family continue in *Indigo's Star,* as the start of school brings a host of worries to each of the Casson siblings (each of whom have been named for a paint color). While mother Eve is busy dealing with the departure of husband Bob and also working on a new creative endeavor, Saffron feuds with best friend Sarah and tries to help youngest sister Rose overcome her difficulty with reading. For nineteen-year-old Cadmium, however, the concern is more with boyfriend issues than schoolwork. Bookish Indigo returns

to school with non-academic worries, battling middle-grade bullies while defended to the end by Saffy, but also making a new friend in guitar-player Tom Levin. Meanwhile Rose summons the confidence to meet her new classmates while sporting a new pair of glasses. Although *Indigo's Star* deals with "the realignment of families, jealousy, [and] violence," the novelist avoids deflating her story's mood with either "earnestness or solemnity," wrote *Horn Book* contributor Sarah Ellis, and a *Publishers Weekly* critic maintained that "McKay's portrayal of the family dynamics and the dialogue among the Cassons are as riotous and refreshing as ever."

After Tom returns to the United States in *Permanent Rose,* he leaves Rose with a loneliness that none of her family or friends understand until the tough-talking but empathetic David helps the eight year old find a positive way of dealing with her feelings. Saffy's loneliness is that of an adopted child, and she and Sarah decide to discover real father's whereabouts. A fast-paced and "rollicking story," according to *School Library Journal* critic Kathryn Kosiorek, *Permanent Rose* "is sure to keep this family's old fans and capture new ones," while

Cover of McKay's young-adult novel **Forever Rose,** *part of her popular "Casson Family" series.* (Photograph © 2008 by Eric Audras/PictureQuest (girl); © 2008 by PhotoSpin, Inc./Alamy (drums). Reprinted with the permission of Margaret K. McElderry Books, an imprint of Simon & Schuster Children's Publishing Division.)

London *Independent* critic Nicholas Tucker concluded that McKay's "charming, affectionate, and perfectly written" story "comes over like a sunny day in the midst of a frosty winter."

The fourth book in the "Casson Family" series, *Caddy Ever After* is narrated by each member of the family in turn—Rose, Indigo, Saffy, and Caddy. Saffy's boyfriend Oscar wins over the family with his easy personality, and when he introduces his older brother, Alex, the soon-to-be-wed Caddy is immediately head over heels in love. Narrated by the wryly humorous Rose, *Forever Rose* ends the popular series and chronicles the adventures, setbacks, and relationships encountered by the loving but eccentric Cassons as the parents reunite, Rose has an exciting adventure, and the older siblings optimistically head into the future. "In McKay's hands, even the things that the Cassons might deem wrong in their lives makes for a narrative that is just right," noted a *Publishers Weekly* contributor in reviewing *Caddy Ever After*. As Ellis asserted in *Horn Book*, McKay's "Casson Family" stories "set the standard of brilliance for the middle-grade mayhem novel." In *Booklist* Engberg praised Rose's "precocious and hilarious" narrative, calling *Forever Rose* a "celebratory view of a messy, imperfect, and fiercely loving family," while Ellis dubbed it a "moving and entirely unsentimental celebration of the virtue of kindness." Praising the "Casson Family" series as a whole, a London *Independent* critic wrote that *Forever Rose* "shines out as a beacon in the otherwise troubled waters" of YA fiction.

McKay plans to continue writing books for children. "Children's minds grow just as their bodies do; it seems very important to me that there should be books worth reading for them right from the start," she wrote in *SAAS*. "To be at home with books is to have a whole world of doorways open to you. Adults who know this already can open or shut the doors at will; what they make of what they find on the other side is up to them. Children have first to discover that the doors are there. That seems to me to be the thing that matters most; to get them wanting to open the doors. That is why I think children's books are so important . . . and why it seems such a privilege, such an enormous stroke of luck, that I have slipped into this job. I am helping to make the worlds behind the doors."

Biographical and Critical Sources

BOOKS

St. James Guide to Children's Writers, fifth edition, St. James Press (Detroit, MI), 1999.
Something about the Author Autobiography Series, Volume 23, Gale (Detroit, MI), 1997.

PERIODICALS

Booklist, January 15, 1995, Carolyn Phelan, review of *The Exiles at Home,* p. 925; November 15, 1995, Carolyn Phelan, review of *Dog Friday,* p. 560; November 15, 1997, Carolyn Phelan, review of *The Amber Cat,* p. 559; May 1, 1998, Carolyn Phelan, review of *Exiles in Love,* p. 1516; January 1, 1999, Lauren Peterson, review of *Where's Bear?,* p. 889; May 15, 2002, Gillian Engberg, review of *Saffy's Angel,* p. 1594; September 1, 2002, Ilene Cooper, review of *Was That Christmas?,* p. 138; March 1, 2005, Carolyn Phelan, review of *There's a Dragon Downstairs,* p. 1204; June 1, 2006, Gillian Engberg, review of *Caddy Ever After,* p. 62; April 1, 2008, Gillian Engberg, review of *Forever Rose,* p. 46.

Guardian (London, England), July 9, 2005, Diana Wynne Jones, review of *Permanent Rose,* p. 33.

Horn Book, July, 1999, review of *Dolphin Luck,* p. 470; July-August, 2002, Natalie Babbitt, review of *Saffy's Angel,* p. 466; November-December, 2002, Martha V. Parravano, review of *Was That Christmas?,* p. 736; September-October, 2004, Sarah Ellis, review of *Indigo's Star,* p. 591; July-August, 2005, Sarah Ellis, review of *Permanent Rose,* p. 473; July-August, 2006, Sarah Ellis, review of *Caddy Ever After,* p. 447; May-June, 2008, Sarah Ellis, review of *Forever Rose,* p. 322.

Independent (London, England), April 1, 2005, Nicholas Tucker, review of *Permanent Rose,* p. 24; December 8, 2006, Nicholas Tucker, review of *Caddy Ever After,* p. 24; October 26, 2007, review of *Forever Rose,* p. 24.

Junior Bookshelf, April, 1994, A.R. Williams, review of *The Exiles at Home,* p. 72; April, 1995, review of *Dog Friday,* p. 72; December, 1996, review of *The Exiles in Love,* p. 271, and *Practically, Perfect,* p. 256.

Kirkus Reviews, November 1, 1992, review of *The Exiles,* p. 1381; May 1, 2002, review of *Saffy's Angel,* p. 661; November 1, 2002, review of *Was That Christmas?,* p. 1622.

New York Times Book Review, August 14, 2005, Jake Coburn, review of *There's a Dragon Downstairs,* p. 16.

Publishers Weekly, October 19, 1992, review of *The Exiles,* p. 79; June 2, 1997, review of *Exiles at Home,* p. 73; March 18, 2002, review of *Saffy's Angel,* p. 104; August 30, 2004, review of *Indigo's Star,* p. 56; March 28, 2005, review of *There's a Dragon Downstairs,* p. 78; May 23, 2005, review of *Permanent Rose,* p. 78; May 22, 2006, review of *Caddy Ever After,* p. 53; May 14, 2009, Sally Lodge, "McElderry to Publish 'A Little Princess' Sequel."

School Librarian, summer, 1999, review of *Strange Bear,* p. 75.

School Library Journal, October, 1995, Ann M. Burlingame, review of *Dog Friday,* p. 136; June, 2000, Kathleen Kelly MacMillan, review of *Pirates Ahoy!,* p. 120; May, 2002, B. Allison Gray, review of *Saffy's Angel,* p. 156; October, 2002, Maureen Wade, review of *Was That Christmas?,* p. 61; September, 2004, Marie Orlando, review of *Indigo's Star,* p. 211; June, 2005, Kathryn Kosiorek, review of *Permanent Rose,* p. 163; May, 2008, Marie Orlando, review of *Forever Rose,* p. 130.

Sunday Times (London, England), September 14, 2003, Nicolette Jones, review of *Indigo's Star,* p. 54; September 24, 2006, Nicolette Jones, review of *Caddy Ever After,* p. 56.

Voice of Youth Advocates, April, 1995, Patricia J. Morrow, review of *The Exiles at Home,* p. 24.

ONLINE

Hilary McKay Home Page, http://www.hilarymckay.co.uk (November 20, 2009).*

* * *

McKAY, Hilary Jane
See McKAY, Hilary

* * *

McMAHON, Bob 1956-

Personal

Born 1956; married; children: one daughter. *Hobbies and other interests:* Taking walks, cooking, visiting the beach.

Addresses

Home—Southern CA. *Agent*—Ronnie Herman, The Herman Agency, 350 Central Park W., New York, NY 10025. *E-mail*—bob@bobmcmahon.com.

Career

Illustrator. Commercial artist for products and advertising; clients include Mattel Toys, Leapfrog Interactive, and Saban Entertainment.

Illustrator

Teresa Dahlquist and Raf Dahlquist, *Mr. Halley and His Comet,* Polestar Nexus (Canoga Park, CA), 1985.

Christina Mia Gardeski, *All Kinds of Kids,* Children's Press (New York, NY), 2002.

Dennis Fertig, *Something Rotten at Village Market,* Steck-Vaughn (Austin, TX), 2003.

Larry Dane Brimner, *Silent Kay and the Dragon,* Children's Press (New York, NY), 2007.

Elizabeth Keeler Robinson, *Making Cents,* Tricycle Press (Berkeley, CA), 2008.

Contributor to periodicals, including *Atlanta* magazine, *Go!,* and *Weekly Reader.*

Biographical and Critical Sources

PERIODICALS

Kirkus Reviews, May 1, 2008, review of *Making Cents.*

School Library Journal, August, 2008, Barbara Katz, review of *Making Cents,* p. 101.

ONLINE

Bob McMahon Home Page, http://www.bobmcmahon.com (November 15, 2009).*

* * *

MEYERHOFF, Jenny 1972-

Personal

Born October 18, 1972; married; children: three. *Education:* University of Michigan, degree (English and psychology); Northwestern University, M.Ed.

Addresses

Home—Deerfield, IL. *E-mail*—mail@jennymeyerhoff.com.

Jenny Meyerhoff focuses on the concerns of elementary-grade readers in **Third Grade Baby,** *a story featuring Jill Weber's pen-and-ink art.* (Illustration copyright © 2008 by Jill Weber. Used by permission of Farrar, Straus & Giroux, LLC.)

Career

Author. Worked previously as a kindergarten teacher.

Writings

Third Grade Baby, illustrated by Jill Weber, Farrar, Straus & Giroux (New York, NY), 2008.

Queen of Secrets, Farrar, Straus & Giroux (New York, NY), 2010.

Sidelights

A former kindergarten teacher, author Jenny Meyerhoff penned her first book for children, *Third Grade Baby,* in 2008. A novel for elementary-school children, *Third Grade Baby* shares with readers the story of a young girl named Polly Peterson as she begins a new school year. When the teacher assigns her class a science project, Polly learns that she is the only student in her class who still has all of her baby teeth. This fact earns her a good bit of teasing from a classmate, a new boy named Zachary. When Polly does lose a baby tooth, the tooth fairy fails to make the usual under-the-pillow deposit, so the next night she takes a camera to bed in order to catch an image of the magical creature. Much to her surprise, the tooth fairy in the photograph looks a lot like Polly's mom.

In addition to finding Meyerhoff's debut humorous, a *Kirkus Reviews* critic wrote that *Third Grade Baby* deals with "very real issues [that] . . . readers will recognize," among them "bullying and the constant need to measure up." In *Booklist* critic Hazel Rochman wrote that Meyerhoff's narrative "gets the young grade-schooler's viewpoint just right," and expresses emotions in a way that is "authentic" to children.

Biographical and Critical Sources

PERIODICALS

Booklist, December 1, 2008, Hazel Rochman, review of *Third Grade Baby,* p. 52.

Kirkus Reviews, August 15, 2008, review of *Third Grade Baby.*

School Library Journal, November, 2008, Debbie S. Hoskins, review of *Third Grade Baby,* p. 96.

ONLINE

Jenny Meyerhoff Home Page, http://www.jennymeyerhoff. com (November 22, 2009).

Jenny Meyerhoff Web Log, http://www.thepurpledesk. blogspot.com/ (November 22, 2009).*

MONTGOMERY, Michael G. 1952-

Personal

Born 1952; married; children: one son, one daughter. *Education:* Attended Georgia Southern College; attended University of Georgia; attended School of Visual Arts.

Addresses

E-mail—mgmont@bellsouth.net

Career

Illustrator.

Writings

SELF-ILLUSTRATED

Night, America, Contemporary Books (Chicago, IL), 1989.

(Collector, with Wayne Montgomery)*Over the Candlestick: Classic Nursery Rhymes and the Real Stories behind Them,* Peachtree (Atlanta, GA), 2002.

ILLUSTRATOR

H.I. Peeples, *Meet the Itty Bitty Kiddies,* Contemporary Books (Chicago, IL), 1989.

H.I. Peeples, *The Itty Bitty Kiddies Wake Up,* Contemporary Books (Chicago, IL), 1990.

Samantha Easton, reteller, *The Steadfast Tin Soldier,* Andrew McMeel (Kansas City, MO), 1991.

Della Rowland, *Little Red Riding Hood; The Wolf's Tale,* Carol (New York, NY), 1991.

Patricia Demuth, *Johnny Appleseed,* Grosset & Dunlap (New York, NY), 1996.

Lee Posey, *Night Rabbits,* Peachtree (Atlanta, GA), 1999.

Mike Reiss, *Santa's Eleven Months Off,* Peachtree (Atlanta, GA), 2007.

Elizabeth Van Steenwyk, *First Dog, Fala,* Peachtree (Atlanta, GA), 2008.

Sidelights

As a freelance artist, Michael G. Montgomery has worked in advertising, magazine illustration, and in the field of editorial comics. He has also illustrated children's books written by authors that include Patricia Demuth and Mike Reiss. Although his varied career, with its ups and downs, has sometimes caused him "a 'hmmm. . . . should I have majored in something else?' moment," as Montgomery admitted on his home page, such a moment has "always passed with the start of a new job."

In his work for Elizabeth Van Steenwyk's picture book *First Dog, Fala,* Montgomery depicts the world through the eyes of the pet of U.S. President Franklin Delano

Michael G. Montgomery's illustrations bring to life Elizabeth Van Steenwyk's World War II-era picture book First Dog Fala. (Press, 2008. Illustration © 2008 by Michael G. Montgomery. Reproduced by permission.)

Roosevelt, who was president during World War II. Randall Enos, writing for *Booklist,* noted that the book's "portrait-like illustrations in muted, rich colors gives Fala's story a dignified look." A reviewer for *Kirkus Reviews* also enjoyed the art in *First Dog, Fala,* commenting that Montgomery's "oil-on-canvas illustration, rendered in warm, muted colors, . . . capture the somber mood of the times."

Maureen Wade, a reviewer for *School Library Journal,* praised Montgomery's illustrations for Reiss's story in *Santa's Eleven Months Off,* calling them "amusing and delightful." Hazel Rochman, writing in *Booklist,* described Montgomery's work for *Night Rabbits* as "handsome realistic paintings."

Biographical and Critical Sources

PERIODICALS

Booklist, May 1, 1999, Hazel Rochman, review of *Night Rabbits,* p. 1601; October 1, 2008, Randall Enos, review of *First Dog, Fala,* p. 45.

Kirkus Reviews, August 15, 2008, review of *First Dog, Fala.*

School Library Journal, June, 2002, Margaret A. Chang, review of *Over the Candlestick: Classic Nursery Rhymes and the Real Stories behind Them,* p. 123; October, 2007, Maureen Wade, review of *Santa's Eleven Months Off,* p. 103.

ONLINE

Michael G. Montgomery Home Page, http://www.michaelgmontgomery.com (December 1, 2009).*

* * *

MUÑOZ, Claudio

Personal

Born in Chile; immigrated to England; married Jill Newsome (a painter and children's book author); children: one son, two daughters. *Education:* Universidad de Chile, architectural studies for four years.

Claudio Muñoz (Reproduced by permission.)

Addresses

Home—England. *E-mail*—claudio@claudiomunoz.com.

Career

Illustrator.

Awards, Honors

Prix du Livre de la Mer (France), 1997, for *Le petit capitaine* (French edition of *Little Captain*); Second Prize, Victoria & Albert Museum Illustration Award, 2003, for *Night Walk*.

Writings

SELF-ILLUSTRATED

Little Captain, Bodley Head (London, England), 1995.

Author's work has been translated into French, Italian, and Japanese.

ILLUSTRATOR

Jon Ward, *Big Baby,* Walker (London, England), 1986.

Antonia Barber, *Satchelmouse and the Dinosaurs,* Walker (London, England), 1987.

Antonia Barber, *Satchelmouse and the Doll's House,* Walker (London, England), 1987, Barron's (New York, NY), 1988.

Antonia Barber, *Satchelmouse and the Banquet,* Walker (London, England), 1990.

Martin Waddell, *Man Mountain,* Viking (London, England), 1991.

Ivor Cutler, *Doris,* Tambourine Books (New York, NY), 1992, published as *Doris the Hen,* Heinemann (London, England), 1992.

Sue Limb, *Come Back, Grandma,* Knopf (New York, NY), 1993.

Russell Hoban, *The Mouse and His Child,* Puffin Modern Classics (London, England), 1993.

Desmond Lynam and David Teasdale, compilers, *The Sporting World,* BBC Books (London, England), 1994.

Jonathan Shipton, *No Biting, Horrible Crocodile!,* Golden Books (New York, NY), 1995, published as *Horrible Crocodile,* Heinemann (London, England), 1995.

Ivor Cutler, *The New Dress,* Bodley Head (London, England), 1995.

Sally Christie, *Sarah Scarer,* A. & C. Black (London, England), 1995.

Rosemary Debnam, *Runaway Fred,* Mammoth (London, England), 1997.

Fay Weldon, *Nobody Likes Me!,* Bodley Head (London, England), 1997.

Richard Walker, *The Barefoot Book of Trickster Tales,* Barefoot Books (Bath, England), 1998.

Jill Newsome, *Shadow,* DK Publishing (New York, NY), 1999.

Meir Shalev, *Storie Piccole,* Montadori (Milan, Italy), 2000.

Henrietta Branford, *Little Pig Figwort Can't Get to Sleep,* Clarion (New York, NY), 2000, published as *Little Pig Figwort,* HarperCollins (London, England), 2000.

Daniel Laurence, *Captain and Matey Set Sail,* HarperCollins (New York, NY), 2001.

Jill Newsome, *Dream Dancer,* Anderson Press (London, England), 2001, HarperCollins (New York, NY), 2002.

Jill Newsome, *Night Walk,* Clarion (New York, NY), 2002.

Candy Verney, *The Singing Day,* Hawthorne Press (Stroud, England), 2003.

Linda Ashman, *Just Another Morning,* HarperCollins (New York, NY), 2004.

Yannick Murphy, *Ahwoooooooo!,* Clarion (New York, NY), 2006.

Candy Verney, *The Singing Year,* Hawthorne Press (Stroud, England), 2006.

Maria José Thomas, *¡Bravo, Rosina!,* Ekaré (Caracas, Venezuela), 2007.

Ilene Cooper, *Jake's Best Thumb,* Dutton (New York, NY), 2008.

Simon Hoggart, *Life's Too Short to Drink Bad Wine,* Quadrille (London, England), 2009.

Contributor of illustrations and cartoons to periodicals, including London *Economist, Financial Times,* and *Courrier Japon.*

Sidelights

Born and raised in Chile, Claudio Muñoz immigrated to England as a young man and continued to advance his career as an illustrator, creating cartoons for British periodicals such as the London *Economist* and also producing artwork for children's picture books. For over twenty years, Muñoz has worked with noted authors, from Martin Waddell to Ivor Cutler and Antonia Barber. In addition, the artist has teamed with his wife, children's book author Jill Newsome, to publish several well-received works.

Since the appearance of *Shadow,* their first collaboration, in 1999, Muñoz and Newsome have produced the books *Dream Dancer* and *Night Walk*. In *Dream Dancer* a young girl named Lily loves to dance, practicing ballet both in the studio and in her dreams. A fall from a tree, however, puts Lily's favorite form of expression on hold, as she must allow her broken leg time to heal. To help lift the girl's spirits, her grandmother brings Lily a beautiful ballerina doll and the young dancer can pirouette vicariously through the toy, which she names Peggy. When her leg finally heals, Lily is hesitant to take to the barre again, but with the help of doll friend Peggy, she gathers her courage and begins to twirl pirouettes with the same energy as before her accident. Calling *Dream Dancer* "a polished pas de deux from a pair of pros," a *Kirkus Reviews* critic commended the quality of Muñoz's artwork, naming the illustrator "a master at depicting a dancer in motion." A *Publishers Weekly* reviewer wrote that Muñoz's art expresses the energy and emotions of Newsome's young heroine, "captur[ing] the graceful arch of an arm and extension of a leg, as well as the emotional underpinnings of the story."

Night Walk follows the story of two household pets, a cat named Flute and a Dog named Daisy, who enjoy separately paced lives. Daisy likes to start the day by taking a rigorous walk as soon as she awakens, while Flute prefers a leisurely breakfast in the ensuing calm. After hearing the canine describe some of the creatures she encounters on her walks, Flute decides to secretly join her owner and pal on their evening walk. Despite becoming overwhelmed by the sensory overload she encounters while outdoors, the feline nonetheless fights her fears and rescues Daisy after the dog becomes trapped by a fierce cat. Resting at home after the incident, Flute declines the dog's invitation of another outing at the park, deciding that she prefers the safe, quiet confines of her owner's home rather than the exhilarating adventures of the outside world. For his work with Newsome, Muñoz earned high marks from reviewers, *Booklist* critic Ellen Mandel suggesting that the artwork "reflects a loving familiarity with canine and feline personalities." In *School Library Journal* Linda L. Walkins noted that Muñoz's "gracefully executed watercolors . . . illustrate the bond of friendship between Daisy and Flute in an expressive manner." In addition to praising his "almost cinematic ability to advance the story line," a *Publishers Weekly* wrote that the artist's "pet protagonists exhibit an Oscar-worthy range of expressions."

In addition to his work with Newsome, Muñoz has also paired with Daniel Laurence to produce *Captain and Matey Set Sail* and with Ilene Cooper to produce *Jake's Best Thumb.* A beginning-to-read chapter book, *Captain and Matey Set Sail* features the quarrelsome relationship of two seamen, Captain and Matey. Both men could not be more opposite: Captain is a short, coarse, and boisterous sailor while Matey is tall, thin, and meticulous. Without each other, however, each man would be lost, leading to much disagreement but always an amicable solution. In *Horn Book* Kitty Flynn predicted that Muñoz's illustrations for *Captain and Matey Set Sail* will "provide visual clues to help new readers decode the text," while *Booklist* reviewer Hazel Rochman maintained that the same pictures "capture the boisterous action of the silly outlaws."

Jake's Best Thumb tackles a problem common to many children: thumb sucking. Although he is old enough to enter kindergarten, Jake refuses to give up his favorite comfort routine and insists that he can manage anything he needs with only one hand. Despite warnings from his mother that his teeth will begin to protrude like a rabbit's, Jake remains confident in his ability to conquer life with his thumb in his mouth. After his bad habit causes him to be teased by a bully at school, however, Jake looks for a way to deflate the bully's aggression and regain his affection for his opposable digit.

Chilean artist Muñoz captures the imaginative elements in Ilene Cooper's picture book **Jake's Best Thumb.** (Illustration © 2008 by Claudio Muñoz. Reproduced by permission of Dutton Children's Books, a division of Penguin Putnam Books for Young Readers.)

Muñoz's "watercolors convey a seemingly effortless physicality, immediacy and empathy," according to a *Publishers Weekly* contributor in a review of *Jake's Best Thumb,* while a *Kirkus Reviews* critic claimed that Muñoz's artwork is the highlight of the book, "investing even minor characters with enormous personality."

Biographical and Critical Sources

PERIODICALS

Booklist, January 15, 1994, Hazel Rochman, review of *Come Back, Grandma,* p. 937; October 15, 1995, April Judge, review of *No Biting, Horrible Crocodile!,* p. 413; January 1, 1999, Helen Rosenberg, review of *The Barefoot Book of Trickster Tales,* p. 874; October 15, 1999, John Peters, review of *Shadow,* p. 456; July, 2001, Hazel Rochman, review of *Captain and Matey Set Sail,* p. 2023; January 1, 2002, Gillian Engberg, review of *Dream Dancer,* p. 867; June 1, 2002, Ilene Cooper, review of *Little Pig Figwort Can't Get to Sleep,* p. 1733; February 15, 2003, Ellen Mandel, review of *Night Walk,* p. 1075; August 1, 2006, Jennifer Mattson, review of *Ahwooooooooo!,* p. 92.

Horn Book, January-February, 2002, Kitty Flynn, review of *Captain and Matey Set Sail,* p. 79.

Kirkus Reviews, January 15, 2002, review of *Dream Dancer,* p. 106; February 15, 2002, review of *Little Pig Figwort Can't Get to Sleep,* p. 59; May 1, 2004, review of *Just Another Morning,* p. 437; May 1, 2006, review of *Ahwooooooooo!,* p. 464; June 15, 2008, review of *Jake's Best Thumb.*

Publishers Weekly, November 9, 1992, review of *Doris,* p. 85; August 21, 1995, review of *No Biting, Horrible Crocodile!,* p. 64; November 17, 1997, review of *Nobody Likes Me!,* p. 61; December 17, 2001, review of *Dream Dancer,* p. 90; January 14, 2002, review of *Little Pig Figwort Can't Get to Sleep,* p. 59; February 17, 2003, review of *Night Walk,* p. 73; April 19, 2004, review of *Just Another Morning,* p. 60; June 2, 2008, review of *Jake's Best Thumb,* p. 45.

School Library Journal, November, 2001, Devon Gallagher, review of *Captain and Matey Set Sail,* p. 127; March, 2002, Karen Scott, review of *Dream Dancer,* p. 198; July, 2002, Marian Drabkin, review of *Little Pig Figwort Can't Get to Sleep,* p. 84; April, 2003, Linda L. Walkins, review of *Night Walk,* p. 134; May, 2004, Maryann H. Owen, review of *Just Another Morning,* p. 100; June, 2006, Marianne Saccardi, review of *Ahwooooooooo!,* p. 123; March, 2009, Susan Weitz, review of *Jake's Best Thumb,* p. 108.

ONLINE

Claudio Muñoz Home Page, http://www.claudiomunoz. com (November 28, 2009).

N-P

NIVOLA, Claire A. 1947-

Personal

Born October 10, 1947, in New York, NY; daughter of Costantino (a sculptor) and Ruth (a jewelry maker) Nivola; married Timothy Gus Kiley (in publishing), September 18, 1982; children: Anther N. Kiley, Alycia A. Kiley. *Education:* Radcliffe College, B.A. (magna cum laude), 1970.

Addresses

Home—Newton Highlands, MA.

Career

Author, illustrator, painter, sculptor, and graphic designer. Freelance illustrator, 1970-78, 1994—, and author, 1997—. Freelance graphic designer, 1980-86; worked in *Newsweek* magazine art department, 1980-83. *Exhibitions:* Murals and sculpture bas-reliefs have been installed in Tennessee, 1992, and Boston, MA, 1998.

Awards, Honors

Publishers Weekly Best Children's Books of the Year inclusion, 2001, for *The Mouse of Amherst* by Elizabeth Spires; Amelia Bloomer Project selection, Notable Children's Book designation, American Library Association, Honor Book designation, Society of School Librarians International, International Reading Association Notable Books for a Global Society designation, and Teachers' Choice selection, Cooperative Center for Children's Books honor, Parents' Choice Honor Book designation, Africana Book Award Honor Book designation, ASA, Green Earth Book Award, Jane Addams Children's Book Award, Outstanding Science Trade Books for Children designation, National Science Teacher's Association/Children's Book Council (CBC), Notable Trade Book in the Field of Social Studies designation, National Council of the Social Studies/CBC, and Capitol Choices Noteworthy Titles for Children and Teens designation, all 2009, all for *Planting the Trees of Kenya.*

Writings

SELF-ILLUSTRATED

Elisabeth, Frances Foster Books (New York, NY), 1997.
The Forest, Frances Foster Books (New York, NY), 2002.
Planting the Trees of Kenya: The Story of Wangari Maathai, Farrar, Straus & Giroux (New York, NY), 2008.

ILLUSTRATOR

Maria Cimino, *The Disobedient Eels and Other Italian Tales,* Pantheon Books (New York, NY), 1970.
Henry Horenstein, *Black and White Photography,* Little, Brown (Boston, MA), 1974.
Betty Miles, *Save the Earth! An Ecology Handbook for Kids,* Knopf (New York, NY), 1974.
Ruth Nivola, *The Messy Rabbit,* Pantheon Books (New York, NY), 1978.
Betty Jean Lifton, *Tell Me a Real Adoption Story,* Knopf (New York, NY), 1994.
Elizabeth Spires, *The Mouse of Amherst,* Frances Foster Books (New York, NY), 1999.
Amy Hest, *The Friday Nights of Nana,* Candlewick Press (Cambridge, MA), 2001.
Susan Campbell Bartoletti, *The Flag Maker,* Houghton Mifflin (Boston, MA), 2004.
Robin Friedman, *The Silent Witness: A True Story of the Civil War,* Houghton Mifflin (Boston, MA), 2005.
Linda Glaser, *Emma's Poem: The Voice of the Statue of Liberty,* Houghton Mifflin Harcourt (Boston, MA), 2009.

Sidelights

Raised in an artistic family, Claire A. Nivola became an artist herself and now works as a sculptor, painter, and graphic designer. Although much of her work has involved illustrating texts by other writers, Nivola has also earned critical praise for her work has a writer: her original picture books include *Elisabeth, The Forest,* and the award-winning *Planting the Trees of Kenya: The Story of Wangari Maathai*. Praising Nivola's illustrations for Susan Campbell Bartoletti's nonfiction picture book *The Flag Maker, Booklist* critic Jennifer Mattson maintained that the artist's "delicate watercolors" act as "a ringing counterpoint to the chaos" of the story's subject: the British attack on Fort McHenry. The "finely executed watercolor and gouache paintings" Nivola contributes to Robin Friedman's *The Silent Witness: A True Story of the Civil War* were described as "reminiscent of primitive art" by *Horn Book* critic Betty Carter and in Rebecca Sheridan added in *School Library Journal* that the illustrations "add a sense of comfort to the turmoil and destruction of . . . war."

"As the daughter of an artist father and a mother equally gifted with her hands, I drew and sculpted from earliest childhood, often by my father's side in his studio," Nivola once recalled to *SATA*. "Having grown up surrounded by art, I took art somewhat for granted, like breathing and walking, and once out of college, found that I did not approach my trade with drive or ambition, and certainly not with the savvy of self-promotion. Because of this, my course was uncertain: I tried illustration, mural painting, exhibiting works done on my own, and graphic design—all attempts to find an application of my skills to something that might become a profession."

Nivola was introduced to book illustration when her father asked her to illustrate a collection of Italian fables for Fabio Coen, then head of Pantheon children's-book division. During the next eight years, Coen gave Nivola encouragement and assigned her two more books to illustrate. However, creating books was not Nivola's first priority. Married at age thirty-five, she stayed home to raise her two children. Unwilling to sacrifice her time as a mother, she only took on work that could be done at home: at one point Nivola created dozens of bas-relief panels for the Aquarium in Chattanooga, Tennessee, while working at home, "with my son and daughter commenting on each panel before it was shipped off for casting," as the artist recalled.

Nivola's first original self-illustrated picture book, *Elisabeth,* is based on an episode from her mother's childhood. The story revolves around a little Jewish girl who flees Nazi Germany, leaving behind all her possessions, including her doll Elisabeth, who had once been chewed on by the family dog. Many years later—and now a mother herself—the once-little-girl is browsing in an antique store, looking for a gift for her daughter, and discovers her long-lost doll with its dog-tooth scar. Betsy Hearne, writing in the *Bulletin of the Center for Children's Books,* described Nivola's narrative tone as "moving" and noted that her "precisely painted compositions" are "appropriately melancholy yet without self-pity." In *Horn Book* Susan P. Bloom praised the "vibrant watercolors" and "graceful, lean language" in *Elisabeth*. In the opinion of a *Publishers Review* critic,

Robin Friedman tells a Civil-War story in **The Silent Witness,** *which features art by Claire A. Nivola.* (Illustration copyright © 2005 by Claire A. Nivola. Reproduced by permission of Houghton Mifflin Company.)

the author/illustrator "proves herself a sure-handed storyteller," the critic going on to call *Elisabeth* "a story that will linger in the reader's heart."

Dubbed "a true gem" by Grace Oliff in *School Library Journal,* Nivola's original picture book *The Forest* features pointillistic illustrations and a "poetic, graceful and remarkably evocative" text, according to Oliff. In the book, a mouse that fears what might be lurking in the forest, decides to conquer its fear by venturing into the woods. Several reviewers commented on the universality of Nivola's theme, including a *Kirkus Reviews* commentator who predicted that "any reader who has felt fear of the unknown will identify with its solitary narrator." *The Forest* presents young children with a "beautifully illustrated parable about overcoming fears," according to *Booklist* critic Gillian Engberg.

Nivola honors Nobel prize-winning activist Wangari Maathai in her picture book *Planting the Trees of Kenya,* a self-illustrated work that weaves Maathai's writing into a text that possesses "the simple eloquence of a traditional tale," according to *Horn Book* contributor Barbara Bader. As a child growing up in Kenya, Maathai had enjoyed the natural beauty of the rural highlands, but during her time spent away at college studying biology in the United States, that region's farms were abandoned and its villages and natural resources decimated by war. Through her Green Belt movement, begun in 1977, Maathai was able to regenerate Kenya's forests by encouraging woman as well as school children to plant tree seedlings; eventually she even recruited Kenyan soldiers as part of the horticultural army that has been credited with planting over thirty million trees throughout Africa. Nivola brings to life Maathai's story in "absorbing" images rendered "in the manner of folk paintings," explained Bader, the critic describing *Planting the Trees of Kenya* "as much a pleasure as an inspiration." The author/illustrator's "delicately detailed illustrations suit the equally low-key writing style," wrote Carol S. Surges in *School Library Journal*, and in *Booklist* Gillian Engberg maintained that Nivola's "beautiful picture-book biography echoes the potent simplicity of Maathai's message." A *Publishers Weekly* contributor had special praise for the artwork in *Planting the Trees of Kenya*, writing that "Nivola's painting have the detail of tapestry and the dignity of icons."

Other illustration projects by Nivola include Elizabeth Spires' *The Mouse of Amherst*, a picture book about famous American poet Emily Dickinson and the fictional poetry-composing mouse, Emmaline, that lives in the wainscot of Emily's room, and Amy Hess's *The Friday Nights of Nana*. Described by *Booklist* contributor Carolyn Phelan as a "quiet, yet precise and sustaining" story, *The Friday Nights of Nana* focuses on young Jennie and her grandmother Nana during their Orthodox Jewish family's preparations for and celebration of the Sabbath. In her *School Library Journal* review of the book, Amy Lilien-Harper complimented Nivola's use of rich colors in *The Friday Nights of Nana*, and a *Publishers Weekly* critic noted that the artist creates a mood of "peace and deep contentment" in her illustrations.

"Having passed many years reading to my own children . . . the books I loved as a child, as well as discovering new ones, my appreciation for the best of children's literature has only grown stronger," Nivola once noted, reflecting on the importance of children's books. "Writing for children, I feel, is a serious business. The words and the images become a vivid part of a child's childhood and that is a responsibility I would never take lightly."

Biographical and Critical Sources

PERIODICALS

Booklist, February 1, 1997, Hazel Rochman, review of *Elisabeth*, p. 946; October 1, 2001, Carolyn Phelan, *The Friday Nights of Nana*, p. 334; April 15, 2002, Gillian Engberg, review of *The Forest*, p. 1408; October 1, 2002, Ilene Cooper, review of *The Friday Nights of Nana*, p. 344; March 1, 2004, Jennifer Mattson, review of *The Flag Maker*, p. 1206; February 15, 2008, Gillian Engberg, review of *Planting the Trees of Kenya: The Story of Wangari Maathai*.

Bulletin of the Center for Children's Books, March, 1997, Betsy Hearne, review of *Elisabeth*, pp. 253-254.
Horn Book, May-June, 1997, Susan P. Bloom, review of *Elisabeth*, pp. 310-311; May-June, 2004, Martha V. Parravano, review of *The Flag Maker*, p. 343; May-June, 2005, Betty Carter, review of *The Silent Witness: A True Story of the Civil War*, p. 349; May-June, 2008, Barbara Bader, review of *Planting the Trees of Kenya*, p. 339.
Kirkus Reviews, April 1, 2002, review of *The Forest*, p. 497; May 1, 2005, review of *The Silent Witness*, p. 538.
New York Times Book Review, September 14, 2008, Simon Rodberg, review of *Planting the Trees of Kenya*, p. 19.
Publishers Weekly, January 6, 1997, review of *Elisabeth*, p. 73; January 25, 1999, review of *The Mouse of Amherst*, p. 96; March 19, 2001, review of *The Mouse of Amherst*, p. 102; August 27, 2001, review of *The Friday Nights of Nana*, p. 82; October 8, 2001, review of *Elisabeth*, p. 67; March 18, 2002, review of *The Forest*, p. 102; March 10, 2008, review of *Planting the Trees of Kenya*, p. 81.
School Library Journal, April, 1997, Susan Pine, review of *Elisabeth*, p. 114; May, 1999, Susan Marie Pitard, review of *The Mouse of Amherst*, p. 98; October, 2001, Amy Lilien-Harper, review of *The Friday Nights of Nana*, p. 120; June, 2002, Grace Oliff, review of *The Forest*, p. 106; April, 2004, Dona Ratterree, review of *The Flag-Maker*, p. 102; June, 2005, Rebecca Sheridan, review of *The Silent Witness*, p. 137; April, 2008, Carol S. Surges, review of *Planting the Trees of Kenya*, p. 135.

ONLINE

Our White House Web site, http://www.ourwhitehouse.org/ (November 20, 2009), "Claire A. Nivola."*

* * *

O'LEARY, Chris

Personal

Born in Youngstown, OH; married; wife's name Tricia; children: Lily, Kate. *Education:* Attended Columbus College of Art and Design. *Hobbies and other interests:* Playing guitar, bicycling.

Addresses

Home—Columbus, OH. *Agent*—Lindgren & Smith, Inc., 676-A 9th Ave., New York, NY 10036. *E-mail*—chris@olearyillustration.com.

Career

Illustrator. Gibson Greeting Card Company, former illustrator; freelance artist.

Illustrator

David A. Adler, *Mama Played Baseball*, Gulliver Books (San Diego, CA), 2003.

Shana Corey, *Paul Revere's Ride*, Random House (New York, NY), 2004.

Mike Leonetti, *In the Pocket: Johnny Unitas and Me*, Chronicle Books (San Francisco, CA), 2008.

Contributor to periodicals, including *Atlantic Monthly, Vegetarian Times*, the *Los Angeles Times, Readers Digest*, the *Boston Globe, Barrons Weekly*, and *Ohio Magazine*.

Sidelights

A father of two who spends most of his time either with his daughters or painting, Chris O'Leary has been a freelance illustrator since leaving a job at the Gibson Greeting Card Company. Born and raised in Ohio, O'Leary freelances for a wide variety of clients, including picture-book publishers and magazines such as the *Atlantic Monthly, Readers Digest*, and *Ohio Magazine*.

O'Leary worked with Shana Corey on her book *Paul Revere's Ride*, an introductory history to the American silversmith and rebel. Reviewing the work in *Booklist*, Carolyn Phelan commented that O'Leary's illustrations have "a warm palette and a sense of boundless energy that propels each character and scene." Pamela K. Bomboy, writing for *School Library Journal*, praised O'Leary's pictures as "charming illustrations, reminiscent of [early-twentieth-century American artist] Thomas Hart Benton's energetic mural style."

O'Leary's interest in sports has inspired his illustrations for two sports-related books, including his picture-book debut, *Mama Played Baseball*, which features a text by

Chris O'Leary captures the life of noted athlete Johnny Unitas in his artwork for Mike Leonetti's picture book In the Pocket. (Illustration © 2008 by Chris O'Leary. Used with permission of Chronicle Books, LLC, San Francisco. Visit ChronicleBooks.com.)

David A. Adler. During World War II, many women moved into areas of the workforce that were previously held by men as the nation's military went off to war. One such area was professional sports, and soon female athletes were being recruited for groups such as the All-American Girls Professional Baseball League. In this book, young Amy's mother tries out for and joins the league, viewing it as an opportunity to make extra money. Steven Englefried, writing for *School Library Journal*, noted that O'Leary's "full-page oil paintings evoke the time and place," and their "figures and faces stand out nicely against the comfortable olive and brown tones in the background." A *Kirkus Reviews* critic maintained that the artwork "enhances the emotions described in an impressive debut." "The high point here is the work of debut artist O'Leary," noted a *Publishers Weekly* critic in a review of *Mama Played Baseball*, that critic adding that the artist's "sinewy artistic style recalls Depression-era murals."

In the Pocket: Johnny Unitas and Me, a picture book featuring a text by Mike Leonetti, follows a young football fan who gets to meet his hero. A *Kirkus Reviews* contributor noted of this book that "O'Leary's acrylic paintings have a soft focus that gives them a proper period feel."

Biographical and Critical Sources

PERIODICALS

Booklist, February 1, 2005, Carolyn Phelan, review of *Paul Revere's Ride*, p. 962.

Bulletin of the Center for Children's Books, April, 2003, review of *Mama Played Baseball*, p. 302

Kirkus Reviews, February 15, 2003, review of *Mama Played Baseball*, p. 298; August 15, 2008, review of *In the Pocket: Johnny Unitas and Me*.

Publishers Weekly, February 3, 2003, review of *Mama Played Baseball*, p. 76.

School Library Journal, April, 2003, Steven Englefried, review of *Mama Played Baseball*, p. 114; May, 2005, Pamela K. Bomboy, review of *Paul Revere's Ride* p. 106.

Tribune Books (Chicago, IL), April 6, 2003, review of *Mama Played Baseball*.

ONLINE

Lindgren & Smith Web site, http://www.lindgrensmith.com/ (December 2, 2009), "Chris O'Leary."*

*   *   *

O'MALLEY, Donough

Personal

Born in Ireland. *Education:* University of the West of England, Bristol, B.A. (illustration), 2000; University of

Brighton, M.A. (illustration). *Hobbies and other interests:* Travel, flying kites.

Addresses

Home—Dublin, Ireland. *E-mail*—pencilrobot@yahoo.ie.

Career

Illustrator and author.

Writings

SELF-ILLUSTRATED

Monkey See, Monkey Do, Frances Lincoln Children's (London, England), 2007, Frances Lincoln (New York, NY), 2008.
Panda in the City, Frances Lincoln Children's (London, England, 2010.

Contributor of illustrations to periodicals, including *Overload, Prospects, Management Today, Mongrel, Irish Times, Irish Independent Weekend,* and London *Guardian.*

Biographical and Critical Sources

PERIODICALS

Kirkus Reviews, June 15, 2008, review of *Monkey See, Monkey Do.*

ONLINE

Donough O'Malley Home Page, http://www.pencilrobot.net (November 15, 2009).*

*   *   *

PAULEY, Kimberly 1973-

Personal

Born January 24, 1973, in San Mateo, CA; married; husband's name Tony; children: Max. *Education:* University of Florida, B.A.

Addresses

Home and office—P.O. Box 303, Grayslake, IL 60030. *E-mail*—kim@kimberlypauley.com; kim@yabookscentral.com.

Career

Writer and book reviewer. Young Adult (and Kids!) Book Central Web site, founder. Formerly worked as a graphics designer, technical writer, Web developer, and manager.

Awards, Honors

Quick Pick for Reluctant Readers designation, Young Adult Library Services Association/American Library Association, 2009, for *Sucks to Be Me.*

Writings

Sucks to Be Me: The All-True Confessions of Mina Hamilton, Teen Vampire (Maybe), Wizards of the Coast (Renton, WA), 2008.
Still Sucks to Be Me: The All-True Confessions of Mina Hamilton, Teen Vampire, Wizards of the Coast (Renton, WA), 2010.

Contributor to *Weekly Planet, Scriptorium, Reflections, Legacy,* and *Hardboiled,* and to online sites including About.com and GLBTQ.com.

Sidelights

Kimberly Pauley pursued her interest in young-adult literature and in science fiction and fantasy in an academic sphere before launching her own career as a writer. After college, Pauley pursued several different careers, from graphics designer to Web developer, before becoming a full-time writer. In 1998, she launched the Young Adult (and Kids!) Books Central Web site, which is devoted to reviewing books for children and teens, interviewing authors, and hosting contests and giveaways to promote teen reading. The site began as part of the About.com network and soon evolved into a much-larger project, which Pauley continues to manage.

The road to publication was not instant for Pauley. After finishing her first manuscript, she sent it out to agents who liked her writing but explained that there was no market for teen vampire fiction. She put her work on the shelf for about two years. Then, at the urging of a friend, Pauley contacted an editor who was looking for paranormal young-adult novels. The manuscript was a good fit for the West Coast publisher, and in 2008 the book was published as *Sucks to Be Me: The All-True Confessions of Mina Hamilton, Teen Vampire (Maybe).*

In *Sucks to Be Me* Mina Hamilton has to make a choice: should she become a vampire, like her parents have, or should she remain human? The Northwest Regional Vampire Council is pressuring Mina to make her decision now that she has turned sixteen years old, so the teen balances high school with vampire camp and a social life juggling three potential Romeos. Gillian Engberg, writing for *Booklist,* called *Sucks to Be Me* a "breezy, often uproarious debut novel" enlivened by "Mina's wisecracking, authentic teen voice," while *Locus* critic Carolyn Cushman noted Pauley's "pleasantly light, bizarrely heartwarming treatment" of the teen vampire trope. Mina's adventures continue in the sequel, *Still Sucks to Be Me.*

Pauley explained on her home page that she did not set out to write a novel about vampires. "I'd recently read this YA vampire book . . . that had all these references

Cover of Kimberly Pauley's middle-grade novel Sucks to Be Me, *an entertaining account of a teenage vampire wannabe.* (Art by Emi Tanji. Cover photograph by Allison Shinkle. Book design by Emi Tanji and Kate Irwin. Reproduced by permission.)

to *Dracula* . . . and it got so much stuff wrong. I was annoyed. And late one night the first line of [*Sucks to Be Me*] came in my head and I got up and wrote it down. And then wrote up the first couple of paragraphs. And then I went to bed. I figured that was it, but when I got up the next day, I had more of Mina in my head and (in the immortal words of John Lee Hooker) it had to come out." Asked for advice, Pauley responded: "The most important thing to do is to write. The more you write, the better you get at it."

Biographical and Critical Sources

PERIODICALS

Booklist, November 15, 2008, review of *Sucks to Be Me: The All-True Confessions of Mina Hamilton, Teen Vampire,* p. 58.
Kirkus Reviews, August 15, 2008, review of *Sucks to Be Me.*
Locus, November, 2008, review of *Sucks to Be Me.*

ONLINE

Kimberly Pauley Home Page, http://kimberlypauley.com (December 2, 2009).
Macleans Online, http://www.macleans.ca/ (July 16, 2008), Brian Bethune, "Love at First Bite."
YA (and Kids!) Book Central Web site, http://www. yabookscentral.com/ (December 2, 2009), profile of Pauley and review of *Sucks to Be Me.**

*   *   *

PILUTTI, Deb

Personal

Married; children.

Addresses

Home—Ann Arbor, MI.

Career

Writer, illustrator, and designer. Oliebollen (online children's retailer), cofounder with Margaret Schankler and designer, 1998.

Awards, Honors

Best of the Best designation, Chicago Public Library, 2009, for *The City Kid and the Suburb Kid.*

Writings

The City Kid and the Suburb Kid, illustrated by Linda Bleck, Sterling Pub. (New York, NY), 2008.
(Illustrator) Susan Collins Thomas, *The Twelve Days of Christmas in Michigan,* Sterling Publishing, 2010.

Sidelights

Deb Pilutti is a Michigan-based illustrator and designer who has also become a children's book author and illustrator. Her self-illustrated picture book *The City Kid and the Suburb Kid* is actually two stories in one: it has two covers and requires only a flip upside down to move from one tale to the other. Pilutti is also one half of the creative talent behind Oliebollen.com, an online retailer of children's products that boasts a colorful Web site of Pilutti's design.

In *The City Kid and the Suburb Kid* readers meet Jack and Adam, two boys who learn about another way of life by while visiting one another. Jack lives in the city, and he enjoys leaving the downtown bustle behind for a week's stay at Adam's suburban home. For Adam, his quiet neighborhood seems boring compared to Jack's urban life, but after a few days both boys realize that home is also friends and family and the comfort of familiar surroundings. A *Kirkus Reviews* critic wrote that a "classic fable gets an update and a clever book design" in Piutti's tale, adding that *The City Kid and the Suburb Kid* may inspire children to wish for a similar change of surroundings. Also commenting on Piutti's inspiration in Aesop's fables, Marge Loch-Wouters wrote that the "retro cartoon" illustrations contributed by illustrator Linda Bleck "perfectly capture" the story's varied settings.

Biographical and Critical Sources

PERIODICALS

Kirkus Reviews, April 15, 2008, review of *The City Kid and the Suburb Kid.*

School Library Journal, May, 2008, Marge Loch-Wouters, review of *The City Kid and the Suburb Kid,* p. 106.

ONLINE

Deb Pilutti Home Page, http://www.debpilutti.com (December 1, 2009).

Oliebollen Web log, http://www.oliebollen.com/ (December 1, 2009).*

*   *   *

PRATT, Pierre 1962-

Personal

Born February 8, 1962, in Montréal, Québec, Canada; son of Marcel and Sylvianc Pratt. *Education:* Studied graphic design at the college level. *Hobbies and other interests:* Music, playing instruments, travel.

Addresses

Home—Montréal, Québec, Canada. *E-mail*—pierre@pierrepratt.com.

Career

Children's book author and illustrator.

Awards, Honors

Canadian Governor General's Award, and Mr. Christie Award for best illustration, both 1991, both for *Uncle Henry's Dinner Guests;* UNICEF-Bologna Book Fair Award, 1992; Golden Apple Award (Bratislava), for *Follow That Hat!;* Governor General's Award for Illustration, and Mr. Christie Book Award in French-language category, both for *My Dog Is an Elephant;* "Totem" for Best French Album in Montreuil, France, 1994, for *Marcel and André;* Governor General's Literary Award for Children's Literature (French) Illustration, 1998, for *Monsieur Ilétaitunefois* by Rémy Simard; Elizabeth Mrazik-Cleaver Picture Book Award, 2004, for *Where's Pup?* by Dayle Ann Dodds; Hans Christian Andersen Award nomination, 2008.

Writings

SELF-ILLUSTRATED

Follow That Hat!, Firefly Books (Richmond Hill, Ontario, Canada), 1992.

Marcel et André, Gallimard (Paris, France), 1994.

Hippo Beach, Seuil Jeunesse (Paris, France), 1996, Firefly Books (Richmond Hill, Ontario, Canada), 1997.

Beaux dimanches, Seuil (Paris, France), 1996.

Léon sans son chapeau, Autrement (Paris, France), 1997.

Collection pied de nez, 4 volumes, Éditions Chouette (Montréal, Québec, Canada), 1997.

La vie exemplaire de Martha et Paul, Seuil (Paris, France), 1998.

I See . . . My Mom; I See . . . My Dad, Annick Press (Toronto, Ontario, Canada), 2001.

I See . . . My Sister; I See . . . My Cat, Annick Press (Toronto, Ontario, Canada), 2001.

Le jour où Zoé zozota, Les 400 Coups (Montréal, Québec, Canada), 2005.

SELF-ILLUSTRATED; "VERY BUSY LIFE OF OLAF AND VENUS" SERIES

Shopping, Candlewick Press (Cambridge, MA), 2000.

Park, Macmillan Children's Books (London, England), 2000, Candlewick Press (Cambridge, MA), 2001.

Home, Macmillan Children's Book (London, England), 2000, Candlewick Press (Cambridge, MA), 2001.

Car, Macmillan Children's Books (London, England), 2000, Candlewick Press (Cambridge, MA), 2001.

Series has been translated into French.

ILLUSTRATOR

Benedicte Froissant, *Les fantasies de l'oncle Henri,* 1990, translated by David Homel as *Uncle Henry's Dinner Guests,* Firefly Books (Richmond Hill, Ontario, Canada), 1990.

Rémy Simard, *Mon chien est un éléphant!,* Casterman, 1994, translated by David Homel as *My Dog Is an Elephant,* Firefly Books (Richmond Hill, Ontario, Canada), 1994.

Rémy Simard, *La bottine magique de Pipo,* [Paris, France], translated as *The Magic Boot,* Firefly Books (Richmond Hill, Ontario, Canada), 1995.

Hannah Roche, *Corey's Kite,* Stewart, Tabori & Chang (New York, NY), 1996.

Hannah Roche, *Sandra's Sun Hat,* Stewart, Tabori & Chang (New York, NY), 1996.

Hannah Roche, *Su's Snowgirl,* Stewart, Tabori & Chang (New York, NY), 1996.

Hannah Roche, *Pete's Puddles,* Stewart, Tabori & Chang (New York, NY), 1996.

Hannah Roche, *Soleil,* Hatier (Paris, France), 1996.

Hannah Roche, *Vent,* Hatier (Paris, France), 1996.

Hannah Roche, *Pluie,* Hatier (Paris, France), 1996.

Jacques Godbout, *Une leçon de chasse,* Boréal (Montréal, Québec, Canada), 1997.

François Gravel, *Klonk* (novel), Hachette (Paris, France), 1997.

François Gravel, *Le cauchemar de Klonk* (novel), Québec/ Amérique (Montréal, Québec, Canada), 1997.

François Gravel, *Klonk et le Beatle mouillé* (novel), Québec/Amérique (Montréal, Québec, Canada), 1997.

James Sage, *Sassy Gracie,* Dutton (New York, NY), 1998.

Rémy Simard, *Monsieur Ilétainunefois,* Annick Press (Toronto, Ontario, Canada), 1998, translated by David Homel as *Mister Once-upon-a-Time,* 1998.

Hannah Roche, *Have You Ever Seen a Chicken Hatch?,* Zero to Ten (New York, NY), 1998.

Hannah Roche, *Have You Ever Picked a Dandelion?,* Zero to Ten (New York, NY), 1998.

Joceline Sanschagrin, *Le cercle des magiciens,* La Courte Échelle (Montréal, Québec, Canada), 1998.

Hannah Roche, *Have You Ever Seen a Frog Leap?,* Zero to Ten (New York, NY), 1999.

Hannah Roche, *Have You Ever Seen a Cat Purr?,* Zero to Ten (New York, NY), 1999.

Joceline Sanschagrin, *La marque du dragon,* La Courte Échelle (Montréal, Québec, Canada), 1999.

François Gravel, *Klonk et le treize noir* (novel), Québec/ Amérique (Montréal, Québec, Canada), 1999.

Laurent Chabin, *La machine à manger des brocolis,* Boréal (Montréal, Québec, Canada), 2000.

François Gravel, *Klonk et la queue du Scorpion* (novel), Québec/Amérique (Montréal, Québec, Canada), 2000.

François Gravel, *David et le fantôme,* Dominique et Cie. (Saint-Lambert, Québec, Canada), 2000.

Joceline Sanschagrin, *Le labyrinthe des rêves,* La Courte Échelle (Montréal, Québec, Canada), 2000.

Joël des Rosiers, *Métropolis opéra: suivi de Tribu* (poetry), Triptyque (Montréal, Québec, Canada), 2000.

Matthieu de Laubier, *Une joyeux Noël,* Bayard Jeunesse (Paris, France), 2000.

François Gravel, *David et les monstres de la forêt,* Dominique et Cie. (Saint-Lambert, Québec, Canada), 2000.

François Gravel, *Coca-Klonk* (novel), Québec/Amérique (Montréal, Québec, Canada), 2001.

François Gravel, *David et le précipice,* Dominique et Cie. (Saint-Lambert, Québec, Canada), 2001.

Hannah Roche, *Une fleur est né!,* Millepages (Paris, France), 2001.

Hannah Roche, *Un poussin est né!,* Millepages (Paris, France), 2001.

Ron Hirsch, *No, No Jack!,* Dial Books for Young Children (New York, NY), 2002.

François Gravel, *David et la maison de la sorcière,* Dominique et Cie. (Saint-Lambert, Québec, Canada), 2002.

François Gravel, *La racine carrée de Klonk* (novel), Québec/Amérique (Montréal, Québec, Canada), 2002.

Jacques Godbout, *Mes petites fesses,* Les 400 Coups (Montréal, Québec, Canada), 2002.

Dayle Ann Dodds, *Where's Pup?,* Dial Books (New York, NY), 2003.

François Gravel, *La testament de Klonk* (novel), Québec/ Amérique (Montréal, Québec, Canada), 2003.

François Gravel, *David et l'orage,* Dominique et Cie. (Saint-Lambert, Québec, Canada), 2003.

Cynthia Zarin, *Albert, the Dog Who Liked to Ride in Taxis,* Atheneum (New York, NY), 2003.

François Gravel, *David et les crabes noirs,* Dominique et Cie. (Saint-Lambert, Québec, Canada), 2004.

François Gravel, *Klonk contre Klonk* (novel), Québec/ Amérique (Montréal, Québec, Canada), 2004.

Mary Stolz, *Belling the Tiger,* new edition, Running Press, 2004.

François Gravel, *David et le salon funéraire,* Dominique et Cie. (Saint-Lambert, Québec, Canada), 2005.

Emily Jenkins, *That New Animal,* Farrar, Straus & Giroux (New York, NY), 2005.

L.C. Gomes, *A galinha que cantava ópera,* Dom Quixote (Lisbon, Portugal), 2005.

Halfdan Wedel Rasmussen, *The Ladder* (originally published as *Stigen*), translation by Marilyn Nelson, Candlewick Press (Cambridge, MA), 2005.

Jacques Godbout, *Bizarres, les baisers,* Les 400 Coups (Montréal, Québec, Canada), 2006.

Marsha Diane Arnold, *Roar of a Snore,* Dial Books for Young Readers (New York, NY), 2006.

Carol Lexa Schaefer, *Big Little Monkey,* Candlewick Press (Cambridge, MA), 2008.

Emily Jenkins, *Skunkdog,* Farrar, Straus & Giroux (New York, NY), 2008.

Sidelights

Award-winning Québec-based artist and author/ illustrator Pierre Pratt creates exuberant, distinctive illustrations for children's books. In addition to producing images for the texts of French-language authors such as Rémy Simard, Hanna Roche, and François Gravel, he has also paired his brightly colored illustrations with English-language texts as well as with original stories such as his board-book series following the adventures of Olaf the elephant and Venus the mouse. Praising Pratt's award-winning contribution to Dayle Ann Dodds' humorous rhyming picture book *Where's Pup?,* about a small dog that is mislaid by its circus-clown owner, *Horn Book* writer Betty Carter cited the artist's "near-sunshine palette" and added that Pratt's illustrations "provide . . . a colorful, but uncluttered circus setting" for Dodds' "engaging story." In *School Library Journal,* Linda M. Kenton dubbed *Where's Pup?* "a visually exciting charmer for storytime," and Susan Perren wrote in the Toronto *Globe & Mail* that the "spellbinding" picture book "showcases . . . Pratt's considerable artistic talent."

Pratt decided on his career course as a child, when drawing was his favorite pastime. "As far back as I can remember, I always drew," the illustrator noted on the Annick Press Web site. "When my father took me to

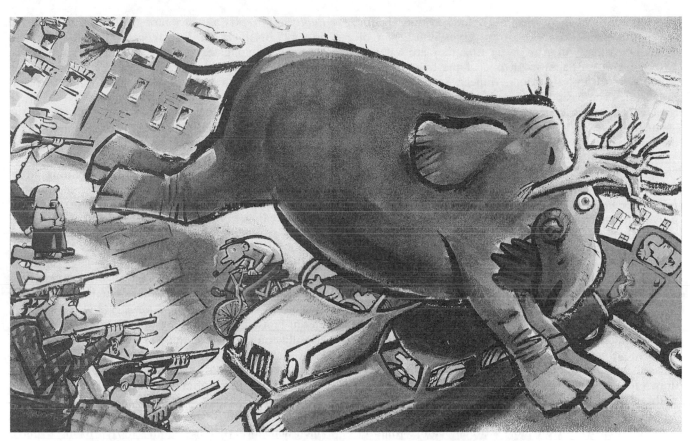

Pierre Pratt creates the engaging artwork that captures the nonsense in Rémy Simard's picture book **My Dog Is an Elephant.** (Annick Press, 1994. Illustration © 1994 by Pierre Pratt. Reproduced by permission.)

hockey games, I would go home and draw the players!" During his teen years, Pratt became a fan of the French-language "Tintin" comics and was inspired to write and illustrate his own comic strips; following high school he enrolled in college to study graphic design.

Using oil pastel and acrylic paint in his works and incorporating heavy black lines, Pratt often plays with perspective and draws on influences from Matisse to Edward Hopper to give his works an absurdist or sometimes merely silly slant. In fact, Pratt's illustrations are sometimes more successful with critics than the stories they accompany. "Pratt is undoubtedly one of the most original of the many gifted children's illustrators Québec has given us in the last decade," remarked McNaughton in a 1992 *Quill & Quire* article, reflecting the award-winning artist's growing stature.

Pratt's first illustration project was a story by Benedicte Froissant that was published in English translation in 1990 as *Uncle Henry's Dinner Guests.* It is a surreal fantasy in which the chickens pictured on Uncle Henry's T-shirt come alive during an otherwise quiet dinner, although only the children at the table seem to notice. Pratt's drawings are "zany and inventive," averred Anne Denoon in *Books in Canada;* "although his characters are pretty grotesque, they seem ideally suited to the strange goings-on at the dinner table." While *Quill & Quire* reviewer Frieda Wishinsky termed Froissant's story "nothing but silly," she called Pratt's

illustrations "exaggerated but in a quirky, stylized manner. The colours are warm and inviting and the pages well designed." *Uncle Henry's Dinner Guests* earned Pratt two major illustration honors, and established him as a contender in the arena of children's book illustration.

Pratt teams up with children's author Rémy Simard in several books that have been noted for their absurdist tendencies. In *My Dog Is an Elephant,* for example, a boy tries to save an elephant from being sent back to the zoo by disguising the creature as a moose, a dinosaur, a butterfly, and finally, as the boy's father. "Both author and illustrator draw their jokes from within the fantasy they have created," Janet McNaughton observed in a *Quill & Quire* review of *My Dog Is an Elephant,* adding: "This state of serious silliness is a worthwhile achievement in a children's book." Although Lucinda Snyder Whitehurst, a contributor to *School Library Journal,* remarked that "most of the humor is rather mature" for its intended audience and the illustrations are "bright, but not particularly attractive," other critics maintained that the positive value of Simard's story equals that of Pratt's illustrations. As Diana Brebner commented in *Books in Canada,* "the high quality of the artwork" and the "delightful absurdity of the text" keep readers turning the pages until the unexpected ending.

In *The Magic Boot* Pratt and Simard team up to explain why the land mass of Italy looks like a boot when viewed from the air. Little Pipo's feet are too big for any boots made, so a good fairy gives him a pair of magic boots that will grow every time they are watered. After several mishaps occur, one of the boots is accidentally tossed into the Mediterranean Sea, and Italy is the result. "The basic idea . . . is excellent," declared a reviewer in *Junior Bookshelf,* who added, however, that "somehow, we are left dissatisfied." Some critics faulted the book's narrative rather than its artwork; a *Publishers Weekly* contributor wrote that Pratt's illustrations "heighten the absurdity but don't deepen the story." *The Magic Boot* "isn't quite the tour de force that *My Dog Is an Elephant* was," McNaughton allowed, "but it proves that this pair is far from exhausting the creative potential of their partnership." Another collaboration, *Mister Once-in-a-Time*, won Pratt one of several Governor General awards for illustration that he has received over his career.

Working with English-language writers has won Pratt new fans in both western Canada and the United States. Collaborating with Cynthia Zarin, he produced the artwork for *Albert, the Dog Who Liked to Ride in Taxis,* an amusing story about a cab-hopping dachshund that is drawn into the dreams of every traveler he meets. Paired with what Ilene Cooper described in *Booklist* as a "droll" narrative, Pratt's "chunky, acrylic illustrations catch the density" of the story's urban setting, while in

Publishers Weekly a contributor wrote that the "stylized artwork" in *Albert, the Dog Who Liked to Ride in Taxis* "brims with elongated vehicles, buildings and trees that seem tailored to a dachshund." Another dog stars in *Roar of a Snore,* a picture-book pairing of Pratt's paintings with Marsha Diane Arnold's cumulative story. In the tale a boy hears a loud roar in the middle of the night. He and his loyal hound dog decide to investigate, waking snorer after snorer from their sleep. "Done in vivid, warm colors," Pratt's detailed acrylic images "add motion and energy" to Arnold's rhyming story, maintained Rebecca Sheridan in her *School Library Journal* review of *Roar of a Snore.*

That New Animal, a picture book by Emily Jenkins, allows Pratt to capture the arrival of a new baby in the family from a dog's perspective, as family pets Fudge-Fudge and Marshmallow fret that all the human attention in their home is directed at a small, pink, wailing creature in a crib. In *School Library Journal* Rosalyn Pierini praised the sensitivity demonstrated in both text and illustrations, concluding of *That New Animal* that Pratt's characteristic use of bright colors and "elongated" shapes "strikes just the right note of humor and whimsy." Another collaboration between Jenkins and Pratt, *Skunkdog,* finds Dumpling the dog an outcast in her neighborhood because her long nose is useless as a smell-detector. After her family moves to the country,

The skewed perspectives in Pratt's blocky acrylic paintings reflect the whimsy of Dayle Ann Dodds' story for **Where's Pup?** (Copyright © 2003 by Pierre Pratt. Used by permission of Dial Books for Young Readers, a division of Penguin Putnam Books for Young Readers.)

however, the pup's lack of a sense of smell allows her to befriend a creature that has even fewer friends: a lonely skunk. Noting the book's "themes of loneliness, tolerance, [and] friendship," *School Library Journal* critic Mary Jean Smith also praised Pratt's "sunlit illustrations" for adding to a book that will "enrich any storytime."

Follow That Hat! marks Pratt's entry into children's literature in the role of writer. In the award-winning book, Leon chases his hat around the world, utilizing every form of transportation imaginable in the process. "Pratt's plot is admirable in its simplicity," McNaughton remarked in a *Quill & Quire* review. While Jane Robinson maintained in a *Canadian Review of Materials* appraisal that the story is "too 'clever' and too sophisticated for the younger reader," she added that experienced story-readers, if alerted, can sidestep "this pitfall and, that way, everyone could enjoy the work of this talented artist." Also expressing reservations about the book's text, Robin Baird Lewis wrote in *Canadian Children's Literature* that Pratt's illustrations, featuring "richly deep and textural colours, yummily scrumbled across black underpainting," more than compensate.

"I have lots of ideas, but sometimes it's difficult to get them out," Pratt noted on the Annick Press Web site, referring to the fact that his work sometimes requires him to tap into the visual inspiration behind other people's stories. "Once I start working, though, the ideas usually begin to flow," he added.

His lighthearted, quirky approach reflects the enjoyment Pratt continues to take in his work. In fact, he often incorporates musical interludes into his working day. "Often while I'm waiting for a painting to dry," he admitted, "I have fun playing the accordion, or the double bass, or the piano, or the guitar."

Biographical and Critical Sources

PERIODICALS

Booklist, January 1, 2002, Ilene Cooper, review of *No, No Jack!,* p. 864; December 15, 2003, Ilene Cooper, review of *Albert, the Dog Who Liked to Ride in Taxis,* p. 749.

Books in Canada, April, 1991, Anne Denoon, review of *Uncle Henry's Dinner Guests,* p. 37; December, 1994, Diana Brebner, review of *My Dog Is an Elephant,* p. 55.

Canadian Children's Literature, number 72, 1993, Robin Baird Lewis, review of *Follow That Hat!,* pp. 80-81.

Canadian Review of Materials, January, 1991, Adele M. Fasick, review of *Uncle Henry's Dinner Guests,* p. 26; January, 1993, Jane Robinson, review of *Follow That Hat!,* p. 23.

Globe and Mail (Toronto, Ontario, Canada), May 31, 2003, Susan Perren, review of *Where's Pup?,* p. D15; September 27, 2008, Susan Perren, review of *Big Little Monkey,* p. D28.

A happy dog with an unfortunate name is captured in Pratt's art for Skunkdog *by Emily Jenkins.* (Illustration copyright © 2008 by Pierre Pratt. Used by permission of Farrar, Straus & Giroux, LLC.)

Horn Book, March-April, 2003, Betty Carter, review of *Where's Pup?,* p. 201; March-April, 2005, Jennifer M. Brabander, review of *That New Animal,* p. 189; January-February, 2006, Susan Dove Lempke, review of *That New Animal,* p. 16.

Junior Bookshelf, June, 1996, review of *The Magic Boot,* p. 103.

Kirkus Reviews, January 15, 2002, review of *No, No Jack!,* p. 106; January 15, 2003, review of *Where's Pup?,* p. 141; July 1, 2004, review of *Belling the Tiger,* p. 638; August 1, 2008, review of *Big Little Monkey.*

New York Times Book Review, January 18, 2004, review of *Albert, the Dog Who Liked to Ride in Taxis,* p. 18.

Publishers Weekly, August 28, 1995, review of *The Magic Boot,* p. 113; June 11, 2001, reviews of *Park, Shopping, Car,* and *Home,* p. 87; April 7, 2003, review of *Where's Pup?,* p. 69; January 19, 2004, review of *Albert, the Dog Who Liked to Ride in Taxis,* p. 74; February 28, 2005, review of *That New Animal,* p. 66; August 28, 2006, review of *Roar of a Snore,* p. 52; April 14, 2008, review of *Skunkdog,* p. 53.

Quill & Quire, January, 1991, Frieda Wishinsky, review of *Uncle Henry's Dinner Guests,* p. 22; October, 1992, Janet McNaughton, review of *Follow That Hat!,* p. 33; September, 1994, Janet McNaughton, review of *My Dog Is an Elephant;* April, 2001, review of *I See . . . My Mom/I See . . . My Dad,* pp. 33-34; June, 2003, Sarah Ellis, review of *Where's Pup?*

San Francisco Chronicle, May 29, 2005, Regan McMahon, review of *That New Animal,* p. E3.

School Library Journal, February, 1995, Lucinda Snyder Whitehurst, review of *My Dog Is an Elephant,* p. 82; November, 2001, Olga R. Kuharets, review of "Very Busy Life of Olaf and Venus" series, p. 133; July, 2003, Linda M. Kenton, review of *Where's Pup?,* p. 95; September, 2004, Bina Williams, review of *Belling the Tiger,* p. 181; March, 2005, Rosalyn Pierini, review of *That New Animal,* p. 174; August, 2006, Rebecca Sheridan, review of *Roar of a Snore,* p. 74; April, 2008, Mary Jean Smith, review of *Skunkdog,* p. 114; October, 2008, Amy Lilien-Harper, review of *Big Little Monkey,* p. 123.

Tribune Books (Chicago, IL), July 1, 2001, review of *Home,* p. 3.

ONLINE

Annick Press Web site, http://www.annickpress.com/ (November 15, 2009).

Pierre Pratt Home Page, http://www.pierrepratt.com (November 15, 2009).*

* * *

PULVER, Robin 1945-

Personal

Born August 14, 1945, in Geneva, NY; daughter of Willard B. (a biochemist) and Alice Robinson; married Donald Pulver (a physician), June 12, 1971; children: Nina, David. *Education:* William Smith College, B.A., 1967; attended Syracuse University School of Journalism. *Hobbies and other interests:* Hiking, swimming, bird-watching, reading.

Addresses

Home—Pittsford, NY.

Career

Writer. Has worked in public relations.

Member

Society of Children's Book Writers and Illustrators, National Coalition against Censorship, Authors' Guild, Association for Retarded Citizens, Sierra Club, Rochester Area Children's Writers and Illustrators.

Awards, Honors

Pick of the Lists selection, American Booksellers Association, 1990, for *Mrs. Toggle's Zipper,* and 1994, for *Homer and the House Next Door;* Children's Choice designation, International Reading Association/Children's Book Council, 1992, for *The Holiday Handwriting School; Smithsonian* magazine Notable Children's Book designation, Nest Literary Classic selection, and nominations for six state reading awards, all 1999, all

for *Axle Annie;* Best Books designation, Bank Street College of Education, Chapman Award, PlanetEsme. com, and Children's Choice award, all 2003, all for *Punctuation Takes a Vacation.*

Writings

Mrs. Toggle's Zipper, illustrated by R.W. Alley, Four Winds Press (New York, NY), 1990.

The Holiday Handwriting School, illustrated by G. Brian Karas, Four Winds Press (New York, NY), 1991.

Mrs. Toggle and the Dinosaur, illustrated by R.W. Alley, Four Winds Press (New York, NY), 1991.

Nobody's Mother Is in Second Grade, illustrated by G. Brian Karas, Dial Books for Young Readers (New York, NY), 1992.

Homer and the House Next Door, illustrated by Arnie Levin, Four Winds Press (New York, NY), 1994.

Mrs. Toggle's Beautiful Blue Shoe, illustrated by R.W. Alley, Four Winds Press (New York, NY), 1994.

Alicia's Tutu, illustrated by Mark Graham, Dial Books for Young Readers (New York, NY), 1997.

Way to Go, Alex!, illustrated by Elizabeth Wolf, Albert Whitman (Morton Grove, IL), 1999.

Axle Annie, illustrated by Tedd Arnold, Dial Books for Young Readers (New York, NY), 1999.

Mrs. Toggle's Class Picture Day, illustrated by R.W. Alley, Scholastic (New York, NY), 2000.

Christmas for a Kitten, illustrated by Layne Johnson, Albert Whitman (Morton Grove, IL), 2003.

Punctuation Takes a Vacation, illustrated by Lynn Rowe Reed, Holiday House (New York, NY), 2003.

Author Day for Room 3T, illustrated by Chuck Richards, Clarion Books (New York, NY), 2005.

Axle Annie and the Speed Grump, illustrated by Tedd Arnold, Dial Books for Young Readers (New York, NY), 2005.

Nouns and Verbs Have a Field Day, illustrated by Lynn Rowe Reed, Holiday House (New York, NY), 2006.

Silent Letters Loud and Clear, illustrated by Lynn Rowe Reed, Holiday House (New York, NY), 2008.

Never Say Boo!, illustrated by Deb Lucke, Holiday House (New York, NY), 2009.

Contributor of articles and stories to periodicals, including *Highlights for Children, Jack and Jill, Pockets, Cricket, Spider,* and *Ranger Rick.*

Sidelights

Robin Pulver has loved writing and reading throughout her life, and although she authored articles for magazines throughout her early adulthood, sharing books with her own two children inspired her first picture books. In addition to her popular "Mrs. Toggle" books, a series about a lovable, frumpy schoolteacher that features artwork by R.W. Alley, Pulver has worked with a range of other illustrators in producing picture books such as *Axle Annie, Punctuation Takes a Vacation,* and *Author Day for Room 3T.*

Robin Pulver's picture book Way to Go, Alex *features illustrations by Elizabeth Wolf.* (Illustration copyright © 1999 by Elizabeth Wolf. Reproduced by permission.)

Introduced in *Mrs. Toggle's Zipper,* Pulver's well-received "Mrs. Toggle" series of books focuses on a group of students that often comes to the rescue of its instructor, Mrs. Toggle. In *Mrs. Toggle's Zipper* the accident-prone teacher cannot remove her winter jacket after its zipper jams, and no amount of tugging will free her. After asking the school nurse for help, the children turn to their clueless principal, who in turn sends for the custodian, Mr. Abel. Using the right tool, Mr. Abel is able to un-stick the jacket zipper, much to the relief of the children and the overheated Mrs. Toggle. A *Publishers Weekly* critic called *Mrs. Toggle's Zipper* "a funny, slightly subversive story," adding that Alley's illustrations "complement the witty tale perfectly."

A new student proves to be a problem in *Mrs. Toggle and the Dinosaur,* when Mrs. Toggle is led to believe that her new pupil is actually a dinosaur. The teacher fears she does not have enough time to prepare her classroom for the large creature and wonders what she will do when the dinosaur arrives at its first day of school. Much to the relief of Mrs. Toggle, when the new student arrives, it proves to be, not a prehistoric beast, but a girl named Dina Sawyer. *Mrs. Toggle and the Dinosaur* is "a fine sequel to the equally delightful *Mrs. Toggle's Zipper,*" wrote a contributor to *Kirkus Reviews.*

More strange events transpire in *Mrs. Toggle's Beautiful Blue Shoe* and *Mrs. Toggle's Class Picture Day.* In the first book, the accident-prone teacher loses her shoe while joining her students in a game of kickball. Landing high up in a tree, the shoe stays stubbornly put, resisting all attempts by the children and their not-very-helpful principal, Mr. Stickler, to retrieve it. Finally, Mr. Abel the custodian comes to everyone's rescue with a simple solution: use a stepladder. A different sort of emergency arises in *Mrs. Toggle's Class Picture Day* when the teacher arrives at school with a less-than-perfect coiffure. After scaring the children with her disheveled locks, Mrs. Toggle turns to the school nurse, then the custodian, principal, librarian, and art teacher for help before the photographer arrives. Calling *Mrs. Toggle's Beautiful Blue Shoe* "another winner," *School Library Journal* critic Joyce Richards predicted that "older [children] will enjoy the [story's] problem-solving aspect." In *Booklist* Julie Corsaro wrote that Pulver's "simple text has appealing repetition," and her story's ending "serves up the right dose of schoolyard justice."

Schooltime is also a key element in *Axle Annie* and *Axle Annie and the Speed Grump,* both of which focus on a good-hearted school-bus driver. Much to the disappointment of her bus-driving colleague Shifty Rhodes, Axle Annie will not let a snowstorm prevent her from getting the children of Burskyville to school on time. Because the school's superintendent follows Axle Annie's lead, students never enjoy a day off from school to enjoy a heavier-than-normal snowfall. Wanting to enjoy a day off from work, Shifty conspires with the owner of a local ski resort to cover a particularly dangerous stretch of road with a heavy coat of manmade snow and ice, using a snow-making machine. What the scheming duo does not count on, however, is the generosity of the other Burskyville residents who help push Axle Annie's bus up the slippery incline as repayment for the many times she gave them a ride in inclement weather. "With hilarious, over the top characters, this satisfyingly outrageous tale will tickle readers' funny bones," suggested a *Kirkus Reviews* critic. Other reviewers cited Pulver's well-drawn characters, a *Publishers Weekly* contributor remarking that the author "creates a memorable character in Annie."

Readers return to Burskyville in *Axle Annie and the Speed Grump,* as the helpful bus driver goes head to head with a local leadfoot. Rush Hotfoot breaks the speed limit and several safety rules besides, and his driving puts Annie's young riders in danger. The man's good luck does not last forever, however, and when Rush escapes a tragic accident with the help of Annie and the students, he turns in his car keys for a three-wheeled bike. Pulver's story will "keep kids laughing out loud," observed Julie Cummins in *Booklist,* and Tedd Arnold's colored pencil-and-watercolor illustrations are "as over the edge as Rush's car." *School Library Journal* critic Susan Weitz also praised Arnold's cartoon art, noting that his "enormously appealing" cartoons combine with Pulver's "bouncy language" to "present a lesson in road safety that's both goofy and memorable."

In *Alicia's Tutu* Pulver tells a tale about a girl who learns to deal with life's disappointments and priorities with help from her loving family, while *Homer and the House Next Door* featuring a dog that becomes upset when it learns its owner intends to sell the family house. In the picture book *Way to Go, Alex!* Carly wishes that she could feel proud of her mentally handicapped younger brother, Alex, and is ashamed that she does not. Nonetheless, she agrees to coach him to compete in the upcoming Special Olympics, where he wants to race in the fifty-yard dash. Although Alex stops short of the finish line on race day, Carly's experience as a coach helps her realize that her brother is still a success because he had the courage to try. Remarking on Pulver's ability to capture Carly's conflicting emotions in *Way to Go, Alex!, Booklist* contributor Susan Dove Lempke claimed that the book "will fill a need for materials on disabilities and is a solid story in its own right."

Pulver returns to school in a story of an inspiring visit in *Author Day for Room 3T*, while *Christmas for a Kitten* pairs her quiet story about a stray kitten's meeting with Santa with what a *Kirkus Reviews* writer described as "glowing" paintings by artist Layne Johnson. "A wacky take on an Author's Day that goes awry," according to *Booklist* critic Ilene Cooper, *Author Day for Room 3T* captures what happens to a group of normal third graders when a chimpanzee takes the place of a visiting teacher and all manner of antics result. Capturing the humor of Pulver's silly story in "goofy caricatures" and "topsy-turvy settings," illustrator Chuck Richards contributes to making *Author Day for Room 3T* "sublimely silly" and "a surefire hit," according to *School Library Journal* critic Marian Creamer.

A collaboration between Pulver and artist Lynn Rowe Reed has produced several entertaining picture books set in a third-grade classroom that take grammar as their subject. In *Punctuation Takes a Vacation* Mr. Wright's students play fast and loose with commas, periods, apostrophes, colons, and hyphens, and their ac-

***Tedd Arnold's collaborations with Pulver include his illustrations for* Axel Annie.** (Illustration © 1999 by Tedd Arnold. Reproduced by permission of Puffin Books, a division of Penguin Putnam Books for Young Readers.)

tions worry the symbols in question. A casual remark from the teacher convinces the punctuation marks to depart the classroom for a holiday, and they leave behind a room full of incomprehensible books, reports, and signs. While Mr. Wrights class is away on a field trip, the classroom's nouns and verbs are left to their own devices in *Nouns and Verbs Have a Field Day* and the students return to find some entertaining messages spelled out on the class bulletin boards. When Mr. Wright's students decide to start a move to ban silent letters in *Silent Letters Loud and Clear,* they are taught yet another lesson after Silent e and his associates depart. Reed's brightly colored, naïve-styled art adds a playful element to Pulver's text, creating books that are "brightly colored, boldly labeled, and packed with personality," according to Gloria Koster in her *School Library Journal* review of *Nouns and Verbs Have a Field Day.* "Although the emphasis is on silliness," wrote *Booklist* critic Kay Weisman, the same book "makes [its] . . . point about the parts of speech," and a *Kirkus Reviews* writer called *Silent Letters Loud and Clear* "a book so clever and fun that both teachers and students alike will be enthralled." "Pulver has outdone herself in this ingenious take on learning," concluded another *Kirkus Reviewer,* commenting on *Punctuation Takes a Vacation.* A *Publishers Weekly* contributor, reviewing the same book, wrote that the author "manages to teach a good deal about punctuation. . . . between the verbal shenanigans and the eye-popping illustrations."

Pulver once told *SATA:* "I have always enjoyed writing and reading. As a child, I was shy about speaking and relied on writing to express what I knew and felt. I think I unwittingly served an apprenticeship in writing for children when I studied journalism in graduate school, then short story writing. Both forms require economy of language and respect for every word.

"My appreciation of children's books deepened when my own children were born. I remember carrying my newborn infant daughter into a children's bookstore in 1978 and being swept off my feet by the beautiful language and extraordinary art. Reading to my two children from their earliest days gave me a profound appreciation of the impact of literature on children and families. Sharing books with my bright, language-loving daughter has been a joy. Reading to my son, who is handicapped but also bright and language-loving in his own way, has been a salvation. It has brought us precious moments of calm and touchstones for moments of recognition and laughter.

"It came as a happy surprise when I found that I could write and sometimes publish stories for children. . . . My goal is to write well enough to move people and offer them a good story to share. I would like to give back to children's literature the kind of gifts I have received from it."

Pulver gives words an interesting twist in **Nouns and Verbs Have a Field Day,** *featuring illustrations by Lynne Rowe Reed.* (Illustration copyright © 2006 by Lynn Rowe Reed. Reproduced by permission of Holiday House, Inc.)

Biographical and Critical Sources

PERIODICALS

Booklist, June 15, 1992, Stephanie Zvirin, review of *Nobody's Mother Is in Second Grade,* p. 1851; March 1, 1994, Julie Cosaro, review of *Mrs. Toggle's Beautiful Blue Shoe,* p. 1270; January 1, 1995, Ilene Cooper, review of *Homer and the House Next Door,* p. 826; September 1, 1997, Helen Rosenberg, review of *Alicia's Tutu,* p. 134; January 1, 2000, Susan Dove Lempke, review of *Way to Go, Alex!,* p. 936; February 15, 2000, Ilene Cooper, review of *Axle Annie,* p. 1120; September 15, 2003, Ilene Cooper, review of *Christmas for a Kitten,* p. 248; May 1, 2005, Ilene Cooper, review of *Author Day for Room 3T,* p. 1592; November 1, 2005, Julie Cummins, review of *Axle Annie and the Speed Grump,* p. 54; April 1, 2006, Kay Weisman, review of *Nouns and Verbs Have a Field Day,* p. 49.

Horn Book, May-June, 2003, Peter D. Sieruta, review of *Punctuation Takes a Vacation,* p. 335; May-June, 2006, Vicky Smith, review of *Nouns and Verbs Have a Field Day,* p. 299; May-June, 2008, Kitty Flynn, review of *Silent Letters Loud and Clear,* p. 298.

Kirkus Reviews, August 15, 1991, review of *Mrs. Toggle and the Dinosaur;* July 15, 1992, review of *Nobody's Mother Is in Second Grade;* March 15, 1994, review of *Mrs. Toggle's Beautiful Blue Shoe,* p. 402; August 1, 1999, review of *Axle Annie,* p. 1230; February 15, 2003, review of *Punctuation Takes a Vacation,* p. 315; November 1, 2003, review of *Christmas for a Kitten,* p. 1319; May 1, 2005, review of *Author Day for Room 3T,* p. 544; August 15, 2005, review of *Axle Annie and the Speed Grump,* p. 920; April 15, 2008, review of *Silent Letters Loud and Clear.*

Publishers Weekly, March 30, 1990, review of *Mrs. Toggle's Zipper,* p. 60; August 24, 1992, review of *Nobody's Mother Is in Second Grade,* p. 79; September 19, 1994, review of *Homer and the House Next Door,* p. 69; August 23, 1999, review of *Axle Annie,* p. 58; January 20, 2003, review of *Punctuation Takes a Vacation,* p. 82.

School Library Journal, May, 1990, Patricia Pearl, review of *Mrs. Toggle's Zipper,* p. 90; June, 1991, Lisa Dennis, review of *The Holiday Handwriting School,* p. 88; November, 1991, Marie Orlando, review of *Mrs. Toggle and the Dinosaur,* p. 106; January, 1993, Virginia E. Jeschelnig, review of *Nobody's Mother Is in Second Grade,* p. 84; May, 1994, Joyce Richards, review of *Mrs. Toggle's Beautiful Blue Shoe,* p. 103; February, 1995, Margaret C. Howell, review of *Homer and the House Next Door,* p. 79; October, 1997, Amy Kellman, review of *Alicia's Tutu,* p. 108; October, 1999, Kathy Piehl, review of *Axle Annie,* p. 123; November, 1999, Christine A. Moesch, review of *Way to Go, Alex!,* p. 128; October, 2003, Eva Mitnick, review of *Christmas for a Kitten,* p. 67; April, 2005, Marian Creamer, review of *Author Day for Room 3T,* p. 110; December, 2005, Susan Weitz, review of *Axle Annie and the Speed Grump,* p. 120; March, 2006, Gloria Koster, review of *Nouns and Verbs Have a Field Day,* p. 200; June, 2008, Lynne Mattern, review of *Silent Letters Loud and Clear,* p. 113.

ONLINE

Robin Pulver Home Page, http://www.robinpulver.com (December 1, 2009).*

R

RIORDAN, Rick 1964-

Personal

Born June 5, 1964, in San Antonio, TX; married; children: two sons.

Addresses

Home— San Antonio, TX *Agent*—Nancy Gallt Literary Agency, 273 Charlton Ave., S. Orange, NJ 07079. *E-mail*—rick@rickriordan.com.

Career

Writer. Middle-school English teacher in San Francisco, CA, 1990-98; middle-school social studies and American history teacher, St. Mary's Hall, San Antonio, TX, 1999-2004; freelance writer. Presenter at workshops for educational organizations, including Texas Library Association, National Council for Teachers of English, International Reading Association, California Association of Independent Schools, and Colonial Williamsburg Teacher Institute.

Awards, Honors

Anthony Award for Best Original Paperback, and Shamus Award for Best First Private-Eye Novel, both 1997, both for *Big Red Tequila;* Anthony Award for Best Original Paperback, Edgar Allan Poe Award for Best Original Paperback, Mystery Writers of America, and Shamus Award nomination, all 1998, all for *The Widower's Two-Step;* Shamus Award nomination for Best Hardcover Private-Eye Novel, 2002, for *The Devil Went down to Austin;* Master Teacher Award, St. Mary's Hall, 2002; inducted into Texas Hall of Letters, 2003; Cooperative Children's Book Council Choice designation, and Notable Children's Book citation, National Council for Teachers of English, both 2006, both for *The Lightning Thief.*

Writings

"PERCY JACKSON AND THE OLYMPIANS" YOUNG-ADULT NOVEL SERIES

The Lightning Thief, Miramax/Hyperion (New York, NY), 2005.
The Sea of Monsters, Miramax/Hyperion (New York, NY), 2006.
The Titan's Curse, Miramax/Hyperion (New York, NY), 2007.
The Battle of the Labyrinth, Hyperion (New York, NY), 2008.
(Editor, with Leah Wilson) *Demigods and Monsters: Your Favorite Authors on Rick Riordan's "Percy Jackson and the Olympians" Series,* Benbella Books (Dallas, TX), 2008.
The Last Olympian, Hyperion (New York, NY), 2009.
Percy Jackson: The Demigod Files, Hyperion (New York, NY), 2009.

"TRES NAVARRE" MYSTERY NOVELS; FOR ADULTS

Big Red Tequila, Bantam (New York, NY), 1997.
The Widower's Two-Step, Bantam (New York, NY), 1998.
The Last King of Texas, Bantam (New York, NY), 2000.
The Devil Went down to Austin, Bantam (New York, NY), 2001.
Southtown, Bantam (New York, NY), 2004.
Mission Road, Bantam (New York, NY), 2005.
Rebel Island, Bantam Books (New York, NY), 2007.

OTHER

Cold Springs (adult novel), Bantam (New York, NY), 2003.
Thirty-nine Clues: The Maze of Bones (children's novel), Scholastic Press (New York, NY), 2008.

Contributor to periodicals, including *Mary Higgins Clark Mystery Magazine* and *Ellery Queen's Mystery Magazine.*

Adaptations

The Lightning Thief was adapted as an audiobook by Listening Library/Books on Tape, 2005, and optioned for film by Twentieth Century-Fox. The other titles in the "Percy Jackson and the Olympians" series have also been adapted for audiobook. Film rights to *Thirty-nine Clues: The Maze of Bones* were sold to Steven Spielberg and DreamWorks.

Sidelights

Known to adult readers as the award-winning author of the "Tres Navarre" mystery novels, Rick Riordan has also earned fans among teens who enjoy his "Percy Jackson and the Olympians" series of young-adult novels. In the *San Antonio Express-News,* Bryce Milligan reflected on the popularity of Riordan's teen fiction, wondering "how it is that Rick Riordan can consistently write novels that, although they begin with

Cover of Rick Riordan's young-adult fantasy novel The Lightning Thief, *featuring artwork by John Rocco.* (Illustration © 2008 by John Rocco. Reproduced by permission of Disney-Hyperion, an imprint of Disney Book Group LLC. All rights reserved.)

dire prophecies and end with narrow escapes from cosmic oblivion, are such delightful romps to read." The popularity of Riordan's "Percy Jackson" series may result from its unusual hero: Percy is actually Perseus, a hyperactive middle schooler who, as Milligan explained, also "happens to be the bona fide son of the Greek god Poseidon."

Riordan spent eight years teaching English in a San Francisco middle school before returning to his hometown of San Antonio in the summer of 1998. When his older son, Haley, turned eight years old, Riordan began retelling original Greek myths at the boy's request. "I'd taught mythology for years, so I began telling him myths for bedtime," the novelist explained to an interviewer for the Powells Web site. Haley had recently been diagnosed with ADHD and dyslexia, and Riordan was heartened to see the boy focus his attention on stories about the Greek gods. For fun, he decided to craft a modern retelling of the myths, focusing on a young boy named Percy, who also suffers from ADHD. Percy's quest is to retrieve the lightning bolt of Zeus from twenty-first century America. After Percy's saga played out, Haley asked his dad to write the story down, and this manuscript was the genesis of *The Lightning Thief.*

In *The Lighting Thief* Percy Jackson is a trouble-making middle schooler who is diagnosed with ADHD and dyslexia. Percy now discovers that the things that have always made him feel different from his classmates are actually due to the fact that he IS different: he is actually a demi-god and his ADHD hones his awareness during battle and dyslexia enables him to read ancient Greek. Pursued by monsters, Percy stays one step ahead of them and ultimately winds up at Camp Half-Blood, a summer camp for young demigods. Embracing his destiny, Percy becomes embroiled in a quest to find Zeus's lightning bolt before the Olympians declare war on Earth. Percy's friends Grover and Annabeth accompany him into the Underworld, where they discover that Kronos, the Titan who once ruled the Olympians, is plotting against all of Western civilization.

Diana Tixier Herald, reviewing the first "Percy Jackson and the Olympians" novel for *Booklist,* called *The Lightning Thief* a "clever mix of classic mythologies, contemporary teen characters, and an action-packed adventure." Despite the many allusions to ancient myths that Riordan incorporates into his tale, "one need not be an expert in Greek mythology to enjoy" the adventure, according to a *Kirkus Reviews* contributor, although the critic added that "those who are familiar . . . will have many an ah-ha moment." In *School Library Journal* Patricia D. Lothrop praised Riordan's story as "an adventure-quest with a hip edge," and in *Booklist* Chris Sherman called Percy "an appealing, but reluctant hero" and "the modernized gods are hilarious."

In *The Sea of Monsters* Percy searches for the Golden Fleece in order to save Thalia's tree, which generates the magical border protecting Camp Half-Blood. On his quest Percy is haunted by dreams in which his friend

Cover of Riordan's adventure-filled teen novel The Sea of Monsters, *featuring artwork by John Rocco.*

Grover is threatened. In other plot developments a homeless campmate turns out to be both a Cyclops and Percy's half-brother. "Percy has a sarcastically entertaining voice and a refreshing lack of hubris," wrote Anita L. Burkam in her *Horn Book* review of *The Sea of Monsters,* the critic describing the preteen as "wry, impatient, [and] academically hopeless, with the sort of cut-to-the-chase bluntness one would wish for in a hero." A *Kirkus Reviews* contributor wrote that "Percy's sardonic narration and derring-do will keep the pages turning." and a *Publishers Weekly* reviewer concluded that the novel's "cliffhanger [ending] leaves no question that Percy's high-stakes battle for Western Civilization will continue to surprise even himself."

Another year has passed and Percy is fourteen years old when he returns in *The Titan's Curse.* Not only is his good friend Annabeth missing, but Artemis, goddess of the hunt, has also vanished. Percy and Grover join the search party despite the promise of danger ahead and a disturbing prophecy that has been revealed by the Oracle. To make matters worse, the giant monsters of legend are growing restless; rising from their sleep after thousands of years, they now threaten Olympus with certain destruction if Percy and his friends do not stop them. Riordan's introduction of two new half-bloods, Nico and Bianca, further fleshes out Percy's fighting forces. Herald commented in *Booklist* that *The Titan's Curse* is an "exciting installment" that adds "even more depth to the characters," while a contributor for *Kirkus Reviews* maintained that Riordan's entertaining depiction of "the contests between the gods will have readers wondering how literature can be this fun." Alison Follos, writing for *School Library Journal,* dubbed *The Titan's Curse* "a winner of Olympic proportions and a surefire read-aloud."

Riordan's "Percy Jackson and the Olympians" series continues in *The Battle of the Labyrinth,* as Kronos once again plans to gain control of the underworld and all the evil forces dwelling there. Along with Annabeth and the mortal Rachel Elizabeth Dare, Percy journeys into the mysterious labyrinth in order to put a stop to Kronos's machinations. There the trio encounters all manner of adventures, confronting giants, the Sphinx, Daedalus, Hephaestus, Calypso, and finally Kronos himself. "Kids will devour Riordan's subtle satire of their world," noted Tim Wadham, the critic adding in his *School Library Journal* critique of the novel that "the cliff-hanger ending will leave readers breathless." A contributor for *Kirkus Reviews* praised Riordan's fourth "Percy Jackson" novel, writing that "the often-philosophical tale zips along with snappy dialogue, humor and thrilling action." Similar praise came from a *Publishers Weekly* reviewer who wrote that the author's "high-octane clashes with dark forces [are] . . . laced with hip humor and drama."

The "Percy Jackson" series ends in *The Last Olympian,* as soon-to-be-sixteen-year-old Percy gains virtual invulnerability in the river Styx and then joins Tyson, head of the Cyclops army, to lead Gordon, Annabeth, and many others into battle. As the war to save Mount Olympus from the Titan king Kronos wages on, the lines are drawn between satyrs, driads, cenaurs, tree nymphs, and other godlike Olympians and Kronos's rogue band of hellhounds, dragons, Hyperboreans, and Laestrygonian cannibals. Citing Riordan's "winning combination of high-voltage adventure and crackling wit" in her *Booklist* review, Carolyn Phelan added that *The Last Olympian* addresses serious themes and values. In *Horn Book* Burkham explained that "Percy and his friends have matured into battle-tested veterans," and romance has finally bloomed between Annabel and Riordan's teen hero. As "the fate of Western civilization" is decided, wrote a *Kirkus Reviews* writer, *The Last Olympian* treats readers to "a compelling conclusion to the saga" while hinting at the possibility of more adventures.

Riordan also addresses young-adult readers in *The Thirty-nine Clues: The Maze of Bones,* "a sensational mix of reading, online gaming, card-collecting, and even a grand-prize sweepstakes," according to *Booklist* contributor Ian Chipman. Designed by Riordan and encompassing a total of ten volumes (each by a different author) the novel's story arc involves the legacy of Grace Cahill, a member of the world's richest family. Grace promises to either give each of her descendant a million dollars or allow them the opportunity to participate in the search for a world-shattering secret by giving them one of thirty-nine clues. Eleven-year-old Dan and older sister Amy opt for the quest and, with the help of their teen au pair, find themselves on a path through their family's amazing history. *The Thirty-nine Clues* "ought to have as much appeal to parents as it does to kids," noted a *Publishers Weekly* contributor, the critic describing the work as "a rollicking good read." In *School Library Journal* Joy Fleishaker also praised the interactive work, writing that it "dazzles with suspense, plot twists, and snappy humor" while also drawing readers into an exploration of history.

Geared for adults, Riordan's "Tres Navarre" mysteries focuses on a San Antonio, Texas-based private detective with a Ph.D. in medieval studies, as well as a few degrees from the streets and an active interest in the martial art Tai Chi Chuan. Commenting in the *Chicago Tribune*, Dick Adler noted of the "Tres Navarre" books that "Riordan writes so well about the people and topography of his Texas hometown that he quickly marks the territory as his own." The author employs a unique "Tex-Mex" style in describing his south Texas settings. As a *Publishers Weekly* critic stated, his "dialogue is terse and the long first person descriptions show an unbeatable flair for detail. You can almost feel the summer storms rolling over south Texas."

While Riordan began his career writing for adults, creating fiction for a younger audience meshes nicely with his love of teaching. Along with visiting schools, he also produces a Web log where he updates readers on his books and discusses the writing process.

Biographical and Critical Sources

PERIODICALS

Booklist, December 1, 1999, Jenny McLarin, review of *The Last King of Texas,* p. 688; May 1, 2001, Jenny McLarin, review of *The Devil Went down to Austin,* p. 1640; March 15, 2003, Connie Fletcher, review of *Cold Springs,* p. 1279; April 15, 2004, Connie Fletcher, review of *Southtown,* p. 1428; May 1, 2005, Frank Sennett, review of *Mission Road,* p. 1534; September 15, 2005, Chris Sherman, review of *The Lightning Thief,* p. 59; July 1, 2006, Diana Tixier Herald, review of *The Sea of Monsters,* p. 52; August, 2007, Steve Glassman, review of *Rebel Island,* p. 48; October 15, 2008, Ian Chipman, review of *Thirty-nine Clues: The Maze of Bones,* p. 39; May 15, 2009, Carolyn Phelan, review of *The Last Olympian,* p. 55.

Bookseller, August 19, 2005, review of *The Lightning Thief.*

Chronicle, April, 2005, Mike Jones, review of *The Lightning Thief,* p. 19.

Guardian (London, England), June 9, 2007, Philip Ardagh, review of *The Titan's Curse.*

Horn Book, July-August, 2005, Anita L. Burkam, review of *The Lightning Thief,* p. 479; May-June, 2006, Anita L. Burkam, review of *The Sea of Monsters,* p. 326; May-June, 2007, Anita L. Burkam, review of *The Titan's Curse,* p. 290; July-August, 2008, Anita L. Burkam, review of *The Battle of the Labyrinth,* p. 456; July-August, 2009, Anita L. Burkham, review of *The Last Olympian,* p. 430.

Kirkus Reviews, April 1, 2003, review of *Cold Springs,* p. 503; May 15, 2005, review of *Mission Road,* p. 566; June 15, 2005, review of *The Lightning Thief,* p. 690; April 1, 2006, review of *The Sea of Monsters,* p. 355;; April 1, 2007, review of *The Titan's Curse,*; April 1, 2008, review of *The Battle of the Labyrinth;* September 1, 2008, review of *Thirty-nine Clues;* May 15, 2009, review of *The Last Olympian.*

Kliatt, September, 2006, Heather Rader, review of *The Lightning Thief,* p. 34; March, 2006, Paula Rohrlick, review of *The Sea of Monsters,* p. 16.

Riordan's "Percy Jackson" series includes **The Battle of the Labyrinth,** *featuring cover art by John Rocco.* (Illustration © 2008 by John Rocco. © 2008 by Rick Riordan. Reproduced by permission of Disney-Hyperion, an imprint of Disney Book Group, LLC. All rights reserved.)

Library Journal, December, 1999, Craig L. Shufelt, review of *The Last King of Texas,* p. 188; May 1, 2001, Rex Klett, review of *The Devil Went down to Austin,* p. 129; May 15, 2003, Ken St. Andre, review of *Cold Springs,* p. 132.

New York Times Book Review, November 13, 2005, Polly Schulman, "Harry Who?," p. 42.

Publishers Weekly, December 20, 1999, review of *The Last King of Texas,* p. 58; April 30, 2001, review of *The Devil Went down to Austin,* p. 59; April 7, 2003, review of *Cold Springs,* p. 45; April 5, 2004, review of *Southtown,* p. 44; May 16, 2005, review of *Mission Road,* p. 40; July 18, 2005, review of *The Lightning Thief,* p. 207; April 24, 2006, review of *The Sea of Monsters,* p. 61; June 18, 2007, review of *Rebel Island,* p. 34; April 14, 2008, review of *The Battle of the Labyrinth,* p. 55; May 18, 2009, review of *The Last Olympian,* p. 55.

San Antonio Express-News, May 4, 2008, Bryce Milligan, review of *The Battle of the Labyrinth.*

School Library Journal, August, 2005, Patricia D. Lothrop, review of *The Lightning Thief,* p. 134; May, 2006, Kathleen Isaacs, review of *The Sea of Monsters,* p. 135; May 1, 2007, Alison Follos, review of *The Titan's Curse,* p. 142; May, 2008, Tim Wadham, review of *The Battle of the Labyrinth,* p. 138; September 22, 2008, review of *Thirty-nine Clues,* p. 58; November, 2008, Joy Fleishhacker, review of *The Thirty-nine Clues,* p. 136; June, 2009, review of *The Olympian,* p. 136.

Texas Monthly, July, 2005, Mike Shea, review of *Mission Road,* p. 64; June, 2007, "Rick Riordan," p. 60.

Times Educational Supplement, July 21, 2006, Fiona Lafferty, "Inspired by Mount Olympus," p. 29.

Voice of Youth Advocates, August, 2005, Dave Goodale, review of *The Lightning Thief,* p. 237.

ONLINE

Cynsations Web log, http://cynthialeitichsmith.blogspot.com/ (December 27, 2005), Cynthia Leitich Smith, interview with Riordan.

Percy Jackson Web site, http://www.percyjackson.co.uk/ (January 13, 2009).

Powells Web site, http://www.powells.com/ (November 3, 2006), interview with Riordan.

Rick Riordan Home Page, http://www.rickriordan.com (December 1, 2009).

Rick Riordan Web log, http://rickriordan.blogspot.com (December 1, 2009).

Scholastic Web site, http://www2.scholastic.com/ (December 1, 2009), "Rick Riordan."

Write Away Web site, http://www.writeaway.org.uk/ (December 1, 2009), Nikki Gamble, interview with Riordan.*

ROSALER, Maxine

Personal
Female.

Addresses
Home—New York, NY.

Career
Freelance writer.

Writings

JUVENILE NONFICTION

Bionics, Blackbirch Press (San Diego, CA), 2003.
Hamas: Palestinian Terrorists, Rosen (New York, NY), 2003.
A Timeline of the First Continental Congress, Rosen (New York, NY), 2004.
Botulism, Rosen (New York, NY), 2004.
Coping with Asperger Syndrome, Rosen (New York, NY), 2004.
Listeriosis, Rosen (New York, NY), 2004.
Measles, Rosen (New York, NY), 2005.
The Department of Agriculture, Rosen (New York, NY), 2006.
Cystic Fibrosis, Rosen (New York, NY), 2007.
(With Philip Margulies) *The Devil on Trial: Witches, Anarchists, Atheists, Communists, and Terrorists in America's Courtrooms,* Houghton Mifflin (Boston, MA), 2008.

Biographical and Critical Sources

PERIODICALS

Booklist, October 15, 2003, John Peters, review of *Hamas: Palestinian Terrorists,* p. 424; March 1, 2005, Carolyn Phelan, review of *Coping with Asperger Syndrome,* p. 1151; November 15, 2008, Ilene Cooper, review of *The Devil on Trial: Witches, Anarchists, Atheists, Communists, and Terrorists in America's Courtrooms,* p. 44.

School Library Journal, March, 2004, Eva Elizabeth VonAncken, review of *Bionics,* p. 241; August, 2004, Christine A. Moesch, review of *Botulism,* p. 137; December, 2004, Lynn Evarts, review of *Coping with Asperger Syndrome,* p. 169; March, 2005, Deanna Romriell, review of *A Timeline of the First Constitutional Congress,* p. 193; February, 2007, Caroline Geck, review of *Cystic Fibrosis,* p. 143; September, 2008, Emma Burkhart, review of *The Devil on Trial,* p. 207.*

S

SALMIERI, Daniel 1983-

Personal
Born 1983.

Addresses
Home—Brooklyn, NY. *Agent*—Rebecca Sherman, Writer's House, 21 W. 26th St., New York, NY 10010. *E-mail*—daniel@danielsalmieri.com.

Career
Illustrator and artist.

Awards, Honors
Borders New Voices Award, and Children's Choice Book Award nomination, both 2009, both for *Those Darn Squirrels!* by Adam Rubin.

Illustrator
Adam Rubin, *Those Darn Squirrels!,* Clarion Books (New York, NY), 2008.
Amy Gibson, *Around the World on Eighty Legs (More or Less),* Scholastic (New York, NY), 2010.
Adam Rubin, *Those Darn Squirrels and the Cat Next Door,* Clarion Books (New York, NY), 2011.
Noah Lukeman, *Capitol City,* Scholastic (New York, NY), 2011.

Biographical and Critical Sources

PERIODICALS

Children's Bookwatch, September, 2008, review of *Those Darn Squirrels!*
Kirkus Reviews, August 15, 2008, review of *Those Darn Squirrels!*
School Library Journal, October, 2008, Susan Weitz, review of *Those Darn Squirrels!,* p. 121.

ONLINE

David Salmieri Home Page, http://www.danielsalmieri. com (November 21, 2009).*

* * *

SCHMID, Susan Maupin

Personal
Married; children: two daughters. *Education:* Earned college degree (speech and theatre).

Addresses
Home—IA.

Career
Writer.

Writings

Lost Time, Philomel Books (New York, NY), 2008.

Sidelights
In her science-fiction novel *Lost Time,* Susan Maupin Schmid tells a story inspired by Schmid's interest in history and archaeology. She takes readers to Lindos, a planet where only a handful of humans live. Twelve-year-old Violynne Vivant lives there with her archeologist parents, a couple hunting for artifacts left on Lindos by the Croon Empire a thousand years before. Violynne's parents have been missing for a year, however, and now the preteen is worried that the Arbiter of Lyrling, ruler of Lindos, may be involved in their disappearance. After someone breaks into the Vivant family home and steals her father's violin, the girl senses a threat and goes into hiding, continuing the search for her parents while avoiding the Arbiter's henchmen.

In *Booklist* Shelle Rosenfeld enjoyed Schmid's heroine, a preteen the critic described as "engaging, . . . vulnerable and courageous" as well as self-reliant. "The concept of *Lost Time* is a good one: combining a suspenseful mystery with an otherworldly science-fiction tale," wrote Saleena L. Davidson in *School Library Journal*, the critic nonetheless noting that Schmid's conclusion "seems rushed." *Lost Time* marked a "promising" debut, noted a *Kirkus Reviews* writer, the critic adding that a sequel by Schmid would be welcome because "well-crafted interstellar tales for [preteens] . . . are rare."

Biographical and Critical Sources

PERIODICALS

Booklist, May 15, 2008, Shelle Rosenfeld, review of *Lost Time,* p. 59.
Kirkus Reviews, April 15, 2008, review of *Lost Time.*
School Library Journal, September, 2008, Saleena L. Davidson, review of *Lost Time,* p. 193.*

Cover of Susan Maupin Schmid's young-adult novel Lost Time, *featuring artwork by Steve Stone.* (Illustration © 2008 by Steve Stone. Reproduced by permission of Philomel Books, a division of Penguin Putnam Books for Young Readers.)

SCHULMAN, Janet 1933-

Personal

Born September 16, 1933, in Pittsburgh, PA; daughter of Albert C. (in insurance) and Edith Schuetz; married Lester M. Schulman (a writer and editor), May 19, 1957; children: Nicole. *Education:* Antioch College, B.A., 1956. *Hobbies and other interests:* Tennis.

Addresses

Home—New York, NY. *Office*—Random House, 1540 Broadway, New York, NY 10036.

Career

Writer and publishing company executive. Macmillan Publishing Co., Inc., New York, NY, member of advertising staff, beginning c. 1961, then vice president and juvenile marketing manager, 1965-74; Random House, Inc., New York, NY, manager, 1978, director of library marketing, 1978-80, vice president and editor-in-chief of children's books, beginning 1980, vice president and editor-in-chief of Knopf and Pantheon children's books, beginning 1983, associate publisher, editor-in-chief, and divisional vice president of Books for Young Readers imprint, 1987, publisher and divisional vice president of Knopf, Random House, and Crown juvenile imprints, beginning 1988, editor-at-large of Random House juvenile division, beginning 1994. Worked in advertising in New Orleans, LA, c. 1950s. Member of New York publishing industry committees, including Freedom-to-Read committee, 1980-84, and M.S. Read-a-Thon committee, 1984; Children's Book Council, member of board of directors and president, 1983; consultant to juvenile publishers.

Member

American Library Association.

Writings

FOR CHILDREN

The Big Hello, Greenwillow Press (New York, NY), 1976.
Jack the Bum and the Halloween Handout, Greenwillow Press (New York, NY), 1977.
Jack the Bum and the Haunted House, Greenwillow Press (New York, NY), 1977.
Jenny and the Tennis Nut, Greenwillow Press (New York, NY), 1978.
Jack the Bum and the UFO, Greenwillow Press (New York, NY), 1978.
Camp Kee Wee's Secret Weapon, Greenwillow Press (New York, NY), 1979.
The Great Big Dummy, Greenwillow Press (New York, NY), 1979.
(Adaptor) *The Nutcracker,* Dutton (New York, NY), 1979, illustrated by Renée Graef, HarperCollins (New York, NY), 1999.

(Selector) *The Twentieth-Century Children's Book Treasury: Celebrated Picture Books and Stories to Read Aloud,* Knopf (New York, NY), 1998.

(Adaptor) Felix Salten, *Bambi,* illustrated by Steve Johnson and Lou Fancher, Atheneum (New York, NY), 1999.

(Selector) *You Read to Me and I'll Read to You: Twentieth-Century Stories to Share,* Knopf (New York, NY), 2001.

Countdown to Spring! An Animal Counting Book, illustrated by Meilo So, Knopf (New York, NY), 2002.

A Bunny for All Seasons, illustrated by Meilo So, Knopf (New York, NY), 2003.

(Reteller) *Sergei Prokofiev's Peter and the Wolf* (with CD), illustrated by Peter Malone, Knopf (New York, NY), 2004.

(Editor) *Your Favorite Seuss: Thirteen Stories Written and Illustrated by Dr. Seuss,* Random House Children's Books (New York, NY), 2004.

Ten Trick-or-Treaters: A Halloween Counting Book, illustrated by Linda Davick, Knopf (New York, NY), 2005.

Pale Male: Citizen Hawk of New York City, illustrated by Meilo So, Knopf (New York, NY), 2008.

Ten Trim-the-Tree'ers: A Christmas Counting Book, illustrated by Linda Davick, Knopf (New York, NY), 2010.

Abridger of books, including the "Chronicles of Narnia" series by C.S. Lewis, and other literary classics, for Caedmon Records.

Adaptations

Bambi was recorded on audiocassette by Audio Bookshelf, 2002.

Sidelights

During her many years working in the publishing industry, Janet Schulman has influenced the quality and character of contemporary children's literature. Beginning her career at Macmillan in New York City during the 1960s, she developed a love of children's books while updating jacket copy for a new edition of British author C.S. Lewis's classic "Narnia" books. "When I read the books I thought, 'Wow, if this is what children's literature is like, this is where I want to be,'" she recalled in an interview posted on the Random House Web site. Schulman has gone on to hold executive positions at Random House, working with authors Theodor Geisel ("Dr. Seuss"), Marc Brown, Jack Prelutsky, and Stan and Jan Berenstain as an editor while also creating original stories such as *The Big Hello, Countdown to Spring! An Animal Counting Book,* and *Bunny for All Seasons.*

Born in 1933, Schulman grew up in the shadow of the Great Depression. As she once recalled, "My mother literally counted pennies to put food on the table for us." When the United States entered World War II, her older siblings joined the military, which forced Schulman to "keep a wary eye on reality." Both these experiences shaped the kinds of stories she would later write. "I try to show children operating not in a vacuum but surrounded by circumstances of reality which do affect their lives," she explained. "In *The Big Hello* a little girl moves to California because her father has gone there to find a new job. In *Camp Kee Wee's Secret Weapon* Jill has to go to summer camp because her mother has just gotten a job and Jill is too young to stay home alone during the day. In *Jenny and the Tennis Nut* Jenny's father wants to see Jenny take up tennis enthusiastically because tennis is his game."

Schulman views her editorship of works such as *The Twentieth-Century Children's Book Treasury: Celebrated Picture Books and Stories to Read Aloud, You Read to Me and I'll Read to You: Stories to Share from the Twentieth Century,* and *Your Favorite Seuss: Thirteen Stories Written and Illustrated by Dr. Seuss* as providing a service to parents of preschoolers who would otherwise be lost in a children's book department. *The Twentieth-Century Children's Book Treasury* includes forty-four picture books, among them the twentieth-century classics *Madeline, Curious George, Goodnight Moon, Stellaluna, Millions of Cats,* and *Make Way for Ducklings.* Each story is accompanied by selected illustrations from its original publication, making the volume valuable for its collection of artwork by popular illustrators James Marshall, Maurice Sendak, and Quentin Blake, although *Horn Book* reviewer Roger Sutton bemoaned the fact that many illustrations in the book "have gone missing," "making hash out of some selections." Commenting on her vision for the anthology, Schulman noted on the Kids@Random Web site that she hopes *The Twentieth-Century Children's Book Treasury* "will change the tide for many children and send them on the path to a lifelong love of books and reading. But most of all, I hope it will bring parents and children closer together."

In addition to anthologies, Schulman has also adapted several major childhood classics. Felix Salten's 1923 story *Bambi: A Life in the Woods* was popularized several decades later in an animated film directed by Walt Disney. An Austrian Jew, Salten wrote his novel—originally intended for adults—as a response to the horrors of World War I, and Schulman began contemplating adapting the original book for young readers as early as 1985. In her adaptation of *Bambi,* which is illustrated by Steve Johnson and Lou Fancher, she worked hard to preserve the language of Salten's original while condensing the text for younger readers. As she told *Publishers Weekly* contributor Cindi di Marzo, "I reread the novel a number of times and then I went through and highlighted the dialogue and poignant sentences Salten had written. It was easy for me to work with the text because Salten's language is so poetic."

While *School Library Journal* reviewer Arwen Marshall wrote of *Bambi* that "the hard realities of life in the wild are still evident" in Schulman's adaptation, "and some of the events may be disturbing to younger, more sensitive children," *New York Times Book Review* contributor Elizabeth Spires cited the book for preserving

Janet Schulman joins with artist Linda Davick to tell a holiday counting story in **Ten Trick-or-Treaters.** (Illustration copyright © 2005 by Linda Davick. Used by permission of Alfred A. Knopf, an imprint of Random House Children's Books, a division of Random House, Inc.)

Salten's "mystical, exultant evocation of nature, and its unwavering depiction of savage human nature." Noting that the retelling "restores the depth of Bambi's character," a *Publishers Weekly* contributor added that Schulman expresses "the heart of Salten's lessons, namely, the importance of thinking for oneself and of acknowledging that no living creature is all-powerful."

Schulman adapts another childhood classic in *Sergei Prokofiev's Peter and the Wolf,* a picture book illustrated by Peter Malone. Although Prokofiev's story was originally designed to be told by the instruments of a symphony orchestra, Schulman's version uses words and includes a CD with a musical version performed by the Cincinnati, Ohio, Pops orchestra. The author "softens the traditional text" by allowing both the ravenous wolf (a French horn) and the ill-fated duck (oboe) to go free, wrote a *Publishers Weekly* contributor, the critic adding that "Malone's . . . jewel-toned paintings will give [readers] pause." In *School Library Journal,* Wendy Lukehart also praised the book's Slavic-styled art but noted that Prokofiev purists "will have issues" with Schulman's decision to include an ending in which "the impact of the drama is considerably lessened." Also citing Shulman's retelling as a "kinder, gentler version" of the children's classic, Rebecca Boggs Roberts added in the *New York Times Book Review* that *Sergei Prokofiev's Peter and the Wolf* is "engaging" and "delightful."

While the bulk of Schulman's work has involved editing or adapting texts by others, she has also produced several original stories for children. Featuring artwork by Meilo So, *A Bunny for All Seasons* was praised by a *Kirkus Reviews* writer as a "charming romp" featuring "brilliant watercolors [that] bounce off the page." In Schulman's story, a brown rabbit spends the summer feasting on the bounty growing in a nearby garden, and then plays among the pumpkins in the fall before curling up for a long winter's nap. The *Kirkus Reviews* writer cited the book's "comforting, well-paced" story, and in *Publishers Weekly* a critic described the author's prose as "economical and straight-forward." *A Bunny for All Seasons* serves as "a delightful educational story," according to Andrea Tarr in *School Library Journal,* the critic adding that So's soft-edged watercolor images "are as lovely as [Schulman's] . . . understated" tale.

Schulman focuses her fiction close to home In *Pale Male: Citizen Hawk of New York City,* a picture book that again teams her with So. The volume is one of several works for children that focus on the red-tailed hawk that nested on an upper ledge of an upscale apartment building on New York City's Fifth Avenue. From his lofty perch, Pale Male raised over twenty chicks with the help of a succession of female nest mates, and his efforts to hunt for the pigeons, squirrels, or other urban wildlife that fed his family sometimes put him at great risk. Recommending Schulman's book as the best of the genre, Joanna Rudge Long added in *Horn Book* that the author's "admirably easygoing and lucid style" pairs well with art that impresses with its "impressionistic virtuosity." In *Booklist* Gillian Engberg also praised

Schulman's true story of a hawk that made Manhattan its home is captured in Meilo So's art for Pale Male. (Illustration copyright © 2008 by Meilo So. Used by permission of Alfred A. Knopf, an imprint of Random House Children's Books, a division of Random House, Inc.)

So's "stunning watercolor-and-pencil" illustrations, calling *Pale Male* a "leisurely, engaging story" that "will ignite children's curiosity."

Schulman credits her daughter, Nicole, for helping to shape her career as a children's writer. "I doubt if I would have written the kinds of stories I write if I had not started just at the time Nicole was in the first grade," she once admitted to *SATA.* "I wanted to write stories for her, stories she could read and would like. None of my stories are based directly on anything that has happened in our family, but all of them have grown or been inspired by my daily life with Nicole."

Biographical and Critical Sources

PERIODICALS

Booklist, October 15, 1998, Hazel Rochman, review of *The Twentieth-Century Children's Book Treasury: Celebrated Picture Books and Stories to Read Aloud,* p. 428; January 1, 2002, Gillian Engberg, review of *Countdown to Spring! An Animal Counting Book,* p. 861; February 15, 2008, Gillian Engberg, review of *Pale Male: Citizen Hawk of New York City,* p. 92.

Horn Book, November, 1998, Roger Sutton, review of *The Twentieth-Century Children's Book Treasury,* pp. 717-718; March-April, 2008, Joanna Rudge Long, review of *Pale Male,* p. 230.

Kirkus Reviews, January 1, 2002, review of *Countdown to Spring!,* p. 50; December 1, 2002, review of *A Bunny for All Seasons,* p. 1773; August 1, 2005, review of *Ten Trick-or-Treaters: A Halloween Counting Book,* p. 858.

Los Angeles Times Book Review, December 6, 1998, Karla Kuskin, review of *The Twentieth-Century Children's Book Treasury,* p. 5.

New York Times Book Review, November 21, 1999, Elizabeth Spires, review of *Bambi,* p. 5; April 21, 2002, review of *Countdown to Spring!,* p. 24; November 14, 2004, Rebecca Boggs Roberts, review of *Sergei Prokofiev's Peter and the Wolf,* p. 42; June 1, 2008, John Schwartz, review of *Pale Male,* p. 27.

Publishers Weekly, September 21, 1998, review of *The Twentieth-Century Children's Book Treasury,* p. 101; September 27, 1999, review of *The Nutcracker,* p. 54; October 18, 1999, review of *Bambi,* p. 80; October 25, 1999, Cindi di Marzo, "A New Look for Bambi," p. 29; August 6, 2001, review of *You Read to Me and I'll Read to You,* p. 89; October 1, 2001, Sally Lodge, "Making the Transition," p. 28; December 24, 2001, review of *Countdown to Spring!,* p. 62; November 25, 2002, review of *A Bunny for All Seasons,* p. 65; November 8, 2004, review of *Sergei Prokofiev's Peter and the Wolf,* p. 54; January 28, 2008, review of *Pale Male,* p. 68.

School Library Journal, December, 1998, Margaret Bush, review of *The Twentieth-Century Children's Book Treasury,* pp. 91-92; October, 1999, Arwen Marshall, review of *Bambi,* p. 126, and Lisa Falk, review of *The Nutcracker,* p. 68; December, 2001, Maryann H. Owen, review of *You Read to Me and I'll Read to You,* p. 110; January, 2002, Melinda Piehler, review of *Countdown to Spring!,* p. 124; February, 2003, Andrea Tarr, review of *A Bunny for All Seasons,* p. 122; October, 2004, Wendy Lukehart, review of *Sergei Prokofiev's Peter and the Wolf,* p. 128; August, 2005, Marge Loch-Wouters, review of *Ten Trick-or-Treaters,* p. 106; January, 2008, Ellen Fader, review of *Pale Male,* p. 111.

ONLINE

January Online, http://januarymagazine.com/ (March 11, 2008), review of *Pale Male.*

Random House Web site, http://www.randomhouse.com/kids/ (November 15, 2009), "Janet Schulman."*

*   *   *

SLEATOR, William 1945-
(William Warner Sleator, III)

Personal

Surname pronounced "*Slay*-tir"; born February 13, 1945, in Havre de Grace, MD; son of William Warner, Jr. (a physiologist and professor) and Esther (a physician) Sleator. *Education:* Harvard University, B.A., 1967; studied musical composition in London, England, 1967-68. *Politics:* "Independent."

Addresses

Home—Boston, MA; Thailand. *Agent*—Russel Galen, Scovil, Galen, Ghosh Literary Agency, 276 5th Ave., Ste. 708, New York, NY 10001. *E-mail*—wsleator@gmail.com

Career

Author, composer, and musician. Royal Ballet School, London, England, accompanist, 1967-68; Rambert School, London, accompanist, 1967-68; Boston Ballet Company, Boston, MA, rehearsal pianist, 1974-83; freelance writer, 1983—. Composer of scores for professional ballets and amateur films and plays.

Awards, Honors

Bread Loaf Writers' Conference fellowship, 1969; *Boston Globe/Horn Book* Award for Illustration honor designation, Caldecott Medal Honor Book designation, and American Library Association (ALA), both 1971, and American Book Award for Best Paperback Picture Book, 1981, all for *The Angry Moon;* Children's Book of the Year Award, Child Study Association of America, 1972, and Notable Book citation, ALA, both for *Blackbriar;* Best Books for Young Adults citation, ALA,

William Sleator (Photograph by Andrew Biggs. Reproduced by permission.)

1974, for *House of Stairs,* 1984, for *Interstellar Pig,* 1985, for *Singularity,* 1987, for *The Boy Who Reversed Himself;* Children's Choice Award, International Reading Association/Children's Book Council, 1979, and CRABbery Award honor book designation, Maryland Library System, 1980, both for *Into the Dream;* Notable Book citation, ALA, and Honor List citation, *Horn Book* magazine, both 1984, both for *Interstellar Pig;* Best Book of the Year designation, *School Library Journal,* 1981, for *The Green Futures of Tycho,* 1983, for *Fingers,* 1984, for *Interstellar Pig;* Golden Pen Award, Spokane, WA, Public Library, 1984, 1985; Notable Book selection, and Best Book for Young Adults designation, both ALA, both 1993, both for *Oddballs.*

Writings

FOR CHILDREN

(Reteller) *The Angry Moon,* illustrated by Blair Lent, Little, Brown (Boston, MA), 1970.

Blackbriar, illustrated by Blair Lent, Dutton (New York, NY), 1972, reprinted, Marshall Cavendish (New York, NY), 2009.

Run, Dutton (New York, NY), 1973.

House of Stairs, Dutton (New York, NY), 1974.

Among the Dolls, illustrated by Trina Schart Hyman, Dutton (New York, NY), 1975.

Into the Dream, illustrated by Ruth Sanderson, Dutton (New York, NY), 1979.

Once, Said Darlene, illustrated by Steven Kellogg, Dutton (New York, NY), 1979.

The Green Futures of Tycho, Dutton (New York, NY), 1981.

That's Silly (easy reader), illustrated by Lawrence DiFiori, Dutton (New York, NY), 1981.

Fingers, Atheneum (New York, NY), 1983.

Interstellar Pig, Dutton (New York, NY), 1984.

Singularity, Dutton (New York, NY), 1985.

The Boy Who Reversed Himself, Dutton (New York, NY), 1986.

The Duplicate, Dutton (New York, NY), 1988.

Strange Attractors, Dutton (New York, NY), 1990.

The Spirit House, Dutton (New York, NY), 1991.

Oddballs: Stories (semi-fictionalized autobiography), Dutton (New York, NY), 1993.

Others See Us, Dutton (New York, NY), 1993.

Dangerous Wishes (sequel to *The Spirit House*), Dutton (New York, NY), 1995.

The Night the Heads Came, Dutton (New York, NY), 1996.

The Beasties, Dutton (New York, NY), 1997.

The Boxes, Dutton (New York, NY), 1998.

Rewind, Dutton (New York, NY), 1999.

Boltzmon!, Dutton (New York, NY), 1999.

Into the Dream, Puffin (New York, NY), 2000.

Marco's Millions, Dutton (New York, NY), 2001.

Parasite Pig, Dutton (New York, NY), 2002.

The Boy Who Couldn't Die, Amulet Books (New York, NY), 2004.

The Last Universe, Amulet Books (New York, NY), 2005.

Hell Phone, Amulet Books (New York, NY), 2006.

Test, Amulet Books (New York, NY), 2008.

Contributor of short stories to anthologies, including *Am I Blue? Coming out from the Silence,* edited by Marion Dane Bauer, and *Things That Go Bump in the Night,* edited by Jane Yolen and Martin H. Greenberg.

OTHER

(With William H. Redd) *Take Charge: A Personal Guide to Behavior Modification* (adult nonfiction), Random House (New York, NY), 1977.

Adaptations

The Angry Moon was adapted for audiocassette by Read-Along-House; *Interstellar Pig* was adapted for audiocassette by Listening Library, 1987.

Sidelights

A popular and prolific writer of fiction for children and young adults, William Sleator is regarded as a particularly original and imaginative author whose works use the genres of fantasy, mystery, and science fiction to explore personal relationships and growth. Sleator incorporates current scientific theories, suspense, and the su-

pernatural in his books, which challenge readers to take active roles in the stories while allowing them to resonate with the feelings and experiences of his characters. Depicting boys and girls who are often reluctant heroes, Sleator takes his characters from their everyday lives into confrontations with unusual, even unnerving situations. His protagonists encounter alien beings, doppelgangers, ESP, telepathy, telekinesis, black holes, evil spirits, malevolent dolls, weird scientific experiments, time travel into the past and the future, and other strange phenomena. In addition, they must learn to deal with brothers and sisters—sibling rivalry is a consistent theme—as well as with parents and peers. Through their physical and emotional journeys, the young people in Sleator's stories discover strength and confidence within themselves while developing a greater understanding of life in general. Characteristically, Sleator ends his books with the situations seemingly resolved and his characters secure; however, he is also fond of including surprising twists, hinting that perhaps things are not quite so rosy as readers may think.

Cover of Sleator's quirky sci-fi novel **Interstellar Pig,** *featuring artwork by Broeck Steadman.* (Illustration © 1995 by Broeck Steadman. Reproduced by permission of Puffin Books, a division of Penguin Putnam Books for Young Readers in the U.S. In the U.K. by Steadman Broeck.)

As a writer, Sleator is often credited for setting a darkly humorous tone. Although many of his books are scary, he often laces suspense with tongue-in-cheek humor. The author is praised as a skilled creator of plot and character who is able to blend the real with the surreal. In addition, Sleator has been lauded for his insight into human nature, especially in the area of family relationships, and for creating fully realized worlds in haunting, thought-provoking page-turners. Although his books are often considered demanding and disturbing, and his use of ambiguous endings is sometimes questioned, he is generally considered a talented author of rich, fascinating books that appeal to young readers on several levels. *School Library Journal* contributor David Gale commented on the author's "singular talent for writing astonishing science fiction novels," while in *Horn Book* Roger Sutton dubbed Sleator a "master of the juvenile creepy-crawly." Writing in *English Journal*, Margaret L. Daggett stated: "Sleator succeeds with adolescents because he blends enough scientific realities with supernatural possibilities to tantalize the mind and the imagination. Readers feel refreshed after the intellectual and emotional challenges in Sleator's novels. . . . He sets us in a reality and helps us stretch our imaginations."

Born in Havre de Grace, Maryland, Sleator is the eldest son of William Warner Sleator, Jr., a physiologist and professor, and Esther Sleator, a physician. He and his siblings—brothers Daniel and Tycho and sister Vicky—grew up in University City, Missouri, a predominantly Jewish suburb of St. Louis, where the family moved after the author's father was hired by the University of St. Louis. "My parents," Sleator once explained, "always encouraged us to be whoever we were." Sleator began studying the piano at the age of six and at around the same time he wrote his first story. In high school, he continued writing poems and stories and composing music; he also learned to play the cello. "I wasn't a complete nerd," the author was quick to explain. "I rebelled with drugs, sex—all the things every kid goes through. My parents weren't happy about it, but they were looser about it than most."

In his book *Oddballs: Stories,* Sleator shares ten short autobiographical and semi-autobiographical vignettes that provide fans with a window into his childhood and adolescence. The stories show four creative, talented children growing up in a household run by free-thinking parents who provide minimal supervision. The book is credited with depicting how, through all of their sibling rivalry and joke-playing, the Sleator children developed individuality, confidence, and independence. Writing in *Kirkus Reviews,* a critic favorably commented on the author's "splendid sense of comic timing" in *Oddballs,* as well as his "vivid characterizations." Betsy Hearne, writing in *Bulletin of the Center for Children's Books,* added that "Sleator evidently thrived without pause on his permissive parents' steady encouragement to violate social taboos."

Cover of Sleator's young-adult novel The Boxes, *featuring cover art by Victor Lee.* (Illustration copyright © 1998 by Victor Lee. Used by permission of Dutton, a division of Penguin Putnam Books for Young Readers.)

After high school, Sleator attended Harvard University, where he intended to study musical composition. However, when he found the music program to be too restrictive, he become an English major, continuing to write music for student plays and films. After receiving his bachelor's degree in 1967, he moved to London, England, where he studied musical composition for a year while working as a pianist at the Royal Ballet School and the Rambert School. During this period, he lived in the middle of a forest in an ancient cottage that had once been a "pesthouse" for people with smallpox. He shared the cottage with his landlady, a sixty-ish woman who treated the young American as a son. This experience would become the subject of Sleator's young-adult novel *Blackbriar.*

In *Blackbriar,* which is illustrated by Sleator's friend Blair Lent, teenager Danny struggles for independence from his middle-aged guardian, Philippa, with whom he shares a haunted, isolated cottage in the English countryside. Danny and Philippa are shunned by the locals because of the perception that they are linked to Satanism. After Philippa and her cat are kidnapped, Danny and his friend Lark search for her. In the process, Danny discovers a lot about himself and learns the secret of the cottage, which functioned as a pesthouse during a seventeenth-century outbreak of the bubonic plague. As a critic in *Kirkus Reviews* advised readers tackling *Blackbriar:* "Bolt the cellar door, watch your cat closely for personality changes, and follow him—vicariously." Although Ashley Darlington Grayson, writing in *Fantasy Review,* described Danny as "thick as a post," Paul Heins concluded in *Horn Book* that "the effectiveness of the story lies in its characterization and in its [author's] narrative skill."

Sleator also collaborated with Lent on the picture book *The Angry Moon,* which became his first published book. A retelling of a Tlingit Indian legend, *The Angry Moon* describes how a girl named Lapwinsa is taken away by the moon after she laughs at it. Her friend, the boy Lupan, rescues Lapwinsa by making a ladder out of arrows and climbing into the sky. A reviewer in *Publishers Weekly* noted that "books like *The Angry Moon* appear only once in a blue moon." Lent "has topped himself with this one," the critic added, "perhaps because William Sleator gave him such a strong story to illustrate." Writing in *School Library Journal,* Ann D. Schweibish deemed *The Angry Moon* a "highly successful adaptation and visualization" of the traditional tale.

In 1974, Sleator began working as a rehearsal pianist for the Boston Ballet while continuing to write fiction. With the dancers, he toured the United States and Europe and wrote three ballets that were performed by the company. He also published *House of Stairs,* a young-adult novel set in a huge room that contains a labyrinthine maze of stairways leading nowhere. Sleator's story outlines how five orphaned sixteen year olds learn to survive in this world without walls, ceilings, or floors. The young people, who eat only if they perform dance-like rituals in front of a machine, eventually realize that they are part of a stimulus/response experiment in which food is dispensed when the subjects display hostile behavior toward each other. When two of the protagonists refuse to perform the cruel acts that are required to obtain food, the scientists end the experiment. Compared by critics to such works as *Brave New World* and *Lord of the Flies, House of Stairs* was called "brilliant, [and] bone-chilling" by a reviewer in *Publishers Weekly.* Sleator's "forceful sci fi based on Skinnerian precepts . . . will have readers hanging by the skin of their teeth," according to *School Library Journal* reviewer Pamela D. Pollack, and in *Thursday's Child: Trends and Patterns in Contemporary Children's Literature,* Sheila A. Egoff described the plot of *House of Stairs* as "one of the most brutal in science fiction, all the more sickeningly compelling because of its finely controlled, stark writing."

Sleator considers his middle-grade novel *The Green Futures of Tycho* to be a watershed book in his career. While working in his family's garden, eleven-year-old Tycho finds a strange silver egg that was buried by aliens thousands of years before. The egg, a time-travel

device, allows the preteen to go into both the past and the future. At first, Tycho uses his abilities to tease his four brothers and sister. He then meets his adult self in the future and finds that the figure is becoming more and more evil and manipulative. For example, the adult Tycho uses his knowledge of the future dishonestly and also wreaks destruction on his siblings. At the end of the story, Tycho's love for his family leads him to reject his powerful but vile grownup persona; he risks death to bury the egg so far back in the past that his childhood self will never discover it.

In a *School Library Journal* review of *The Green Futures of Tycho,* Pollack noted that "Sleator's expert blend of future and horror fiction is unusually stark, dark, and intriguing," while in *Horn Book* Paul Heins added that, although "the combination of logic and horror gives the telling a Poe-like quality, . . . the moral significance" of the happenings becomes clear. As Sleator once noted, "I really got in touch with my weirdness in [*The Green Futures of Tycho*]. That was the first book into which I was able to inject humor, and I feel

Cover of Sleator's middle-grade sci-fi novel Rewind, *in which a preteen finds a way to undo his own death.* (Illustration copyright © 1999 by Cliff Nielsen. Used by permission of Dutton Children's Books, a division of Penguin Putnam Books for Young Readers.)

humor is important. Even in a basically serious, or even a scary piece, there must be comic relief to reduce the tension. Humor is also very attractive to kids."

In 1983, Sleator left his job as an accompanist for the Boston Ballet to become a full-time author. The next year he produced the young-adult novel *Interstellar Pig*. In this work, sixteen-year-old Barney faces a boring summer at the beach with his doltish parents. He is intrigued when an interesting trio of strangers—Joe, Manny, and Zena—moves in next door and invites him to join in playing a role-playing board game called Interstellar Pig. The object of the game is to possess the Piggy, a card named for a pink symbol and is an integral part of the game. When Barney's neighbors turn out to be hostile aliens masquerading as humans, the game turns deadly, placing the teen in a life-and-death struggle for survival.

Writing in *School Library Journal,* Trev Jones called *Interstellar Pig* "compelling on first reading—but stellar on the second." In her *New York Times Book Review* appraisal, Rosalie Byard cited Sleator's humor, describing the story as "a riveting adventure that should satisfy readers in the 12-to-14-year-old range, especially any who happen to be hooked on strategy games." In *Junior Bookshelf,* Marcus Crouch called *Interstellar Pig* a "remarkable story" that is "surprisingly readable," adding that "the curious details of the game get right into the reader's system."

In *Parasite Pig,* a sequel to *Interstellar Pig,* Barney is once again playing the dangerous game Interstellar Pig. The Piggy, the game's goal, is located on the planet J'koot and Barney and friends must travel there to find it. However, terrible creatures, including flesh-eating crabs, must be overcome before Barney can retrieve the Piggy and win the game. Michele Winship, writing in *Kliatt,* believed that "Sleator's SF adventure is filled with tongue-in-cheek humor and likeable characters," and Betty Carter noted in *Horn Book* that "the aliens are well-developed characters, and the action proceeds at a furious pace." Miranda Doyle, writing in *School Library Journal,* dubbed *Parasite Pig* "a sometimes dark, sometimes silly, always entertaining read."

Inspired by Sleator's interest in Thai culture—he spends a part of each year in Thailand—his young-adult novel *The Spirit House* incorporates Thai beliefs. Considered a stylistic departure from Sleator's other works, the story focuses on fifteen-year-old Julie, who meets Bia, an exchange student from Thailand, when he comes to stay with her family. Julie's younger brother, Dominic, builds Bia a "spirit house," or a traditional household shrine, in the backyard to make him feel at home. When Bia becomes convinced that the house is inhabited by a vengeful spirit, Julie leaves offerings for the spirit, who appears to grant her wishes. However, Julie's health begins to decline, and things begin to go badly for her, her family, and Bia. Ultimately, Julie travels to Thailand with a jade carving containing the spirit, hoping to

Cover of Sleator's young-adult thriller The Boy Who Couldn't Die, *a story of zombies, voodoo, and a teen's search for immortality.* (Amulet Books, a division of Harry N. Abrams, Inc. 2004. Cover art © by Ira Block/National Geographic Image Collection/Getty Images. Reproduced by permission.)

set things right by restoring it to its rightful place. Calling *The Spirit House* "both scary and convincing," *Bulletin of the Center for Children's Books* reviewer Roger Sutton commented that "all of the events of the story are entirely possible, if unremittingly frightening." According to *Washington Post Book World* reviewer S.P. Somtow, *The Spirit House* "provides no easy answers . . . and the ending packs a satisfying punch." Writing in *Kirkus Reviews,* a contributor enjoyed Sleator's "logical explanation of seemingly supernatural events: the reader suspends belief only to have it systematically restored. That's a feast—and a treat."

Dangerous Wishes, a sequel to *The Spirit House,* focuses on Julie's fourteen-year-old brother Dominic. After three years of bad luck have passed for Dom and his family, he and his parents travel to Bangkok for an extended stay. When everything goes awry, Dom suspects that the cause may be the jade carving his sister had attempted to deliver three years earlier. Dom and Kik, a Thai boy, now try to find the charm and take it to its temple, but in the process they are pursued by a malevolent creature from the spirit world. Although they escape and restore the jade charm to its rightful place, the boys remain unconvinced that the bad luck will end. According to Sutton, in *Dangerous Wishes* Sleator crafts "narrative coincidences that would be trite in realistic fiction [but] here have an otherworldly eeriness that makes them convincing." *Booklist* critic Merri Monks called deemed *Dangerous Wishes* "fast-moving," while a *Horn Book* critic dubbed the novel "vintage Sleator."

Marco's Millions finds twelve-year-old Marco traveling to a distant planet via a mysterious tunnel he has discovered in the basement of his house. The aliens Marco encounters worship what they call a "naked singularity," a force that interconnects multiple universes and allows travel between them. They need the assistance of Marco and his sister, Lilly, to appease this powerful force. Beth Wright, writing in *School Library Journal,* called *Marco's Millions* "a good choice for readers who enjoy *The X-Files* or creepier episodes of *Star Trek.*" "Sleator achieves some dazzling effects here," a *Horn Book* reviewer admitted in reviewing the novel, while a critic for *Publishers Weekly* predicted that Sleator's "curious fantasy will spark readers' imaginations."

Sleator writes of zombies and voodoo in *The Boy Who Couldn't Die.* After teenager Ken Pritchard loses his best friend in a plane crash, he begins to think about ways of avoiding death himself and discovering the key to immortality. When a strange woman offers to remove his soul from his body and keep it safe, thus ensuring him everlasting life, Ken accepts. He finds out too late, however, that the deal has unexpected and dangerous consequences. Only with the help of a new friend, Sabine, can Ken reclaim his soul and save himself. A critic for *Publishers Weekly* called Ken "an interesting, conflicted hero," while *School Library Journal* contributor Beth Wright labeled *The Boy Who Couldn't Die* a "fast-paced, suspenseful book." Paula Rohrlick, reviewing the novel in *Kliatt,* stated that Sleator's "horror story is gripping and fast moving, and deliciously creepy."

The Last Universe focuses on Susan, as she spends the summer caring for her older brother Gary, now that he is confined to a wheelchair with a strange illness. The siblings live next to a strange garden that was originally designed by a scientist. As Susan cares for her brother and tries to discover the source of his malady, she also begins to notice that the garden's many mazes have remarkable powers; a walk through a maze can alter the entire world. Susan soon wonders whether the garden's powers may include the ability to cure her brother. A *Kirkus Reviews* critic predicted that *The Last Universe* "will keep readers turning pages until the very end of this exploration of multiple universes," and in *Kliatt* Janis Flint-Ferguson called *The Last Universe* "a perfect 'what if' story."

Set in the near future, *Test* draws readers into a world where the rich have every convenience while the poor are relegated to a life in housing projects and menial jobs. The dividing line comes with a standardized test

that determines the course of every child's future and is now the only focus of education. For Ann, the disparity between these worlds is all too apparent: her father works for the man who runs the lower-class slums and also publishes the test that forces people to live in them. When her friend Lep, a Thai immigrant, learns that the answers to the test are available through bribery, he takes that information to Ann, and the two teens attempt to expose a corrupt system that has breached the highest levels of government. By featuring short, "fast-paced" chapters and suspenseful endings, Sleator's novel provides "a good read for moderately reluctant readers," according to *School Library Journal* contributor Marie C. Hansen. With its contemporary slant, *Test* may also inspire readers to take a closer look at "their [own] political/social environment," Hansen added, while in the *Journal of Adolescent and Adult Literacy* James Blasingame described Sleator's novel as a "brilliant work of social satire and commentary" that points a clear finger at "many issues affecting education in the United States."

Described by a *Publishers Weekly* contributor as a "lean, fast-paced horror tale [that] moves from fascinating to far-fetched," *Hell Phone* finds middle-grader Nick hop-

A phone with a party line to the damned is the subject of Sleator's YA thriller **Hell Phone,** *featuring cover art by Jonathan Beckerman.* (Amulet Books, 2007. Illustration copyright © 2006 by Jonathan Beckerman. Reproduced by permission.)

ing to connect more with girl friend Jen by purchasing a cell phone. Budget constraints force him to go the discount route, and his used phone has no caller ID. It also comes loaded with unpleasant games, such as "Torture Master," and the unidentified callers range from sinister to demonic. As conversations with these callers begin to influence the preteen, Nick realizes that the phone is a portal, and it is up to him to discover a way to permanently put these hellions on hold. *Hell Phone* features "sinister suspense" and its wealth of "nasty detail" will appeal to horror fans, according to *Kliatt* contributor Paula Rohrlick.

Regarding his development as a writer, the prolific Sleator once explained: "At the beginning, I was copying other things, but with each book, I've learned to tap deeper into my subconscious. The more books I write, the more they represent who I really am . . . Also, my style has improved; I'm a better writer, but that goes up and down." He added, "I try to make my books exciting. I also provide incentives in the sense of giving kids a more active role in the story. . . . My goal is to entertain my audience and to get them to read. I want kids to find out that reading is the best entertainment there is. If, at the same time, I'm also imparting some scientific knowledge, then that's good, too. I'd like kids to see that science is not just boring formulas. Some of the facts to be learned about the universe are very weird." Sleator also noted, "In any idea for a book, I want to see how I can explore the personal relations that would manifest from that idea."

Biographical and Critical Sources

BOOKS

Children's Books and Their Creators, edited by Anita Silvey, Houghton (Boston, MA), 1995, pp. 605-606.

Davis, James E., and Hazel K. Davis, *Presenting William Sleator,* Twayne (New York, NY), 1992.

Egoff, Sheila A., *Thursday's Child: Trends and Patterns in Contemporary Children's Literature,* American Library Association, 1981, p. 142.

Lerner, Fred, *A Teacher's Guide to the Bantam Starfire Novels of William Sleator,* Bantam (New York, NY), 1990.

Meet the Authors and Illustrators: Sixty Creators of Favorite Children's Books Talk about Their Work, edited by Deborah Kovacs, Scholastic (New York, NY), 1993.

Roginski, Jim, *Behind the Covers: Interviews with Authors and Illustrators of Books for Children and Young Adults,* Libraries Unlimited, 1985.

St. James Guide to Young-Adult Writers, 2nd edition, St. James Press (Detroit, MI), 1999.

Sleator, William, *Oddballs: Stories* (autobiographical fiction), Dutton (New York, NY), 1993.

PERIODICALS

Booklist, August, 1995, Merri Monks, review of *Dangerous Wishes,* p. 1942; November 15, 2002, Frances Bradburn, review of *Parasite Pig,* p. 589.

Bulletin of the Center for Children's Books, October, 1991, Roger Sutton, review of *The Spirit House,* p. 30; May, 1993, Betsy Hearne, review of *Oddballs,* pp. 295-296; October, 1995, Roger Sutton, review of *Dangerous Wishes,* p. 70; April, 2004, Elizabeth Bush, review of *The Boy Who Couldn't Die,* p. 349.

English Journal, March, 1987, Margaret L. Daggett, "Recommended: William Sleator," pp. 93-94.

Fantasy Review, December, 1986, Ashley Darlington Grayson, "Two by Sleator," pp. 41-42.

Horn Book, August, 1972, Paul Heins, review of *Blackbriar,* p. 378; August, 1981, Paul Heins, review of *The Green Futures of Tycho,* p. 426; March, 1996, review of *Dangerous Wishes,* p. 200; May-June, 1998, Roger Sutton, review of *The Boxes,* p. 349; May, 2001, review of *Marco's Millions,* p. 337; November-December, 2002, Betty Carter, review of *Parasite Pig,* p. 764.

Journal of Adolescent and Adult Literacy, September, 2008, James Blasingame, review of *Test,* p. 84.

Junior Bookshelf, June, 1987, Marcus Crouch, review of *Interstellar Pig,* p. 137.

Kirkus Reviews, April 15, 1972, review of *Blackbriar,* p. 486; October 15, 1991, review of *The Spirit House,* p. 1350; February 1, 1993, review of *Oddballs,* p. 154; September 15, 2002, review of *Parasite Pig,* p. 1400; February 15, 2004, review of *The Boy Who Couldn't Die,* p. 185; April 15, 2005, review of *The Last Universe,* p. 482.

Kliatt, November, 2002, Michele Winship, review of *Parasite Pig,* p. 15; March, 2004, Paula Rohrlick, review of *The Boy Who Couldn't Die,* p. 16; March, 2005, Janis Flint-Ferguson, review of *The Last Universe,* p. 16; September, 2006, Paula Rohrlick, review of *Hell Phone,* p. 18.

New York Times Book Review, September 23, 1984, Rosalie Byard, review of *Interstellar Pig,* p. 47.

Publishers Weekly, November 23, 1970, review of *The Angry Moon,* p. 39; May 6, 1974, review of *House of Stairs,* p. 68; July 10, 2000, review of *The Boxes,* p. 65; May 21, 2001, review of *Marco's Millions,* p. 108; February 9, 2004, review of *The Boy Who Couldn't Die,* p. 82; May 2, 2005, review of *The Last Universe,* p. 200; August 28, 2006, review of *Hell Phone,* p. 56; March 10, 2008, review of *Test,* p. 83.

School Library Journal, February, 1971, Ann D. Schweibish, review of *The Angry Moon,* p. 50; March, 1974, Pamela D. Pollack, review of *House of Stairs,* p. 120; April, 1981, Pamela D. Pollack, review of *The Green Futures of Tycho,* p. 133; August, 1985, David Gale, review of *Singularity,* p. 82; September, 1984, Trev Jones, review of *Interstellar Pig,* p. 134; August, 1993, Michael Cart, review of *Oddballs,* p. 189; June, 2001, Beth Wright, review of *Marco's Millions,* p. 156; October, 2002, Miranda Doyle, review of *Parasite Pig,* p. 172; April, 2004, Beth Wright, review of *The Boy Who Couldn't Die,* p. 162; July, 2005, Elaine Fort

Weischedel, review of *The Last Universe*, p. 108; July, 2008, Marie C. Hansen, review of *Test*, p. 107.

Voice of Youth Advocates, June, 2004, review of *The Boy Who Couldn't Die*, p. 147; April, 2005, Kathleen Beck, review of *The Last Universe*, p. 62.

Washington Post Book World, December 1, 1991, S.P. Somtow, "Something Weird in the Neighborhood," p. 25.

ONLINE

Fantastic Fiction Web site, http://www.fantasticfiction.co. uk/ (November 20, 2009), "William Sleator."

William Sleator Home Page, http://cs.cmu.edu/~sleator/ (November 20, 2009).*

* * *

SLEATOR, William Warner, III
See SLEATOR, William

* * *

SNOW, Carol 1965-

Personal

Born 1965; married; children: two. *Education:* Brown University, B.S. (psychology), 1987; Boston College, M.Ed., 1992.

Addresses

Home—Fullerton, CA. *Agent*—Stephanie Kip Rostan, Levine Greenberg Literary Agency, 307 7th Ave., New York, NY 10001. *E-mail*—carolsnow@roadrunner.com.

Career

Author. Worked previously in marketing and teaching.

Awards, Honors

Quick Picks for Reluctant Young Adult Readers selection, American Library Association, 2009, for *Switch*.

Writings

YOUNG-ADULT NOVELS

Switch, HarperTeen (New York, NY), 2008.
Snap, HarperTeen (New York, NY), 2009.

ADULT NOVELS

Been There, Done That, Berkley (New York, NY), 2006.
Getting Warmer, Berkley (New York, NY), 2007.

Here Today, Gone to Maui, Berkley (New York, NY), 2009.
Just like Me, Only Better, Berkley (New York, NY), 2010.

Contributor to *Park City* magazine and *Salon.com*.

Sidelights

Although she wanted to be a writer from a young age, Carol Snow took a practical career track, earning degrees in psychology and education before pursuing her literary career. "Eventually, I decided that I could accept failing as a writer," she explained on her home page, "but I couldn't live with myself unless I at least gave it a shot." After her byline was attached to articles published in several magazines, Snow published her first book, the adult novel *Been There, Done That*. she earned notice from reviewers for her next novel, *Getting Warmer*. A romantic comedy, the novel focuses on a woman in her late twenties who is attracted to a man she meets while out with her girlfriends. Unfortunately, she told the man untruths about her life, and she now regrets the lying game she and her girlfriends often play when meeting new people. Writing in *Booklist*, John Charles called *Getting Warmer* an "entertaining combination of a realistically flawed heroine, sharp writing, and tart humor."

Snow turns to a teen readership in *Switch*, a story with a supernatural bent. Much like her deceased grandmother with whom she still communicates, fifteen-year-old Claire Martin possesses the ability to take over the body of another individual whenever electricity strikes. After a fierce thunderstorm, Claire finds herself in the body of a rich and popular girl named Larissa. While enjoying the romantic attention paid the girl by a handsome lifeguard, Claire realizes that Larissa faces stresses in her private life and these stresses convince Claire to return to her own body. Unlike other times, when she has easily moved in and out of different people, Claire cannot end this switch. Complicating matters, her dead grandmother has claimed Claire's unoccupied body, hoping to fulfill a secret desire to relive her younger days and leaving the teen without a corpus to return to. *Switch* "will be enjoyed by teens drawn to light fantasy/ science fiction," predicted *Kliatt* contributor Cara Chancellor. Writing in *Kirkus Reviews*, a critic applauded Snow's "quick-paced narration," which "comes laced with bolts of sarcasm," and concluded of *Switch* that Claire's "realistic problems blend successfully into a suspenseful, mystical story."

Biographical and Critical Sources

PERIODICALS

Booklist, December 15, 2006, John Charles, review of *Getting Warmer*, p. 30.
Kirkus Reviews, August 1, 2008, review of *Switch*.

Kliatt, September, 2008, Cara Chancellor, review of *Switch,* p. 22.

Publishers Weekly, November 20, 2006, review of *Getting Warmer,* p. 38.

ONLINE

Carol Snow Home Page, http://carolsnow.com (November 24, 2009).*

*   *   *

SPIRO, Ruth

Personal

Married; children: two daughters. *Education:* University of Illinois, B.S. (advertising), 1986; Loyola University, M.B.A., 1990. *Hobbies and other interests:* Reading, cooking, yoga.

Addresses

Home—Deerfield, IL.

Career

Writer. Formerly worked in advertising, in broadcast production and account management. Founder, Writing for Moms program; presenter at schools.

Member

Society of Children's Book Writers and Illustrators, Authors Guild, Authors League, Association of Booksellers for Children, Society of Midland Authors, Illinois Art Education Association, Illinois Reading Council.

Awards, Honors

Writer's Digest Annual Writing Contest winner; Kate Snow Writing Contest winner, Willamette Writers.

Writings

Lester Fizz, Bubble-gum Artist, illustrated by Thor Wickstrom, Dutton Children's Books (New York, NY), 2008.

Contributor to periodicals, including *Chicago Parent, FamilyFun, Child, Redbook, Writer,* and *Woman's World.* Stories included in *The Right Words at the Right Time,* Volume 2, edited by Marlo Thomas, Atria Books, 2006, and in several "Chicken Soup for the Soul" anthologies.

Sidelights

When Ruth Spiro traded a career in business for life as a busy mom, she also discovered a talent for writing. After honing her talent by attending workshops and writing classes, Spiro successfully submitted articles to anthologies and magazines. When she finished her first

***Ruth Spiro's cartoon art captures the humor in Thor Wickstrom's* Lester Fizz, Bubble-Gum Artist.** (Illustration copyright © 2008 by Thor Wickstrom. Reproduced by permission of Dutton Children's Books, a division of Penguin Putnam Books for Young Readers.)

children's-book manuscript and started looking for a publisher, she found she had made the contacts needed to find success: Featuring illustrations by Thor Wickstrom, Spiro's debut *Lester Fizz, Bubble-gum Artist* was published in 2009.

For Lester Fizz, family life seems like a mismatch. While all the other Fizzes—relatives with evocative names like Frida, Claude, Edouard, and Georgia—find creative expression in art, Lester remains uninspired by pens, paper, pencils, paint brushes, or canvas. Fortunately, the young boy eventually discovers a creative outlet that is uniquely Lester: blowing bubbles with pink chewing gum. The problem now is finding a way to exhibit his novel art form at the upcoming school art contest! "Brimming with the improbable and silly," and full of puns and other wordplay, *Lester Fizz, Bubble-gum Artist* also serves as "a roundabout introduction to art history," according to a *Publishers Weekly* critic. In *School Library Journal* Susan Weitz dubbed Spiro's story "endearing," adding that the author's alliterative language "make[s] delicious sounds" that are reflected in Wickstrom's "clever illustrations." As a *Kirkus Reviews* writer quipped, *Lester Fizz, Bubble-gum Artist* is "pop art in the most literal sense."

Spiro takes her writing career seriously, attending conferences to learn more about the business of publishing. Commenting on her experiences in *Writer,* she noted that finding a publisher for a manuscript does not mark the end of an author's job. "After submitting my original manuscript, I thought the hardest part was over," she recalled. "But it was still to come. Yet, by working through the changes, I learned about story rhythm and character development, lessons I'll apply to future manuscripts." Her final recommendation? "Listen to the advice of professionals, and keep an open mind."

Biographical and Critical Sources

PERIODICALS

Kirkus Reviews, July 1, 2008, review of *Lester Fizz, Bubble-gum Artist.*

Publishers Weekly, July 28, 2008, review of *Lester Fizz, Bubble-gum Artist,* p. 73.

School Library Journal, October, 2008, Susan Weitz, review of *Lester Fizz, Bubble-gum Artist,* p. 124.

Writer, June, 2009, Ruth Spiro, "Lots of Revisions, Waiting Led to 'Overnight' Success," p. 14.

ONLINE

Ruth Spiro Home Page, http://www.ruthspiro.com (December 2, 2009).*

*   *   *

STEVENS, April 1963-

Personal

Born February 6, 1963, in New Milford, CT; daughter of Leonard (a writer) and Carla (a writer) Stevens; married Alexander Neubauer (a writer), October 1, 1988; children: Samuel. *Education:* New School for Social Research (now New School University), B.A., 1984.

Addresses

Home—Cornwall, CT.

Career

Novelist.

Writings

Angel Angel (adult novel), Viking (New York, NY), 1995.

Waking up Wendell (picture book), illustrated by Tad Hills, Schwartz & Wade (New York, NY), 2007.

Sidelights

New England author April Stevens charmed critics with her first novel, *Angel Angel,* which was published in 1995. The story of a highly dysfunctional family, the book follows the Irises through a series of crises that begins when family patriarch, Gordie Iris, runs off to England with his mistress. Gordie's wife, Augusta, responds by retreating to her darkened bedroom for months on end, while youngest son Henry—who has just failed to graduate from high school—devotes himself to creating a sculpture in his father's studio. When older brother Matthew returns home to help his family, he fails to stir them from their seclusion; however, he is seduced by Henry's live-in girlfriend Bette Mack, a vivid personality who finally manages to revive the entire family.

Reviewing *Angel Angel,* several critics compared the work to novels by John Updike, Anne Tyler, and Laurie Colwin. Writing in the *New York Times Book Review,* Gary Krist deemed Stevens as "a writer who can move us in unexpected ways" and described *Angel Angel* "a surprisingly potent study of emotional healing."

Stevens turns to a younger readership in the picture book *Waking up Wendell.* Featuring colorful illustrations by Tad Hills, *Waking up Wendell* takes young readers to Fish Street, as one pig family after another is awakened by a succession of noises sparked by the cheerful morning song of a little bird. The bird awakens Mr. Krudwig, the grouchy pig living at Number 2 Fish Street, and when Mr. Krudwig's dog starts barking it wakes up Mrs. Musky, living next door at Number 3. And so it goes, until a young piglet named Wendell Willamore, asleep in his crib at Number 10, opens his eyes to the new day. Praising Hills' "bright" paintings with their "simple lines and contracting colors," Donna Cardon added in *School Library Journal* that *Waking up Wendell* serves as "both a clever and original counting book and a great read-aloud." "Stevens's text often

April Stevens introduces an engaging family in her picture book **Waking up Wendell,** *featuring artwork by Tad Hills.* (Illustration copyright © 2007 by Tad Hills. Used by permission of Schwartz & Wade Books, an imprint of Random House Children's Books, a division of Random House, Inc.)

reads like poetry as she describes her characters and their mornings," observed a *Kirkus Reviews* writer, and in *Publishers Weekly* a reviewer praised *Waking up Wendell* for its "well-developed characters, plenty of noise and enough humor to keep readers wanting more."

Biographical and Critical Sources

PERIODICALS

Booklist, February 1, 1995, Melanie Duncan, review of *Angel Angel,* p. 991.

Kirkus Reviews, November 1, 1994, review of *Angel Angel,* p. 1442; August 1, 2007, review of *Waking up Wendell.*

Library Journal, March 1, 1995, Kathy Helmond, review of *Angel Angel,* p. 104.

New York Times Book Review, January 29, 1995, Gary Krist, review of *Angel Angel,* p. 10.

Publishers Weekly, November 21, 1994, review of *Angel Angel,* p. 66; September 3, 2007, review of *Waking up Wendell,* p. 58.

School Library Journal, September, 2007, Donna Cardon, review of *Waking up Wendell,* p. 176.*

*   *   *

SUDYKA, Diana

Personal

Born in IL; married; husband's name Jay (a printer).

Addresses

Home—Chicago, IL. *E-mail*—diane@dianasudyka.com.

Career

Print artist and illustrator. Master printer for Big Cat Press, Chicago, IL, and Landfall Press, Santa Fe, NM. Volunteer for Chicago Field Museum of Natural History.

Awards, Honors

E.B. White Read Aloud Award, Notable Children's Book designation, American Library Association, Top Ten Youth Science-Fiction and Fantasy designation,

Booklist, Best of the Best designation, and Chicago Public Library, all 2009, all for *The Mysterious Benedict Society and the Prisoner's Dilemma* by Trenton Lee Steward.

Illustrator

Trenton Lee Stewart, *The Mysterious Benedict Society and the Perilous Journey,* Little, Brown (New York, NY), 2008.

Trenton Lee Stewart, *The Mysterious Benedict Society and the Prisoner's Dilemma,* Little, Brown (New York, NY), 2009.

Contributor to periodicals, including *Poetry.*

Biographical and Critical Sources

PERIODICALS

Booklist, March 15, 2008, Ilene Copper, review of *The Mysterious Benedict Society and the Perilous Journey,* p. 51.

Horn Book, May-June, 2008, Anita L. Burkam, review of *The Mysterious Benedict Society and the Perilous Journey,* p. 328.

Kirkus Reviews, April 15, 2008, review of *The Mysterious Benedict Society and the Perilous Journey.*

School Library Journal, May, 2008, Eva Mitnick, review of *The Mysterious Benedict Society and the Perilous Journey,* p. 140.

ONLINE

Diana Sudyka Home Page, http://www.dianasudyka.com (November 21, 2009).

Diana Sudyka Web log, http://thetinyaviary.blogspot.com/ (November 21, 2009).*

* * *

SUMMY, Barrie

Personal

Born in Ontario, Canada; married; children: four. *Education:* Earned degrees in French, Canadian literature, and speech pathology.

Addresses

Home and office—CA. *E-mail*—barrie.summy@gmail.com.

Career

Novelist.

Writings

I So Don't Do Mysteries, Delacorte (New York, NY), 2008.
I So Don't Do Spooky, Delacorte (New York, NY), 2009.
I So Don't Do Makeup, Delacorte (New York, NY), 2010.

Sidelights

When Barrie Summy was growing up in Toronto, Ontario, Canada, her parents had a very firm rule: she could read as many "dessert" books as she wanted as long as she matched each one with a "meat-and-potatoes" book. According to Summy's parents, "Nancy Drew" novels counted as dessert books. As Summy explained on the Random House Web site, "[I] loved Nancy Drew mysteries more than anything in world. [I] . . . vowed to [my] . . . sisters that [I] . . . would grow up and write a Nancy Drew mystery. Maybe even two, in a row."

In her career as a novelist, Summy has fulfilled that vow to her sisters. In her fiction debut, *I So Don't Do Mysteries,* seventh grader Sherry (short for Sherlock) Holmes Baldwin wants to spend time at the beach, hang out with friends at the local mall, and date her middle-grade crush. Sherry's father, a widower, has just gotten remarried, and while he and his bride are on their honeymoon he makes plans to send Sherry to stay with relatives in San Diego. Sherry objects until she is visited by the ghost of her mother, a police officer, asking for help in solving a mystery. Until the person poison-

Cover of Barrie Summy's novel **I So Don't Do Mysteries,** *featuring artwork by Helen Dardik.* (Illustration © 2008 by Helen Dardik. Used by permission of Delacorte Press, an imprint of Random House Children's Books, a division of Random House, Inc.)

ing the rhinos at the San Diego Wild Animal Park is not caught, Sherry's late mom will not travel on to her afterlife in the Academy of Spirits. With the help of her friend Junie and the ghosts of her mother and grandmother, Sherry reluctantly sets out to solve the case.

"Summy keeps the fizz in her effervescent premise for most of this debut novel, using a punchy first-person narration," wrote a contributor to *Publishers Weekly* in appraising *I So Don't Do Mysteries*. A *Kirkus Reviews* contributor commented that, although the author's "fluffy" and "chick-lit-y" text almost becomes "hokey," Sherry's personality, particularly as she develops a new relationship with her ghostly mom, adds "sincerity and warmth" to her story.

Sherry's adventures continue in *I So Don't Do Spooky* and *I So Don't Do Makeup*. Although Sherry has had enough of sleuthing, when someone begins stalking her new stepmom she and Junie resolve to keep the woman safe in *I So Don't Do Spooky*. Once again, the teen's ghostly relatives help solve the mystery. If Sherry solves the case, she may also earn five minutes of "Real Time" with her mother. In a review of *I So Don't Do Spooky* a *Kirkus Reviews* contributor noted that, while the idea of the stalker might be frightening for middle-grade read-

ers, "Sherry's silly, over-the-top inner dialogue helps defuse the situation and provide comic relief."

Biographical and Critical Sources

PERIODICALS

Kirkus Reviews, November 15, 2008, review of *I So Don't Do Mysteries*; November 1, 2009, review of *I So Don't Do Spooky.*

Publishers Weekly, October 20, 2008, review of *I So Don't Do Mysteries*, p. 50.

School Library Journal, January, 2009, Robyn Zaneski, review of *I So Don't Do Mysteries*, p. 120.

ONLINE

Barrie Summy Web log, http://barriesummy.blogspot.com/ (December 2, 2009).

Cynsations Web site, http://cynthialeitichsmith.blogspot.com/ (December 15, 2008), interview with Summy.

Random House Web site, http://www.randomhouse.com/ (December 2, 2009), "Barrie Summy."*

T

TESTA, Dom

Personal
Male.

Addresses
Home—Castle Rock, CO.

Career
Author and radio personality. Radio host, beginning 1977; KIMN, Mix 100, Denver, CO, morning cohost, beginning 1993. Profound Impact Group (educational and literacy advocacy group), founder and host of nonprofit Big Brain Club Web site; presenter at workshops and at schools and libraries.

Member
Colorado Independent Publishers Association.

Awards, Honors
Numerous broadcasting awards; EVVY Award for Best Young Adult Book, Colorado Independent Publishers Association, and *Writer's Digest* magazine International Grand Prize, both 2009, both for *The Comet's Curse.*

Writings

"GALAHAD" SCIENCE-FICTION NOVEL SERIES

The Comet's Curse, Profound Impact Group (Castle Rock, CO), 2005, published as *The Comet's Curse: A Galahad Book,* Tor (New York, NY), 2009.
The Web of Titan, Profound Impact Group (Castle Rock, CO), 2006, published as *The Web of Titan: A Galahad Book,* Tor (New York, NY), 2010.
The Cassini Code, Profound Impact Group (Denver, CO), 2008.

Sidelights
"From the time I was a teenager I knew that I wanted to do two things: goof around on the radio, and write. So that's exactly what I've done." So admits Dom Testa on the Web site of Mix 100, the Denver, Colorado, radio station where Testa has co-hosted the morning program since 1993. In addition to his day job—"goofing around" on the radio—Testa has also achieved his second life goal as the author of the "Galahad" science-fiction novels. Originally self-published, the first volume of the series, *The Comet's Curse,* won several awards before being released by New York publisher Tor. *The Comet's Curse* "grabs readers' attention with the very first page and never lets go," concluded a *Kirkus Reviews* critic in discussing Testa's fiction debut.

As the futuristic "Galahad" saga opens in *The Comet's Curse,* the tail of a passing comet releases a contagious disease into Earth's atmosphere that kills any human who has reached adulthood. As humankind slowly perishes, scientists hope that by evacuating the world's most promising children to a planet far away the species can survive. Powered by an advanced computer called Roc and commanded by sixteen-year-old Triana, the ship *Galahad* carries 251 teens . . . along with someone far more threatening. In *The Web of Titan* the crew of the *Galahad* reaches Saturn and its orange moon Titan, but a small metal object orbiting Titan triggers the concern of the young travelers. The third "Galahad" novel, *The Cassini Code,* follows the ship as it reaches the edge of Earth's solar system and problems on board reach a crisis level.

Describing *The Comet's Curse* as a mix of suspense and space opera, Kim Ventrella wrote in *School Library Journal* that Testa's story features "well-placed hooks, . . . a strong premise," and "solid characterizations." In *Booklist* Daniel Kraus recommended the "Galahad" series to readers who do not necessarily reach for science fiction, calling Testa's saga "one part *Lord of the Flies* and one part TV reality show."

When he is not writing or working on the radio, Testa advocates on behalf of reading and literacy for younger

Cover of Dom Testa's young-adult sci-fi thriller The Comet's Curse, *part of his "Galahad" series.* (Tom Doherty Associates, 2009. Reproduced by permission.)

children. In addition to visiting schools and libraries to encourage reading, he has created the Big Brain Club Web site, which empowers children to ignore peer pressure in favor of embracing the academic challenges that will allow them to follow their dreams.

Biographical and Critical Sources

PERIODICALS

Booklist, December 15, 2008, Daniel Kraus, review of *The Comet's Curse: A Galahad Book,* p. 38.

Kirkus Reviews, November 15, 2008, review of *The Comet's Curse.*

School Library Journal, March, 2009, Kim Ventrella, review of *The Comet's Curse,* p. 156.

Voice of Youth Advocates, April, 2009, Angela Carstensen, review of *The Comet's Curse,* p. 69.

ONLINE

Dom Testa Home Page, http://www.domtesta.com (December 2, 2009).

Macmillan Web site, http://us.macmillan.com/ (December 2, 2009), "Dom Testa."

Mix 100 Web site, http://mix100.com/ (December 2, 2009), "Dom Testa."*

*   *   *

TINGLE, Tim 1948-

Personal

Born November 24, 1948. *Education:* University of Texas, bachelor's degree; graduate study at University of Oklahoma.

Addresses

Office—StoryTribe Publishing, 4417 Morningside Way, Canyon Lake, TX 78133. *E-mail*—timtingle@hotmail.com.

Career

Writer, entrepreneur, performer, musician, public speaker, and storyteller. New Canaan Farms (gourmet food manufacturer), San Marcos, TX, co-owner and operator, 1979-97; StoryTribe Publishing, Canyon Lake, TX, founder and publisher. Worked variously as a marketing workshop presenter for Texas Department of Agriculture, touring storyteller in Germany for U.S. Department of Defense, and as a performer at Six Flags over Texas theme park. Teller-in-residence, International Storytelling Center, 2004; featured storyteller at numerous festivals, including National Storytelling Festival, Minnesota Storytelling Festival, Keepers of the Word at Amherst College, Texas Storytelling Festival, Pete Seeger's Clearwater Revival Festival, and Mississippi Storytelling Festival.

Awards, Honors

Storytelling World Honor designation, 1998, for "Rabbit and Buffalo," and 1999, for *Texas Ghost Stories;* named Contemporary Storyteller of the Year, Wordcraft Circle of Native American Writers and Storytellers, 2001; *Storytelling World* Award, 2002, for "Crossing Bok Chitto"; May-November, 2005 declared "Walking the Choctaw Road" months by Oklahoma Governor Brad Henry; Teddy Award for Best Children's Book, Texas Writer's League, Oklahoma Book Award, and Texas Institute of Letters Best Children's Book, all 2006, American Library Association (ALA) Notable Book designation, 2007, and American Indian Youth Literature Award for Picture Book, American Indian Library Association/ALA, 2008, all for *Crossing Bok Chitto.*

Writings

FOR CHILDREN

Walking the Choctaw Road, Cinco Puntos Press (El Paso, TX), 2003.

(With Doc Moore) *Texas Ghost Stories: Fifty Favorites for the Telling,* Texas Tech University Press (Lubbock, TX), 2004.

(With Doc Moore) *Spooky Texas Tales,* illustrated by Gina Miller, Texas Tech University Press (Lubbock, TX), 2005.

Crossing Bok Chitto: A Choctaw Tale of Friendship and Freedom, illustrated by Jeanne Rorex Bridges, Cinco Puntos Press (El Paso, TX), 2006.

Spirits Dark and Light: Supernatural Tales from the Five Civilized Tribes, August House (Little Rock, AR), 2006.

When Turtle Grew Feathers: A Folktale from the Choctaw Nation, illustrated by Stacey Schuett, August House LittleFolk (Atlanta, GA), 2007.

Saltypie, illustrated by Karen Clarkson, Cinco Puntos Press (El Paso, TX), 2010.

Contributor to periodicals, including *Storytelling World.*

RECORDINGS

Children of the Tracks, and Other San Antonio Ghost Stories (sound recording), StoryTribe (Canyon Lake, TX) 1994.

Grandma Spider Brings the Fire, and Other Native American Stories (sound recording), StoryTribe (Canyon Lake, TX), 1998.

(With Doc Moore) *Texas Ghost Stories,* StoryTribe (Canyon Lake, TX), 1999.

(With Doc Moore) *Texas Christmas Stories,* StoryTribe (Canyon Lake, TX), 2000.

The Choctaw Way, StoryTribe (Canyon Lake, TX), 2000.

Archie's War, and Other Choctaw Stories, StoryTribe (Canyon Lake, TX), 2002.

(With Doc Moore) *Ghostly Tales of Texas,* StoryTribe (Canyon Lake, TX), 2009.

Adaptations

Walking the Choctaw Road was adapted for audiobook, read by the author, Cinco Puntos Press (El Paso, TX), 2005. Stories from *Walking the Choctaw Road* were adapted as the ballet *Trail of Tears: Walking the Choctaw Road,* produced by Ballet Austin and Polyanna Theatre Company.

Sidelights

Tim Tingle is a professional storyteller and musician who has appeared at conferences and festivals throughout the United States and abroad. A member of the Choctaw Nation of Oklahoma, Tingle tells stories that reflect his Native-American heritage, combining personal tales with historical events and traditional lore. He is a frequent performer at schools and libraries, where he tells stories and promotes literacy. His works have attracted the attention of Choctaw chief Gregory Pyle, who has requested a story from Tingle at the Annual State of the Nation Address at the Choctaw Labor

Day Gathering every year since 2002. Tingle often complements his sessions with performances on the Native-American flute and frequently accompanies himself on a variety of gourd rattles and drums.

In *Walking the Choctaw Road* Tingle tells twelve stories, ranging from accounts of his father's experiences on the infamous Trail of Tears during the late 1800s to traditional Choctaw folk tales and personal accounts of Tingle's modern-day experiences. In the story "Trail of Tears," a child carries along his mother's bones during the tragic days of Native Americans' forced migration by U.S. cavalry troops. Other stories cover topics such as slave escapes, the morality of paying the price for one's own crimes, and Tingle's own experiences as an adolescent coming of age during the Vietnam War. Many of the stories include lessons from traditional Choctaw culture, folk practices, and social values. The book also includes a glossary of Choctaw words, a bibliography of suggested readings on Choctaw history and tradition, and Tingle's lengthy introduction, which discusses Choctaw story sources, motifs, and historical events. Reviewing *Walking the Choctaw Road,* a *Kirkus Reviews* contributor called Tingle a "superb storyteller" whose "poetic language and . . . compelling but quiet

Storyteller Tim Tingle presents an unusual variant of a traditional tale in **When Turtle Grew Feathers,** *featuring artwork by Stacey Schuett.*
(August House LittleFolk, 2007. Illustration copyright © 2007 by Stacey Schuett. Reproduced by permission of the publisher.)

voice honor . . . Native American traditions." John Peters, writing in *Booklist,* predicted that the storyteller's "evocative language, expert pacing, and absorbing subject matter will rivet readers and listeners both."

Tingle shares over two dozen stories designed to send a shiver up one's spine in *Spirits Dark and Light: Supernatural Tales from the Five Civilized Tribes.* As the pages turn, readers meet shape shifters, witches, snakes, and other devilish creatures, all brought to life in the storyteller's engaging prose. In addition to presenting stories that draw from diverse tribal cultures such as Cherokee, Creek, Chicksaw, Choctaw, and Seminole, Tingle also crafts introductory essays that include a wealth of facts about the history and culture of each tribe. Reviewing *Spirits Dark and Light* in *Booklist,* Hazel Rochman dubbed the collection "deliciously scary" and praised Tingle's text as "clear and informal." Teri Markson described the collected tales as "highly readable," adding in her *School Library Journal* review that the stories in *Spirits Dark and Light* are "eerie and compelling, sometimes gruesome, and always satisfying."

Featuring paintings by Cherokee artist Jeanne Rorex Bridge, Tingle's award-winning picture book *Crossing Bok Chitto: A Choctaw Tale of Friendship and Freedom* features one of the storyteller's most popular tales: a story about a young Choctaw girl living near the Bok Chitto river that threads between the cotton-growing lands of Mississippi and what was once the Choctaw nation. In the story, a young Choctaw girl aids a slave family in a daring nighttime escape by leading them to freedom along a secret path under the river's waters. Praising Tingle's tale as "a moving and wholly original story about the intersection of cultures," a *Publishers Weekly* critic added that *Crossing Bok Chitto* is enhanced by Bridge's "utterly mesmerizing" paintings. Author and artist "join forces with stirring results," declared Jennifer Mattson in her *Booklist* review of the picture book, the critic adding that Tingle's "sophisticated endnotes" add to the story's "powerful impact on young readers."

Tingle shares another story with young children in *When Turtle Grew Feathers: A Folktale from the Choctaw Nation.* Here he joins with artist Stacey Schuett to retell the traditional Choctaw folktale about the race between Rabbit and Turtle, a variant of Aesop's "The Tortoise and the Hare" that also features trickster and porquoi

elements. In Tingle's tale, heavy-footed Turkey accidentally shatters Turtle's fragile shell, and in mending the pieces back together he gives the shell's surface its intricate patterns. In gratitude, Turtle allows Turkey to wear the beautiful shell. Enter Rabbit, who challenges Turkey to a race believing him to be Turtle. The outcome of the race is a familiar one. Recommending *When Turtle Grew Feathers* as an effective "introduction to Native American lore," Suzanne Myers Harold added in *School Library Journal* that the book "stands out for its humor and expressive illustrations," and a *Kirkus Reviews* contributor predicted that Tingle's "lively" and "amusing" rendition will entrance story-hour audiences.

Biographical and Critical Sources

PERIODICALS

Booklist, June 1, 2003, John Peters, review of *Walking the Choctaw Road,* p. 1758; April 15, 2006, Jennifer Mattson, review of *Crossing Bok Chitto: A Choctaw Tale of Friendship and Freedom,* p. 64; November 1, 2006, Hazel Rochman, review of *Spirits Dark and Light: Supernatural Tales from the Five Civilized Tribes,* p. 45.

Childhood Education, winter, 2003, Irene A. Allen, review of *Walking the Choctaw Road,* p. 92.

Kirkus Reviews, June 1, 2003, review of *Walking the Choctaw Road,* p. 812; May 15, 2007, review of *When Turtle Grew Feathers.*

Publishers Weekly, April 21, 2003, "Native American Connections," review of *Walking the Choctaw Road,* p. 65; March 13, 2006, review of *Crossing Bok Chitto,* p. 65.

School Library Journal, March, 2005, Francisca Goldsmith, review of *Walking the Choctaw Road,* p. 89; July, 2006, Cris Riedel, review of *Crossing Bok Chitto,* p. 88; January, 2007, Teri Markson, review of *Spirits Dark and Light,* p. 140; May, 2007, Suzanne Myers Harold, review of *When Turtle Grew Feathers,* p. 125.

ONLINE

Educational Paperback Association Web site, http://www.edupaperback.org/ (March 13, 2006), "Tim Tingle."

Tim Tingle Home Page, http://www.timtingle.com (November 15, 2009).*

V-Y

VIAU, Nancy

Personal
Female.

Career
Writer.

Writings

Samantha Hansen Has Rocks in Her Head, Amulet (New York, NY), 2008.

Contributor to *Highlights for Children* and *Ladybug.*

Sidelights

Nancy Viau grew up developing her talent for making up songs and stories, but she did not take writing seriously as a career option until her youngest child began preschool. Now experiencing the free time that had been so rare, she "thought it might be fun to take my experiences, mix in the experiences of kids I've known, and twist them into stories," as Viau explained on her home page.

Viau's first published book, *Samantha Hansen Has Rocks in Her Head,* is a novel for elementary-school-aged readers. Samantha wants to be a scientist when she grows up. She is particularly interested in geology, and when her mother announces a family trip to the Grand Canyon, Sam is ecstatic. Unfortunately, in order to go on the trip, the girl has to learn to control her volatile temper. The challenge is made even greater when Sam's older sister tries to deliberately provoke her younger sibling. Eventually, Sam reins in her temper and, in addition to visiting some of the world's biggest rock formations, she gets answers to her questions about her father's death and gains a greater appreciation of her sometimes-annoying older sister.

Reviewing *Samantha Hansen Has Rocks in Her Head* for *School Library Journal,* Kim Dare called Sam "an engaging and realistically drawn protagonist" and added that the girl's "love of science is refreshing." A *Kirkus Reviews* contributor predicted that Viau's novel will be a good bridge between the popular "Amber Brown" and

Cover of Nancy Viau's chapter book **Samantha Hansen Has Rocks in Her Head,** *featuring artwork by LeUyen Pham.* (Amulet Books, 2008. Illustration © 2008 by LeUyen Pham. Reproduced by permission.)

"Junie B. Jones" series for younger readers and Beverly Cleary's "Ramona Quimby" novels, although Sam's "passion for science distinguishes her from other franchise heroines." Julie M. Prince, writing on the YA (and Kids!) Books Central Web site, described Viau's heroine as "lovable," adding that the author "weaves in seamless science lessons . . . [that are] sure to slide by young readers as casual plot, until they pop up and help them during science tests."

In addition to her novel, Viau has contributed stories to *Highlights* and *Ladybug*. She noted on her Web log that she hopes to publish a picture book, because writing in that format has always been her goal as an author.

Biographical and Critical Sources

PERIODICALS

Kirkus Reviews, August 15, 2008, review of *Samantha Hansen Has Rocks in Her Head.*
School Library Journal, March, 2009, Kim Dare, review of *Samantha Hansen Has Rocks in Her Head,* p. 156.

ONLINE

Abrams Books Web site, http://www.abramsbooks.com/ (December 2, 2009), "Nancy Viau."
Nancy Viau Home Page, http://www.nancyviau.com (December 2, 2009).
YA (and Kids!) Books Central Web site, http://www.yabookscentral.com/ (December 2, 2009), Julie M. Prince, review of *Samantha Hansen Has Rocks in Her Head.**

*   *   *

WHITMAN, Candace 1958-

Personal

Born 1958. *Education:* Yale University, B.A. (art); New York University, M.A.T; attended Parson's School of Design, Cleveland Institute of Art, Art Students League, and National Academy of Design. *Hobbies and other interests:* Backgammon, swimming, the beach.

Addresses

Home—NY. *E-mail*—info@candacewhitman.com.

Career

Author and illustrator. Currently works for a church.

Awards, Honors

New York Times Outstanding Picture Book designation, for *The Night Is like an Animal.*

Writings

SELF-ILLUSTRATED

If I Met a Dinosaur, Derrydale Books (Avenel, NJ), 1994.
The Night Is like an Animal, Farrar, Straus & Giroux (New York, NY), 1995.
Bring on the Blue, Abbeville Kids (New York, NY), 1998.
Ready for Red, Abbeville Kids (New York, NY), 1998.
Yellow and You, Abbeville Kids (New York, NY), 1998.
Now It Is Morning, Farrar, Straus & Giroux (New York, NY), 1999.
Lines That Wiggle, illustrated by Steve Wilson, Chronicle Books (Maplewood, NJ), 2009.

ILLUSTRATOR

Mem Fox, *Zoo-looking,* Mondo (Greenvale, NY), 1996.
Christine Ford, *Snow!,* HarperFestival (New York, NY), 1999.
May Garelick, *Sounds of a Summer Night,* Mondo (Greenvale, NY), 2000.
Jeannine Atkins, *Robin's Home,* Farrar, Straus & Giroux (New York, NY), 2001.
Cynthia Vance, *Red, Yellow, Blue, and You,* Abbeville Kids (New York, NY), 2008.

Contributor to periodicals, including *Highlights High Five.*

Sidelights

Candace Whitman is a collage artist whose unique, brightly colored arwork has appeared in many books for young children. Describing her illustrations for Mem Fox's *Zoo-looking, Booklist* critic Susan Dove Lempke gave special praise to Whitman's "unusual," soft-edged collage images, calling them "both powerful and tender." While she sometimes contributes illustrations to the stories of other writers, Whitman is also known for creating original, self-illustrated stories such as *The Night Is like an Animal* and *Now It Is Morning,* as well as her color-filled "My First Colors" series: *Ready for Red, Bring on the Blue,* and *Yellow and You.*

In *Night Is like an Animal* Whitman creates a rhyming text in which she uses a shaggy brown bear to symbolize night. As the bear slowly stretches across the globe, and as children all over the world curl up to sleep, the bear sleeps with them, waking up and slipping slowly away at dawn. The rising of the sun brings the bustle of activity, as Whitman shows in her companion volume, *Now It Is Morning.* Called an "arrestingly illustrated concept book" by a *Publishers Weekly* critic, *Now It Is Morning* follows both farm children and city children as they engage in their early morning routine, whether it is feeding the animals and collecting eggs from the family's chicken coop or letting the dog out, waving their working parents goodbye, and visiting the playground with their babysitter. Praising *Night Is like an*

Candace Whitman's collage arts brings a sense of fun to Cynthia Vance's picture book **Red, Yellow, Blue and You.** (Abbeville Press, 2008. Illustration © 2008 by Candace Whitman. Reproduced by permission.)

Animal in *Booklist,* Lauren Peterson wrote that Whitman's "exquisite" images "perfectly complement" her story's "gentle rhyming text," while *Now It Is Morning* complements the nighttime story with its "short sentences, simple language, and . . . onomatopoeia."

Describing her colorful collage technique on her home page, Whitman noted that selecting the colored papers she will use is the first step. "By tearing my shapes, the fibers of the paper are separated," she explained. "This creates the soft edge. Tearing is one of the hardest parts of my work, because even the slightest mistake means I have to start again! But I love the effect for children's illustrations."

Whitman moved to collage from painting while attending a course on children's book illustration. "I remembered . . . collages I had made some years back and on the last day brought them into class. The teacher and other students encouraged me to pursue this style. That was lucky! So I made some sample collages, this time of people, different animals, and other storybook objects. I took my portfolio to show to publishers in New York City where I was living at the time. It was very exciting when I was asked to do my first book!"

Biographical and Critical Sources

PERIODICALS

Booklist, November 15, 1995, Lauren Peterson, review of *The Night Is like an Animal,* p. 566; June 1, 1996, Su-

san Dove Lempke, review of *Zoo-looking,* p. 1731; February 15, 1999, Lauren Peterson, review of *Now It Is Morning,* p. 1077; January 1, 2000, Kathy Broderick, review of *Snow!,* p. 936; March 15, 2001, Connie Fletcher, review of *Robin's Home,* p. 1402.

Publishers Weekly, June 17, 1996, review of *Zoo-looking,* p. 64; January, 25, 1999, reviews of *Yellow and You, Bring on the Blue,* and *Ready for Red,* p. 94; May 10, 1999, review of *Now It Is Morning,* p. 66; February 26, 2001, review of *Robin's House,* p. 84.

School Library Journal, April, 2001, Carolyn Jenks, review of *Robin's Home,* p. 98.

ONLINE

Candace Whitman Home Page, http://www.candacewhitman.com (November 20, 2009).*

*   *   *

WILLIAMS, Sue 1948-2007
(Sue Machin)

Personal

Born December 3, 1948, in Sydney, New South Wales, Australia; died February 4, 2007, in Adelaide, South Australia, Australia. *Education:* Flinders University, B.A. (with honors).

Career

Author, artist, and publisher. Formerly worked as a commercial artist and set designer. Omnibus Books, Adelaide, South Australia, Australia, cofounder and publisher, with Jane Covernton, 1981; Working Title Press, Adelaide, cofounder with Covernton, 1997. Flinders University, academic.

Awards, Honors

Distinguished Alumni Award, Flinders University, 2006.

Writings

I Went Walking, illustrated by Julie Vivas, Harcourt Brace Jovanovich (San Diego, CA), 1990.
Let's Go Visiting, illustrated by Julie Vivas, Harcourt Brace (San Diego, CA), 1998.
Dinnertime!, illustrated by Kerry Argent, Harcourt (San Diego, CA), 2001.

Also author of books published by Rigby, Ltd. Books, some published as Sue Machin.

Author's work has been translated into Spanish.

Biographical and Critical Sources

PERIODICALS

Booklist, April 1, 2002, Ilene Cooper, review of *Dinnertime!,* p. 1323.

Kirkus Reviews, March 1, 2002, review of *Dinnertime!,* p. 348.

Publishers Weekly, August 31, 1990, review of *I Went Walking,* p. 63; September 4, 2000, review of *Let's Go Visiting,* p. 110; March 11, 2002, review of *Dinnertime!,* p. 70.*

* * *

WILSON, Sarah 1934-

Personal

Born October 8, 1934, in Syracuse, NY; daughter of Homer Arthur (an engineer) and Elizabeth (an artist) Turpin; married Herbert Eugene Wilson (an architect), September 30, 1956; children: Leslie Anne, Robert Murray. *Education:* University of Madrid, Diploma de estudios Hispanicos, 1955; Ohio University, B.A. (English and art), 1956.

Addresses

Home—Dublin, CA. *E-mail*—sarahwilsonbooks@ sbcglobal.net.

Career

Denver General Hospital, Denver, CO, medical social worker, 1963-64; Laguna Pre-School and Laguna Beach School of Art & Design, Laguna Beach, CA, and Newport Harbor Art Museum, Newport Beach, CA, art teacher, 1965-77; freelance artist and illustrator, 1977—. Co-owner of Art Workshop West, Los Angeles, CA, 1971-73; workshop leader; resource teacher in public schools of Orange County, CA. *Exhibitions:* Work exhibited at museums and galleries in southern California.

Member

Authors Guild, Society of Children's Book Writers and Illustrators (past regional adviser), Bay Area Illustrators for Children, Virginia Kittredge Crosley Society.

Awards, Honors

Don Freeman memorial grant, Society of Children's Book Writers and Illustrators, 1982.

Writings

FOR CHILDREN; SELF-ILLUSTRATED

I Can Do It! I Can Do It!, Quail Street (Newport Beach, CA), 1976.

Beware the Dragons!, Harper (New York, NY), 1985.

Muskrat, Muskrat, Eat Your Peas!, Simon & Schuster (New York, NY), 1989.

The Day That Henry Cleaned His Room, Simon & Schuster (New York, NY), 1990.

Three in a Balloon, Scholastic (New York, NY), 1990.

Uncle Albert's Flying Birthday, Simon & Schuster (New York, NY), 1991.

June Is a Tune That Jumps on a Stair, Simon & Schuster (New York, NY), 1992.

Dragon Tooth Trouble, Henry Holt (New York, NY), 2006.

FOR CHILDREN

Garage Song, illustrated by Bernie Karlin, Simon & Schuster (New York, NY), 1991.

Christmas Cowboy, illustrated by Peter Palagonia, Simon & Schuster (New York, NY), 1993.

Good Zap, Little Grog, illustrated by Susan Meddaugh, Candlewick Press (Cambridge, MA), 1995.

Hats, illustrated by Mary Mayberry, Wright Group (Bothell, WA), 1996.

Disney Babies on the Go, illustrated by Ron Cohee and Adam Devancy, Mouse Works (New York, NY), 1997.

What Do People Do?: A Learn-about Book, illustrated by Josie Yee, Joshua Morris Publishing (Westport, CT), 1997.

The Guide Dog, illustrated by Graham Meadows, Wright Group (Bothell, WA), 1997.

Going to the Bank, illustrated by Damon McPhail, Wright Group (Bothell, WA), 1997.

Going to the Hairdresser, illustrated by Damon McPhail, Wright Group (Bothell, WA), 1997.

(With Susan Hood) *The Curious Little Lamb,* illustrated by Josie Yee, Reader's Digest (Pleasantville, NY), 1997.

Spotty Can't Sleep, illustrated by Thompson Brothers, Reader's Digest (Pleasantville, NY), 1997.

A Baby's Got to Grow, illustrated by Peter Panas, Simon & Schuster (New York, NY), 1997.

What Should Eddie Pack?, illustrated by Carolyn Bracken and Jim Durk, Joshua Morris Publishing (Westport, CT), 1998.

Sleepytime Farm, illustrated by Susan Calitri, Reader's Digest (Pleasantville, NY), 1999.

Love and Kisses, illustrated by Melissa Sweet, Candlewick Press (Cambridge, MA), 1999.

George Hogglesberry: Grade School Alien, illustrated by Chad Cameron, Tricycle Press (Berkeley, CA), 2002.

Big Day on the River, illustrated by Randy Cecil, Henry Holt (New York, NY), 2003.

A Nap in a Lap, illustrated by Akemi Gutierrez, Henry Holt (New York, NY), 2003.

Friends and Pals and Brothers, Too, illustrated by Leo Landry, Henry Holt (New York, NY), 2008.

The Day We Danced in Underpants, illustrated by Catherine Stock, Tricycle Press (Berkeley, CA), 2008.

ILLUSTRATOR

Elizabeth Rush, *The House at the End of the Lane,* Green Tiger (La Jolla, CA), 1982.

Phyllis Hoffman, *Baby's First Year,* Harper (New York, NY), 1988.

Elizabeth Winthrop, *Sledding,* Harper (New York, NY), 1989.

Phyllis Hoffman, *We Play,* Harper (New York, NY), 1990.

OTHER

Author/illustrator of column "The World of Food," for *Valley Times,* 1981; illustrator of monthly newsletter "The Letter Bear," 1982-86.

Sidelights

Author and illustrator Sarah Wilson is noted by critics for creating children's books that are full of quirky characters and downright silly situations. "Humor is something I'm drawn toward in artwork and in the world in general," Wilson once told *SATA.* In her many books for children, Wilson has had much opportunity to practice her particular blend of humor: from a little boy who finally cleans his room, to an alien facing his first day in school on Earth, she treats young readers to playful interpretations of everyday childhood events. Her humorous perspective enlivens topics such as eating peas and growing up, allowing children to view such common situations from a reassuring distance. In both narrative and verse, Wilson charts the daily lives of children and has proven herself to be an able illustrator, preparing the artwork for other authors, as well as illustrating seven of her own titles. She has also authored a score of titles illustrated by others.

Born in Syracuse, New York, in 1934, Wilson was an only child who early on discovered the joys of art. "I've always loved children's books and illustrations from the time my mother read to me as a small child," she once told *SATA.* From age four, she began putting together her own self-illustrated booklets, assembling them with paper clips. She had her first art lesson at the age of seven, an experience that added to her fertile imagination. "There was something very appealing to me about being able to carry art around in my pockets and enjoy it in a compact form," Wilson once reported. By the time she was in the fifth grade, her output had increased so much that a teacher told her she should consider becoming a children's author and illustrator when she grew up.

With her father in the Navy, Wilson and her family moved frequently, attending several different elementary schools and three high schools. Far from being a liability, this constant moving aided Wilson's artistic growth, allowing her to see how color and expression changed in varying climates and surroundings. A very special place for her, in the midst of all her moving, was her grandparents' rambling house in New York State which she often visited. Full of curios from around the world, an attic packed with old junk, and a massive basement, this house filled her with amazement and ideas.

Wilson spent a year abroad in college, studying at the University of Madrid in 1955. Returning to Ohio University, she graduated the following year and also married. Two children soon followed and then time spent as a social worker and art teacher. In 1976, Wilson published her first picture book, *I Can Do It! I Can Do It!,* featuring her own illustrations. She also began writing and illustrating a weekly newspaper column and a monthly newsletter for children. Artwork for other authors occupied the early part of her career. Working with Phyllis Hoffman, she illustrated both *Baby's First Year* and *We Play.* Reviewing the first title, a miniature chronicle of a baby's first year of life, Anna Biagioni Hart, writing in *School Library Journal,* pronounced the work "pretty," and predicted that the book's colorful cover "will easily move this one off the shelves." A reviewer for *Publishers Weekly* also praised Wilson's "gently humorous and always affectionate" illustrations in *Baby's First Year.* A day at nursery school is portrayed in *We Play,* captured in Wilson's "action-filled pictures," according to *Horn Book* critic Carolyn K. Jenks. Working with author Elizabeth Winthrop, Wilson also contributed artwork to *Sledding,* a verse celebration of sled riding. Ann Stell, reviewing *Sledding* in *School Library Journal,* drew attention to Wilson's "animated, cheerful watercolor illustrations" for the book.

Branching out into writing, Wilson has also illustrated a variety of original tales. *Muskrat, Muskrat, Eat Your*

Sarah Wilson's humorous story plays out in Catherine Stock's fun-filled art for **The Day We Danced in Underpants.** (Illustration copyright © 2008 by Catherine Stock. Used by permission of Tricycle Press, an imprint of Crown Publishing Group, a division of Random House, Inc.)

ber 15, 1998, review of *Love and Kisses,* p. 1805; October 1, 2002, review of *George Hogglesberry: Grade School Alien,* pp. 1483-1484; March 1, 2003, review of *Big Day on the River,* p. 401; May 1, 2008, review of *The Day We Danced in Underpants.*

Magpies, March, 1996, Anne Hanzl, review of *Good Zap, Little Grog,* pp. 27-28.

Publishers Weekly, October 14, 1988, review of *Baby's First Year,* p. 70; May 11, 1990, review of *The Day That Henry Cleaned His Room,* p. 259; June 14, 1991, review of *Uncle Albert's Flying Birthday,* pp. 56-57; June 22, 1992, review of *June Is a Tune That Jumps on a Stair,* p. 61; September 20, 1993, review of *Christmas Cowboy,* pp. 34-35; September 4, 1995, review of *Good Zap, Little Grog,* pp. 68-69; December 3, 2001, review of *Love and Kisses,* pp. 62-63; January 13, 2003, review of *Big Day on the River,* p. 59; January 5, 2004, review of *A Nap in a Lap,* p. 59.

School Library Journal, January, 1989, Anna Biagioni Hart, review of *Baby's First Year,* p. 64; August, 1989, Jeanne Marie Clancy, review of *Muskrat, Muskrat, Eat Your Peas!,* p. 134; November, 1989, Ann Stell, review of *Sledding,* p. 96; March, 1990, May Lou Budd, review of *Three in a Balloon,* p. 202; September, 1991, Marge Loch-Wouters, review of *Uncle Albert's Flying Birthday,* p. 244; January, 1992, Nancy A. Gifford, review of *Garage Song,* p. 101; July, 1992, Nancy Seiner, review of *June Is a Tune That Jumps on a Stair,* p. 71; October, 1993, Jane Marino, review of *Christmas Cowboy,* p. 49; January, 1996, Judith Constantinides, review of *Good Zap, Little Grog,* pp. 98-99; February, 1999, Lisa Gangemi Kropp, review of *Love and Kisses,* p. 94; December, 2002, Sally R. Dow, review of *George Hogglesberry,* pp. 112-113; April, 2003, Kathleen Kelly MacMillan, review of *Big Day on the River,* p. 144; January, 2004, Liza Graybill, review of *A Nap in a Lap,* p. 108; December, 2006, Susan Lissim, review of *Dragon Tooth Trouble,* p. 118; May, 2008, Wendy Woodfill, review of *Friends and Pals and Brothers, Too,* p. 111; July, 2008, Marge Loch-Wouters, review of *The Day We Danced in Underpants,* p. 84.

ONLINE

Sarah Wilson Home Page, http://www.sarahwilsonbooks.com (November 15, 2009).*

*   *   *

WOJTUSIK, Elizabeth

Personal
Female.

Addresses
Home—Florence, MA.

Career
Writer, teacher, director, and actor. Old Deerfield Productions, Deerfield, MA, director of children's summer theatre program; The Fabulists, Martha's Vineyard, MA, co-founder and contributing playwright.

Writings

Kitty Up!, illustrated by Sachiko Yoshikawa, Dial Books for Young Readers (New York, NY), 2008.

Adaptor of plays for children.

Biographical and Critical Sources

PERIODICALS

Kirkus Reviews, April 15, 2008, review of *Kitty Up!*
School Library Journal, August, 2008, Kara Schaff Dean, review of *Kitty Up!,* p. 106.*

*   *   *

YATES, Kelly 1971-

Personal
Born 1971. *Education:* Attended Elon College and University of North Carolina at Greensboro; Guilford Tech, degree (commercial art and computer graphics).

Addresses
Home—Greensboro, NC. *E-mail*—kellyyates@att.net.

Career
Illustrator and comics creator. Tsunami Studios, Greensboro, NC, cofounder, c. 2000. Hanesbrands, graphics manager and artist for Marvel Comics clothing line; K-mart, graphic artist and artist for Sesame Street clothing line.

Illustrator
Christopher Krovatin, *Venomous,* Atheneum Books for Young Readers (New York, NY), 2008

Creator of "Amber Atoms" comic-book series, published by Image Comics. Contributor to comic-book series, including *Doctor Who: The Forgotten,* IDW Publishing.

Sidelights
For Kelly Yates, being an avid comic-book reader and a fan of the long-running *Doctor Who* television series proved to be the key to a job as a comic-book illustrator and author. Yates was pursuing a career in sports science when he realized that his class time spent doo-

Cover of **Amber Atoms,** *number 2, a comic-book series by Kelly Yates.*
(Copyright 2009 by Kelly Yates. Reproduced by permission.)

dling signaled a talent of a different sort. He switched degrees and trained as a graphic artist, then worked creating the images of well-known characters from Marvel, Lucasfilm, and Sesame Street that these companies licensed for use on sheets, clothing, and other non-

comic-book applications. Yates' talent and persistence eventually led to his job illustrating the "Doctor Who" comic book, as well as to his children's-book debut as illustrator of Christopher Krovatin's young-adult novel *Venomous.*

Venomous features fourteen black-and-white images by Yates that illustrate Krovatin's young-adult novel about Locke Vinetti, a high schooler whose darker, more violent side sometimes takes over à la Mr. Hyde. The teen's gradual acceptance of his aggressive nature is aided by new friendships with two other troubled teens, and his efforts to integrate the two sides of his personality are captured in "graphic-novel-style illustrations mirroring Locke's ongoing battle with his inner self," according to *School Library Journal* critic Jeffrey Hastings. Calling *Venomous* "a brooding, electric exploration" of a teen's coming of age, Thom Barthelmess added in *Booklist* that "Yates' . . . comic-style illustrations . . . amplify . . . the epic tone" of Krovatin's story.

Biographical and Critical Sources

PERIODICALS

Booklist, September 15, 2008, Thom Barthelmess, review of *Venomous,* p. 50.
Bulletin of the Center for Children's Books, October, 2008, April Spisak, review of *Venomous,* p. 82.
Kirkus Reviews, August 15, 2008, review of *Venomous.*
School Library Journal, January, 2009, Jeffery Hastings, review of *Venomous,* p. 108.
Voice of Youth Advocates, December, 2008, Steven Kral, review of *Venomous,* p. 454.
Winston-Salem Journal, Tim Clodfelter, "Greensboro Artist Gets a Shot at His Dream Project."

ONLINE

Kelly Yates Home Page, http://www.kellyyatesart.com (November 25, 2009).